THOMAS CRANMER'S
DOCTRINE OF REPENTANCE

Thomas Cranmer's Doctrine of Repentance

Renewing the Power to Love

ASHLEY NULL

OXFORD

UNIVERSITY PRESS

OXFORD
UNIVERSITY PRESS

Great Clarendon Street, Oxford OX3 6DP

Oxford University Press is a department of the University of Oxford.
It furthers the University's objective of excellence in research, scholarship,
and education by publishing worldwide in

Oxford New York

Auckland Cape Town Dar es Salaam Hong Kong Karachi
Kuala Lumpur Madrid Melbourne Mexico City Nairobi
New Delhi Shanghai Taipei Toronto

With offices in

Argentina Austria Brazil Chile Czech Republic France Greece
Guatemala Hungary Italy Japan Poland Portugal Singapore
South Korea Switzerland Thailand Turkey Ukraine Vietnam

Oxford is a registered trade mark of Oxford University Press
in the UK and in certain other countries

Published in the United States
by Oxford University Press Inc., New York

© John Ashley Null 2000

The moral rights of the author have been asserted
Database right Oxford University Press (maker)

First published 2000
First published in paperback 2006

British Library Cataloguing in Publication Data

Data available

Library of Congress Cataloging in Publication Data
Data available

Typeset by Joshua Associates Ltd., Oxford
Printed in Great Britain
on acid-free paper by
Biddles Ltd., King's Lynn

ISBN 0–19–827021–6   978–0–19–827021–8
ISBN 0–19–921000–4 (Pbk.)   978–0–19–921000–8 (Pbk.)

1 3 5 7 9 10 8 6 4 2

Deo sit gloria, laus, et imperium in saecula saeculorum.

('Cranmer's Great Commonplaces' II, 202r)

ACKNOWLEDGEMENTS

My Kansas forebears built their homestead from blocks of fresh-cut sod made firm by the tightly intertwined root system of prairie grasses. As I look back over the long process which has led to the publication of this book, I am keenly aware of my debt to a similarly foundational network of close friends and family, teachers and colleagues, churches and communities. They have strengthened my resolve, sharpened my work, and steadied my progress.

I especially want to thank my thesis supervisors: Dr Peter Newman Brooks, who encouraged me to come to Cambridge and under whom I began my research; Prof. Diarmaid MacCulloch, under whose vigilant guidance I completed my work; and Dr Eamon Duffy, who provided advice and analysis throughout this project, in addition to supervising me for a term. I also have benefited greatly from the comments and suggestions of my two examiners, Prof. Christopher N. L. Brooke and Revd David G. Selwyn, as well as those of my anonymous readers for Oxford University Press. In addition, I have been aided by the expertise and encouragement of Prof. Patrick Collinson, Dr Richard Rex, Revd Dr Bruce Winter, Revd Dr Gerald Bray, Dr Karen Attar, Dr David Crankshaw, Dr Sean Hughes, Dr Thomas Freeman, Colin Armstrong, Ian Garrett, Sonya Merrill, and the members of the Church History Seminar and the Tudor History Seminar of Cambridge University, to whom portions of this thesis were read. As their collective wisdom has assuredly made this a better book, its present faults remain my failings.

I would also like to record my gratitude to those educators who prepared me to pursue doctoral studies, beginning with my teachers in Kansas at Salina High School South, especially Ann L. (Flattery) Howard, Carol J. Brandert, Dr Eloise Lynch, and Llona Steele. Among my subsequent teachers, I would like to thank Prof. Marshall Terry, Prof. Kenneth D. Shields, Prof. Brevard S. Childs, Prof. Rowan

A. Greer III, and Prof. Harry S. Stout who, in addition to many other kindnesses through the years, along with Dr Alister McGrath, were most helpful in my securing a Fulbright scholarship to begin my studies at Cambridge. I would also like to express my appreciation to the staff of the libraries that have been particularly important to my work: the University Library, Cambridge; the Parker Library, Corpus Christi College, Cambridge; Tyndale House; the British Library; the Library of Lambeth Palace; the National Portrait Gallery; the Folger Shakespeare Library; the Library of Congress; the Library of the Episcopal Seminary of the Southwest; the Mennonite Library and Archives, Bethel College, North Newton, Kansas; and the Public Library of Salina, Kansas, especially Linda Grieve, Inter-library Loan Manager. I would also like to thank the National Portrait Gallery for permission to reproduce *Thomas Cranmer* by Gerlach Flicke, and Thames & Hudson, publishers, for permission to reproduce the *Metamorphosis of Acteon* and *The Creation of Eve* by Jean Mignon.

My studies have received financial assistance from the Fulbright Commission, USA, the Overseas Research Students Awards Scheme, the Lightfoot Fund and the Archbishop Cranmer Fund of the Faculty Board of History, the Crosse Fund of the Faculty Board of Divinity, Robinson College, the Jarvis Alumni Fund of Berkeley Divinity School at Yale, the Evangelical Education Society of the Episcopal Church, the Hall Memorial Fund of the Protestant Episcopal Evangelists, the Rupp Memorial Fund, and the Bishop White Prayer Book Society. I am especially indebted to Sir Christopher Wates, Chairman of Governors, and Major General Timothy Toyne Sewell, DL, Director, of the London Goodenough Trust. Their bold decision to appoint me research fellow and Chaplain to Mecklenburgh Square has given me four memorable years, numerous friendships, and the resources necessary to revise my doctoral thesis for publication.

Finally, words cannot express how deeply grateful I am to all those who have faithfully supported me with their prayers and encouragement through the years. I would especially like to thank: Very Revd James Annand, for his good sense and good will; the Clergy, Wardens and Vestry of Grace Church in the City of New York, for enabling me to pursue the studies which led to my initial interest in Cranmer's doctrine of repentance; the people of St Andrew's Episcopal Church, Liberal, Kansas, for rejoicing with me when the opportunity arose for me to study in England, even though that entailed my leaving their parish; the people of Olney, Buckinghamshire, for welcoming me as honorary verger for several Pancake Days; the Governors, Headmaster, staff, and pupils of Fettes College, Edinburgh, for allowing me the privilege of sharing their community as Chaplain for an all-too-short year; Right Revd John F. Ashby and Right Revd Vernon Strickland for their cordial permission to remain canonically resident in the Episcopal Diocese of Western Kansas while living so very far away. Above all others, however, I wish to thank my family for their unstinting support. In the midst of the uncertainties that are the nature of academic research, their loving care has been constant and cherished.

J. A. N.

The Chapel of St Augustine of Canterbury
London House
Pentecost 1999

CONTENTS

ABBREVIATIONS

AC	Augsburg Confession, in B. J. Kidd (ed.), *Documents Illustrative of the Continental Reformation*
ALC	Fisher's *Assertionis Lutheranae Confutatio*
BCP	*The Book of Common Prayer*
BL	British Library
Burnet	Burnet's *The History of the Reformation of the Church of England*, ed. N. Pocock
CCCC	Corpus Christi College, Cambridge
CGC I and II	BL Royal MSS 7B.XI and 7B.XII, 'Cranmer's Great Commonplaces'
COA	Cranmer's copy of the *Opera Augustini*, BL C.79.i.1
Cotton MS	Cottonian Manuscript
Cox I	*Writings and Disputations of Thomas Cranmer . . . relative to the Sacrament of the Lord's Supper*, ed. J. E. Cox
Cox II	*Miscellaneous Writings and Letters of Thomas Cranmer, Archbishop of Canterbury, Martyr, 1556*, ed. J. E. Cox
CR	*Corpus Reformatorum*: Melanchthon, *Opera* (vols. i–xxviii); Calvin, *Institutio* (vol. xxix)
CUL	Cambridge University Library
EW	*The English Works of John Fisher*, ed. J. E. B. Mayor
HMSO	Her Majesty's Stationery Office
LB	Erasmus's *Opera omnia*, ed. J. Leclerc
LCT	Melanchthon's *Loci communes theologici*
Lit. Ed. VI	*The Two Liturgies . . . in the Reign of King Edward VI*, ed. J. Ketley
LP	*Letters and Papers, Foreign and Domestic, of the Reign of Henry VIII, 1509–1547*
LPL	Lambeth Palace Library
MO	Modern order for the enumeration of Augustine's *Epistolae*
PL	Migne's *Patrologia Latina*
PRO SP	Public Record Office, State Papers
RSTC	*Short-Title Catalogue . . . 1475–1640*, revised
Unio (1532)	Hermann Bodius's *Unio dissidentium* (Venice, 1532)
WA	*D. Martin Luthers Werke* ('Weimar Ausgabe')

Introduction:

The Theology of Thomas Cranmer

Ye haue heard that it is sayde, thou shalt loue thyne
neyghbour, and hate thyne enemy. But I saye vnto you:
loue your enemyes. Blesse them that curse you. Do
good to them that hate you. Praye for them which hurt
you and persecute you, that ye maye be the children of
your father which is in heauen: (*'Cranmer's Bible'*,
1540)[1]

Thomas Cranmer devoted the full powers of his position as
Primate of All England to inculcating the Protestant faith
into every fibre of English life and law. In so doing, he
shattered forever medieval Catholicism's hegemony over
English society, stealthily destroying its ingrained religious
semiotics, severely disrupting its instinctive communal
rhythms. The noted Cambridge historian Eamon Duffy
has recently drawn a lush and often lyrical portrait of the
world Cranmer sought to leave behind: a beautiful world
of soaring church towers, newly built, and instructive
iridescent interiors, softly candlelit; a balanced world
where affective personal piety grieved over the sufferings
of Christ but festive parish bonfires abetted neighbourly
fellowship made jolly with ale; a supernatural corporeal
world where saints and sacramentals diverted demonic fury
and fecundated husbandry and home; a supernatural spiritual world where human tears averted the doom of divine
wrath as well as celebrating the indwelling presence of
divine love; and, above all else, a supernatural sacramental
world where liturgy marked life's milestones and offered
the daily miracle of seeing one's Maker.[2] What would make

[1] The Gospell of S. Mathew 5[: 44–5], *The Byble in Englyshe, that is to saye the
content of al the holy scrypture, both of the olde, and newe testament, with a prologe
therinto, made by the reuerende father in God, Thomas archbysshop of Cantorbury*
([London]: Edward Whytchurche, Apryll 1540), fol. 3v.
[2] Eamon Duffy, *The Stripping of the Altars: Traditional Religion in England, c.
1400–c. 1580* (New Haven, Conn.: Yale University Press, 1992).

an archbishop of Canterbury want to end such a world as
this?

CRANMER IN RECENT SCHOLARSHIP

For most commentators, the answer has been decidedly
straightforward, although their opinions as to its exact
nature have been widely divergent.[3] For many admirers of
medieval English Catholicism, Thomas Cranmer was
clearly just a real-life 'Tom Snout', the tinker-turned-
would-be-actor as in Shakespeare's *A Midsummer Night's
Dream*. As a time-serving sycophant promoted beyond his
promise, Cranmer could only play-act being a real wall
between the royal will and the English church. From
necessity, he was only too willing to accommodate a monarch's lusts and so by the work of his hand provided Henry
with the chinks the king needed to see his way through to
seizing whatever he desired, including a comely new wife
and the church's ancient wealth.[4]

For those traditionalists willing to concede Cranmer some
theological sincerity, he was a sad 'Doubting Thomas', a
recipient of apostolic authority who was uncertain about the
church's received teaching and his own ability to decide. An
innocent in high office, he was too amicable to his opponents
and too amenable to political pressure. While the second
prayer book bent so far to the prevailing wind of 'Swiss'
Protestantism as to refuse to see the Lord in a raised host,
his liturgy of 1549 remained truly Catholic, providing a sure
footing for the historic faith in the Church of England.[5]

---

[3] For a review of Cranmer historiography, see Jasper Ridley, *Thomas Cranmer*
(Oxford: Clarendon Press, 1962), 1–12; Peter Newman Brooks, *Cranmer in Context: Documents from the English Reformation* (Minneapolis, Minn.: Fortress Press,
1989), 117–27.

[4] 'And shortly after, Doctor Warham being dead, [the King] bestowed upon him
the archbishopric of Canterbury. Then loe had Cranmer the sweet soppe he looked
for, that made him so drunk that he wist not nor cared what he did so he might
serve the King's pleasure and appetite', Nicholas Harpsfield, *A Treatise on the
Pretended Divorce between Henry VIII and Catharine of Aragon*, ed. Nicholas
Pocock (Westminster: Camden Society, New Series, 21, 1878), 290; '[Cranmer's]
life was the life of a cowardly time-serving hypocrite, a perjured person, and a
traitor', *The Saturday Review*, 25 July 1868, 123.

[5] 'Whatever else he was, Cranmer was no crafty dissembler. He was as artless as

Yet for churchmen in favour of a decidedly Protestant Anglican tradition, Cranmer was the only true 'St Thomas of Canterbury'.[6] Motivated by a deep and abiding commitment to *sola scriptura*, he was cruelly martyred as the chief trophy of a papist British monarch's reactionary persecution, primarily because of his public support for justification and Holy Communion *sola fide*.[7] Despite his unfortunate vacillation under duress, Cranmer's long-held biblical faith and last-minute reconversion to it secured his name for the Protestant cause. Thus, he is fit for invocation by all those seeking to legitimize their working within Anglicanism to advance a more scripturally-sound faith and practice.[8]

For those less fervent about circumscribing all liturgy and learning exclusively within the sphere of scriptural warrant, but reluctant to embrace the more supernatural (some would say even superstitious) beliefs and practices of England's medieval past, Cranmer was not unlike Thomas

a child . . . He may sometimes have deceived himself; he never had any intention to deceive another. Trustful towards others, even to a fault, he had little confidence in himself. His humility amounted almost to a vice. His judgement was too easily swayed by those who surrounded him—especially by those in authority. In this way he frequently did or consented to things imposed upon him by others, which he would never have thought of by himself . . . [Nevertheless, if] our country possesses a Church of unbroken lineage, true to the agelong inheritance in its framework of government, doctrine, and worship, yet open to every form of progress . . . the thanks are due, under God, to the sagacity, the courage, the suppleness combined with firmness, of Archbishop Cranmer', Arthur James Mason, *Thomas Cranmer* (London: Methuen, 1898), 200, 202.

[6] According to Foxe, Cranmer was 'much more worthy the name of *S. Thomas* of Caunterbury then he whom the the [*sic*] *Pope* falsly before dyd Canonise', *Ecclesiasticall history contaynyng the Actes and Monumentes of thynges passed in every Kynges tyme in this Realme, especially in the Church of England principally to be noted* (London: Iohn Daye, 1570), 2066. Cf. Marcus L. Loane's description of Cranmer's death in the language of Elijah's exit from this life: 'On that cold, wet morning of March 21st, 1556, in the sixty-seventh year of his life, Thomas Cranmer was caught away in a chariot of fire to soar aloft at the call of God in glory; while to those who stood by, the doom of the Primate of All England, his sorrow and triumph, struck home with a moral grandeur such as no mere words could ever inspire', *Masters of the English Reformation* (London: Church Book Room Press, 1954), 240–1. Cf. 2 Kings 2: 11.

[7] *Sola scriptura* (by Scripture alone), *sola gratia* (by grace alone) and *sola fide* (by faith alone) were the three hallmarks of the Protestant Reformation.

[8] 'Cranmer was a prototype Anglican "evangelical", one for whom Scripture was both supreme and straightforward. His was an essentially simple faith based on reading, understanding and obeying what the Bible taught, and it is precisely here that we, his successors, must begin to hear and heed his voice', Maurice Elliott, 'The Giant and the Dwarfs', *Churchman* 109 (1995), 327–32, at 328.

Jefferson, whose pen gave America *The Declaration of Independence*. As the author of an exceptionally eloquent literary legacy, Cranmer bequeathed to the English people a liturgy that expressed the deepest aspirations of the human spirit with rhetorical potency and rational clarity. Thoroughly imbued with humanist assumptions and aspirations, Cranmer was the founding father of Anglicanism as a theological equipoise.[9]

Self-serving lackey, self-deceiving puppet, Swiss Protestant partisan or sensible Erasmian humanist, was Cranmer one of these, none of these or some combination thereof? The question is an important one for the current lively debate on the nature of the English Reformation. A. G. Dickens's work on the period has focused on the 'theme of Protestant conversion', arguing that the religious alterations in England were brought about by a popular movement arising as a natural response to the 'rational appeal of a Christianity based upon the authentic sources of the New Testament'.[10] Dr Duffy, however, has used his study of the vibrancy of pre-Reformation English liturgical life to argue that religious change during the period came as 'a violent disruption' of popular practice, 'a stripping of the altars' by an act of state.[11] Whether religious transformation in Tudor England was the result of inevitable progress or intimidating proclamation, understanding Cranmer's doctrinal sympathies is essential. On the one hand, tracing Cranmer's intellectual progression towards Protestant doctrine would

---

[9] 'As a man deeply influenced by humanist studies and as one subject to the Word of God, Cranmer was also an eminently reasonable man, and the Book of Common Prayer, contrasted with that which went before, was a book for reasonable persons', *The Book of Common Prayer 1559: The Elizabethan Prayer Book*, ed. John E. Booty (Washington, D.C.: Folger Books, 1976), 362; '[Cranmer] had stood for decency and order in public worship, and had laboured with uncommon skill to express it in language of dignity and beauty . . . There are words of his which have found a place in every edition of the Prayer book from 1549 to our own day: "Christ's Gospel . . . is a religion to God, not in bondage of the figure or shadow, but in the freedom of spirit"', F. E. Hutchinson, *Cranmer and the English Reformation* (London: English Universities Press, 1951), 182–3.

[10] A. G. Dickens, 'The Shape of Anti-clericalism and the English Reformation', in *Politics and Society in Reformation Europe: Essays for Sir Geoffrey Elton on his Sixty-Fifth Birthday*, ed. E. I. Kouri and Tom Scott (London: Macmillan, 1987), 379–410, at 380.

[11] Duffy, *Stripping of the Altars*, 4.

offer an important 'case study' of 'conversion' among the learned in Henrician England. On the other, determining what Cranmer's Protestant convictions actually were, and when he held them, would provide invaluable insight into the theological debates behind the acts of state which fostered the ecclesiastical changes.

Yet such an enquiry is immediately confronted with a vexing question of methodology. Which doctrinal positions should be considered sufficiently foundational as to determine definitively Cranmer's theological orientation? Much of the diversity of opinion on Cranmer stems from how historians have answered this question, for Catholics and Protestants of the era differed over even how to define their differences.

At his trial before both papal and royal officials in September 1555, Cranmer was accused of two chief doctrinal errors. He repudiated papal authority and denied transubstantiation.[12] So important was the latter issue, that previously in April 1554 the Convocation of Canterbury had arranged a public disputation, the sole subject of which was the Mass, in order that the best doctors of Oxford and Cambridge might publicly refute Cranmer, Latimer, and Ridley on their heretical Eucharistic teaching.[13] Although without a doubt the Marian authorities considered Cranmer's teaching on justification to be in serious error as well, his solifidianism was raised neither at the disputation nor at his trial.[14] In their eyes, Cranmer was clearly not Catholic because he had both broken with the pope and

---

[12] The third charge was a matter of discipline, unchastity. For an account of Cranmer's trial before Bishop James Brooks of Gloucester, the papal delegate, and Thomas Martin, John Story and David Lewis, the proctors for the Crown, see Diarmaid MacCulloch, *Thomas Cranmer: A Life* (London: Yale University Press, 1996), 573–9.

[13] According to Foxe, the three questions considered at the April 1554 disputation were: '1 whether the naturall body of Christ bee really in the sacrament after the wordes spoken by the Priest, or no? 2 whether in the sacrament, after the words of consecration, any other substance do remaine, then the substance of the body and bloud of Christ? 3 whether in the Masse be a sacrifice propiciatory for the synnes of the quicke and the dead?', $\overline{A}$*ctes and Monumentes*, 1591. For an account of the proceedings, see MacCulloch, *Cranmer*, 563–7.

[14] Derived from *sola fide*, solifidianism is the technical term for adherence to justification by faith alone.

denied that Christ's natural body was offered as a propitiatory sacrifice during the sacrament of the altar.

Martin Luther, however, drew a different line between
Catholics and Protestants. He considered the doctrine of
justification by faith alone to be the chief article of Christian
doctrine, the sun which illuminated the holy church of God,
the article of faith by which the church stood or fell into
ruin. Once solifidianism was lost, Christ was lost; and the
church was left without any knowledge of doctrine or the
Spirit.[15] So essential did Luther consider justification by
faith that in his Smalcald Articles he declared:

> Nothing in this article can be given up or compromised, even if
> heaven and earth and things temporal should be destroyed . . . On
> this article rests all that we teach and practice against the pope, the
> devil, and the world. Therefore, we must be quite certain and
> have no doubts about it. Otherwise all is lost, and the pope, the
> devil, and all our adversaries will gain the victory.[16]

Although Luther clearly thought the power of the papacy
and the nature of the Lord's Supper were very substantial
issues, rejecting the Catholic position on both,[17] he considered them secondary behind the all-surpassing importance of the Bible's message that salvation was by faith alone.
Since only trusting in God's promises brought sinful
humanity into a relationship with its Maker, Luther held
solifidianism to be the plumb-line for the true gospel belief
for which he stood.

Somewhere between these two standards lay the church of
Henry VIII. The king demanded that the church in Eng-

---

[15] 'Iste psalmus [130] . . . tractat illum principalem locum doctrinae nostrae,
nempe iustificationem . . . hoc amisso amittitur Christus et Ecclesia nec relinquitur
ulla cognitio doctrinarum et spiritus', Martin Luther, *D. Martin Luthers Werke:
Kritische Gesamtausgabe*, ed. J. K. F. Knaake, G. Kawerau, et al. (Weimar, 1883–)
[henceforth *WA*], 40³.335; 'iste versus sit Summa doctrinae Christianae et ille sol,
qui illuminat Sanctam ecclesiam dei, quia isto articulo stante stat Ecclesia, ruente
ruit Ecclesia', *WA* 40³.352.

[16] *The Book of Concord: The Confessions of the Evangelical Lutheran Church*, ed.
Theodore G. Tappert (Philadelphia, Pa.: Fortress Press, 1959), 292; for the
original German, see *WA* 50.199. Cf. *Die Promotionsdisputation von Palladius
und Tilemann* (1537): 'Articulus iustificationis est magister et princeps, dominus,
rector, et iudex super omnia genera doctrinarum, qui conservat et gubernat omnem
doctrinam ecclesiasticam et erigit conscientiam nostram coram Deo', *WA* 39¹.205.

[17] See, for example, *The Babylonian Captivity*.

land repudiate papal authority in favour of his own head-ship, but he refused to endorse justification by faith and publicly defended the presence of Christ's natural body in the Eucharist. For Henry, obedience was the chief theo-logical virtue;[18] and he expected his subjects to demonstrate their Christian faith by submitting to royal authority and doing works of charity, both as necessary conditions for their salvation. To exhibit this balance of being equally opposed to treasonous papists and Lutheran heretics, Henry had three of each burned in 1540, including Robert Barnes, his sometime ambassador to the German Luther-ans.[19] As a result of the king's opinions, the official for-mularies of the Henrician church were neither clearly Catholic nor definitely Protestant, but an uncertain, unstable *tertium quid*.

For the Marian authorities, the foremost mark of true Christianity was papal obedience and proper Eucharistic piety. For Luther it was justification by faith. For Henry it was manifest obedience to God through the king. What was the key doctrine for Cranmer?

This crucial question is only made more complex by Cranmer's self-confessed gradualism in matters theological. He was not like Calvin 'whose mind on everything was perfectly formed by the time he was twenty-five'.[20] By his own admission, Cranmer at one time believed in 'transub-stantiation, of the sacrifice propitiatory of the priests in the mass, of pilgrimages, purgatory, pardons, and many other superstitions and errors that came from Rome'. And he put away his 'former ignorance' only 'by little and little', coming to his final opinion on the Eucharist only in his late fifties.[21]

Many in the past have found this shifting of allegiance to be a sign of theological instability evincing Cranmer's lack of any determinative doctrinal commitment.[22] Canon Dixon

---

[18] See Richard Rex, 'The Crisis of Obedience: God's Word and Henry's Reformation', *The Historical Journal* 39 (1996), 863–94.

[19] See MacCulloch, *Cranmer*, 274–5.

[20] J. I. Packer, 'Introduction', in *The Work of Thomas Cranmer*, ed. G. E. Duffield (Appleford: Sutton Courtenay Press, 1964), xiii.

[21] *Writings and Disputations of Thomas Cranmer . . . relative to the Sacrament of the Lord's Supper*, ed. J. E. Cox (Cambridge: Parker Society, 1844) [henceforth Cox I], 374.

[22] Dr Martin said at his trial, 'For you, Master *Cranmer*, haue taught in this

expressed the judgement of many when he wrote of Cranmer in the nineteenth century, 'In doctrine he ran from one
position to another, until at last he seemed ready to
surrender the Catholicity of the Church to the Sacramen-
tarians'.[23] More recently, Jasper Ridley has continued this
critical attack but on a fresh front. Recognizing Cranmer's
unquestioned loyalty to Henry VIII, Ridley has suggested
that Cranmer's only real theological principle was the
Protestant notion of obedience to the godly prince.[24] His
other doctrinal positions were expediently provisional,
depending on the current prince's current preference.[25]
Ridley aptly summarized his assessment of Cranmer when
he described his death as coming at a propitious moment for
Protestantism—'Perhaps if he had lived for another hour, he
would have recanted again . . .'[26]

Other scholars, however, have interpreted Cranmer's
changing doctrinal positions as a sign of intellectual progress, seeing in his theological gradualism 'all the caution
and integrity of the true scholar accustomed to weigh both
sides of a question before committing himself'.[27] Indeed,
Cranmer's theological progression can be properly characterized as instability only if the same charge were made
against 'every theologian of worth', including St Paul, St
Augustine, St Thomas, and Karl Barth.[28] In his quatercen-

hygh Sacrament of the aultar three contrary doctrines, and yet you pretended in
euery one, *Verbum Domini*', Foxe, *Actes and Monumentes*, 2053.

[23] R. W. Dixon, *History of the Church of England from the Abolition of the Roman
Jurisdiction* (Oxford: Oxford University Press, 1878–1902), i.155–6.

[24] 'Cranmer was an agent of Tudor despotism. He glorified the King, denounced
enemies of the regime to the Council, punished political opposition, applied torture
to suspects and sent heretics to the stake. Yet he was not a cruel man; and if he was
sometimes influenced, usually unconsciously, by selfish motives, he tried far harder
than most of his contemporaries to adhere to the principles in which he believed . . .
His evil actions were nearly all the result of his fidelity to the doctrine of Christian
obedience to the Prince', Jasper Ridley, *Thomas Cranmer* (Oxford: Clarendon
Press, 1962), 410.

[25] 'Cranmer believed in royal absolutism. He believed that his primary duty as a
Christian was to strengthen the power of the King, and was prepared if necessary to
sacrifice all his other doctrines to accomplish this', ibid., 12; cf. ibid., 65–6.

[26] Ibid., 409.

[27] G. W. Bromiley, *Thomas Cranmer, Archbishop and Martyr* (London: Church
Book Room, 1956), 37.

[28] E. Gordon Rupp, *Studies in the Making of the English Protestant Tradition*

tenary survey of Cranmer scholarship, Peter Newman Brooks rejected Ridley's approach.[29] Drawing upon Professor Sir Isaiah Berlin's use of the ancient comparison between the hedgehog and the fox,[30] Brooks likened Ridley's unitary description of the Archbishop to 'an ecclesiastical hedgehog knowing but one big thing to perfection'.[31] Brooks, however, thought Cranmer 'a very foxy Archbishop of Canterbury' who knew many things. Those scholars who credit Cranmer with a sound but developing doctrinal integrity see him at best as a crafty fox, intellectually agile enough to adapt his ways to evolving new ideas and situations.[32] At worst, they see him simply as an old dog willing to learn new lessons from his theological trainers, for even among those scholars sympathetic to Cranmer disagreement exists as to the nature of his intellectual capacities.[33] Now to

(Cambridge: Cambridge University Press, 1947), 130; C. W. Dugmore, *The Mass and the English Reformers* (London: Macmillan, 1958), 176.

[29] Peter Brooks, 'Cranmer Studies in the Wake of the Quartercentenary', *Historical Magazine of the Protestant Episcopal Church*, 31 (1962), 365–74.

[30] 'There is a line among the fragments of the Greek poet Archilochus which says, "The fox knows many things, but the hedgehog knows one big thing"', Isaiah Berlin, *The Hedgehog and the Fox: An Essay on Tolstoy's view of History* (New York, N.Y.: Simon & Schuster, 1953), 1.

[31] Brooks, 'Studies', 374.

[32] Some scholars consider Cranmer to have been a first-class mind: 'We are suggesting . . . that he was, in fact, in his unobtrusive way, a theologian of the first rank . . . he was neither prolific nor original nor argumentative, but this does not of itself mark him down as a second-rater . . . Cranmer's genius was not for system-building, nor yet for polemics . . . but for crystallising a stock of tested material into confessional definitions (the Articles), forms for worship (the Prayer Books) and plain practical expositions, like the three great homilies of 1547 . . . and the *Defence*', Packer, in Duffield, *Cranmer*, xviii; 'As the man upon whom fell the weight of the English Reformation Thomas Cranmer is without doubt such a "giant". The preceding articles, while not ignoring his weaknesses, have demonstrated both the depth and the breadth of his thinking', Elliott, 'The Giant and the Dwarfs', 327–8.

[33] Other commentators have seen in Cranmer's lack of originality an equal lack of intelligence: 'As a scholar Cranmer was thorough and painstaking rather than quickminded and brilliant,' Maria Dowling, 'Cranmer as Humanist Reformer', in *Thomas Cranmer: Churchman and Scholar*, ed. Paul Ayris and David Selwyn (Woodbridge: Boydell, 1993), 89–114, at 91; 'Cranmer was a distinguished scholar, a reasonably competent theologian' but he 'was not an original systematic theologian', Basil Hall, 'Cranmer's Relations with Erasmianism and Lutheranism', in Ayris and Selwyn, *Churchman and Scholar*, 3–37, at 36, and 'Cranmer, the Eucharist and the Foreign Divines in the Reign of Edward VI', in ibid., 217–58, at 232; '[N]o scholar would claim that Thomas Cranmer was one of the great systematic theologians of the Reformation in the sense that Melanchthon or Calvin

snare a fox, a trapper must first identify his den and from there trace back his runs. In the light of both Henry's strictures and Cranmer's gradualism, many of these scholars have sought to classify the archbishop's true theological sympathies by similarly first identifying his final doctrinal den, and then following his trail backwards.

Only under Edward VI did Cranmer find the freedom to express his own theological views as well as gain the authority to shape the doctrinal formularies of the new reign accordingly. Consequently, the two benchmarks of Cranmer's mature theology date from this period: his three homilies on justification—'Of Salvation', 'Of the True, Lively and Christian Faith', and 'Of Good Works annexed unto Faith'—(1547); and his writings on the Eucharist, *A defence of the true and catholike doctrine of the sacrament of the body and blood of Christ* (1550), *An answer of . . . Thomas archebyshop of Canterburye, vnto a crafty cauillation by S. Gardiner* (1551), and *An answere against the false calumniacions of D. Richarde Symth who hath taken vpon him to confute the Defence* (1551) as well as *The Book of Common Prayer* (1549 and 1552). In the Parker Society's presentation of the material, Cranmer's writings on the Lord's Supper total 379 pages (not including the two different prayer books), whereas his teaching on soteriology yields a mere twenty-one.[34]

Whether commentators have associated Cranmer's mature theological home with his views on the Eucharist or his position on justification naturally depends on whether the scholar perceived Cranmer as more a humanist non-papist Catholic whose broadly Catholic Eucharistic piety moderated his solifidianism or as more a humane non-predestinarian Protestant whose solifidianism brought about a moderate Reformed Eucharistic piety. Once the *terminus ad quem* had been determined, historians then

can be so regarded', Peter Newman Brooks, *Thomas Cranmer's Doctrine of the Eucharist: An Essay in Historical Development*, 2nd edn. (London: Macmillan, 1992), 370.

[34] For his Eucharistic writings see Cox I, 1–379; For the homilies, see *Miscellaneous Writings and Letters of Thomas Cranmer, Archbishop of Canterbury, Martyr, 1556*, ed. J. E. Cox (Cambridge: Parker Society, 1846) [henceforth Cox II], 128–49.

read back into Henry's reign a pattern of development consistent with Cranmer's mature views as they understood them. Two contrasting studies of his Eucharistic doctrine will suffice to illustrate this approach.

In his book *The Mass and the English Reformers*, Professor Clifford Dugmore took as his premise that Continental theological trends were not determinative in shaping the doctrine of the leading English Reformers.[35] Hence, when he examined Cranmer's Eucharistic writings, he concluded that the Archbishop had made his own study of the patristic sources and was then decisively influenced by Nicholas Ridley to adopt Ratramn's teaching that Christ's real presence in the sacrament was not corporal but spiritual and 'without any destruction of the substance of the bread and wine'.[36] The result was that Cranmer held a 'non-papist Catholic doctrine of the real presence'. Christ was spiritually, but still objectively, present as the real Consecrator at every Eucharist, and by his presence throughout the whole Eucharistic action he spiritually fed the worthy receiver. Dugmore styled this position as 'the Reformed Catholic, or Augustinian realist-symbolist tradition of eucharistic doctrine handed down from the days of the early Church'.[37]

Reading this 'Reformed Catholicism' back into Henry's reign, Dugmore acknowledged the existence of a party 'among the bishops and higher clergy' who wanted to extend ecclesiastical reforms beyond merely repudiating papal jurisdiction. These 'Reformed Catholics', who included Bilney, Latimer, Barnes, and Cranmer, embraced justification by faith and sought to remove superstitious practices in accordance with Erasmian principles. Yet their soteriology did not effect their 'orthodoxy' on the sacrament of the altar; for 'whatever ideas about justification by faith may have been held by the English Reformers in common

---

[35] '[O]ne is so tired of reading that everything said by Cranmer or Ridley, Frith or Latimer or Jewel was derived from Luther, Zwingli or Calvin, as if they had no theological training, no knowledge of the Schoolmen or the Fathers and were utterly incapable of thinking for themselves . . . Of course the English Reformers took note of what Luther, Melancthon, Bucer, Calvin and Zwingli believed and achieved . . . But the influence was not necessarily one-sided; it was more likely to have been mutual', Dugmore, *Mass*, vii–viii.

[36] Ibid., 82–3.   [37] Ibid., 200.

with the Lutherans, an unbridgeable gulf separated them on the doctrine of the Eucharist'.[38] The Henrician Reformers never followed a Lutheran view of the sacrament, but held instead to a conventional Catholic Eucharistic piety, including transubstantiation, until almost the very eve of Edward's accession.[39]

Thus, for Dugmore, Cranmer was a reforming Catholic both under Henry and also under Edward; and the foundation for his theology was not solifidianism, but a consistent, Catholic, realist approach to understanding the Eucharist. Although Cranmer was mainly responsible for the second, substantially less Catholic prayer book of 1552, the revisions did not necessarily reflect his own preferences. By then the more extreme Protestant John Dudley had taken control of the boy-king's council. 'It is obvious that Cranmer had to allow very substantial concessions to be made to the radical Reformers, but it does not follow that he interpreted the rite of 1552 in exactly the same sense as they did, or that he welcomed all the changes made.'[40]

Dr Brooks, on the other hand, began his monograph *Thomas Cranmer's Doctrine of the Eucharist* with a premise which was directly the reverse of Dugmore's: 'In almost every respect the English Reformation is Act II of a Continental drama played out earlier and on a different stage.'[41] Not surprisingly then, Brooks located the key to Cranmer's thinking not in an adherence to Catholic tradition but in his adoption of Protestant soteriology. Brooks evaluated Cranmer's Eucharistic writings in the light of the 'Homily on Salvation' and found that the central themes of redemption and solifidianism ran 'like a scarlet thread throughout his exposition of both the *Defence* and the *Answer*'.[42]

---

[38] Dugmore, *Mass*, 208.

[39] Ibid., 90–6, 109, 173, 176–83. NB, however, that Dugmore comments that Barnes's Eucharistic doctrine 'can best be described, not as Lutheran, but as anti-papal, although there is not sufficient evidence to enable us to determine exactly how he conceived of the mode of the eucharistic presence', ibid., 96.

[40] Ibid., 141, 163, 171.

[41] Brooks, *Eucharist*, xxii. For a succinct account of his position, see also Brooks, 'Studies', 370.

[42] Brooks, *Eucharist*, 83; cf., 'Studies', 367.

Brooks concluded that Cranmer built 'his whole sacramental superstructure on that doctrine basic to all Reformed theology—the concept of *Justificatio sola fide*' because Cranmer believed that 'faith is the one instrument that, from the human angle, can bring communion with Christ'.[43] The logical result of this solifidianism was a mature Eucharistic theology which made personal faith the determinative factor. Brooks described Cranmer's final position as the Swiss 'True Presence' doctrine of the Eucharist in which Christ is truly but only spiritually present and only to those with saving faith. In fact, Brooks suggested that Cranmer chose to write so extensively on the Eucharist precisely because he wanted to ensure that the Romish doctrine of the Mass as a propitiatory sacrifice for sin would no longer impede people seeking a right relationship with God *sola fide*.[44] Naturally, Brooks saw the 1552 *Book of Common Prayer* as completing Cranmer's mission 'to turn the Mass into a Communion'.[45]

Confident that Cranmer eventually held the same Eucharistic theology as Bucer, Melanchthon, Bullinger, and Calvin,[46] Brooks in his monograph traced the historical development of Cranmer's Eucharistic doctrine through three phases: from holding to transubstantiation at the beginning of his archiepiscopate to adopting a doctrine of the real presence similar to the Lutheran view later in Henry's reign, through to its final culmination in his accepting the Swiss Protestant position and its expression in the prayer books under Edward. Significantly, Brooks buttressed his argument for a gradual development toward Reformed Protestant thought by citing evidence drawn from Cranmer's manuscript notebooks, including the 'Great

---

[43] Brooks, *Eucharist*, 94; cf., 'Studies', 367; *Eucharist*, 106.

[44] 'Thus, only as all ". . . such popish masses are clearly taken away out of Christian Churches, and the true use of the Lord's Supper . . . restored again" can the principle of Justification by Faith be truly operative so that "godly people assembled together may receive the sacrament every man for himself, to declare that he remembereth what benefit he hath received by the death of Christ, and to testify that he is a member of Christ's body, fed with his flesh, and drinking his blood spiritually"', Brooks (glossing a quotation from Cranmer's *Defence*), *Eucharist*, 83; cf. ibid., 78–9.

[45] Ibid., 162.

[46] Ibid., 68–9.

Commonplaces'.[47] In the process, he definitively demonstrated Cranmer's use of Continental Protestant sources in his theological reflections.

Influenced by Brooks's work, many recent scholars conclude that Cranmer came to move within broadly Protestant parameters during Henry's reign and most likely as early as 1532 when he took advantage of an extended stay in Germany as ambassador to marry a woman who was the relative of the Nuremberg Reformer Andreas Osiander.[48] Not all, of course, agree.[49] But if Cranmer did come under the influence of Luther's teachings by the early 1530s, to what extent did he do so? Cranmer himself asserted that he had 'come to the conclusion that the writings of every man must be read with discrimination'.[50] Moreover, Cranmer's emphasis on holy living as evidence of justification has suggested to some that he muddled the key doctrine of Protestant theology even in his Edwardian 'Homily of Salvation'. They argue that while Cranmer accepted the Lutheran means for justification as by faith alone, he continued to hold to the Catholic notion of its nature as being made personally righteous.[51] In recent years the

---

[47] See the Appendix.

[48] See, e.g., Patrick Collinson, 'Thomas Cranmer', in *The English Religious Tradition and the Genius of Anglicanism*, ed. Geoffrey Rowell (Wantage: Ikon, 1992), 79–103, at 91; Hall, in Ayris and Selwyn, *Churchman and Scholar*, 18–20. Cf. Packer, in Duffield, *Cranmer*, xv. Jasper Ridley also saw Cranmer's marriage as the decisive act by which he decided to move within more Protestant parameters; Ridley, *Cranmer*, 45–7.

[49] David Loades holds the view that Cranmer did not become a Protestant until 1548, after he had written the 'Homily of Salvation', and that he remained an orthodox Catholic on the Eucharist during the life of Henry VIII; 'Thomas Cranmer: A Biographical Introduction', in Margot Johnson (ed.), *Cranmer—A Living Influence for 500 years: A Collection of Essays by Writers Associated with Durham* (Durham: Turnstone Ventures, 1990), 1–24, at 16. John T. Wall, Jr., however, argues that Cranmer was an Erasmian humanist under Edward VI and enshrined his convictions in his homilies and prayer books, in 'Godly and Fruitful Lessons: The English Bible, Erasmus' Paraphrases, and the Book of Homilies', in *The Godly Kingdom of Tudor England: Great Books of the English Reformation*, ed. John E. Booty (Wilton, Conn.: Morehouse-Barlow, 1981), 47–135. For earlier opinions, see Chapter 4.

[50] '[D]idicique omnium hominum omnia cum delectu esse legenda', Cranmer's letter to Joachim Vadianus, Cox II, 342; this translation, Cox II, 344.

[51] See Alister E. McGrath, *Iustitia Dei: A History of the Christian Doctrine of Justification*, 2nd edn. (Cambridge: Cambridge University Press, 1998), 288. Cf. *A Catechism set forth by Thomas Cranmer: From the Nuremberg Catechism translated*

debate over Cranmer's doctrine has focused on the degree to which he agreed with developing Continental Protestant doctrine.

Yet even among those scholars who agree that Cranmer was clearly Protestant, some see him as more Lutheran, while others considered him more Reformed. This was the fundamental point of contention in Basil Hall's vociferous disagreement with Peter Brook's assessment of Cranmer's mature doctrine of the Eucharist.[52] Hall agreed that the key to understanding Cranmer was found in his Edwardian writings, and especially in the moderate solifidianism of his homilies, with their emphasis on both saving faith and a subsequent life of righteousness.[53] However, Hall strongly disputed Brooks's suggestion that justification by faith inevitably led to a more Reformed view of the Eucharist.[54] After all, Hall duly noted, such was obviously not the case with Luther himself, the very font of sixteenth-century solifidianism.[55] Hall also rightly flagged an underlying weakness in Brooks's landmark study, the fact that Brooks never actually defined what he meant by Cranmer's adherence to Reformed soteriology.[56] In the absence of any evidence of Cranmer's holding to the predestinarianism characteristic of Reformed theologians, Hall argued that Cranmer should be characterized as a moderate Lutheran in his Eucharistic theology as well as in his soteriology, his mature views on both being more like Melanchthon than Calvin.[57] Naturally, Hall argued that the 1549 prayer book, and not the 1552 edition, reflected the real Cranmer.[58]

into Latin by Justus Jonas, ed. D. G. Selwyn (Appleford: Sutton Courtenay Press, 1978), 'Introduction', 46.

[52] Hall, in Ayris and Selwyn, *Churchman and Scholar*, 251–8.

[53] Ibid., 1, 18–19.

[54] Ibid., 256, responding to Brooks, *Eucharist*, 120–1.

[55] Hall, in Ayris and Selwyn, *Churchman and Scholar*, 257.

[56] Ibid., 257.

[57] Ibid., 36 n. 132, 254; 'When in doubt as to a possible influence on Cranmer . . . it is always safer to go to moderate Lutheranism and avoid Swiss notions', ibid., 254. Cf. Collinson's comment that Cranmer's assertion in the 'Homily of Good Works' that if the thief on the cross had lived 'and not regarded faith, and the works thereof, he should have lost his salvation again' reflected a doctrinal stance which seventy years later 'would have been called grossly Arminian', 'Cranmer', 97.

[58] Hall, in Ayris and Selwyn, *Churchman and Scholar*, 238–40.

Thus, Cranmer studies as recently as the quincentenary celebrations of his birth were left with a conundrum.[59] To find a recognizable, if evolving, consistency in the performance of his ecclesiastical duties under Henry and in all his theological writings under Edward, Cranmer needed to have been committed to the Protestant cause early in his archiepiscopate and to have continued to develop his views along lines similar to the emerging Reformed tradition of such second-generation leaders as Calvin and Bullinger. However, in the absence of any firm evidence to suggest that Cranmer actually held to such doctrines as unconditional election and effectual grace—not to mention lingering questions about his commitment to the basic Protestant premise of forensic justification—the portrait of Cranmer as an early Reformed theologian could at best only be judged 'not proven'. And in the light of Cranmer's universally acknowledged moderation, such an assessment could at worst be considered to miss the mark very widely. As a result, the most convincing account scholars could construct for Cranmer was as a *tertium quid* Protestant, clearly not a sixteenth-century Catholic but neither clearly Lutheran nor Reformed, holding an uncertain, unstable *via media* muddle that, as with Henry, would not outlive its author.[60]

Such was the state of Cranmer scholarship on the eve of the publication of Diarmaid MacCulloch's well-received recent biography, *Thomas Cranmer: A Life*. Taking as his premise that Cranmer was indeed a committed Protestant by 1532, Prof. MacCulloch has presented a compelling portrait of the Archbishop as working for the evangelical cause throughout his years in office, gradually adapting his theology in accordance with emerging developments in the incipient Reformed theology of the 'Strassburg-St Gall network'.[61] Nicely turning Ridley's assessment on its head,

---

[59] Publications associated with Cranmer's quincentenary included: Paul Ayris and P. N. Brooks, *Cranmer—Primate of all England: Catalogue of a Quincentenary Exhibition at The British Library, 27 October 1989–21 January 1990* (London: British Library, 1989); Brooks, *Cranmer in Context*; Johnson, *Living Influence*; Ayris and Selwyn, *Churchman and Scholar*.

[60] For an excellent description of Cranmer in this vein, see Collinson, 'Cranmer'.

[61] MacCulloch, *Cranmer*, 173–4.

MacCulloch argues that Cranmer eagerly supported royal supremacy as the necessary means to advance his doctrinal agenda, not as the necessary altar on which to sacrifice it.[62] If Duffy's scholarship raises the question of why Cranmer presided over the destruction of medieval England's deeply entrenched Catholicism, MacCulloch's magisterial study convincingly answers that Cranmer was simply a deeply committed English evangelical.

MacCulloch's book is persuasive not only because of the plausible unity it offers to Cranmer's life but also because of its detailed documentary support. Among other evidence MacCulloch cites is 'Thomas Cranmer's Doctrine of Repentance', a recent Ph.D. dissertation which was prepared under his supervision.[63] Using evidence drawn from previously unstudied manuscript sources, including 'Cranmer's Great Commonplaces',[64] this dissertation sought to establish the development of Cranmer's soteriology, from his initial medieval Catholic focus on sacramental penance to his mature Reformed Protestant view of justification by faith of the elect alone. In order to make this dissertation available to a wider audience as well as to submit its argument to more general critical scrutiny, its text has been revised and is published as the present volume.[65]

THE HEART OF CRANMER'S THEOLOGY

If MacCulloch has provided the answer to what Cranmer's theology was during his years as Primate of all England, the question raised by Dickens's work—Why did Cranmer choose to become a Protestant?—still remains largely unanswered. MacCulloch has noted the great difficulty in ascertaining the motives of a man who has left us no account

---

[62] Ibid., 150–1.

[63] John Ashley Null, 'Thomas Cranmer's Doctrine of Repentance', Ph.D. thesis (Cambridge, 1994).

[64] See the Appendix.

[65] For the purpose of this study, the word 'Protestant' will be used to describe an adherent to solifidianism, thus including both Lutheran and Reformed theologians. The word 'Lutheran' will be used to refer to views in agreement with the writings of Luther and Melanchthon. The word 'Reformed' will be used to refer primarily

of his own *Turmerlebnis*[66] and who was notoriously circum-
spect among his contemporaries. Consider the witness of
Ralph Morice, his principal secretary:

[H]e was a man of suche temperature of nature, or rather so
mortified, that no maner of prosperitie or adversitie coulde alter or
change his accustumed conditions: for, being the stormes never so
terrible or odious, nor the prosperous estate of the tyme never so
pleasante, joyous, or acceptable, to the face of [the] worlde his
counteynance, diete, or sleape comonlie never altered or changed,
so that thei whiche were mooste nerest and conversante aboute
hym never or syldome perceyvid by no signe or token of
counteynance howe th'affaires of the prince or the realme wente.
Notwithstanding privatelie with his secrete and speciall frends he
wolde shede forth many bitter teares, lamenting the miseries and
calamities of the worlde.[67]

Reflecting on these famous remarks, MacCulloch writes,
'Those friends have not betrayed their confidence, and
Cranmer's private face remains for the most part inscrutable.'[68] Yet Cranmer did choose to leave behind clues as to
what had captured the affections of the heart concealed
behind his famous poker face. The most well-known is his
portrait of 1545 where various elements are designed to alert
the knowledgeable viewer to Cranmer's Protestant Augustinianism.[69] Here, however, art is not so much explaining
life as imitating it. For true to his evangelical creed,
Cranmer intended his treatment of others to be a public

to views most similar to the positions held by Bucer and Calvin. The word
'Catholic' will be used to refer to the views permissible in the Church of England
prior to its break with Rome. The word 'Conservative' will be used to refer to those
who agreed to the repudiation of papal authority but none the less continued to
hold to other views recognized as 'Catholic' prior to the Church of England's
rupture of relations with Rome. The word 'Augustinian' will be used to refer to
theologians who sought to remain faithful to Augustine's principle of the primacy
of grace in salvation, regardless of how accurately they reflected Augustine's own
views. Finally, in keeping with recent scholarship and their own custom, the word
'evangelical' will be used to refer to those Henrician reformers who sought to
introduce Protestant theology into England.

[66] A German term meaning literally, 'tower experience', *Turmerlebnis* refers to
the moment when Martin Luther understood that justification was by faith alone.
Later in life Luther said this breakthrough insight had come to him while he was in
his study in the tower of the Augustinian monastery at Wittenberg, hence the term.

[67] John Gough Nichols (ed.), *Narratives of the Days of the Reformation* (London:
Camden Society, First Series, 77, 1859), 244.

[68] MacCulloch, *Cranmer*, 1.   [69] See Chapter 3.

parable whose meaning he believed the elect of God would be given to perceive.

Despite the pressures of his office and his era, Cranmer's most striking characteristic was to forgive his enemies. To be sure, Cranmer could act sternly toward evangelicals who, in his view, endangered the whole reforming enterprise by contravening authority with their 'outeragious doings'.[70] He could also be equally harsh with religious conservatives he considered as recalcitrant recidivists.[71] Nevertheless, his customary response to personal wrongs was unmerited forgiveness, often to the irritation of his friends and the delight as well as abuse of his foes. According once more to Morice,

[a] notable qualitie or virtue he hadd: to be benficiall unto his enemyes, so that in that respecte he wolde not be acknowne to have anye enemy atall. For whosoever he hadd byn that hadd reportid evill of hym, or otherwaies wrought or done to hym displeasure, were the reconciliation never so meane or symple on the behalf of his adversarye, yf he hadd any thing attall relentid, the matter was both pardoned and clerelie forgotten, and so voluntarilie caste into the sachell of oblivion behinde the backe parte, that it was more clere nowe oute of memorie, than it was in mynde before it was either commensid or committed: insomuche that if any suche person sholde have hadd any sute unto hym afterwardes, he might well recken and be as suer to obteyn (yf by any meanes he might lawfullie do it) as any other of his special frendes. So that on a tyme I do remember that D. Hethe late archebisshopp of Yorke, partelie mislyking this his overmoche lenitie by hym used, saided unto hym, 'My lorde, I nowe knowe howe to wynne all thinges at your handes welenough.' 'How so?' (quoth my lorde.) 'Mary, (saied D. Hethe,) I perceyve that I muste firste attempte to do unto you some notable displeasure, and than by a litle relenting obteyne of you what I can desire.'[72]

---

[70] For Cranmer's attitude toward disobedient evangelicals, see Nichols, *Narratives*, 247. Perhaps Cranmer's willingness to repress evangelicals who were 'too progressive' accounts for Foxe's slight qualification in his description of Cranmer's moderation: 'Surely if ouermuch pacience may be a vice, this man may seeme peraduenture to offend rather on this part then on the contrary. Albeit for all his doinges I cannot say: for the most part . . .', a qualification not found in Morice, his primary source on this point; *Actes and Monumentes*, 2036.

[71] For an example of Cranmer's remorseless punishment of a traditionalist priest he considered a repeat offender, see Cox II, 333–4, 361–2.

[72] Nichols, *Narratives*, 245–6. For examples of this leniency, see ibid., 157, 251–2, 269–72 and MacCulloch, *Cranmer*, 318, 321.

Such habitual benevolence was not merely the naivety of an innocent in high office, the guilelessness to be expected from one as 'artless as a child'.[73] Rather, Cranmer's demonstrated love for those who opposed him was the conscious decision of a dedicated evangelist. When queried why he was so lenient with 'papists', Cranmer replied:

What will ye have a man do to hym that ys not yet come to the knowledge of the trueth of the gospell, nor peradventure as yet callid, and whose vocation ys to me uncerteyne? Shall we perhapps, in his jorney comyng towards us, by severitie and cruell behaviour overthrowe hym, and as it were in his viage stoppe hym? I take not this the wey to alleure men to embrace the doctrine of the gospell. And if it be a true rule of our Saviour Christe to do good for evill, than lett suche as are not yet come to favour our religion lerne to folowe the doctrine of the gospell by our example in using them frendlie and charitablie.[74]

Cranmer certainly was not unique in his day for emphasizing the love of enemies as the essence of true Christianity. So taught Erasmus of Rotterdam in his widely influential early book, the *Enchiridion militis christiani*.[75] Bishop Edmund Bonner did likewise in his sermon on charity which appeared in both Edwardian and Marian books of homilies.[76] Even Cranmer's arch-opponent, the conservative bishop Stephen Gardiner, vigorously sought to portray himself in his dispute with the Lutheran Robert Barnes as the true Christian who obediently forgave the wrongs done him by his opponent.[77] Nor was Cranmer particularly innovative in seeing Christ-like conduct as more persuasive

[73] Mason, *Cranmer*, 200.

[74] Nichols, *Narratives*, 246–7.

[75] Erasmus's *Enchiridion*, as translated into English in *The Handbook of the Christian Soldier*, trans. Charles Fantazzi, *Collected Works of Erasmus*, 66, ed. John W. O'Malley (Toronto: University of Toronto Press, 1988), 93–107.

[76] *Certain Sermons or Homilies (1547) AND A Homily against Disobedience and Wilful Rebellion (1570): A Critical Edition*, ed. Ronald B. Bond (Toronto: University of Toronto Press, 1987), 120–5, esp. 123–4. Edmund Bonner, *Homelies . . . not onely promised before in his booke, intituled, A necessary doctrine, but also now of late adioyned therevnto* (London: Ihon Cawodde, 1555), fols. 21v–27r, esp. 24v–25v).

[77] '[Barnes] cryed out to me, and asked me forgiuenes with a maruelous circumstance, as though the worlde shuld thinke, I had had nede of suche a publique obtestacion . . . So it lyked hym with a courage to playe with me . . . and therwith to boste his own charitie, and bringe myne in doubt'; printed

than syllogistic bombast. Once again, Erasmus urged this very approach in his *Enchiridion*.[78] What did set Cranmer apart from his former Catholic humanist colleagues was his mature theological understanding of this command. For Erasmus, Gardiner, and traditional Catholicism in general, love of enemies was a matter of obedience, a necessary condition for salvation. For Cranmer, such unmerited love for others was necessarily a response to and the inevitable result of receiving the assurance of unmerited salvation. Consequently, he intended his well-known reputation for giving grace to the unworthy to be a cardinal signal, a scarlet cord hung openly from the window of Canterbury, so that in the midst of the battles of his times and since, those with eyes to see should spot where the wall of the old order was first breached in England and recognize as comrades those in the household where the gospel conspiracy was first forged.

For Cranmer's commitment to love his enemies was more than just the outward fruit of his living Protestant faith. It was its very foundation. The logic is breathtakingly simple. Christ commands us to love our enemies so that we show ourselves sons of our Father in heaven. If the highest expression of divine love is to love one's enemies, that must be the very same kind of love by which God saves sinners. And that, in fact, is what the apostle Paul himself wrote in Romans 5: 10—'when we were enemies, we were

marginalium: 'Barnes was not appoynted thus to do, nor it was not nedefull, for I was in no auctoritie . . . and had forgiuen him before'; 'For so moche the tale may be profitable to the (reader) to considre howe thinges be blowed and blustered abrode with lyes, and how Barnes death is layde to my charge, that haue onely suffred at Barnes hand, and neuer dyd any thing to him, but euer forgaue him, and he euer vsed forgeuenes, neuer to amende, but to delude and tryfle'; 'And one of that company tolde me (whom I take for my frende) that he had not thought to heare so muche diuinitie of me, ne se so moche charitie in a Bysshop', Stephen Gardiner, *A declaration of such true articles as George Ioye hath gone about to confute as false* (London: Iohannes Herford, 1546), fols. 9v, 10v.

[78] 'Exteriorly let your friendliness, affability, good nature, and obligingness win over your brother, who should be attracted to Christ in an appealing manner and not put off by harshness of behaviour. In a word, you must express your sentiments not in thundering utterances, but in your conduct. On the other hand you must not be so indulgent to the weakness of the common person that you do not have the courage to defend the truth vigorously when the occasion arises. Men must be corrected, not deceived, by kindness', Erasmus, *Enchiridion*, 104.

reconciled to God through the death of His Son'. Since God loved those who had not a right to be loved, Cranmer reached out to his opponents with unmerited forgiveness and favour in hopes that they would realize that God did likewise when he brought salvation. This emphasis on God's love for the unworthy is the common thread which runs throughout Cranmer's theological writings.

Like Ockham's razor, the radical simplicity of this principle cut through key tenets of medieval teaching. In keeping with the etymological meaning of the Latin Vulgate's *justificare* 'to make righteous', the Catholic understanding of justification was as a process of transformation. Hence, the primary interest of much of late scholastic penitential instruction lay in encouraging sinners to demonstrate through genuine sorrow and good works that they no longer wanted to be God's enemy. Penitents who did their best to show an increasing love for God gradually acquired an acceptable degree of worthiness which was the necessary preparation for divine forgiveness. Influenced by the Augustinian revival, the Cambridge theologian John Fisher insisted that human actions needed the special assistance of prevenient grace to be effective towards justification,[79] and Gardiner, a Cambridge-trained lawyer, agreed.[80] In accordance with his *philosophia Christi*, Erasmus declared that this requisite preparation should consist of sound spiritual activities and not mere vain superstitions.[81] Nevertheless, all three continued to teach a transition period where sinners co-operated with God to make progress toward their justification. And all taught that a final supernatural gift of divine goodness infused into worthy penitents finished the process of making them fully acceptable to God so he could grant them justification.

Luther, however, believed that the inevasible human

---

[79] See Chapter 1.

[80] '[N]o man hath ben so madde, to say that a synner, that is so blynded with synne, as he can not see god, can of hym selfe, turne as he shuld do, to god frutefully, without the lyght and grace of god. Who can wake out of synne, without god cal him and faith', Gardiner, *Declaration of true articles*, fol. 94v; 'that god doth ministre speciall grace, and helpe man to turne to god from synne, it is agreed with you', ibid., fol. 95r.

[81] See Chapter 2.

tendency toward self-centredness rendered it impossible for anyone to be truly righteous in this life. Therefore, humanity was constrained to seek another righteousness as the objective basis for justification, not relying on something within them, but looking beyond themselves to the perfect human righteousness which belonged to Christ alone.[82] Noting that the Greek New Testament word for *justificare* was δικαιουν, a legal term meaning to pronounce a defendant 'not guilty', Protestants taught that when sinners trusted God's promise to forgive them their sin because of Christ's death on their behalf, God credited them with Christ's own righteousness.[83] Although they would still struggle with sin working in their lives, God would continue to declare them to be 'not guilty' through their faith in Christ. Thus, justification came in a moment of belief that changed a sinner's status before God without changing his personal worthiness for acceptance.

Cranmer eventually agreed. In his early forties, he became convinced that any attempt to make ourselves acceptable to God as the basis for forgiveness was an insult to the depth of the divine love shown for an unworthy humanity by Christ's death on the cross.[84] In his view, 'it is the work and glory of God alone to justify the ungodly, to forgive sins, to give life freely out of his goodness, not from any merits of our own'.[85] Parting company with Fisher and Erasmus, Cranmer denied the possibility of any middle transitional stage between the children of God and of the devil.[86] He also rejected their traditional factitive understanding of justification where God first made sinners inherently righteous so that he could then accept them. Believing God justified people

---

[82] See Paul Althaus, *The Theology of Martin Luther*, trans. Robert C. Schultz (Philadelphia, Pa.: Fortress Press, 1966), 142–60, 224–45.

[83] For Philip Melanchthon's role in establishing forensic justification as the norm for Protestantism, see McGrath, *Iustitia Dei*, 210–12.

[84] 'Sanguis Christi, multis modis contumelia afficitur. Primum, ab iis qui praeter Christi sanguinem, alia excogitant aut supponu[n]t remedia, satisfactiones, aut pretia pro abluendis peccatis', BL Royal MS 7B.XII [henceforth 'Cranmer's Great Commonplaces' (CGC) II], 226r.

[85] 'Solius dei opus est et gloria, iustificare impium, remittere peccata, donare vitam ex sua bonitate gratis, non ex ullis nostris meritis', CGC II, 226v.

[86] 'Nec medium est ullum inter filios dei et diaboli', CGC II, 213r.

'although they were sinners',[87] Cranmer embraced the forensic understanding in which God imputed Christ's righteousness to the ungodly who turned to him in faith.[88]

Yet he did not believe that justification based on the external merits of Christ had no internal effect in the justified. Quite to the contrary. For if the glory of divine love was to love the unworthy, the duty and joy of the justified was to return that love to God and to others. Consequently, in the moment of justification Cranmer held that God imparted both faith and love. The believer's faith laid hold of the extrinsic righteousness of Christ on which basis alone his sins were pardoned. At the same time, however, the Holy Spirit indwelt the believer, stirring in him a love for God and his commandments. This renewal of a person's will would naturally issue forth in a godly life marked by obedience to divine precepts and repentance for on-going shortcomings caused by the infirmities of human nature. In short, Cranmer believed that justification was being made 'right-willed' by faith, not being made inherently righteous, and its evidence was love and repentance toward God and neighbour.

Cranmer's insistence on the personal unworthiness of the justified did indeed lead him to hold to predestination. Since divine love loves those who have no right to be loved, God saves sinners unconditionally, without any regard for personal merit, whether acquired or infused. Yet if divine love requires that salvation comes as an unconditional gift, then God's love must also be able to ensure the full acceptance of that gift, otherwise human response to divine love would

---

[87] *Marginalium*: 'Iustificavit nos deus cum peccatores essemus', CGC II, 257r.

[88] 'Iustificare subinde significat, iustum pronuntiare, declarare, aut ostendere', CGC II, 84r; 'Because all men be sinners and offenders against God, and breakers of his law . . . no man by his own acts . . . be justified and made righteous before God; but every man of necessity is constrained to seek for another righteousness, or justification, to be received at God's own hands, that is to say, the remission, pardon, and forgiveness of his sins . . . And this justification or righteousness, which we receive by God's mercy and Christ's merits, embraced by faith, is taken, accepted, and allowed of God for our perfect and full justification . . . Christ is now the righteousness of all them that truly believe in Him', 'Homily of Salvation', Cox II, 128, 130. Cf. '[Christ's] sanctified body offered on the cross is the only sacrifice of sweet and pleasant savour, as St. Paul saith; that is to say, of such sweetness and pleasantness to the Father, that for the same he accepted and reputeth of like sweetness all them that the same offering doth serve for', Cox II, 114.

become a necessary condition. Therefore, God's love must have the power both to awaken love for God among God-haters and to ensure the perseverance of that love for eternity. Consequently, Cranmer believed that the justified were also the elect, so that God gave saving faith only to those whom he had chosen to deliver from eternal damnation before the foundation of the world.

This assurance of salvation was crucial for Cranmer's understanding of how God drew the justified to love him and to obey his commandments. In Catholic teaching, the justified who subsequently marred their personal righteousness by committing a mortal sin forfeited divine favour and incurred once again the threat of eternal damnation until they should regain a fresh infusion of sanctifying grace. Hence, Christians were to face the future with a sober uncertainty about their eternal fate, striving to lead a godly life in a constant state of both hope and fear. The former guarded against despair of ever reaching final salvation, the latter against presumption and its moral careless-ness which would lead to everlasting damnation. Cranmer, however, accepted the Protestant approach. He based justi-fication on the never-changing external righteousness of Christ, so that the elect could have an assurance of salvation which drove out all fear. Since God was certain to save 'from everlasting damnation by Christ' those who trusted in his promises, a grateful love was to be the exclusive motive for a godly life.[89] For

if the profession of our faith of the remission of our own sins enter within us into the deepness of our hearts, then it must needs kindle a warm fire of love in our hearts towards God, and towards all other for the love of God . . .[90]

Naturally, Cranmer intended such benevolence to be extended to foes as well as friends, for 'they be his creation and image, and redeemed by Christ as ye are'.[91] Therefore, God's gracious love inspired a grateful love in his children, turning their wills from wrong to right and binding them to their heavenly Father as well as to one another forever.

[89] Cox II, 133.   [90] Cox II, 86.   [91] Cox II, 149.

The ultimate expression of Cranmer's vision of God's gracious love inspiring grateful human love was the 1552 Holy Communion service. In what he intended to be the central act of English worship, Cranmer wove together his great themes of free justification, on-going repentance, communal fellowship, and godly living and placed them in a setting which clarified God's incomprehensible sacrificial love for the unworthy as their sole source. He deleted an explicit invocation of the Holy Spirit over the elements and made their reception the immediate response to the words of Institution. As a result, receiving the sacramental bread and wine, not their prior consecration, became the liturgy's climax. And since he repositioned the prayer of oblation as a post-communion prayer, the community's sacrifice of praise, thanksgiving, and service was their newly empowered *response* to God's grace at work in them, not its grounds as previously. Now, human gratitude clearly flowed from divine grace.[92] The first change indicated that the sacramental miracle was not changing material elements but reuniting human wills with the divine. The second showed that grateful service was the necessary effect of that gracious reunion, that godly love was the natural response to remembering God's love. In the final analysis, Cranmer transferred the traditional factitive nature of justification from righteousness to 'right-willedness'. Likewise, in his last Eucharistic liturgy he transferred the miracle of Communion from Christ's corporeal presence in the bread to Christ's spiritual renewal of the communicants' intrinsic will to love all as they have been loved by God.[93]

What, then, can be said to be the hallmark of Cranmer's theology? Ultimately, Cranmer's Eucharistic teaching was determined by his doctrine of justification. Yet his understanding of salvation was but in turn a consequence of an even more basic premise: that godly love is a love for enemies. As a result, Cranmer conceived of God's work in

---

[92] See Colin Buchanan, *What Did Cranmer Think He Was Doing?*, 2nd edn. (Bramcote: Grove Books, 1982); Brooks, *Eucharist*, 112–62.

[93] '[I]n the Lord's supper neither the substance nor accidences of bread and wine be changed . . . but the alteration is inwardly in the souls of them that spiritually be refreshed and nourished with Christ's flesh and blood', Cox I, 254.

the world as changing human wills, not human worthiness, and he believed God did so by loving the unworthy elect so unconditionally as to inspire in them a reciprocal love for him and others. Thus, Cranmer taught and lived a gospel of gracious divine love inspiring gratefully human love. Here his motives found their force and focus. Here his doctrine found its foundation and inner coherence. Here is his true hallmark.

Cranmer's Medieval Inheritance:
Contrition as Repentance

> We be not suffycyent and able of our selfe, as of our
> selfe, to thynke ony maner thynge, but our suffycyency
> and habylyte dependeth and cometh of god onely,
> therfore this thynge is to be asked of god that he
> vouchesaue to moue our soules perfytely by his grace
> vnto the excercysynge & doynge of many good werkes,
> that they may vtterly be wyped and made clene from all
> contagyousnes of synne.[1]

'Thomas, et ego baptizo te in nomine patris, et filii, et
spiritus sancti'—with these words shortly after his birth
on 2 July 1489 Thomas Cranmer was baptized into the one,
holy, catholic, and apostolic church.[2] This early act of
parental affection on his behalf was considered necessary
because of two basic precepts of historic Western Christian
teaching. On the one hand, every human being was born a
sinner estranged from God and in need of salvation from the
divine threat of just eternal damnation. On the other, in his
infinite love and mercy God the Father sent his son Jesus
Christ to be humankind's saviour. As the sinless God-Man,
Jesus gave himself up to death on a cross to be an atoning
sacrifice for the sins of the whole world, thus making
possible humanity's reconciliation with their Maker.
According to the medieval Catholic church, this redemption
from sin bought by Christ's passion was first made available
to guilty humanity through the sacrament of baptism.
Accordingly, once the Latin baptismal formula was spoken
over him, new-born Thomas's inherited sinfulness was

---

[1] John Fisher, *The English Works of John Fisher*, Part I, ed. J. E. B. Mayor,
(London: Early English Text Society, Extra Series, 27, 1876) [henceforth *EW*],
100.

[2] The baptismal formula in the Sarum Rite; F. E. Brightman, *The English Rite*
(London: Rivingtons, 1915) ii. 740.

understood to be pardoned, and a supernatural goodness imparted to his soul. Now pleasing to God, he was adopted as God's child and made an heir to eternal life.

Nevertheless, even now his salvation from hell was not yet certain. In the normal course of events, upon emerging from the water, young Thomas would have been dressed with the chrisom, a white robe which symbolized his newly received purity, and instructed so to live his life as to be able to present his soul to God just as spotless on the day of judgement.[3] For baptism remitted the guilt (*reatus*) of original sin inherited from Adam but did not remove its stirrings (*actus*), the *fomes peccati*.[4] This 'tinder-box' remained within the pilgrim (*viator*) throughout his mortal life, always ready to spark the Christian's consent to the sins and offences which Satan and his demons ceaselessly suggested to him. Once the Christian had decided to commit a mortal sin, he would instantly lose both the supernatural goodness imparted by baptism and its concomitant promise of eternal salvation, until such time as he chose to restore himself to God's favour by penance.[5] And so the robing and the warning represented the twin hope and threat under which the Christian *viator* made his earthly pilgrimage. Thus, within days of his birth Thomas Cranmer had his first encounter with the issue that would come to dominate his life and legacy—the Christian doctrine of justification.

[3] See J. D. C. Fisher, *Christian Initiation: Baptism in the Medieval West: A study in the disintegration of the primitive rite of initiation* (London: SPCK, 1965), 174.

[4] Since concupiscence was not formally sin but the material from which sin sprang when consent was given to its motions, scholastic theologians referred to it as the '*fomes peccati*', literally the 'tinder of sin' which can best be rendered in English as the 'spark' or 'fuel for sin'.

[5] For the history of penance see, E. Amann and A. Michel, 'Pénitence', *Dictionnaire de théologie catholique*, ed. Jean Michel Alfred (Paris, 1899–1950), xii(i). 722–1050; John T. McNeill, *A History of the Cure of Souls* (London: SCM, 1952); Bernhard Poschmann, *Penance and the Anointing of the Sick*, trans. and rev. Francis Courtney (London: Burns & Oates, 1964); Amédée Teetaert, *La Confession aux laïques dans l'église latine depuis le VIIIe jusqu'au XVIe siècle* (Paris: Universitas Catholica Lovaniensis, 1926); Oscar D. Watkins, *A History of Penance*, 2 vols. (London: Longmans Green, 1920). For period studies, John Gray Nicholas, 'A Study of Piers Plowman in relation to the Medieval Penitential Tradition', Ph. D. thesis (Cambridge, 1984); Thomas N. Tentler, *Sin and Confession on the Eve of the Reformation* (Princeton: Princeton University Press, 1977); and Gordon J. Spykman, *Attrition and Contrition at the Council of Trent* (Kampen: Kok, 1955).

As Thomas emerged from childhood into early adolescence, he would have had the promise and the peril of the Christian life impressed on him during his annual Lenten duty of auricular confession. At the behest of Innocent III the Fourth Lateran Council (1215) had imposed this yearly obligation on all Christians in order that the faithful might confront their sins, receive pardoning grace, and so be restored to eternal salvation. As a result of this decree, sacramental penance became the agreed forum for both academic theologians and parish priests to discuss how Christians might avoid hell and eventually achieve entrance into heaven.

SOURCES FOR EARLY TUDOR
PENITENTIAL TEACHING

During Cranmer's youth the advent of commercial printing in early Tudor England helped to standardize the nature of penitential teaching in the English church. Of the new titles printed in England between 1506 and 1515, 52 per cent were concerned with religious subjects.[6] Six books issued in the first two decades of the sixteenth century are of particular interest for penance: The *Pupilla oculi* and the *Manipulus curatorum* (Latin penitentials), *The Ordynarye of Crystyanyte or of crysten men* and *The arte or crafte to lyue Well* (vernacular handbooks), as well as Mirk's *Festyuall* and Fisher's *Sermons on the Penitential Psalms* (vernacular sermons).[7] These publications provided clergy and learned laity ready access to sound teaching. While acknowledging rival schools of interpretation,[8] they popularized an English

[6] Namely, clerical information (2), devotions (23), exegesis (3), sermons (5), and theology (4), for a total of 37 new titles out of 71; based on a table provided by David Birch, *Early Reformation English Polemics* (Salzburg: Institut für Anglistik und Amerikanistik, Universität Salzburg, 1983), 17. See also Richard Rex, *Henry VIII and the English Reformation* (London: Macmillan, 1993), 110–14.

[7] In addition, the more technical description found in Fisher's later, polemical work, the *Assertionis Lutheranae Confutatio* (1523), is also helpful for illuminating the Scotist penitential framework found in many of these other books. All references to the *Confutatio* are based on the text printed in Fisher's *Opera, quae hactenus inveniri potuerunt omnia* (Würzburg: Fleischmann, 1597) [henceforth, *ALC*, Article number in *Confutatio*, column number in *Opera*].

[8] For example, John de Burgh preferred to define the mechanics of the

consensus on penitential doctrine, giving some credence to
the common assumption that

Than be there a great nombre of the doctours | whiche descante
vpon this playne songe [of Scripture]: but for bicause ther is no
discorde | no repugnancy | no contradiction amonge them | at the
leest in any poynt concernyng the substance of our faithe: all their
voyces make but one songe | & one armony.[9]

These books illustrate the penitential doctrine most commonly held by educated clergy at the turn of the sixteenth
century and, thus, the teaching that Thomas Cranmer
would have encountered, at the latest, when as a fourteen-
year-old scholar he came to Jesus College, Cambridge, in
1503.

When John Alcock, the founder of Jesus College, cited
'Johannes et Guido' in his sermon entitled *Ihesus clamabit*,
he was referring to the two most widely used Latin penitentials in England.[10] Written for learned clergy in 1385 by
John de Burgh, the chancellor of the University of Cambridge, the *Pupilla oculi* followed mostly Thomist teachings
and was the most popular penitential manuscript in England
during the fifteenth century. Seven editions were printed on
the Continent between 1510 and 1527, one in 1510 explicitly
for sale in London. If the sixteen surviving copies in the
Cambridge libraries are any indication, the later editions
continued to have a market in England as well.[11] The
sacrament in a Thomist manner. The penitent's acts of contrition, confession, and
satisfaction were the matter of the sacrament, while absolution by the priest was its
form (*Pupilla oculi*, Pars 5, cap. 1). Recognizing the influence of Scotus, however,
he also noted the Subtle Doctor's definition. Sacramental penance was the
absolution of penitent men in which, because of divine institution, the priest's
pronouncement effectively signified the soul's absolution from sin (ibid.). Similarly, Guido de Monte Rocherii acknowledged four different possible positions on
the power of the keys before presenting a fifth with which he agreed, *Manipulus
curatorum*, Pars 2, tract. 3, cap. 10.

[9] Fisher, *A sermon had at Paulis* (London: Berthelet, n.d.), sigs. [D4]v–E1r.

[10] John Alcock, *Ihesus clamabat Qui habet aures audiendi audiat, Luc. viii.*
(Westmynstre: Wynkyn de Worde, n.d.), sigs. [D6]v–[D7]r. William Maskell
offers extracts from both of these handbooks in his *Doctrine of Absolution*
(London: Pickering, 1849), 71–9.

[11] Records attest to over 100 individuals and 40 institutions having manuscript
copies of *Pupilla* during this period; R. M. Ball, 'The Education of the English
Parish Clergy', Ph.D. thesis (University of Cambridge, 1977), 8. H. M. Adams lists
printed editions surviving in Cambridge libraries as follows: 1510 (Rouen), 1510

Manipulus curatorum was another fourteenth-century Latin penitential written by Guido de Monte Rocherii, curate of Teruel, near Madrid. Recommended for parish priests by the noted pastoral authority Jean Gerson, its less learned and essentially Scotist exposition appears to have enjoyed more demand than the *Pupilla*, receiving seven printed editions in England itself between 1498 and 1517.[12] The Cambridge inventories of the mid-sixteenth century offer some additional evidence that the popularity of Guido's work most likely superseded that of de Burgh's in early Tudor England. Of those having taken their BA prior to 1530, three fellows at death had a copy of the *Manipulus* in their possession, while only one of these also had a copy of the *Pupilla*.[13] Still De Burgh continued to have his followers. The churchwardens' accounts for St Mary Major, Exeter, in the year 1533 record two copies of the *Pupilla*, 'whereof one is chained in the body of the church', undoubtedly for use by the priest during confession.[14]

(Paris for London), 1516 (Rouen), Strasbourg (1518), For Paris (1518), Paris (1522) and Paris (1527); *Catalogue of Books Printed on the Continent of Europe 1501–1600 in Cambridge Libraries* (Cambridge: Cambridge University Press, 1967), i. 214–15. All references to this work are based on the 1510 Paris edition (RSTC 4115).

[12] D. Catherine Brown, *Pastor and Laity in the Theology of Jean Gerson* (Cambridge: Cambridge University Press, 1987), 50. The *Manipulus* was printed in 1498, 1500, 1502, 1508 (twice), 1509, and 1517; A. W. Pollard and G. R. Redgrave (eds.), *A Short-title Catalogue of Books Printed in England, Scotland, and Ireland, and of English Books Printed Abroad, 1475–1640*, 2nd edn., W. A. Jackson, F. S. Ferguson, and Katharine F. Pantzer, rev. eds. (London: Bibliographical Society, 1986), i. 545. Although previous scholars had identified Caxton's *Doctrinal of Sapience* as an English translation of the *Manipulus*, Joseph E. Gallagher corrected this error in his detailed study of the origin of the *Doctrinal of Sapience*; 'The Sources of Caxton's *Ryal Book* and *Doctrinal of Sapience*', *Studies in Philology* 62 (1965), 40–62. All citations from the *Manipulus* are based on the London 1508 edition (RSTC 12474).

[13] Those having a copy of *Manipulus*: Pawmer, scholar and fellow of The King's Hall (1508–44) and Bygrave, BA 1518/19, fellow of Queens' (1518–54); having both a copy of *Manipulus* and *Pupilla*, Davy, B.Can.L. in 1520/1, fellow of The King's Hall (1531–43); E. S. Leedham-Green, *Books in Cambridge Inventories* (Cambridge: Cambridge University Press, 1986) i. 42–3, 55–7, 144–6, ii. 164, 403.

[14] Churchwardens' accounts, St Mary Major, Exeter, fol. 11, as quoted by Robert Whiting, *The Blind Devotion of the People* (Cambridge: Cambridge University Press, 1989), 22. For confession routinely taking place in an open area within the church, see McNeill, *Cure of Souls*, 148. For depictions of penitentials used during the course of confession, see Ann Eljenholm Nichols, 'The Etiquette of Pre-Reformation Confession in East Anglia', *The Sixteenth*

Vernacular handbooks were written both to be read and to be heard. Learned laity of means included them in their libraries. Priests used them for their own instruction and as didactic material to read to parishioners. One early English handbook indicated this multiple audience when suggesting that its earlier French version had the promise of indulgences for those priests 'that shal rede this boke to other [i.e. the laity] . . . to alle that shal here it rede: and by them self red it'.[15] The two popular English religious handbooks at the beginning of the sixteenth century were also translated from earlier French versions: *The Ordynarye of crysten men*, published in 1502 and 1506, and *The arte or crafte to lyue Well*, which was brought out under different titles in 1503 and 1505.[16] The first of these two can be directly connected to Lady Margaret Beaufort's reforming circle with which Jesus College was associated.[17] James Morice, clerk of works to the countess, and father of Ralph Morice, principal secretary to Cranmer, recorded his ownership of the 'Ordinarye of cristen men' in his 'Kalender' of English books inscribed on the verso of the first leaf of a copy of Caxton's 1481 edition of Cicero's *De senectute*.[18]

While printed collections of vernacular sermons were to be read to the laity, the degree of education expected of the audience varied. The most popular collection intended for a less learned congregation was John Mirk's sermon-cycle. Written in the late fourteenth century as parochial homilies for Sundays and major feasts of the liturgical year, Mirk's *Festyuall* combined theological teachings with traditional

Century Journal 17 (1986), 145–63, at 148–9, and *The arte or crafte to lyue Well* (London: Wynkyn de Worde, 1505), fol. 42v, the latter reproduced in Duffy, *Stripping of the Altars*, pl. 19.

[15] The *Doctrinal of Sapience* (London: William Caxton, 1487), sig. A1v. The *Doctrinal* emphasized this dual role by twice referring to its audience as 'ye reders and herars' (sigs. L8v–L9r) and once as 'ye that rede or here thys' (sig. L9r).

[16] All citations from *The Ordynarye of Crystyanyte or of crysten men* are based on Wynkyn de Worde's 1502 London edition (RSTC 5198); All citations from *The arte or crafte to lyue Well* are based on Wynkyn de Worde's 1505 London edition (RSTC 792).

[17] D. R. Leader, *A History of the University of Cambridge*, i: *The University to 1546* (Cambridge: Cambridge University Press, 1988), 264–81.

[18] J. C. T. Oates, *Studies in English Printing and Libraries* (London: Pindar, 1991), 22–30.

exempla. The *Festyuall* went through perhaps as many as twenty-three editions between 1483 and 1532.[19] For the more learned, however, John Fisher's sermons on the seven penitential psalms expounded sound doctrine with humanist erudition and eloquence. Published at the insistence of Lady Margaret before whom they were preached, Fisher's *Treatyse concernynge . . . the Seuen Penytencyall Psalmes* went through seven editions between 1508 and 1529.[20] When these penitentials, vernacular handbooks, and sermon collections are examined together, they demonstrate a wide consensus in England on the eve of the Reformation to inculcate contrition, to require confession for the forgiveness of sins, and to encourage human effort but foster a dependency on God for health and salvation.

POENITENTIA AS PENANCE[21]

At its most basic *poenitentia* was simply voluntary self-punishment required by God's justice for sin.[22] A sinner deserved to suffer as much punitive pain as he had previously had illicit pleasure, and only by doing penance could 'the wrath and Ire of so grete a mageste be pacyfyed'. Either a sinner punished his transgression himself, or God did. When a penitent punished himself accordingly, God's wrath against him ceased, and he would require nothing further,

---

[19] The Revised Short-Title Catalogue lists under *Liber festivalis* and *Quatuor Sermones* entries 17957–75, printed in 1483, 1486, 1491, 1493 (three times), 1495 (twice), 1496, 1499 (four times), 1502, 1506?, 1507?, 1508, 1511, *c.*1512, 1515, 1519, 1528 and 1532; RSTC ii. 156–7. All citations from Mirk's *Festyuall* are based on 1508 edition (RSTC 17971).

[20] The Revised Short-Title Catalogue lists pre-Reformation editions of Fisher's sermons on the Penitential psalms as entries 10902–7, printed in 1508, 1509, 1510, [1514?], [1519?], 1525 and 1529; RSTC i. 485. All references to Fisher's *Treatyse concernynge . . . the Seuen Penytencyall Psalmes . . .*, are based on the text of *EW*. According to Rex, of vernacular sermon collections published in Tudor England, only Latimer's and the official *Book of Homilies* were more successful; *Henry and the Reformation*, 112.

[21] *Poenitentia* is the technical Latin word for godly sorrow and is translated variously as 'penitence', 'penance' or 'repentance', depending on the context and the translator's theological commitments.

[22] 'Poenitentia est quaedam dolosis [*sic*] vindicta puniens in se quod se dolet commisisse', *Manipulus curatorum*, Pars 2, tract. 1, cap. 1, fol. 65r.

since God would 'not of ryght punysshe twyse for one and the same cause'.[23]

Poenitentia as self-punishment was both a virtue, an inner quality of character, and one of the church's seven sacraments. As a virtue, penitence was a *dolor*, that is, a manifest pain caused by mental grief, voluntarily assumed because of sin.[24] As a sacrament, penance's three parts of contrition (i.e. *dolor verus*—true sorrow), confession, and satisfaction were individually as well as collectively painful punishment which the penitent willingly undertook for the sins he had committed.[25] All three parts were needed for a completed sacrament, whether in intention or in fact.[26] The interrelatedness of *poenitentia* as a virtue and as a sacrament was ensured not only by the inclusion of contrition as an integral part of the sacrament but also by the universal agreement that true contrition always included the intention to confess.[27]

All the major penitential texts on the eve of the English Reformation taught that sacramental penance was of divine institution. 'For without that no creature may recouer saluecyon nor also with that to goo vnto dampnacyon.'[28] Not yet pressed by the Lutheran controversy, in his *Sermons on the Psalms* Fisher simply stated that confession was ordered to be made to priests because they had been 'sette

[23] Fisher, *EW*, 16, 84, 93, 131, 159; cf. Fisher quoting Ambrose, 'Peccator ergo si sibi ipsi non pepercerit, a Deo illi parcitur. Et si futuras poenas gehenae perpetuas in hoc parvo vitae spacio compensaverit, seipsum ab aeterno iudicio liberat', *ALC*, Art. 5, col. 389; 'Novam vitam a nemine putant rite inchoari posse, nisi quem veteris poeniteat, et qui pro noxis prioribus in se severius ulciscatur', Fisher, *ALC*, Art. 7, col. 413.

[24] *Oxford Latin Dictionary*, ed. P. G. W. Glare (Oxford: Clarendon Press, 1982), 569.

[25] '[H]e the whiche it [sacramental penance] receyueth wyll that his syn be punysshed', *The arte or crafte*, fol. 43r. 'Vltimo aduertendum est quod poenitentia aliquando accipitur pro punitione hominis peccatoris pro peccatis . . . contritio est poenitentia id est punitio pro peccatis. Confessio etiam est punitio peccatoris pro peccatis. et similiter satisfactio. Quandoque vero accipitur pro punitione peccatoris sufficiente pro peccatis secundum forum ecclesiae sed non absolute:' *Pupilla oculi*, Pars 5, cap. 1, v, fol. 27v. *Manipulus curatorum*, Pars 2, tract. 1, cap. 4, fol. 66v.

[26] *Pupilla oculi*, Pars 5, cap. 1, T–V, fol. 27v; *Manipulus curatorum*, Pars 2, cap. 2, fols. 67v–68r.

[27] *Pupilla oculi*, Pars 5, cap. 2, L–M, cap. 3, A, fol. 28r; *Manipulus curatorum*, Pars 2, tract. 2, cap. 2, fol. 68r; *The arte or crafte*, fol. 43v; Fisher, *EW*, 85.

[28] *The Ordynarye*, Part 4, chap. 10, sig. [T6]v.

in this worlde by almyghty god as ouerlokers of the people'.[29] The penitentials, however, often went to greater lengths to establish this point.

According to the *Pupilla*, while only mental confession was mandated by immutable natural law, vocal confession was required by the new law of the Gospel. Appealing to the customary Scripture texts, De Burgh argued that Jesus implicitly instituted auricular confession when he told the leper to go and show himself to the priest (Matthew 8: 4) and that James had promulgated the command to confess when he told Christians to confess their sins to one another (James 5: 16). De Burgh also repeated the traditional argument that the priesthood's power to judge (*potestas iudicandi*) implied a power to investigate (*potestas cognoscendi*) as well. Jesus had given priests the authority to judge sins when he said, 'The sins of those you forgive are forgiven' (John 20: 23). Since priests could not properly exercise this office unless sinners opened their conscience to them, Christ had established priests as judges to whom sinners were bound to confess.[30]

Guido de Monte Rocherii took a very different approach.[31] He also admitted that confession of sins to a priest was not a matter of natural law, only mental confession to God (*coram Deo*) was so required. Nevertheless, in an implicit attempt to dispel any doubts about its universal necessity for Christians which some people might have had as a result, Guido argued that sacramental penance could not have been instituted prior to the Incarnation. Since its purpose was to remove sin and reconcile a sinner to God and the church, the sacrament's aims could only have been accomplished through the grace made possible by the Incarnation. Moreover, a judge had to be able to mediate between the parties, and there was no mediator between

---

[29] Fisher, *EW*, 76–7. For Fisher's later, more elaborate defence, see Chapter 2.

[30] *Pupilla oculi*, Pars 5, cap. 3, R, fol. 29. Although *The arte or crafte* did not directly address the nature of the institution of sacramental penance, its illustration of the sacrament implied agreement with De Burgh. Over three scenes of auricular confession was a depiction of Jesus commanding his disciples to loose Lazarus from his bonds; fol. 42v.

[31] *Manipulus curatorum*, Pars 1, tract. 1, cap. 1, fol. 4r; Pars 2, tract. 3, cap. 1, fols. 74r–75r.

God and humanity until the coming of Jesus Christ, the God-Man.

Having explained why the commandment to confess to a priest could not have been part of natural law, Guido then sought to justify its place in the divine law of the New Testament by reasoning back from his Scotist definition of sacramental penance. Confession had its effect because of absolution, and absolution had its effect because of the keys. Christ gave the keys to Peter and in him to 'many others' when he said 'I give you the keys to the kingdom of heaven' (Matthew 16: 19) and 'the sins of those you forgive are forgiven' (John 20: 23). Therefore, Christ established the leaders of the church as judges in his place with the authority to reconcile sinners to God and to his church. Only after this explanation did Guido add the traditional proof texts of the cleansing of the ten lepers (Luke 17: 14) and the injunction of James to confess (James 5: 16).

CONTRITION

Penitential *dolor* could be either attrition or contrition. De Burgh and *The arte or crafte* distinguished between the two with respect to grace.[32] If the penitent's voluntary displeasure was unformed by *gratia gratum faciens*, it was attrition; if coupled with grace, it was contrition. Guido de Monte Rocherii described attrition and contrition both with respect to grace and with respect to motive. Attrition was simply 'a certain imperfect contrition' that needed to be perfected by grace. Yet since sanctifying grace infused human sorrow with a love for God, Guido chose to emphasize attrition as a sorrow from fear of punishment and contrition as detesting sin for having offended the God one loved. *The Ordynarye of crysten men* also included references to both descriptions, defining contrition as sorrow principally for the love of God and attrition as 'a maner of contrycyon vnparfyte and

---

[32] In this study *Gratia gratis data*, literally 'the grace given freely', will be rendered in English as either 'actual grace' or 'prevenient grace'. *Gratia gratum faciens*, literally the 'grace which makes one pleasing', will be rendered in English as 'sanctifying grace', since *gratia gratum faciens* restored a sinner to a state of justification.

vnsuffycyent for to haue the grace of god'.[33] In his sermons, Fisher distinguished between the two sorrows with respect to their origin in either fear or love.[34] As a virtuous habit, regret for sin was to be consistent and lifelong. Whenever the thought of a past sin came into mind, a penitent was to grieve that he had committed such an act so 'that no thynge of it be vncontryte & vnconfessed'.[35] Everyone agreed that true contrition included the intention to forsake sin.[36]

Although perfect sorrow was a divine gift so that almost every saint 'had nede somtyme to aske of almyghty god the gyfte of contrycyon',[37] all agreed that attrition could serve as

[33] '[D]olor voluntarie assumptus pro peccatis etc. quando est imperfectus et informis propter defectum gratiae gratum facientis dicitur attritio', *Pupilla oculi*, Pars 5, cap. 2, c, fol. 27v, see also cap. 2, A; 'attrycyon is a sorowe imperfyte of his syn . . . whiche is without grace makyng agreable', *The arte or crafte*, fol. 44; '[R]ecogitat se multa mala commisisse quae displicent diuinae bonitati et propter quae est dignus puniri grauiter: timet. quoniam etiam cogitat vlterius dei pietatem et misericordiam qui paratus est omni dolenti et poenitenti parcere et dimittere culpam quantumcumque magnam: sperat de venia et sic mouetur ad detestandum peccatum. Et iste motus vocatur attritio id est quaedam contritio imperfecta . . . ita quod timor seruilis praecedat et praeparat cor peccatoris ad contritionem: sed amor et feruor charitatis perficit ipsum', *Manipulus curatorum*, Pars 2, tract. 2, cap. 6, fol. 72r; *The Ordynarye*, Part 4, chap. 2, sigs. RIV–3v, and chap. 11, sig. VIV.

[34] 'There be two thynges therfore whiche be the very cause that we turne our selfe vnto almyghty god, one is whan we call to mynde his ferefull and greuouse punysshement. The other is the sorowe in our herte whan we remembre the multytude of our synnes, wherby our best and moost meke lorde god is gretely dyscontent with vs . . . the mouynge of the soule fyrst caused of fere, and after of sorowe referred vnto god is called contrycyon', Fisher, *EW*, 30.

[35] Fisher, *EW*, 86; cf. 'Deus quando absoluit hominem a vinculo peccati: ligat eum vinculo perpetuae detestationis . . . poenitens semper doleat et de dolore semper gaudeat', *Pupilla oculi*, Pars 5, cap. 2, G, fol. 28r; '[Q]ualiscumque occurret ei memoria de peccato quod displiceat sibi illud peccatum fecisse . . . Semper doleat et de dolore gaudeat. et sequitur. vbi dolor finitur: ibi poenitentia deficit', *Manipulus curatorum*, Pars 2, tract. 2, cap. 4, fol. 70r.

[36] 'Confitens qui non est contritus nec habet propositum deserendi peccatum', *Pupilla oculi*, Pars 5, cap. 3, af, fol. 30r; 'That penaunce is a vertue by the whiche we playne and hate the ylles and synnes the whiche we haue commytted with purpose vs to amende and by the whiche we purpose no more to commyt the sayd synnes by vs', *The arte or crafte*, fol. 43r. *The Ordynarye* taught that intending to amend was necessary for true penitence; Part 4, chap. 11, sig. VIV. Mirk associated 'not to torne agayne to his synne' with true penitence, *Festyuall*, fol. 24r; cf. his requirement for absolution, 'He muste be contryte sory for his synnes and shryue hym clene | and be in full purpose neuer to synne more', ibid., fol. 12r. According to Fisher, the truly contrite would not willingly 'fall agayne but with a full purpose contynue in vertuous lyuynge', *EW*, 218–19, cf. 85–6, 216, 238.

[37] Fisher, *EW*, 34; cf. the accusation of heresy brought against Margery Kempe that 'she says that she may weep and have contrition when she will'; *The Book of*

preparation. In keeping with the medieval axiom 'facienti quod in se est non Deus denegat gratiam',[38] the *viator* was expected to 'do that that is in hym'. According to *The Ordynarye of crysten men*,

[A purpose and desyre to do penaunce] comyth pryncypally of god by a remorce of conscyence that god gyueth vnto the persone | or by a lytell | and inclynacyon naturall or by a predycacyon | or by the counseyll of a gode confessour or by other vocacyon semblable | And thenne they the whiche dyspose them to receyue and obey vnto that inspyracyon receyuen true contrycyon of theyr synnes | And by the consyguent [*sic*] the grace of the holy gooste |[39]

Reflecting the diversity of scholastic opinion on whether attrition arose from natural human ability unaided by grace (*ex puris naturalibus*) or in response to divine prompting *ex gratia gratis data*, *The Ordynarye* emphasized grace but included an 'inclynacyon naturall' as a possibility as well. Regardless how attrition arose, once the 'inspyracyon' of penitence had come to the *viator*, he was expected to co-operate by persisting in his sorrow until God granted him the sanctifying grace necessary for true contrition.[40] There-fore, much of the medieval penitential tradition was devoted to assisting the penitent to do his best to prepare for this divine gift. Such assistance most often took the form of directing the penitent's attention to the recognized causes which led to contrition. De Burgh offered the traditional six: recognition of sin, shame because of it, the worthlessness of sin, fear of the last judgement with its unbearable punish-ment, sorrow for the loss of heavenly glory, and the triple hope of forgiveness, grace, and glory.[41] Guido de Monte

Margery Kempe, trans. B. A. Windeatt (London: Penguin, 1985), Book 1, chap. 54, 170.

[38] 'God will not deny grace to the man who does his best', McGrath, *Iustitia Dei*, 83–91.

[39] *The Ordynarye*, Part 4, chap. 2, sig. R2r.

[40] *The Ordynarye*, Part 4, chap. 2, sigs. R1v–R2r; 'Nota quod attritio potest fieri contritio . . . si tum maneat huiusmodi motus doloris non interruptus quo usque infundatur gratia gratum faciens et maneat cum ista: tunc dicitur contritio secundum Thomam', *Pupilla oculi*, Pars 5, cap. 2, c, fol. 27v. NB that Aquinas taught that the *attritus* (the person) could become *contritus* but not that *attritio* (the sorrow) itself become *contritio*. See Spykman, *Attrition and Contrition*, 60–1.

[41] *Pupilla oculi*, Pars 5, cap. 2, F, fol. 28r. According to Tentler, this list was first

Rocherii had a similar list: love of God, embarrassment of sin, the vileness of having to serve Satan as a result of sin, being held accountable for every thought, word, and deed on the day of judgement, losing heavenly citizenship, and lastly offending the God who had done so much for humanity in creating them in his image and in redeeming them by the blood of Christ from the cruelty of the demons and from the bitterness of hell. Fisher was somewhat briefer, but consistent with the other two. Repentance came from sinners' examining their conscience, recognizing their sins, remembering their liability for everlasting punishment, and seeing how far and from whom they had fallen.[42] Mirk's *Festyuall* provides an example of a woman who was moved to contrition by the steps recommended in the penitentials:

> For as she bethought her of the streytnesse of Crystes dome | and the grete and horryble paynes of hell that were ordeyned for suche synners as she that was sore aferde and bethought her of Crystes passyon what loue he shewed to all crysten people | she thought she was unkynde to hym | and he suffred so sore for her . . .[43]

Trusting in his childlike mercy, she asked for pardon and was forgiven.

Commonly, the causes which led to contrition were contracted to two chief motives: the fear of punishment and the hope of forgiveness.[44] Under the category of contrition caused by the love of God, Guido de Monte Rocherii described the process as follows. The *viator*, considering

offered by Raymond de Peñaforte in his *Summa confessorum*, widely known as *Raymundina*; *Sin and Confession*, 31, 238–9.

[42] *Manipulus curatorum*, Pars 2, tract. 2, cap. 6, fol. 71v–73r; Fisher, *EW*, 159, 210, 245, 250.

[43] Mirk, *Festyuall*, fol. 69v.

[44] '[F]or too haue perfyte contrycyon it behoueth to haue hope of pardon procedynge of the dyuyne mercy | and fere of payne by consyderacyon of the dyuyne iustyce', *The arte or crafte*, fol. 44r; 'And by the meane of these two thynges | That is to knowe fere on that one partye | and hope on the other | comyth a purpose and desyre to do penaunce', *The Ordynarye*, Part 4, chap. 2, sig. R2r. Cf. 'Notandum tamen quod licet peccator sicut dictum est debeat dolere et conteri de peccatis. tamen semper debet sperare in domino et in pietate et misericordia eius ita quod debet sperare de venia et gloria', *Manipulus curatorum*, Pars 2, tract. 2, cap. 6, fol. 73r.

how he was worthy to be grievously punished by God for his sins and yet how merciful God was that he was prepared to spare a penitent and forgive his sins, no matter how great, hoped for forgiveness and was moved to detest his sin. While still attrition, this servile fear and fervent hope prepared his heart for perfecting grace, which when granted, illuminated the penitent with the love of God and expelled all servile fear.[45] Like upper and lower millstones grinding the wheat kernels between them into flour for baking bread, hope and fear shattered hardened hearts, making the tears of contrition flow, and firing the heart with a love for God that made Christ welcome in the penitent's life.[46] Fear of divine punishment caused grief, but because Christians had hope that this pain would bring about forgiveness, they also had joy.[47]

Pious Christians were always to live in reverent fear and godly hope.[48] The first prevented presumption of assured

[45] '[I]ta quod timor seruilis praecedat et praeparat cor peccatoris ad contritionem: sed amor et feruor charitatis perficit ipsum . . . sic contritionem praecedit timor poenae et iste timor praeparat ad amorem et charitatem dei quae postquam est in anima expellit omnem timorem.' *Manipulus curatorum*, Pars 2, tract. 2, cap. 6, fol. 72r; 'Sicque postquam inceperimus a timore, perveniemus tandem ad amorem, ut subinde timor paulatim desinat, et affectus in nobis iustitiae tandem aliquando regnet ac triumphet', Fisher, *ALC*, Art. 6, col. 413.

[46] 'Et istas duas molas [i.e. spem veniae et timorem poenae] debet tenere semper verus poenitens . . . vt cor peccatoris durum vt lapis emolescat et liquefiat ut cera', *Manipulus curatorum*, Pars 2, tract. 2, cap. 1, fol. 67v; '[E]t ideo verus poenitens granum, id est animiam suam debet tenere inter duas molas scilicet timoris et spei: vt ex farina sic trita barutelo discretionis mundata aqua lachrymarum, id est compunctionie [*sic*] commixta. panem bonum in clibano cordis igne charitatis decoctum faciat hospiti suo scilicet Christo', ibid., cap. 3, fol. 69v.

[47] 'Notandum tamen quod in contritione non solum est dolor | sed etiam est gaudium . . . sed quoniam cogitat se per istum dolorem a peccato liberari et reconsiliari deo: gaudet et non immerito', *Manipulus curatorum*, Pars 2, tract. 2, cap. 1, fol. 68r. Cf. Fisher, *EW*, 42–3. Duffy has rightly noted that for Fisher penitential tears were 'evidence of the recreative work of the Spirit within us'; 'The spirituality of John Fisher', in *Humanism, Reform and the Reformation: The Career of Bishop John Fisher*, ed. Brendan Bradshaw and Eamon Duffy (Cambridge: Cambridge University Press, 1989), 205–31, at 210. However, Fisher would have believed that his tears were a sign of inner renovation because they also represented the meritorious self-punishment of contrition.

[48] 'That persone which soo dooth [i.e. mix dread with hope] shall neyther truste in god without his fere, nor drede hym without hope, for by enclynynge more to the one than to the other we shall soone erre', Fisher, *EW*, 113; 'Multis obfuit solius misericordiae recordatio. Fecit enim ut praesumerent. Multis enim item solius iustitiae, quae fecit ut disperarent. At ambae simul confoederatae profuerunt omnibus', Fisher, *ALC*, Art. 6, col. 413.

salvation. Although the aim of medieval piety was to die in a state of grace, no one could be certain that he would so live his life as for that to happen. Remembering God's determination to punish sin encouraged people to do so themselves so that they would be prepared when called to account at their passing from this life. Godly hope, on the other hand, eliminated despair of inevitable damnation. While the Old Covenant created 'grete fere and drede of the greuous punysshement of god', the New Testament offered 'grete hope & truste of forgyuenes, for the excellent treasure of grace & mercy of god'.[49] The letter of the law may have demanded eternal death for sinners, but its spirit promised forgiveness to all who turn to God in true penance. Judas wept bitterly for his sin, confessed his error to the priests, and offered the thirty pieces of silver as satisfaction. Nevertheless, having no faith in God's mercy, like Cain he lacked hope, and true contrition always included hope.[50] With defective penitence, Judas killed himself in despair.[51] Having an unwavering hope in God's willingness to forgive the penitent delivered sinners from sinking down to the sin of Cain. Like a single millstone, neither hope nor fear were of much use without the other, and nothing was 'more peryllous than lenynge more to the one than to the other'. However, when held together like millstones placed on top of each other and set to move in opposite directions, nothing was 'more profytable to the synner' than the 'Iuste moderacyon of them bothe' which resulted from their conjunction.[52]

Penitents had many aids for reflecting on the causes of contrition. With scenes of the last judgement and shields bearing the emblems of Christ's passion, with rood beams depicting the crucifixion and images of the saints whose presence in paradise witnessed to the hope to which all Christians were called, the fabric and fixtures of the churches were designed to inculcate penitence in those

---

[49] Fisher, *EW*, 169.
[50] '[U]nde debet esse cum spe veniae ita quod vere contritus nunquam debet desperare de venia | sed semper debet spectare de dei misericordia', *Manipulus curatorum*, Pars 2, tract. 2, cap. 3, fol. 69v.
[51] Fisher, *EW*, 81.
[52] Fisher, *EW*, 114.

who worshipped within them. The devout, if extremely excitable, Margery Kempe recorded in her *Booke* that upon seeing a crucifix 'piteously portrayed and lamentable to behold', thoughts of Christ's passion entered her mind and fired a love so strong that she cried out in a loud voice and wept uncontrollably.[53]

Preaching also could encourage contrition.[54] According to Fisher in the *Confutatio*, he could offer very many instances of sermons turning people from their errors towards striving for virtue.[55] *The floure of the commaundements of god* (1510) records the example of such a conversion. A mocker came to hear Saint Bernard preach, but moved to deep contrition by the saint's words he began to weep. With each tear shed by the mocker, Bernard was given to see a link in the invisible chain of sin wrapped around the new penitent's neck break and fall off. By the end of the sermon the contrition brought about by St Bernard's preaching had completely freed the former mocker from his bondage to past misdeeds.[56] Likewise, meditating on the seven penitential psalms was helpful.[57] Since reciting these psalms was both an expression of whatever sorrow the supplicant might have had and a means for contemplating the truths that God used to bring about perfect penitence, praying them was an ideal means for the individual to do what was in him to prepare for the gift of contrition. According to Fisher, who based his penitential

[53] *Margery Kempe*, Book 1, chap. 46, 148; cf. her weeping both on the Via Dolorosa in Jerusalem and subsequently at crucifixes and upon seeing people and animals being beaten; ibid., Book 1, chaps. 28–9, 104–9.

[54] '[A purpose and desyre to do penaunce] comyth . . . by a predycacyon', *The Ordynarye*, Part 4, chap. 2, sig. R2r.

[55] 'Nec desunt exempla plurima, quae proferamus, eorum qui per conciones ab erroribus, ad viam rectam, a turpi luxu, ad vitae sanctitatem, et a maximis demum sceleribus ad virtutem capescendam sunt conversi', Fisher, *A$\overline{L}$C*, Art. 36, col. 692.

[56] *The floure of the commaundementes of god* (London: Wynkyn de Worde, 1510), fol. 136r. For the descent into ever deepening sin, see Fisher, *EW*, 200–9.

[57] i.e. *Domine ne in furore* (Ps. 6), *Beati quorum* (Ps. 31), *Domine ne in furore posterioris* (Ps. 37), *Miserere mei deus* (Ps. 50), *Domine exaudi, prioris* (Ps. 101), *De profundis* (Ps. 129), and *Domine exaudi, posterioris* (Ps. 142). Chief among these was Ps. 50, David's lament over his adultery with Bathsheba and his subsequent murder of her husband to avoid detection; see 2 Sam. 11–12. As an example of the frequency of Ps. 50 in the liturgy during Lent, consider this quotation from Mirk: '[A]nd [to] drawe a man to the more contrycyon those .l. dayes the psalme in the sawter as (Miserere mei deus) is more rehersed these dayes than ony other tyme of the yere'; *Festyuall*, fol. 13r.

sermons on them, these psalms were 'lettres of supplyca-
cyon' which would move God to grant forgiveness and were
more acceptable to him than the penitent's own prayers.[58]

POENITENTIA AS A VIRTUE VERSUS
POENITENTIA AS A SACRAMENT

Despite the universal recognition of their interrelatedness,
the schoolmen differed in their descriptions of the exact
nature of the relationship between contrition and sacramental penance. Peter the Lombard taught that the presence of
the divine gift of contrition remitted a penitent's sin at the
moment he turned to God with such penitence. Priestly
absolution merely declared innocent what God's grace had
already made so.[59] Aquinas, however, sought to make
forgiveness of sin a conjoint result of both the virtue of
penitence and a benefit of Christ's passion that was com-
municated through absolution, i.e. both *ex opere operantis*
and *ex opere operato*.[60] Applying Aristotelian philosophy to
the problem, Aquinas first defined the sacrament as consisting of matter, i.e. the penitent's contrition, confession, and
satisfaction, and form, i.e. the priest's absolution. Next, he
defined the process of justification as the infusion of grace, a
double movement of free will toward God and against sin,
and the remission of sins. Lastly, he defined the interrela-
tionship between justification and the sacrament by the
simultaneous mutual causality of the material (natural)
order and the formal (supernatural) order. By material
causality, contrition and faith (the double movement of
the will) provided the necessary disposition for receiving
grace. In the formal causality, the infusion of grace made

---

[58] Fisher, *EW*, 73–4.

[59] Poschmann, *Penance*, 159–60; Spykman, *Attrition and Contrition*, 44–5.

[60] Sacramental grace bestowed because of a quality in the recipient is said to be
ex opere operantis (literally, 'by the work of the worker'). Sacramental grace
bestowed because of the inherent power of the sacrament to which the recipient
places no spiritual barrier is said to be *ex opere operato* (literally, 'by the working of
the work'). For an excellent survey of Latin terms used in scholastic theology, see
Richard A. Muller, *Dictionary of Latin and Greek Theological Terms: Drawn
Principally from Protestant Scholastic Theology* (Grand Rapids, Mich.: Baker
Book House, 1985).

possible faith and contrition.[61] Since, however, contrition could not exist in the penitent without the infusion of grace, the formal causality had logical, although not temporal, priority.[62] As a result, Aquinas's carefully constructed union of justification and sacramental penance remained fundamentally dependent on the initiation of divine grace, *ex opere operato*. While he accepted the traditional teaching that justification through the gift of contrition received extra-sacramentally was the regular, normal way, Aquinas mostly taught that such contrition cleansed the *viator* immediately by means of the absolution that would follow, since the sacrament existed in intention.[63]

Aquinas may have linked the efficacy of contrition for forgiveness to the power of the keys made available in the sacrament, but his reasoning left contrition as simultaneously both the 'disposition for and fruit of the grace conferred in absolution'.[64] Scotus's solution to this problem was to cut the Gordian knot into two. *De potentia ordinata*,[65] God had established two means by which those whom he had predestined to eternal life might receive divine pardon: either through a sustained level of penitence *ex merito de congruo*[66] or through absolution in sacramental penance.

---

[61] Poschmann, *Penance*, 169–70; Spykman, *Attrition and Contrition*, 63; Charles R. Meyer, *The Thomistic Concept of Justifying Contrition* (Mundelein, Ill.: Seminarius Sanctae Mariae ad Lacum, 1949), 122–31.

[62] 'Because a formal cause is in regard to any acts on the part of the sinner in some way also an efficient and final cause, in these orders of causality also grace and the infused virtues are prior to the acts which are informed by them, and hence proceed from them', Meyer, *Thomistic Contrition*, 123.

[63] Poschmann, *Penance*, 171–2; Spykman, *Attrition and Contrition*, 66–7. For the rare references in Aquinas to the sacrament raising attrition to contrition, see Poschmann, *Penance*, 172–4; Spykman, *Attrition and Contrition*, 68–9.

[64] Spykman, *Attrition and Contrition*, 64.

[65] Scotus distinguished between two powers in God: (i) *potentia absoluta* ('absolute power'), his omnipotent power to shape the universe and everything in it as he saw fit, but without any contradiction; (ii) *potentia ordinata* ('ordained power'), the power by which God creates and sustains the natural order and the means of salvation as he has actually chosen to establish them.

[66] Scholastics distinguished between two forms of merit, the semi-meritorious *meritum de congruo* (congruent merit) of those not yet in a state of justification and the fully meritorious *meritum de condigno* (condign merit) of the justified. For Scotus, *meritum de congruo* was the necessary disposition which God would freely choose to reward with sanctifying grace. For the distinctive nature of Scotus's

Those who persisted in their sorrow *ex naturalibus cum communi influentia* would receive the grace necessary for forgiveness when God determined they had reached a sufficient level of penitential intensity.[67] At that point, always unknowable to the *viator*, God would infuse sanctifying grace so that the same motion that before was *attritio* would then be *contritio*. Those with some sorrow but not a sufficient disposition for pardon *de congruo* could, if they presented no obstacle, receive the same infusion of grace through the sacrament *ex opere operato*. Scotus defined the sacrament simply as the priest's act of absolution, the penitent's sorrow, confession, and satisfaction as a disposition. Scotus justified his 'two-track' approach by arguing that the sacramental way was an easier, more certain way of forgiveness which God had granted as a gracious accommodation to human frailty.[68]

In general, the early sixteenth-century English sources for penitential teaching eschewed the scholastic details of these various positions, presenting instead a general pattern in which contrition could bring forgiveness directly and the sacrament could change attrition to contrition *ex opere operato*. Citing Lazarus, the ten lepers and Ps. 31, Guido de Monte Rocherii taught that those truly contrite were cleansed from their *culpa* at the time of their penitence before they came to confession. Those merely attrite, however, could come to confession and by virtue of the sacrament have their imperfect penitence transformed into true contrition and their *culpa* forgiven.[69] According to *The*

approach to congruent merit, see Richard Cross, *Duns Scotus* (Oxford: Oxford University Press, 1999), 103–7.

[67] On whether Scotus intended God's *communis influentia* (universal sustaining power) to be considered as *gratia gratis data* and, thus, should be distinguished from those theologians who taught justification *ex puris naturalibus*, for the affirmative position, see Harry J. McSorley, *Luther: Right or Wrong? An Ecumenical-Theology Study of Luther's Major Work, The Bondage of the Will* (New York, N.Y.: Newman, 1969), 169. For those opposed, see Spykman, *Attrition and Contrition*, 76–79, and Poschmann, *Penance*, 186.

[68] Poschmann, *Penance*, 184–90; Spykman, *Attrition and Contrition*, 70–83.

[69] 'Ille enim qui accedit ad confessionem aut est perfecte contritus aut non. si est perfecte contritus: tunc deus virtute contritionis remittit sibi peccata . . . ita quod antequam accedat ad confessionem mundatus est a culpa. Si autem non est perfecte contritus tunc virtute confessionis ista imperfecta contritio reducitur ad perfectam. ita quod de attrito fit virtute confessionis contritus et sic virtute confessionis

Ordynarye, a man having true contrition and intending to confess was in a state of grace. Nevertheless, if a man lacked true contrition, he could trust the power of absolution to change his attrition into contrition so that he could be forgiven, 'yf there be none other lettynge'. *The arte or crafte* took substantially the same position. Perfect contrition remitted 'gylte', but attrition was made agreeable by 'confessyon and absolucyon sacramentall', so long as the penitent did not put 'ony obiecte vnto the holy ghost'.[70] The highest praise for this 'two-track' system of forgiveness came from Fisher in the *Confutatio*. Reflecting the English consensus on penitential matters, he attributed this teaching not to Scotus but to the church itself:

And so . . . the church believes that sinners are able to be made acceptable to God in two ways: either through great and bitter sorrow, not having yet received the sacrament of absolution or through the reception of the sacrament, with some sorrow preceding. Certainly, either way God is prepared to give his grace freely. Nevertheless, the second way is easier and more secure for the sinner.[71]

Fisher argued that the scholastics had been faithful to the Gospel when they permitted an easier way as an accommodation to human weakness because, according to Matthew 12: 20, Jesus would not break a bruised reed or quench a smouldering wick.[72]

The only exception to this pattern of two means of justification was the strict contritionism of the Thomist *Pupilla oculi*. De Burgh agreed that contrition remitted sin

---

remittuntur peccata quo ad culpam', *Manipulus curatorum*, Pars 2, tract. 3, cap. 10, fol. 97r.

[70] *The Ordynarye*, Part 4, chap. 3, sig. R3 and chap. 11, sig. VIV; *The arte or crafte*, fol. 44r.

[71] 'Duobus itaque modis . . . Ecclesia credit peccatores Deo posse conciliari. Altero per ingentem et acerbum dolorem, nondum absolutionis suscepto sacramento: Altero per susceptionem sacramenti, dolore nonnullo praecedente. Utroque certe modo suam paratus est Deus elargiri gratiam. Secundus tamen modus facilior est, et peccatori securior', Fisher, *ALC*, Art. 5, col. 385.

[72] 'Illi nimirum spectant illud Evangelicum: arundinem quassatam non confringet, et linum fumigans non extinguet. Condescendunt itaque misericorditer infirmitatibus peccatorum, ac propterea viam struunt faciliorem, et certiorem quo poteruntque ad alliciendos in rectam semitam peccatores', Fisher, *ALC*, Art. 1, col. 339.

prior to confession,[73] but he did not explicitly teach that the sacrament raised attrition to contrition. In fact, De Burgh assumed that the penitent came to sacramental penance already contrite, for he taught that a worthy confession had to arise from love. Nevertheless, he reasoned that the attrite could still benefit from confession. Since a *viator* was commanded to open his sins to the priest, if he were not contrite, he was to confess and submit himself to the power of the keys. Afterwards, should he become contrite and, thus, no longer be guilty of receiving absolution under false circumstances, he would begin to receive its benefits.[74]

Therefore, in the early sixteenth-century English church the typical, although not exclusive, teaching on justification by penance followed a two-tier approach: either extra-sacramentally through true contrition or sacramentally with attrition. Since Guido offered a fairly generic scholastic account of how attrition became contrition, it is difficult to establish whether he was explicitly Scotist in his under-standing of extra-sacramental justification. However, as Tentler has noted, the very fact that Guido was willing to recognize an easier standard for forgiveness through the sacrament in addition to his rigorous contritionism suggests that he worked from a broadly Scotist penitential frame-work.[75] When expounding the scholastic teaching on justi-fication in the *Confutatio*, Fisher himself described the extra-sacramental mode as the *'via contritionis seu attritionis formatae'* ('the way of contrition or formed attrition').[76] Such a Scotist phrase was incompatible with Thomist thought,[77]

---

[73] 'Homo reconsiliatus deo per contritionem debet etiam si facultas assit reconsiliari ecclesiae per confessionem', *Pupilla oculi*, Pars 5, cap. 3, A, fol. 28r.

[74] 'Nota quod confessio secundum quod est actus virtutis non valet sine caritate quae est principium merendi sed confessio secundum quod est pars sacramenti ordinat confitentem ad sacerdotem habentem claves ecclesiae qui per confessionem cognoscit conscientiam confitentis. Et sic potest non contritus confiteri: quia potest peccata sua sacerdoti notificare et clavibus ecclesiae se subicere. Et quamvis tunc non recipiat absolutionis fructum. tamen recedente fictione incipiet obtinere sicut in aliis sacramentis', *Pupilla oculi*, Pars 5, cap 3, C, fol. 28v. For a discussion of this standard Thomist teaching, see Poschmann, *Penance*, 173–4; Spykman, *Attrition and Contrition*, 68.   [75] Tentler, *Sin and Confession*, 273–4.

[76] 'Quoniam igitur via contritionis, seu attritionis formatae, non minus est dura, quam incerta peccatoribus, iccirco viam hanc alteram, per sacramentorum suscep-tionem, multo mitiorem, et securiorem docent', *ALC*, Art. 1, col. 339.

[77] Aquinas argued that since contrition arose from the habit of charity, attrition

and included the Scotist description of the process of information as well.[78] What lay behind the double-method of justification taught in the early sixteenth-century English church was most likely the Scotist notion of justification through divine acceptance, either through attaining a sufficient level of sorrow *ex merito de congruo* or by putting no obstacle to grace during the reception of the sacrament.

CONFESSION

Although art and architecture, self-examination and corporate worship, preaching and praying could inspire a sinner's heart with contrition, the process of auricular confession was itself designed to cultivate as well as to exhibit worthy sorrow. The church required the penitent to recite and grieve for all mortal sins brought to his memory.[79] A general confession was sufficient to blot those deadly sins which a penitent could not remember with due diligence, because God did not require more than a man could do.[80] However, this provision only applied to those mortal sins omitted through invincible ignorance and that did not include failure

could never become contrition. The former ceased to exist at the moment when charity was infused in the soul and created contrition in its place; Meyer, *Thomistic Contrition*, 76–80; cf. Spykman, *Attrition and Contrition*, 60–1.

[78] 'Et in hoc detestationis motu pergere, donec ex congruo tandem infundatur gratia. Infusa vero gratia, iam idem motus (qui pridem dictus erat attritio) contritio dicitur. Vides itaque contritionem (quae modis antedictis paratur) charitate formatam esse. Attritionem vero, quae discussionem illam et collectionem et detestationem peccatorum complectitur, penitus informem esse.' Fisher, *ALC*, Art. 6, col. 407.

[79] *Pupilla oculi*, Pars 5, cap. 3, E, fol. 28v; *Manipulus curatorum*, Pars 2, tract. 3, cap. 5, fol. 83; '[C]ertes a man hym sholde repent syngulerly of euery mortall synne the whiche a man knoweth too haue commyt whan it cometh vnto mynde', *The arte or crafte*, fol. 43v. *The Ordynarye* required confession to be entire, because the penitent had 'to doo that that is in hym', Part 4, chap. [13], sig. [v4]r. Fisher repeated the universal principle that the penitent must show all his 'offences small & grete without ony shadowe or colour, no thynge excusynge or makynge lesse but expresse as moche as we may the very wyckednes with all the circumstaunce as it was done in dede', *EW*, 85, cf. 211, 220.

[80] *Pupilla oculi*, Pars 5, cap. 3, P, fol. 29r; 'Cum enim benignissimus Deus noster, non exigat a nobis impossibilia, non est dubium quin si (facta congrua diligentia) quaedam nos fugerint, ea neutiquam imputabuntur nobis', Fisher, *ALC*, Art. 9, col. 430; cf. ibid., Art. 8, cols. 426–7. Cf. *Manipulus curatorum*, Pars 2, tract. 2, cap. 5, fol. 71.

to come sooner to be shriven.[81] Mirk offered as an ideal
confession the story of a particularly wicked man who, when
struck on his death-bed with contrition, was so determined
to confess all his sins that 'he wepte nyght and day euer
whan his synne came unto his mynde and so lay seuen dayes
and seuen nyghtes | and shroue him clene and toke grete
repentaunce to hym | and euer cryed god mercy.'[82]

Not all sinners, however, had either this man's measure of
compunction or his commitment to a complete confession.
The confessor's initial approach was to encourage contrition
by inspiring hope and fear. He was to remind the penitent of
the goodness of God in his creation and recreation, of the
shortness of life, of the instability of the world, but most
importantly, of the piety and passion of Christ, and that
God was always prepared to restore penitent sinners to his
grace. If, however, 'sweet and pleasant eloquence' failed to
move the penitent to make a complete confession, the
confessor was to threaten him with the terror of the last
judgement and the pains of hell.[83]

The floure of the commaundements records two stories
which warn of the damnation of those who died with
unconfessed sin, one from wilfulness, the other from negligence. In the first, a princess is damned despite her numerous good works for the poor, widowed, and orphaned
because she refused to confess her secret sin of once
engaging in fornication and aborting the child thus conceived. The reader is assured that she would have been
pardoned even if she had engaged in such conduct many

---

[81] 'But yf the ygnoraunce were inexcusable a man were holden hym to repente in
especyall | for euery persone is holden to put all dylygence for too knowe his syynes
to the ende that he repente hym', *The arte or crafte*, fol. 43v. *The Ordynarye* offered
an example of such inexcusable ignorance, negligence to come sooner to confession;
Part 4, chap. 5, sig. [R6]r.

[82] Mirk, *Festyuall*, fol. 12v.

[83] '[E]t si non vult confiteri: proponat ei terrorem extremi iudicii poenas inferni
et huiusmodi', *Pupilla oculi*, Pars 5, cap. 7, A, fol. 38r. 'Et si forte ex istis omnibus
peccator non velit confiteri. proponat ei confessor terrorem iudicii et poenas
inferni. et quanta mala parata sunt peccatoribus. et quam dire punit deus eos qui
nolunt poenitere. et quam misericorditer parcit poenitentibus', *Manipulus curatorum*, Pars 2, tract. 3, cap. 8, fol. 89r. Peter Marshall is undoubtedly correct that
the manuals stressed a positive approach, but their injunction to threaten the
recalcitrant should not be overlooked; *The Catholic Priesthood and the English
Reformation* (Oxford: Clarendon Press, 1994), 10.

times, if only she had admitted the offence to her confessor. In the second, another devout woman was damned because shame kept her from admitting her lust. Since she had only formed the intent to have relations with a certain man in her mind, but never had acted upon her decision, she thought she did not need to confess her sin.[84] Fisher repeated the same warning about the deadly nature of mental assent to grievous sin and insisted that even the least mortal sin which occurred to the penitent during confession had to be confessed, even the least of what *seemed* to the him to be mortal sin. Otherwise, absolution had no benefit and even those rare people who came to sacramental penance already justified would be damned because of hypocrisy.[85]

The good confessor sought to enable his people to avoid this fate by assisting them to make as complete a confession as was possible.[86] First, the confessor was to listen carefully and in silence to the penitent's confession. The *Pupilla* offered an example of a penitent's opening confession that included a long list of sins: the seven deadly sins of pride, wrath, envy, greed, gluttony, sloth and luxury; other potential sins such as presumption or despair, lacking contrition,

---

[84] *The floure of the commaundements*, fols. 203v–204r, 213v–214r. Cf. Mirk's story about a man who remained ill because he had not confessed his venial sins, since he did not realize that their collective *gravitas* added up to a mortal sin, *Festyuall*, fol. 22.

[85] 'But whan Adam (that is to say mannes reason & wyll) agreeth to the eatyng of this apple, whan he doth assent & is content to take any pleasure contrary to the commaundement of god: than is synne done, than is synne commytted in thy soule, though thou neuer wade further in doyng the dede. This consent is syn . . . Thou man seest peraduenture a fayre woman, & thou haste a carnall lykynge of her, & a pleasure to beholde her | so that thy body is styred & moued with an vnclene desyre to haue her at thy wyll . . . yf thy wyll ones assent to this desyre of thy flesshe, though they neuer go any forther, or though thou neuer come to the actuall dede, thou doost offende and synne deedly by this only consent of thy selfe', John Fisher, *Two fruytfull sermons*, ed. M. D. Sullivan (Ann Arbor: University of Michigan Microfilm Service, 1965), fols. F1v–F2r, 57–8; 'Sed de illis (quae facillime possunt occurrere) si vel minimum tacuerimus, quod nobis visum est esse mortale, nihil nobis proderit absolutio', Fisher, *ALC*, Art. 9, col. 430; 'Sed si sancti, vel minimum mortale, quod menti occurrisset tempore confessionis, sponte subticuissent, ausim dicere, nec sanctos eos esse, nec iustificatos, immo si quam ante iustitiam habuissent, iam propter hyprocrisim penitus amiserunt', ibid., Art. 8, col. 427.

[86] e.g., 'Istud ostendas oportet, quod peccatori (qui fructum absolutionis consequi velit) peccatum aliquod mortale vel minimum, quod menti occurrit, ex industria tegere licebit', Fisher, *ALC*, Art. 8, col. 428.

faltering in love, oppressing the poor or failing to govern oneself as one ought; and, finally, sins associated with the five senses and sin done in thought, word, will, and work.[87]

Since human memory was often frail and since the will to disclose secret sins was even less reliable, after the penitent's confession of his sins, the priest was to probe for further sins by careful questioning.[88] The *Pupilla* based these questions on the outline of Christian teaching required by Archbishop John Pecham's canon, *Ignorantia Sacerdotum*.[89] The penitent was to be questioned about sins against the articles of the Creed and the Ten Commandments, about sins that fell under the broad category of the seven deadly sins and the circumstances surrounding them, about sinful thoughts, about sins of the five senses, about sins of the tongue, about sins of omission (i.e. neglecting the seven works of corporal mercy and the seven works of spiritual mercy) and, lastly, about sins associated with the penitent's station in life, whether as a prince, soldier, justice, merchant, craftsman, farmer, young scholar, priest, member of religious order, or as a prostitute.[90] The *Manipulus* based its main enquiry on the traditional seven deadly sins, including

---

[87] *Pupilla oculi*, Pars 5, cap. 7, D–S, fols. 38v–39r.

[88] 'Finita narratione siue confessione poenitentis dicat ei modeste confessor. Habes ne plura dicere et si poenitens . . . ¯ dixerit se non habere alia de quibus recolit: poterit confessor dicere: fortasse non omnia quae gessisti occurrunt modo memoriae tuae ideo de aliquibus te interrogabo. Tu ergo caue ne diabolo instigante aliquo peccatorum tuorum occultare praesumas', *Pupilla oculi*, Pars 5, cap. 7, S, fol. 39r.

[89] This canon was enacted at the council of the province of Canterbury at Lambeth in 1281 and required that the laity be taught at least four times a year the fourteen articles of faith, the Ten Commandments, the summary of the Law, the seven works of mercy, the seven deadly sins, the seven virtues, and the seven sacraments; *Councils and Synods with other Documents relating to the English Church, A. D. 1205–1313*, ed. F. M. Powicke and C. R. Cheney (Oxford: Clarendon Press, 1964), ii. 900–5.

[90] *Pupilla oculi*, Pars 5, cap. 8–9, fols. 39r–41v. Cf. John Mirk's fifteenth-century penitential in English Verse, *Instructions for Parish Priests*. The priest was to question the penitent on his knowledge of the Pater Noster, the Ave Maria and the Creed, (vv. 805–10), whether he knew them in English (vv. 811–12), and if he believed the Creed (vv. 813–48). He was also to ask if the penitent had broken the Ten Commandments (vv. 849–972), if he had fallen into the seven deadly sins (Pride, vv. 977–1048; Sloth, vv. 1049–1106; Envy, vv. 1107–36; Wrath, vv. 1137–68; Greed, vv. 1169–1200; Gluttony, vv. 1201–34; and Lechery, vv. 1235–86), and if he had sinned venially by the five senses (vv. 1303–98); ed. Gillis Kristensson (Lund: Gleerup, 1974).

questions about works of mercy under avarice. Then followed questions concerning the penitent's station in society, his knowledge of the Lord's Prayer, the Hail Mary, and the Creed, and any temptations which he faced so that the confessor could teach him how to resist.[91]

Between the penitent trying to be sorry with all his 'power, strength, & good wyll' and the priest asking questions to help him to be sorry, it was expected that the penitent would experience and express *dolor* for the sins he confessed.[92] Although not necessary, the ideal was always sorrow expressed in tears.[93] Dame Julian told Margery Kempe that her constant weeping was a divine gift because the Holy Spirit moved Christians 'to ask and pray with mourning and weeping so plentifully that the tears may not be numbered'.[94] At the other extreme, it was equally clear that a confession done 'by custome' and not principally for the love of God and of the salvation of the soul, was inefficacious. According to Fisher, confession without true sorrow 'profyteth very lytell or no thynge'.[95]

Therefore, a priest could not absolve a penitent who did not have the necessary inward disposition of the mind, although, as has been noted, the Scotist school was less demanding than the Thomist in the level of penitence needed to meet this requirement. While ideally the penitent had deep sorrow for his sin before he confessed, the exhaustive questioning served as an essential part of helping a penitent to recognize the full extent of his sinfulness, the

---

[91] *Manipulus curatorum*, Pars 2, tract. 3, cap. 9, fols. 90r–96v.

[92] Fisher, *EW*, 85; the penitent was to 'make a lamentable and mournynge confessyon', ibid., 153.

[93] *Pupilla oculi*, Pars 5, cap. 2, H, fol. 28r; *Manipulus curatorum*, Pars 2, tract. 2, cap. 2, fols. 68v–69v; The truly contrite 'ought to haue abundance of teerys at the leest spyrytuell the whiche ben sorowe and dyspleasure to haue offended god by synne', *The Ordynarye*, Part 4, chap. 5, sig. [R5]r; 'The yren with rubbynge anone wyll shyne full bryght. So the soule with wepynge is made fayre and whyte', Fisher, *EW*, 17; 'the spiryte of god shall gyue so grete infusyon of grace to them that be penytent that the waters, that is to saye theyr wepynge teres shall flowe and be haboundaunte', ibid., 99.

[94] *Margery Kempe*, Book 1, chap. 18, 78; While affirming the need for a 'grete noyse before our moost mercyfull lord' for to have 'very contrycyon', Fisher added that a penitent also needed a quiet cry from his 'very herte rote' that was 'softe, without noyse of wordes', private, with no outward indication; *EW*, 210–11.

[95] *The Ordynarye*, Part 4, chap. [13], sig. X2r; Fisher, *EW*, 211.

first step in the preparation for contrition. The shame of having to admit the full extent of one's faults to another was the second step. If these means failed to encourage a demonstration of sorrow to the priest, Fisher argued that it was all the more reason for a penitent to be questioned about his *dolor*.[96] Since, however, sacramental penance in the Scotist tradition only required attrition, Fisher added that the priest's task was to establish if the penitent truly grieved, not whether he grieved sufficiently for extra-sacramental forgiveness.[97]

Thus, the penitent's task in auricular confession was to grieve and humble himself before the priest, the confessor's to examine him carefully and to administer absolution in the proper manner.[98] If the priest took his task too far, querying too thoroughly or threatening too much, he risked hindering the penitent in his duty and confirming obstinacy in him rather than correcting it. Such once was the reaction of Margery Kempe. In her youth when a confessor 'was a little too hasty and began sharply to reprove her before she had fully said what she meant', Kempe decided that 'she would say no more in spite of anything he might do'. She attributed the subsequent eight months of being 'amazingly disturbed and tormented with spirits' to feeling caught between the dread of damnation for unconfessed sin and her determination not to submit again to her confessor's sharp probings.[99] Eamon Duffy has argued that the practical limitations of shriving a whole parish during Lent severely limited the time a confessor could spend with each individual so that the penitent would have been encouraged to follow the maxim 'be brief, be brutal, be gone'.[100] If Duffy

[96] 'De dolore igitur interrogandus est inter confitendum peccator, num vere doleat? et maxime si nulla sacerdos interim viderit doloris indicia', Fisher, *ALC*, Art. 14, col. 453.

[97] 'Caeterum de tali poenitudine, nempe quae digna sit, et quae sufficiat, sacerdos (ut diximus) non exquirit. Examinat tantum, an vere doleat confitens, non autem an sufficienter doleat', Fisher, *ALC*, Art. 14, col. 454.

[98] 'Tuum [opus] quidem, ut doleas et humilies te sacerdoti: Sacerdotis vero, ut probe et rite sacramentum ipsum administret', Fisher, *ALC*, Art. 11, col. 440.

[99] *Margery Kempe*, Book 1, chap. 1, 41.

[100] Duffy, *Stripping of the Altars*, 60. Cf. the similar, more detailed argument of Marshall, *Catholic Priesthood*, 11–13. A sermon delivered to Cambridge University about 1510 would seem to suggest that confession and absolution took only fifteen

be correct, when a penitent like the young Margery failed to follow this formula, the priest may well have thought it his responsibility to be brutal, so that the questioning could be brief and the penitent be gone.

SATISFACTION

An act of mortal sin incurred a liability for both eternal damnation (*culpa*) and temporal punishment (*poena*), with contrition remitting the former and satisfactions the latter.[101] In Scotist teaching, however, divine pardon merely commuted *culpa* to *poena*, since God had ordained that sin must be punished, either by himself on the day of judgement or by the *viator*. Therefore, after a penitent had been loosed from his debt of eternal punishment through the infusion of grace, he still remained bound to work off his debt of temporal punishment through the penance which his confessor had assigned him.[102] Although manuals and canons were helpful in assigning appropriate satisfactions, in the end, the judgement was left to the discretion of the confessor.[103] If the penance imposed was worthy of the absolution of all temporal pains, the penitent would not be punished further. If, however, the penances imposed by the priest did not meet this standard, or if the penitent did not finish them all, the remaining debt would be completed in Purgatory.[104]

Still the 'iniunccyon of a good dede in the waye of satysfaccyon of a mannes owne ghostly fader' had great

minutes: 'in quarta parte horae homo potest delere culpam | recuperare gratiam: et promerei gloriam', Stephen Baron, *Sermones Declamati coram alma vniuersitate Cantibrigiensi* (London: Wynkyn de Worde, n.d.), sig. [A2]v. I am most grateful to Dr Richard Rex for drawing my attention to this volume.

[101] *Pupilla oculi*, Pars 5, cap. 1, 0, fol. 27r; Fisher, *EW*, 24.

[102] 'Nam si pusillus dolor antecessit, absolvitur a culpa per sacramentum, at remanet adhuc (soluto reatu) rubigo quaedam quae et poena peccatis debita tolli debent, priusquam anima coelum ingrediatur', Fisher, *ACL*, Art. 5, col. 385.

[103] 'Communis sententia doctorum tenet quod omnes poenitentiae sunt arbitrariae, i.e., arbitrio sacerdotis', *Manipulus curatorum*, Pars 2, tract. 4, cap. 5, fol. 106v; 'Sacerdotis prudentis arbitrio relictum sit, quanti temporis cuique peccatori satisfactio sit imponenda', Fisher, *ALC*, Art. 5, col. 395.

[104] *Manipulus curatorum*, Pars 2, tract. 3, cap. 10, fol. 98r.

efficacy.[105] Through the power of the keys exercised in the sacrament, the priest applied the merit of Christ's passion to the penitent. Consequently, just as absolution could raise attrition to contrition, satisfactions done at the injunction of a priest were held to be more effective in remitting *poena* than self-imposed penances. The amount, however, was always in proportion to the contrition the penitent expressed in performing his satisfactions.[106] Taking this principle to the extreme, Guido taught that works of satisfaction imposed by a priest in auricular confession had very much greater virtue for remitting *poena* than those done at the penitent's initiative. He argued that the temporal debt for mortal sin was infinite rather than finite because a sinner had offended the infinite goodness of God. Only the passion of Christ could satisfy such a debt, and the sacerdotal power of the keys joined this virtue to the penitent. Therefore, one Pater Noster said by the penitent at the injunction of a confessor was more effective for rendering satisfaction than a hundred thousand said by his own desire.[107]

While a priest only had power to loose a penitent from *culpa* and assign penances to satisfy *poena*, the pope had authority to loose not only *culpa* but *poena* as well. In the *Confutatio* Fisher noted that Christ had told the disciples they could bind and loose in 'heaven' (Matthew 18: 18), but he said to Peter that he could bind and loose in the 'heavens' (Mathew 16: 18–19). Christ's greater promise to Peter meant that he alone had been given the superior power to bind and to loose both *culpa* and *poena*.[108] Therefore, the

---

[105] Fisher, *EW*, 26.

[106] 'Et sacerdos potestate clavium partem remittere potest poenae temporalis debitae pro peccato . . . plus vel minus potest de huiusmodi poena remittere secundum quod plus vel minus fuerit poenitens per veram contritionem ad hoc dispositus | sed sacerdos ad huiusmodi remissionem agit instrumentaliter. deus autem principaliter et effectiue', *Pupilla oculi*, Pars 5, cap. 14, ag, fol. 48v.

[107] '[U]nde secundum hanc viam virtus clavium est; quam virtute earum communicatur confitenti passio Christi in cuius virtute potest satisfacere pro peccatis quod non faciebat ante. unde credo quod unum Pater noster impositum in poenitentia a sacerdote efficacius est ad satisfaciendum pro peccatis quam si aliquis diceret centum milia per semetipsum; quia illud habet meritum a passione Christi', *Manipulus curatorum*, Pars 2, tract. 3, cap. 10, fol. 98r. For a discussion of Hugh Payne's use of this principle, see Chapter 4.

[108] 'Caeterum ex iis intelligi datur, quemadmodum in sequentibus apertius

pope as Peter's legitimate successor had the authority to grant indulgences for the loosing of temporal punishment owed for sins to those whose debt of eternal punishment had been remitted.[109]

In principle, however, contrition by itself always had the potential to remit all future penalties. As a form of painful punishment voluntarily assumed for sin, extra-sacramental contrition could be so great as to remit both *culpa* and *poena*, like the case of the thief on the cross.[110] Margery Kempe was convinced that the deep contrition she thought her prolonged periods of weeping represented ensured that she would avoid both hell and purgatory at her death.[111] Having such perfect sorrow, however, did not excuse the penitent from needing to receive sacramental penance for two reasons. On a practical level, despite the conviction of Margery, everyone needed to submit to a priest because no one could be sure that his contrition was sufficient to remit both *poena* and *culpa*.[112] On a doctrinal level, all the penitential literature defined true contrition as including not only the intention to confess but also to make satisfaction as directed by a priest.[113] In the *Confutatio* Fisher's example of true contrition remitting both *poena* and *culpa* subtly reinforced this connection, for the penitent's perfect sorrow was manifested as he was confessing to the priest.[114]

dicemus, quod illis verbis Petro dictis, non solum culpae solvendae potestas accipi debeat, verumetiam poenae peccatis debitae', Fisher, *ALC*, Art. 14, col. 452.

[109] 'Nos vero cum ecclesia credimus, quod plerumque post deletam culpam remanet in peccatore, quaedam ad poenam pro peccatis pristinis debitam, obligatio, quae per summi pontificis condonationem tolli potest . . . quae per quemcunque legitimum Petri successorem, pariter condonari potest', Fisher, *ALC*, Art. 17, col. 485.

[110] *Pupilla oculi*, Pars 5, cap. 2, M, fol. 28r; *The arte or crafte*, fol. 44r; '[F]or a man maye haue so grete and suche contrycyon that it may quenche all the paynes that euer were ordeyned for hym', Mirk, *Festyuall*, fol. 12r; cf. 'posset esse tanta contritio confitentis quod pro maximo peccato esset modica immo quasi nulla poenitentia imponenda', *Manipulus curatorum*, Pars 2, tract. 4, cap. 5, fol. 106v.

[111] *Margery Kempe*, Book 1, chaps. 5 and 22, pp. 50, 87–8.

[112] *Pupilla oculi*, Pars 5, cap. 2, M, fol. 28r.

[113] *Pupilla oculi*, Pars 5, cap. 2, L, cap. 3, A, fol. 28r; *Manipulus curatorum*, Pars 2, tract. 2, cap. 1, fol. 67v; *The arte or crafte*, fol. 43v; cf. Fisher, *EW*, 85.

[114] 'Evenit tamen interdum, ut is qui fuerat absolutus, non multa prius admisisset crimina, et eadem non gravissima, vehementi quoque pulsus occasione, tanta sceleris detestatione venisset ad sacerdotem, tanta poenitudinis acerbitate peccata sua detegisset, tam exundanti lacrymarum profluvio, ut priusquam petiisset

Although much emphasis was placed on *poenitentia* as satisfaction for a debt of punishment, the pre-Reformation English church never lost sight of the other traditional function of penance: healing a soul made sick by sin. Hence, *The Ordynarye* included a chapter which discussed 'the arte of physyke spyrytuall founded in the twelue rules of the scyence of physyke corporall'.[115] Satisfaction was intended to root out the cause of sin to prevent future lapses as well as compensate for past offences: '[F]or mannes flesshe is so wylde and so lusty to synne that it wyll not in no waye leue his luste to serue god but yf it be chastysed with penaunce for it must be chastysed some tyme with payne.'[116] Thus, like medicine, penance was indeed painful but always applied as a means towards a greater joy.

One of the most common descriptions of penance's power to restore the sinner to health was equating the forgiveness of sin with release from captivity to the devil. Committing sin permitted an evil spirit to attach itself to the offender. According to Mirk, Christ would not abide where mortal sin dwelled. And at his leaving 'thenne cometh the fende in and abydeth there | thenne may that soule that is so forsaken of god and betaken vnto the fende'. Fisher employed the same language in his sermons as well: 'The holy ghost shal not dwell or abyde in a body subgecte to synne.' Those falling into sin put themselves in the service of devils, as Paul and the holy fathers thought 'all synners to be vnder the power of an euyl spryrte'.[117]

Receiving the sacrament and doing the penances assigned freed the penitent from sin's demonic influence. Mirk explained the liturgy of Palm Sunday as an expression of this truth. Every Christian processed with palms on that day

---

veniam, accesserit non solum a culpa liberatus, verumetiam a poena, cui fuerit obnoxius', Fisher, *ALC*, Art. 5, col. 385.

[115] *The Ordynarye*, Part 4, chap. 26, fols. [HH5]r–[II4]r.

[116] Mirk, *Festyuall*, fol. 8r. For penance having a double purpose of satisfying God's honour and preventing a return of sin, see *Pupilla oculi*, Pars 5, cap. 4, A, fol. 30v, and *The arte or crafte*, fol. 44v.

[117] Mirk, *Festyuall*, fol. 36v; cf. 'Ryght so the holy goost fleeth frome the soule that is combred with deedly synne | and aungels wyll stoppe theyr noses | for moche more fouler stynketh deedly synne in the syght of god | then dooth ony caryon to the people', ibid., fol. 42r; Fisher, *EW*, 71, 115, 235, 243.

to show that 'he hadde foughten with the fende oure
ennemye and hath the vyctory of hym by shryft of
mouthe | satysfaccyon with dede | mekely doone his
penaunce with grete contrycyon in his herte | and in these
maner of wyse he ouercame his goostly ennemye the fende
of helle.' According to Fisher, sacramental penance drove
away evil spirits; satisfactions freed the sinner from both
God's punishments and the devil's snare.[118]

POENITENTIA AS PASTORAL THEOLOGY

Influenced by the Augustinian revival associated with
Amerbach's first edition of the *Opera omnia Augustini*
published between 1490 and 1506,[119] John Fisher was
committed to preaching the necessity of grace in the process
of salvation.[120] His meditations on the penitential psalms
offer a valuable example of the manner in which an early
sixteenth-century humanist-scholastic translated the details
of the penitential teachings which we have surveyed into a
coherent vision for the Christian life.[121] For Fisher, penitence is both the central act of the Christian life and indicative of the long process of salvation, at once totally
dependent on divine grace and yet still requiring human
effort.

According to Fisher, sinners were helpless in their own
strength to do anything good: 'We be not suffycyent and
able of our selfe, as of our selfe, to thynke ony maner thynge,
but our suffycyency and habylyte dependeth and cometh of

---

[118] Mirk, *Festyuall*, fol. 28r; Fisher, *EW*, 21, 24, 53, 86–8, 154, 209–10.

[119] For the renewed interest in Augustine at the beginning of the sixteenth
century, see Peter Iver Kaufman, *Augustinian Piety and Catholic Reform: August-
ine, Colet, and Erasmus* (Macon, Georgia: Mercer University Press, 1982); Heiko
A. Oberman, *Masters of the Reformation: The Emergence of a New Intellectual
Climate in Europe* (Cambridge: Cambridge University Press, 1981), 64–110; Alister
E. McGrath, *The Intellectual Origins of the European Reformation* (Oxford: Basil
Blackwell, 1987), 175–82. For Fisher's humanism, see Richard Rex, *The Theology
of John Fisher* (Cambridge: Cambridge University Press, 1991), 50–64.

[120] For Fisher's preaching see, Rex, *Fisher*, 30–49; William S. Stafford, 'Repentance on the Eve of the Reformation: John Fisher's Sermons of 1508 and 1509',
Historical Magazine of the Protestant Episcopal Church 54 (1985), 297–338.

[121] For a discussion of Fisher's academic presentation of these principles, see
Chapter 2.

god onely.'[122] Since God required good works as part of the process of salvation, the sinner was to ask for divine grace so as to perform them but never to presume that his execution of them meant that he merited salvation by right.[123] Despite salvation being God's gift, however, no one was damned except by his own fault.[124] Since human beings were composed of body, soul, and spirit, even the most wicked man still had a portion of his being that was spirit. Although the power of sin often usurped the soul, compelling a person to do the thing which he would not do, no matter how great its influence, no matter how strong the demonic bondage, the spirit always continued to struggle against sin. This remaining trace of the image of God in humanity encouraged 'the body so moche as it may to do good yf we be dysposed for to here it, and for to do therafter'. Fisher expected Christians to give heed to this inner inclination, when the Spirit 'pricks the conscience', urging them to make their flesh obey their reason by turning to God and away from sin. If they would make their soul follow the spirit, they would experience such hearty compunction that eventually they would gain the grace of justification.[125]

Since God promised to receive all that would come to him, if they come to him as they should, Fisher outlined

[122] Fisher, *EW*, 50, 99–100.

[123] '[T]herfore this thynge is to be asked of god that he vouchesaue to moue our soules perfytely by his grace vnto the excercysynge & doynge of many good werkes', Fisher, *EW*, 50, 99–100; cf. Fisher's warning against the presumption that living in an uninterrupted state of grace and doing of good works merited a heavenly reward, ibid., 264.

[124] God has redeemed us by his son's blood and will show us mercy. 'Soo noo faute is in almighty god, but onely in the synner yf he be dampned', Fisher, *EW*, 230, cf. 160. Cf. 'For it is a thynge certayn that there was neuer creatour dampned but by his owne defaute', *The Ordynarye*, Part 4, chap. 2, sig. R2r; cf. 'For all the whyle thou louest more synne than god | and haddest leuer to serue the fende than god | thou arte cause of thyn owne dampnacyon', Mirk, *Festyuall*, fol. 87v.

[125] Fisher, *EW*, 120, 245; *ALC*, Art. 6, col. 410. NB that the Latin text refers to 'spiritum, animam, et carnem in singulis hominibus esse'. The English sermon is less specific, describing the *spiritus* as 'some sparke remayneth in the soule' and 'the superyoure porcyon of the soule'. In his sermon on All Saints, 1520, Fisher referred to 'the reasonable soule': 'Whan thou folowest the desyres of thy body: Eue is the ruler. Whan thou folowes the desyre of thy soule & of thy reason: than Adam is orderer . . . after that the body be styred to vnclennes, the reasonable soule is at his lyberty whether it wyll assent to the styrynges & vnclene delytes of the flesshe ye or nay. But yf it assent, than Adam eteth of the Apple', *Two Sermons*, fol. F1r, 55–6. See Stafford, 'Repentance', 330.

three steps as necessary for reconciliation with the Creator. A sinner needed to amend his life, to call to God for help, and to have a full trust in his merciful Lord. If a penitent turned to God by renouncing his evil life, God would turn to him and give the sinner the grace which would enable him to 'be tourned to the grete shame & confusyon of the deuylles'. Citing the example of the prodigal son, Fisher urged the penitent to prayer: 'socour me that am about to ryse fro synne & come vnto the. Brynge thyn owne out of the myserable seruytude of deuylles whein it hath be put downe a longe season.'[126]

The sinner was to call on God by first acknowledging the wretchedness to which his sin had brought him and his deep contrition for offending such a good God as his creator.[127] Nevertheless, this penitence was always to be coupled with a firm conviction in God's promise to forgive those who turned to him: 'let vs neuer so moche wayle & sorowe our synnes, confesse them to neuer so many preestes and laste study to purge them by as moche satysfaccyon as we can, all these profyte no thynge without hope'. David had won the remission of his sin by his sure hope in God's goodness towards contrite sinners. Since Scripture spoke of God's great mercy 'in euery corner', and he had exercised it so often on so many sinners, those who failed to believe in God's forgiveness could only be 'ouer moche obstynate & harde herted', whose fate was to be 'dygested & incorporate in to the substaunce of the deuyll'. Like the persistent widow or the Canaanite woman, the penitent needed constantly to go in faith to God to remind him of his promise to cleanse and to restore struggling sinners to himself.[128]

While affirming humanity's moral responsibility, Fisher never denied the weakness of the human will either. He repeated over and over again the frailty to which humankind was heir: 'the lawe & custome of our body is contrary to the lawe & custome of our soule and the custome of our body putteth vs dayly vnder the captyuyte & thraldome of synne'. Like a weak and feeble man trying to roll a great millstone up a high hill, only to be overcome by its great weight and

[126] Fisher, *EW*, 13, 22, 106, 208, 267.   [127] Fisher, *EW*, 74, 101.
[128] Fisher, *EW*, 81, 103, 107, 139, 143-7, 207, 221-30.

roll with the stone back into the valley, so 'we be aboute to brynge this our body vnto thy holy hyll, neuetheless it is thrast downe by the heuy burden of synne that oftentymes it boweth & slyppeth downe backwarde'. 'And we that are the remenaunt beynge without strength or myght, & lefte behynde, are very feble & weyke, lyghtly ouerthrowen with euery blast of temptacyon.' 'And our freylte is so grete that without the mercy of god we all sholde declyne from the ryght way.' Since 'no thynge in this life can be ferme & stable without the helpe of god', Fisher urged penitents to turn to the one who could and would give them victory over sin and Satan.[129]

Following Augustine's maxim, the penitent needed to pray continually that God be to him like a good physician, who would not leave the side of the sick until he had made him well. Yet, Fisher acknowledged that penitents were often not able to persevere in prayer in faith for forgiveness: 'But alas woo is me now, the fyre of vnlawfull concupyscence hath wasted & taken awaye fro me all the fatnes, all the swetnes of prayer, & made my soule drye & voyde from all moystnesse of deuocyon.'[130] Fisher had a lively sense of the demonic in this struggle. Throughout the earthly life of the pilgrim, wicked spirits sought to deceive and to destroy him through sin. The harder he fought, the more he came under attack. If a sinner fled to penance, intending to amend his life, the demon he chased away by his tears would come back with seven more wicked than himself. In the face of such harsh spiritual attacks, how could any man trust in his own strength to persevere in a state of grace until his death? He could put his trust only in an omnipotent God: 'Truly he that is almighty may socour vs & none other.' Without the help of his grace at all times, a Christian 'must nedes sagge & bowe'.[131]

Therefore, God had given humanity two aids in its turning back to God. Reading 'the worde of God' refreshed the soul, making it strong, causing the flesh to obey reason, producing goodness within it and enabling it to bring forth good works.[132] The other aid God had mercifully provided

[129] Fisher, *EW*, 105, 176, 191, 259. [130] Fisher, *EW*, 147.
[131] Fisher, *EW*, 86–90, esp. 88. [132] Fisher, *EW*, 149–50.

to assist sinners to return to him was, naturally, the 'meke & mercyful lawe' of confession.[133] Ultimately, both means directed the penitent's attention away from trusting in the efforts he was required to exert and towards the promised mercies of his God. As Fisher wrote, 'yf we wyll lene, cleue, or stycke faste with a stedfaste mynde and truste in the grete mercy of almyghty god in maner as we myght holde hym vp in vs, we shall be susteyned & supported in our so doynge rather by hym'.[134]

Guido de Monte Rocherii would have agreed that the ultimate purpose of auricular confession was to point the penitent away from his own actions and to look to those of his Maker. He noted that neither contrition nor confession remitted sin but God alone.[135] The constant uncertainty of living between those twin millstones of hope and fear was not only merely to discourage sloth but also equally, if not more importantly, to foster dependence on God's grace for perseverance. Likening auricular confession to Jacob's ladder which stretched from earth to heaven, de Monte Rocherii attributed the same two aims to sacramental penance. On the penitent's part, the ladder's three rungs represented grief, shame and labour. On God's part, however, the three rungs represented how he would strongly sustain the penitent during his ascent out of sin; how, if necessary, he would reach out his hand to help the penitent, and lastly, how, when the penitent had become tired by the climb, he could look up and throw all his trust on God because he was not so cruel as to let a penitent fall.[136]

---

[133] Fisher, *EW*, 220.   [134] Fisher, *EW*, 221.

[135] '[I]ntelligendum est deum dimittere peccatum. non contritionem vel confessionem . . . Verbum dei peccata dimittit', *Manipulus curatorum*, Pars 2, tract. 3, cap. 10, fol. 97.

[136] 'Poenitentia etiam sic perfecta est illa scala benedicta cum istis tribus gradibus quam vidit Jacob erectam a terra vsque ad caelum et dominum innixum scalae. Et hoc propter tria. Primo vt ascendentem per eam fortiter sustineat. Secundo vt si necessitas forte fuerit ascendenti per eam manum porrigat. Tertio vt ascendens per eam cum fatigatus fuerit in ipsum respiciat et iactet totam fiduciam suam in eum. Non enim ita crudelis (vt ait augustinus) vt ipsum cadere permittat. In primo gradu est dolor. in secundo pudor. in tertio labor. De his ergo tribus partibus poenitentiae', *Manipulus curatorum*, Pars 2, tract. 1, cap. 4, fol. 67r. Cf. 'Sed nos de isto contendimus, qui totis viribus ad Deum converti conatur, quales multos esse nemo dubitat, et his Deum praesto esse, qui manum porrigat', Fisher, *ACL*, Art. 6, col. 410.

Even the analogy of penance as a ladder for human ascent to heaven has its stress on human effort significantly softened by de Monte Rocherii's emphasis on looking to God and leaning on his sustaining grace. Not only was the ladder of penance a divine gift, but the stamina for an ascent out of sin was as well. Thus, the sacrament, with its rigorous demands for human co-operation in contrition, confession, and satisfaction, far from undermining humanity's reliance on divine grace, was construed by the pre-Reformation English church as the indispensable school for teaching sinners their need for utter dependence on God.

Cranmer's Doctrine of Repentance *circa* 1520: Augustinian-Influenced Scotist Penance

Existimant enim peccat[ore]m, ex naturalibus, cum generali influxu, et auxilio dei posse considerare peccatum ab se commissum, ut offensivum dei, et ut aversivum a deo, ut impedivum praemii, et supplicii inductivum, ac proinde posse voluntatem eius, peccatum sic consideratum detestari.[1]

The fourteen-year-old Thomas Cranmer arrived in Cambridge at an auspicious moment in the university's history. The political stability brought about by the Tudor dynasty, coupled with the fervent piety of the king's mother, Lady Margaret Beaufort, had focused fresh attention on the needs of English universities. Cambridge, whose leading figure, John Fisher, was Lady Margaret's confessor, especially benefited from royal patronage, and the result was evident everywhere.[2] For the first two decades of the sixteenth century much of the market town remained a building site as old colleges expanded and new colleges were founded, including Cranmer's own Jesus College.[3] Set off beyond the King's Ditch in a large park to the northeast and reached by Jesus Lane, the college had been

---

[1] 'For we think that a sinner, by his own natural abilities, with the general influence and help of God is able to weigh a sin he has committed as an offense to God and as an aversion from God, as an impediment to reward and an induction to punishment, and then his will is able to detest the sin so weighed', Fisher, *ALC*, Art. 6, col. 407.

[2] For a full description of Lady Margaret's involvement with Oxford and Cambridge, see Michael K. Jones and Malcolm G. Underwood, *The King's Mother: Lady Margaret Beaufort, Countess of Richmond and Derby* (Cambridge: Cambridge University Press, 1992), 202–31.

[3] For a description of the buildings in progress, see H. C. Porter, *Reformation and Reaction in Tudor Cambridge* (Hamden, Conn.: Archon Books, 1972), 16–17, and the map of Cambridge *c*.1500 provided by Leader, *Cambridge*, 12–13.

founded in 1496 by John Alcock, the bishop of Ely and a member of Lady Margaret's circle. For much of Cranmer's student years he would have heard the sounds of workmen dressing stone, cutting timber and winching ropes as the buildings of the former convent which Alcock had suppressed were adapted and enlarged to provide for the needs of his new college.

This physical transformation of the university had been preceded by an equally important change in its course of study. Under the influence of humanism a gradual reform of the university's curriculum had taken place so that by 1503 the BA required two years of study in *Literae Humaniores* followed by a year of logic and a year of scholastic philosophy. For the MA, a bachelor had to study more philosophy and attend lectures on mathematics, music, and astronomy.[4] Only upon the completion of the MA could someone then have read theology, 'the Queen of the sciences'. The BD required two years spent studying the Bible and two years concentrating on Peter the Lombard. In addition, the candidate had to give a year of lectures on the Bible.[5] Despite later developments, in early sixteenth-century Cambridge humanist exegesis and scholastic training were not mutually exclusive. Fisher, chancellor of the university and its leading theologian, sought to combine the rigour of scholastic reasoning with humanism's learning in the *tres linguae* (Greek, Latin, and Hebrew), the *bonae literae* of classical literature, scriptural exegesis, and patristic writings.[6] He thought that historical-linguistic studies were apt for establishing and expressing the knowledge of the past, but he still considered scholastic logic as necessary for defining and defending the church's doctrine.[7] Fisher's

---

[4] Leader, *Cambridge*, 242, 253.

[5] Ibid., 174.

[6] Fisher was chancellor from 1505 to his resignation in 1514 and again later that same year until 1535. For the best study of Fisher's theology and his influence in Cambridge, see Rex, *Fisher*.

[7] 'Qui tametsi triade linguarum instructi sint, tamen si defuerit eis scholasticum exercitium, sensum quem conceperunt, enarrare licebit, at ubi narraverint, iam finis est. Nequeunt enim deinceps, aut suas constabilire sententias, aut aliorum errores fortiter impugnare', Fisher, *De veritate corporis et sanguinis Christi euchar-istia*, *Opera*, col. 871; Presented in translation by Edward Surtz, *The Works and Days of John Fisher* (Cambridge, Mass.: Harvard University Press, 1967), 166.

ultimate goal was to improve the quality of parish life by having well-educated clerics share the fruit of their learning with their people.[8] By coming to the collegiate foundation of John Alcock, Cranmer had entered into a community shaped by this humanist-scholastic vision of Catholic church reform.[9]

Alcock was a noted preacher and his several published sermons combine a humanist emphasis on Scripture with a firm adherence to the centrality of the sacraments.[10] The bishop could take a very pragmatic view of the usefulness of Scripture. Clergy needed to understand the Bible and use it in their preaching, because ignorance was 'the moder of all errowyse'.[11] Yet, Scripture's utility went beyond illumination of a Christian's moral and spiritual duties. The Bible also served as an instrument to convey the necessary grace for him to do what was right. Among its pages were 'medycynes reseruatyf agayn all mortall syknesse or synne'. As a result, 'no thynge more deseuerith a mannes mynde from the desyres of this worlde | and strengthe [sic] the soule ayenst temptacion & helpeth him to do well | as the studye & redynge of holy scripture'. So powerful was the Bible's effect on the soul, that the 'vertue of the worde of god & his scrypture gyueth an Influence of grace to hym that hereth & redeth it though he vnderstondeth it not & be in synne or whretchednesse'.[12]

Although the grace given through Scripture could

---

[8] Such was the purpose of St John's College which Lady Margaret Beaufort founded with advice from John Fisher: 'Ex hoc coetu theologi qui suorum studiorum fructum populo communicent'; *Early Statutes of St. John's College, Cambridge*, ed. J. E. B. Mayor (Cambridge: Cambridge University Press, 1858), 377, as quoted by Rex, *Fisher*, 213 n. 4. For an excellent study of Lady Margaret, John Fisher, and the promotion of Catholic humanist reform, see Jones and Underwood, *King's Mother*.

[9] According to Leader, Jesus College had 'all the hallmarks of the English Renaissance college', including connections with John Fisher and Lady Margaret; *Cambridge*, 270–5. For the traditional view that Alcock and the fellows of his college were Scotists untouched by humanism, see Arthur Gray and Frederick Brittain, *A History of Jesus College Cambridge* (London: Heinemann, 1979), 37; A. F. Pollard, *Thomas Cranmer and the English Reformation 1489–1556* (London: Putnam, 1905), 14.

[10] RSTC 277–87.

[11] John Alcock, *Ihesus clamabat*, sigs. B3v–[B4]r.

[12] John Alcock, *Mons Perfectionis* (Westmestre: Wynkin de Worde, 1497), sigs. [A5]v–[A6]r.

penetrate ignorance and mortal sin, Alcock made clear that Scripture was not an alternative to the sacraments, but rather each was inherently dependent on the other. On the one hand, Scripture expressly commanded Christians to receive the five obligatory sacraments, i.e. Eucharist, baptism, penance, extreme unction and confirmation. On the other hand, God's Word made the sacraments effective when spoken during their proper performance. The power of the Word transformed bread into Christ's flesh and blood, infused faith, hope, and charity into the baptized, and took away all sin during absolution.[13]

Alcock also intertwined Scripture, church Fathers, and scholasticism. The Bible was not open to private interpretation, but was to be understood as the church taught, lest someone fall into heresy. He subtly reinforced this principle by always citing canon law and the schoolmen along with his scriptural text for each major point, then illustrating its implications with quotations from early authorities like Jerome and John Chrysostom as well as scholastics like Anselm and Hugo of St Victor. Alcock wove humanism's emphasis on God's Word and early sources with the scholastic sacramental system to form a three-string ecclesiastical cord which would not be easily broken.

Not only did the founder of his college combine humanism and scholasticism, but Cranmer's principal tutor in philosophy also did as well. Cochlaeus recounted that in 1532 Cranmer told him that Robert Ridley, an uncle of Nicholas Ridley, trained him in his philosophy.[14] Being both a noted humanist and a defender of scholastic doctrine, Ridley was one of the new Cambridge men that Fisher had hoped his efforts would help the university to produce. Ridley gave the Terence lectures in humanities at Cambridge from 1508 to 1510, helped to bring the first printing press to the town in 1521, and assisted his friend Polydore Vergil in editing Gildas's *De calamitate britanniae*. Vergil

---

[13] Alcock, *Ihesus clamabat*, sigs. A2r–A6r.

[14] In the preface of his edition of Isidore which he dedicated to Ridley, Cochlaeus wrote 'dominum Thomam Cranmerum, virum eruditum & Theologum insignem . . . qui non leuia pietati ac eruditioni tuae dabat ille testimonia, affirmans te sibi olim egregium fuisse in Philosophia praeceptorem', J. Cochlaeus, *Beati Isidori . . . De officiis ecclesiasticis* (Leipzig, 1534), sig. A1v; Ridley, *Cranmer*, 21 n. 1.

subsequently used his name as a respondent for his *Dialogi de prodigiis*. On the other hand, Ridley was firmly orthodox and fought against the spread of Protestant ideas in England. He was one of four representatives of Cambridge at Cardinal Wolsey's gathering of scholars in May 1521 which advised the king on the writing of the *Assertio septem sacramentorum*.[15] He was one of two chief complainants who accused Robert Barnes of heresy in his Christmas Eve homily at St Edward's Church, Cambridge, in 1525.[16] He also served as the assessor in the Diocese of London's heresy trials and was active in suppressing the spread of Tyndale's English New Testament, criticizing its neglect of penance and bias against scholasticism, among other concerns.[17] When the king's 'privy matter' replaced Lutheranism as the greatest threat to the established religious order, Ridley spoke on behalf of the queen's cause at the 'divorce' proceedings at Blackfriars, although like his patron Tunstall, he did eventually subscribe to the royal supremacy.[18]

Some literary evidence of Ridley's dual interests has survived. From his own pen is a commonplace book in the Cambridge University Library. Reflecting both a humanist's emphasis on preaching and a scholastic's willingness to use medieval sources, Ridley transcribed a set of sermons for the liturgical year by the eleventh-century monk William of Merula. He also appended brief extracts from an ancient authority, John Chrysostom, and a modern writer, Laurentius Valla's *De mysterio eucharistiae*.[19] Another indication of Ridley's interests occurs in the two works that his

[15] Leader, *Cambridge*, 251–2, 318, 320; A. B. Emden, *Biographical Register of the University of Cambridge* (Cambridge: Cambridge University Press, 1963), 480–1; Richard Rex, 'The English Campaign Against Luther in the 1520s', *Transactions of the Royal Historical Society*, Fifth Series, 39 (1989), 85–106, at 87–9.

[16] Barnes identifies his chief accusers as 'doctour Rydley and doctour Preston | chaplens to the bisshope off London', Robert Barnes, *Supplicatyon* [London, 1531?], sig. [c6]v.

[17] For his criticism of Tyndale see his letter to Henry Gold, BL Cotton MS Cleopatra E.v, fol. 392; extracts in *Letters and Papers, Foreign and Domestic, of the Reign of Henry VIII, 1509–47*, ed. J. S. Brewer, J. Gairdner, and R. H. Brodie (London: HMSO, 1862–1910) [henceforth *LP*], iv(ii). 3960; For his association with heresy trials, see *LP* iv(ii). 4029 (3), 4038 (2), 4175; *LP* v. 589.

[18] Henry Ansgar Kelly, *The Matrimonial Trials of Henry VIII* (Stanford: Stanford University Press, 1976), 93–4, 188 n. 27.

[19] CUL MS Dd.v.27. Leader has demonstrated that the sermons which were

friend Cochlaeus dedicated to him: *Aliquot articulis* and an edition of Isidore of Seville's *De ecclesiasticis officiis*. *Aliquot*, a refutation of Anabaptist errors, offers evidence of their mutual concern for Catholic orthodoxy, while *De ecclesiasticis officiis* reflects their shared interest in ancient sources.[20]

Older historians have failed to grasp the dual nature of the training which Cranmer would have received in Fisher's Cambridge. Hence, they have adopted uncritically the anonymous biographer's rigid division of Cranmer's education: training in Scotus until his BA at twenty-two, humanist studies for four or five more years, three years of biblical studies and, finally, studies in the Fathers until he was made Doctor of Divinity in 1526 at thirty-four.[21] According to Morice, Cranmer then held the lectureship on the Bible which had been established at Jesus College.[22] To those predisposed to consider pre-Reformation theology as 'a scholastic learning then in the last stage of senile decay', this division demonstrates a pattern of gradual enlightenment.[23] However, for a strongly Roman Catholic historian like Philip Hughes, such a stratified programme is evidence that Cranmer lacked any real 'formation' in scholastic theology. Having turned away from the schoolmen 'at the very outset of his theological studies', the Archbishop remained 'an enthusiastic student' rather than a theologian 'as long as he lived'.[24] Neither depiction of his education appears

previously thought to be Ridley's composition were actually his transcriptions for a commonplace book; *Cambridge*, 189–90.

[20] The preface to *Aliquot articulis*, a very rare book, is reprinted in Cochlaeus's *Commentaria . . . de actis et scriptis Martini Lutheri* (Mainz, 1549), 172–4; *De ecclesiasticis officiis*, sigs. A1v–A2v; Rex, 'English Campaign against Luther', 104.

[21] Nichols, *Narratives*, 218–19; Mason, *Cranmer*, 4–5; Pollard, *Cranmer*, 3, 19–20; Philip Hughes, *The Reformation in England*, rev. edn. (London: Burns & Oates, 1963), i. 344–5; Loane, *Masters of the English Reformation*, 181–2; Ridley, *Cranmer*, 15–16, 20; Packer, in Duffield, *Cranmer*, xiii–xiv; Brooks, *Cranmer in Context*, 1, 4–5. MacCulloch has put forward Stephen Nevinson, the son-in-law of Reyne Wolfe, Cranmer's printer, as the anonymous biographer (*Cranmer*, 633–6), a suggestion which David Selwyn has characterized as 'a speculation, albeit an attractive and plausible one', 'Review of *Thomas Cranmer: A Life* by Diarmaid MacCulloch', *Journal of Theological Studies*, NS 48 (1997), 323–30, at 329.

[22] Nichols, *Narratives*, 240; for the lectureship, see Leader, *Cambridge*, 273. Leader suggests *c.*1516 for Cranmer's tenure. MacCulloch favours a date in the late 1520s; *Cranmer*, 23, 31 n. 56.

[23] Pollard, *Cranmer*, 14.

[24] Hughes, *Reformation*, i. 344–5.

consistent with what is now known about Cambridge studies at the beginning of the sixteenth century.

It would seem far more likely that Cranmer studied both humanist learning and scholastic philosophy for his BA in 1511 and his MA in 1515. He would have then begun his work toward the BD with two years devoted to Holy Scripture. Only after his biblical studies would Cranmer most likely have turned to the *Sententiae*, approximately during the years 1517–19. Like Robert Ridley and the other leading reforming clergy of his day, Cranmer undoubtedly studied both scholastic theology and biblical humanism at least until he received his BD in 1521. With the English Campaign against Lutheranism opening in that year, it would have been only natural for Cranmer to have then concentrated his attention on the growing controversy, studying the disputed doctrines in the light of Scripture and the Fathers, the sources the Protestants claimed as their own, as he proceeded towards his DD in 1526.[25] The anonymous biographer's account of Cranmer's academic training probably should be interpreted as a reflection in hindsight of Cranmer's growing preference for humanism over the schoolmen rather than his deciding to study one to the exclusion of the other.

Cranmer readily admitted that he accepted the teachings of the scholastic theology which he had been taught, being 'brought up from youth' in such errors 'as of transubstantiation, of the sacrifice propitiatory of the priests in the mass, of pilgrimages, purgatory, pardons, and many other superstitions and errors that came from Rome' and 'nousled therein for lack of good instruction'.[26] The question remains, then, as to the nature of this scholastic training. Eugene McGee has suggested that Cranmer was educated in the *via moderna* and, thus, the conflict between Gardiner and Cranmer on the nature of Christ's presence in the Eucharist was between a 'non-nominalist' and a 'nominalist'.[27] McGee's argument has several difficulties, not the

---

[25] See Rex, 'English Campaign against Luther', 85–106.
[26] Cox I, 374.
[27] Eugene K. McGee, 'Cranmer and Nominalism', *Harvard Theological Review* 57 (1964), 189–216.

least of which is the evidence he offers for Cranmer's training in theological terminism.[28] According to McGee, Cranmer called his nominalism 'the "Old Learning" which was really new'.[29] In fact, the Archbishop was simply making another reference to his standard claim that Protestant theology returned doctrine to its authentic biblical foundation as known in the patristic era before its corruption by the Antichrist during the last five hundred years, as he makes clear in that very same letter.[30]

Although limited, the surviving evidence indicates that Cranmer was actually trained as a Scotist. In early sixteenth-century Cambridge, the favoured schoolmen were Thomas and Scotus, with Scotus seeming to be slightly more popular.[31] According to Cranmer's anonymous biographer, a source noted by MacCulloch as 'always well-informed', Cranmer 'was nosseled in the grossest kynd of sophistry, logike, philosophy morall and naturall, (not in the text of the old philosophers, but chefely in the darke ridels and quidities of Duns and other subtile questionestes)'.[32] Philip Hughes thought otherwise, suggesting that Cranmer 'was turned by its undoubted difficulty from the task of wrestling with Duns Scotus, and so took to the newer and more congenial business of the historical study of the pre-

[28] For a concise and cogent rebuttal of McGee's main arguments for Cranmer's mature 'nominalism', see William J. Courtenay, 'Cranmer as a Nominalist, *Sed Contra*', *Harvard Theological Review* 57 (1964), 367–80. McGee offers an unpersuasive refutation of Courtenay's criticism in 'Cranmer's Nominalism Reaffirmed', *Harvard Theological Review* 59 (1966), 192–6.

[29] McGee, 'Cranmer and Nominalism', 194; The full quotations cited from Cranmer are as follow: 'But when a good number of the best learned men reputed within this realm, some favouring the old, some the new learning, as they term it, (where indeed that which they call the old is new, and that which they call the new is indeed the old;)', Cox II, 450; 'And yet to deface the old, they say that the new is the old: wherein for my part I am content to stand to the trial', ibid., 453.

[30] Cox II, 450–3; See Richard Rex, 'The New Learning', *Journal of Ecclesiastical History* 44 (1993), 26–44, at 39–42.

[31] Rex, *Fisher*, 19–20; Leader, *Cambridge*, 182, 313–17. Rex and Leader's analysis would seem to be corroborated by Cranmer's statement that Scotus and Aquinas were 'the chief pillars of the papists', Cox I, 64. NB that Henry VIII himself wrote that there were two common views on the sacraments; and, of these, he leaned more towards an instrumentalist understanding of sacramental efficacy (Thomist) rather than to a covenantal understanding (Scotist), although he acknowledged the former as the minority view; Henry VIII, *Assertio septem sacramentorum* (London: Pynson, 1521), sig. [13].

[32] MacCulloch, *Cranmer*, 36; Nichols, *Narratives*, 218–19.

medieval Fathers of the Church'. However, David Selwyn's magnificent reconstruction of Cranmer's library would seem to provide some documentary support for Cranmer's theological as well as philosophical study of Scotus.[33] The Archbishop had two copies of the Subtle Doctor's *Quaestiones super quatuor libris Sententiarum*, an inexpensive 1477 edition crowded with numerous annotations in different hands and a better edition of 1513 with only a few marginalia in Cranmer's own hand.[34] The heavy annotation of the earlier edition suggests that this was a 'second-hand' student's working copy, which he supplemented later with a cleaner text as he moved from struggling student to become a more prosperous scholar.

What would Cranmer have learned from Scotist scholasticism? Firstly, he would have been tutored in the voluntarist tradition that emphasized the native freedom of the human will as the highest faculty of the soul.[35] For the intellectualist tradition of St Thomas, the will naturally desired the good as presented to it by the intellect so that cultivating right reason was the key to right conduct. Scotus, however, was true to the tradition of his Franciscan order. Quoting Augustine's statement that 'nothing is so much in our power as the will itself',[36] the Subtle Doctor argued that the human will was self-determining so that moral choice was the crux of Christian life. From Scotus, Cranmer would have learned that the supreme cause of human good and the

---

[33] David G. Selwyn, *The Library of Thomas Cranmer* (Oxford: Oxford Bibliographical Society, 1996).

[34] Despite similarities with Cranmer's recognized later script, the main hand in the 1477 edition has some significant differences, including the style of final 's', which render it questionable to attribute the hand to Cranmer. For Selwyn's opinion, see *Library*, 28. Note, however, MacCulloch's suggestion that the marking system is Cranmer's customary arabic numerals; *Cranmer*, 20.

[35] See Cross, *Duns Scotus*, 84–9; Bernardine M. Bonansea, 'Duns Scotus' Voluntarism', in *John Duns Scotus, 1265–1965*, ed. John K. Ryan and Bernardine M. Bonansea, Studies in Philosophy and the History of Philosophy, 3 (Washington, D.C.: Catholic University of America Press, 1965), 83–121; Allan B. Wolter, 'Native Freedom of the Will as Key to the Ethics of Scotus', in *The Philosophical Theology of John Duns Scotus*, ed. Marilyn McCord Adams (Ithaca, N.Y.: Cornell University Press, 1990), 148–62.

[36] 'Augustinus *primo lib. retract. cap.* 22 ubi dicit quod *nihil est tam in potestate nostra quam ipsa voluntas*', John Duns Scotus, *Quaestiones in quartum librum sententiarum (Oxon)*, Li. ii, d. 25, q. un; *Opera omnia* (Paris: Vives, 1891–5), xiii. 198.

principal activity of human perfection was selfless love of the good.[37]

Secondly, because of Scotus's rather positive view of fallen human nature, Cranmer would have been taught that human beings had an innate capacity to love moral goodness for its own sake. Like Thomas, the Subtle Doctor taught that human nature's lower sensitive soul with its passions needed to be subordinated to the reason and will of the higher rational soul. Consequently, in paradise God had endowed Adam and Eve with an additional gift of original righteousness (*donum superadditium*) which ensured this requisite internal harmony in the first human beings. Unlike Thomas, however, Scotus argued that the Fall entailed only a loss of this special grace of original righteousness without any concomitant disordering of human faculties as well. In the rational soul, the will retained two native inclinations: (i) a natural desire for self-realization in accordance with the Aristotelian principle that every agent is drawn towards the actualization of its potential (*affectio commodi*); (ii) an innate desire for justice that permitted the will to transcend natural self-interest and to choose the moral good for its own sake in accord with right reason (*affectio iustitiae*).[38] In the sensitive soul, concupiscence was not an inclination towards sin but merely the natural longings of the sensitive appetite with which God created humankind as incarnate beings.[39] Without the *donum superadditium* the ordering of the passions by right reason would not come as easily as before. Nevertheless, human beings still had both the power to choose to love God selflessly without any special assistance of grace and an innate instinct drawing them towards him. While godly love had an

---

[37] Mary Elizabeth Ingham, 'Scotus and the Moral Order', *American Catholic Philosophical Quarterly* 67 (1993), 127–50, at 127.

[38] For a discussion of the two affections of the will, see Cross, *Duns Scotus*, 86–9 and Ingham, 'Scotus and the Moral Order'. For current literature on the subject, see ibid., 127 n. 1. For the relationship between the *affectio iustitiae* and Bonaventura's understanding of the 'spark of conscience' (*syndersis*), see Allan B. Wolter, *Duns Scotus on the Will and Morality*, translation edition ed. William A. Frank (Washington, D.C.: Catholic University of America Press, 1997), 45–6.

[39] For a fuller discussion of the issue, see Cross, *Duns Scotus*, 96–100; Norman Powell Williams, *The Ideas of the Fall and of Original Sin: A Historical and Critical Study* (London: Longmans Green, 1927), 408–16.

emotional dimension, it was primarily an act of the will to put God first.[40] From Scotus Cranmer would have learned of humanity's ability and obligation to love God above all else.

Thirdly, Cranmer would have been taught that salvation was not primarily because of something inherently worthy in humanity but ultimately as a result of God's gracious acceptance. According to Scotus, the supernatural infusion of sanctifying grace was necessary for justification only because of the divine decision to accept its presence as the meritorious basis for salvation *de potentia Dei ordinata*. The same principle applied equally to Scotus's 'two-track' system for receiving this grace. The sacrament was not an instrumental means of grace, nor were morally good works before justification inherently meritorious in God's eyes. Both were the basis for the reception of *gratia gratum faciens* simply because God had chosen to accept them as such. Therefore, although fallen humanity could do morally good acts by stilling their passions and calmly choosing to listen to their *affectio iustitiae*, without the additional divine gift of sanctifying grace such acts were never meritorious for salvation.[41]

Finally, Cranmer would have been taught that ultimately salvation depended on God's predestination of only some to eternal life. According to Scotus, predestination was a matter of God's will rather than his knowledge, that predestination to life was the result of foreordination rather than merely foreknowledge. Applying the Aristotelian principle that every agent that acts in an orderly manner first wills the end and then the means to that end, Scotus argued that God first willed whom he would bring to salvation before any prevision of merits (*ante praevisa merita*). Then he willed for them the means of grace by which they would be saved. Hence, God chose to accept the person by election even before he decided to accept his acts as the basis for the infusion of grace.[42] Thus, from Scotus

---

[40] See Wolter, *Will and Morality*, 92.
[41] See McGrath, *Iustitia Dei*,146–9; Wolter, *Will and Morality*, 89–94; Cross, *Duns Scotus*, 103–11.
[42] See McGrath, *Iustitia Dei*, 134–7, 148–9; B. M. Bonansea, *Man and his*

Cranmer would have learned a system of salvation that both insisted on the necessity of human penitential activity and fully safeguarded its utter gratuity through its doctrines of election and acceptation.

Yet Cranmer was most likely trained not only as a Scotist but also as a humanist. The impact of the dual nature of his education surely influenced his academic instruction in penitential theology. As we have seen, on penance, at least, John Fisher was also a Scotist and a humanist. His synthesis of the two traditions would have been a natural basis for Cranmer's own initial training in justification and penitence.

In the *Confutatio*, Fisher marshalled the full force of his humanist learning to defend the basic Scotist approach to penance. For example, Fisher opened his defence of the divine institution of auricular confession by asserting Scotus's famous argument that the Fathers would never have imposed such a hard obligation on Christians if they had not been persuaded that either the Scriptures commanded it or the apostles instituted it.[43] He then turned to the twin pillars of authority—tradition and Scripture—and proceeded to amass evidence for the command to confess to a priest. He listed numerous examples of patristic biblical interpretation and also the early church historian Sozomen to show that confession had been a private rite from the most distant past in both the Latin and the Greek churches. Fisher then quoted many passages of Scripture, including the Mosaic regulations that lepers had to show themselves to the priest and the injunction of James for Christians to confess their sins to one another. Naturally, he finished with Jesus granting the power to pardon to his apostles in John 20: 23 as well as the associated text in Acts 19: 18

Approach to God in John Duns Scotus (Lanham, N.Y.: University Press of America, 1983), 216–21; Cross, *Duns Scotus*, 100–3.

[43] 'Neque facile crediderim patres ipsos hanc usque adeo duram provinciam nobis imposuisse, nisi persuasissimum habuissent, hanc exomologesin aut ab Apostolis institutam, aut in ipsis scripturis sacris dilucide traditam fuisse', Fisher, *ALC*, Art. 8, col. 418; cf. 'Quod confessio non cadit nisi sub praecepto ecclesiae, non potest faciliter improbari, nisi quia vel ecclesia non attentavisset tam arduum praeceptum imponere omnibus Christianis, nisi esset praeceptum divinum', Scotus, *Quaestiones (Oxon)*, Li. 4, dist. 17, q. unica; *Opera omnia*, xviii. 508.

where penitents come to St Paul and openly confess their sins.[44]

Yet on the key issue of attrition arising *ex puris naturalibus*, Fisher's humanist learning clearly revised Scotus's teaching. The Subtle Doctor sought to protect the gratuity of salvation by his teachings on election and divine acceptance. As a result,

Scotus' doctrine of justification resembles an Iron Age settlement, containing a highly vulnerable central area surrounded by defensive ditches. The two defensive ditches in Scotus' doctrine of justification are his doctrines of absolute predestination and divine acceptation, which emphasise the priority of the divine will in justification. The central area, however, is highly vulnerable to the charge of Pelagianism, in that Scotus insists upon the *activity* of the human will in justification.[45]

Neither of these two defensive ditches were visible in the Scotist penitential teaching we have examined, leaving the 'highly vulnerable central area' clearly exposed. Fisher's answer was not to revive these defences so much as simply to move the basic Scotist penitential framework to higher ground. Within the Scotist 'two-track' means to justification, Fisher simply insisted on the necessity of prevenient grace to enable the penitent to prepare for sanctifying grace. In his harmony of scholastic descriptions of attrition in the Article 6 of the *Confutatio*, Fisher employed language which echoed Scotus but also included Gregory of Rimini's key term for prevenient grace, *auxilium Dei speciale* ('the special help of God'). According to Fisher, the schoolmen had taught that the detestation of sin came from human effort as aided by the *influentia generalis* and *auxilium dei*.[46] And in

[44] Fisher, *ALC*, Art. 8, cols. 418–24.

[45] McGrath, *Iustitia Dei*, 144. See also McGrath, 'The Anti-Pelagian Structure of "Nominalist" Doctrines of Justification', *Ephemerides Theologicae Lovanienses* 57 (1981), 107–19.

[46] Scotus: 'Peccator in peccatis existens . . . potest ex naturalibus cum communi influentia considerare peccatum commissum, ut offensivum dei, et ut contra legem divinam, et ut aversivum a deo, et ut impeditivum praemii, et ut inductivum supplicii, et sub

Fisher: 'Existimant enim peccatorum [recte, peccatorem], ex naturalibus, cum generali influxu, *et auxilio dei* posse considerare peccatum ab se commissum, ut offensivum dei, <u>et</u> ut aversivum a deo, et ut impedivum <u>p</u>raemii, <u>et</u> supplicii inductivum, ac proinde posse

Article 36, Fisher cited the publican's conversion as an example of grace 'knocking, stirring and (as they say) coming before although not yet having been permitted to enter'. With the help of this grace and 'by doing what was in him', the publican 'was able to do morally good works and thus at length merit forgiveness'.[47] While not actually using the term *meritum de congruo*, Fisher insisted that good works done before justification were 'not completely for nothing' in assisting the *viator* to move closer to justification.[48]

Recent scholarship has sought to distance Fisher from any semi-Pelagian connotations associated with Scotus and the later *via moderna* because of their understanding of meritorious attrition *ex puris naturalibus*. While acknowledging that his description of the scholastic doctrine of justification in the Article 6 of the *Confutatio* followed Scotist teaching, these scholars have argued that Fisher's personal position was different from the opinions that he was recounting. Edward Surtz has suggested that Fisher appeared to be 'standing aloof' from his account of how attrition became contrition. His only concern in the matter was merely 'the just exposition of Scholastic doctrine'.[49]

multis talibus rationibus; et potest voluntas ipsum . . . illud peccatum sic consideratum detestari', *Questiones (Oxon)*, Li. 4, dist. 14, q. 2; *Opera omnia*, xviii. 74.

voluntatem eius, peccatum sic consideratum detestari' (italics added), *ALC*, Art. 6, col. 407; cf. *ALC*, Art. 36, cols. 672, 704.

For a discussion of the soteriology of Gregory of Rimini in relation to other medieval theologians, see A. E. McGrath, '"Augustinianism"? A Critical Assessment of the So-called "Medieval Augustinian Tradition" on Justification', *Augustiniana* 31 (1981), 247–67, at 259–61.

[47] 'Sed adfuit gratia pulsans, excitans, et (ut aiunt) praeveniens, nondum intromissa . . . faciendo quantum in se fuerit, non modo non peccare mortaliter, verumetiam divinae gratiae praesentia sic adiuvari, ut posset bene moraliter agere, atque ita tandem promereri veniam', *ALC*, Art. 36, cols. 712–13.

[48] 'Mihi nunquam persuadebis, quod eleemosyna, oratio, iniuriarum dimissio, ac caetera id genus opera, nihil omnino peccatori conferunt, quo posset ad gratiam citius pervenire', *ALC*, Art. 7, col. 414; 'Non est ergo prorsus nihil, si quis peccator extra charitatem existens, studio resipiscendi, faciat aut eleemosynam, aut orationem, aut caetera id genus, quanquam non inde mereatur ex condigno praemium', ibid., col. 414; 'Sed et poenitentiam quae antecedit iustificationem non esse prorsus nihil', ibid., col. 415. Although not acknowledging Fisher's reluctance to use the term 'meritum de congruo', Surtz is correct that 'the sinner, however, acting under the influence of actual grace, can merit from congruity (*ex congruo*) other actual graces which dispose him proximately for justification', Surtz, *Works and Days*, 206, 234.   [49] Surtz, *Works and Days*, 218.

Emphasizing Fisher's patristic concern for grace in the process of salvation, Richard Rex has also stated that 'Fisher never spoke in his own person of attrition, using the term only when citing or reporting the views of others'; thus 'he gives no reason to conclude that he subscribes to those views'.[50] In fact, those rightly concerned to stress Fisher's commitment to grace need not deny that he was expressing his own views on attrition and penance in the *Confutatio*. For in his description Fisher managed to combine both his Augustinian piety and his scholastic training, neither accepting the notion of a meritorious attrition *ex puris naturalibus* nor abandoning his Scotist framework for justification.

Firstly, as we have seen, Fisher's description of attrition from Article 6 significantly modified the Scotist account to conform to his own view on prevenient grace. According to Article 36, Fisher disagreed with the classic Scotist and *via moderna* understanding of how attrition become contrition *ex congruo* because no one was able to prepare himself for grace without 'the help of God', the very phrase he had inserted into his otherwise standard Scotist description of extra-sacramental justification.[51]

Secondly, the discussion of attrition in Article 6 is consistent with Fisher's presentation of justification throughout the *Confutatio*. In Article 1, Fisher introduced the classic Scotist double method of justification, including the description of contrition as formed attrition, by specifically stating that there was nothing in this scholastic teaching which ought not to be received.[52] In Article 5, Fisher once

---

[50] Rex, *Fisher*, 39, 125, 216 n. 61.

[51] 'Quanquam ex disputatoribus nonnulli, quorum iudiciis ipse non subscribo, sentiant eum, qui mortali peccato gravatus sit, absque speciali auxilio gratiae, posse bene mortaliter agere, ac proinde se praeparare posset, non quidem ut ex merito, sed ut ex congruo Deus ei sit daturus gratiam . . . Nam esto, sine *auxilio Dei* qui foris pulsat, nemo posset ad gratiam parare sese', *ALC*, Art. 36, col. 704; cf. 'Existimant enim peccatorum [recte, peccatorem], ex naturalibus, cum generali influxu, et *auxilio Dei* posse considerare peccatum ab se commissum', *ALC*, Art. 6, col. 407; italics added to both quotations.

[52] 'Nihil quod pro [Scholasticis] abs te redditur, non potest non suspectum [*sic*] esse . . . Quoniam igitur via contritionis, seu attritionis formatae, non minus est dura, quam incerta peccatoribus, iccirco viam hanc alteram, per sacramentorum susceptionem, multo mitiorem, et securiorem docent, utpote ob quam nihil exigitur, nisi ut non ponatur obex, vel infidelitatis vel peccati mortalis', *ALC*,

again described justification according to the Scotist framework, linking it to his earlier discussion, 'as we have said
above', and specifically attributing this teaching to the
church, not just the scholastics. It is important to note as
well that Fisher here based extra-sacramental forgiveness on
'a great and bitter sorrow' rather than contrition.[53] In
Article 7, he specifically equated such sorrow with the
scholastic teaching on attrition, not contrition.[54]

Lastly, in Article 36 which Surtz and Rex both see as
representative of Fisher's personal position, his final discussion of the subject continued to follow the same Augustinian-influenced Scotist description which he had presented
earlier. The process of justification began when divine grace
stimulated the soul of the sinner to detest his sins. If
unformed, this newly conceived penitence could gain the
grace of justification in either of two ways, through the
sinner's persisting in sorrow until God directly infused
gratia gratum faciens or by his receiving the sacrament.
Echoing his initial description of the '*via contritionis*' as
'*attritionis formatae*', Fisher once again stated that the same
sorrow that was unformed became formed through the
infusion of grace.[55] While Fisher deviated from Scotus by
stipulating that attrition arose through prevenient grace, he
continued to hold to Scotus's two ways for attrition, once
arisen, to become the basis for justification.

Thus, under the influence of the Augustinian Catholic
revival, Fisher moved his Scotist doctrine of penitential
justification to higher ground, choosing to defend salvation
from Pelagian influences by insisting on the necessity of

Art. 1, col. 339. While rejecting the discussion of attrition in Art. 6, col. 407, Surtz
accepted this passage as reflecting Fisher's personal view; Surtz, *Works and Days*,
161.

[53] *ALC*, Art. 5, col. 385.

[54] Sed timorem et concussionem, et dolorem, quem dicunt atterentem', *ALC*,
Art. 7, col. 416.

[55] 'Ordo igitur quo peccator ad gratiam redit, eiusmodi statui potest. Stimulatur
primum auxilio divinae gratiae peccatoris animus, ut peccata detestetur. Subinde
poenitet illum eadem admisisse. Verum quoniam haec poenitentia non semper
illico formata est, sed potest adhuc informis manere, ideo tandem, aut continuato
poenitentiae motu, aut sacramentorum virtute, Deus gratiam infundit poenitenti,
quo poenitentia quae prius informis erat, iam evadat formata.' *ALC*, Art. 36, col.
701.

prevenient grace to prepare for the reception of sanctifying grace. Under the influence of *gratia gratis data*, the *viator* could perform works which were good (*de congruo*) in the eyes of God for his progress toward justification, persisting in them until by the reception of *gratia gratum faciens* he himself was made 'good' (intrinsically righteous) in the eyes of God.

In brief, then, Fisher's doctrine held that by the inspiration of divine grace before justification good works assisted the penitent in the process leading him to become 'good' himself in justification. The difficulty of this *ex opere operantis* method of pardon was balanced by the requirement that those who chose the easier means of forgiveness through the sacrament still had to work off the temporal punishments through penances which the confessor imposed. In either case, Fisher considered the struggle to punish sin, so that God might not, to be a powerful reminder of humanity's need for complete dependence on divine grace. When Cranmer came to decide that permitting good works a role in justification hindered complete dependence on grace rather than fostered it, he abandoned the Scotist-humanist training of his youth. In essence, Cranmer came to associate Fisher's higher ground with Mount Sinai, whereas he became convinced that the Protestant interpretation of Augustine had finally returned to Calvary.

1. *Metamorphosis of Actaeon* by Jean Mignon

2. *The Creation of Eve* by Jean Mignon

3. *Thomas Cranmer* by Gerlach Flicke, National Portrait
Gallery, no. 535

3

Cranmer's Doctrine of Repentance during the 1520s: Erasmian Penitence

S[ic] non expedit [apud] quoslibet, q[uovis] loco et tempor[e] verum dicere.[1]

The Augustinian-influenced scholastic humanism of John Fisher taught that good works assisted in the process of the *viator* becoming good in God's eyes, but the goodness of both the works and the worker was the result of divine grace—*gratia gratis data* for the former and *gratia gratum faciens* for the latter. In the 1530s Cranmer would reject the notion that penitential acts aided a sinner in becoming worthy of forgiveness because no work could be considered good before its worker was. What brought about this transition? Cranmer appears to have left us a guide in the careful iconography of Gerlach Flicke's 1545 painting.[2] Depicted as archbishop of Canterbury, Cranmer sits in front of a window framed by a curtain on his left and with an intricately carved jamb on his right. He reads one book while two others lie on the table in front of him. Although the title of the volume farthest from him is now illegible, the book directly in front of Cranmer bears the title 'Augu[stini] *De fide et operibus*' and the one in his hands is designated as 'Pauli Epistolae'.[3] It has been suggested that the first volume was originally labelled 'Erasm[i] [t]estam[en]tum'.[4] While certain difficulties preclude this as a possibility,[5] a work

---

[1] 'Thus, it is not expedient to speak the truth to just anyone in every place and time', Cranmer's *De libero arbitrio* [BL 697.b. 3.(1)], sig. A5r.

[2] London, National Portrait Gallery, No. 535.

[3] That is, 'Augustine's *On Faith and Works*' and 'Paul's Epistles'.

[4] That is, 'The *Testament* of Erasmus'; John N. King, *English Reformation Literature: The Tudor Origins of the Protestant Tradition* (Princeton: Princeton University Press, 1982), 122; Brooks, *Cranmer in Context*, viii.

[5] While the first letter is definitely an 'E' and the second letter most likely an 'r', the remaining letters are so incomplete as to make any suggestion mere supposition. However, a long stem in the second half of the title is clearly visible, either

from Erasmus would have been a natural choice. For together, these three books represent the crucial intellectual steps that Cranmer took to his mature position on justification, the key issue for a Protestant Reformer.

ERASMUS

That Cranmer greatly respected Erasmus cannot be doubted.[6] The anonymous biographer included his name among the humanists whom Cranmer studied;[7] and when as the new archbishop Cranmer continued Warham's pension to Erasmus, Thomas More wrote to his friend that he rejoiced that 'the present prelate of Canterbury shows not a little love toward you'.[8] Indeed, Cranmer's personal motto '*Nosce teipsum et deum*' ('Know yourself and God') could easily have originated as an epitome of Erasmus's famous guide to Christian living, the *Enchiridion Militis Christiani*.[9]

The Dutch reformer's emphasis on a practical Christian piety of ethical conduct arising from the knowledge of Scripture was integral to Cranmer's admiration for him. According to Erasmus, true Christianity was drawn not from the syllogistic subtleties of scholastic thought but

from an 'f' or a 'p'. According to Sir Roy Strong, the inscription is: '[E (?)] p[ote?] n | te'; *Tudor and Jacobean Portraits* (HMSO, 1969), no. 535.

[6] For two recent studies on Cranmer's relationship to Erasmus and to humanism in general, see Hall, in Ayris and Selwyn, *Churchman and Scholar*, 6–16; Dowling, in ibid., 89–114.

[7] Nichols, *Narratives*, 219.

[8] 'Praesentem Cantuariae Praesulem non minorem erga te amorem', Letter 2831 in *Opus epistolarum Des. Erasmi Roterodami*, ed. P. S. Allen, H. M. Allen, and H. W. Garrod, 12 vols. (Oxford: Clarendon Press, 1906–58), x. 258; Erasmus reciprocated Cranmer's goodwill, calling him 'vir integerrimus candidissimisque moribus', Letter 2879, ibid., x. 318. For Cranmer continuing the pension, see Letter 2815, ibid., x. 233; for Erasmus's concern that a member of Warham's household, whom he described as 'is usque ad insaniam est Evangelicus', would seek to discontinue his pension, see Letter 2761, ibid., x. 151.

[9] For the motto itself, see MacCulloch, *Cranmer*, 10, illustration no. 3. Cf. 'The beginning of this wisdom [that we must ask of God . . . and extract like a treasure from the veins of divine Scripture] is to know thyself'; 'the first rule [of true Christianity] should be to understand fully what the Scriptures tell us about Christ and his Spirit', Erasmus, *Enchiridion*, 40, 55.

from the plain teaching of the New Testament. Its authentic precepts were more concerned with what effected the internal dispositions of humankind than with the outward trappings of ritualistic conduct. Indeed, the battle for which Erasmus sought to prepare his Christian knight was the spiritual struggle within each person to follow the good leadings of reason rather than the deceitful passions of the body.[10] When Paul spoke of the flesh lusting against the spirit and the spirit against the flesh, he described this contest between reason and passion to influence the will.[11] Erasmus, however, like the Scotists before him, taught that there were no 'impulses' which were 'so violent that they cannot be restrained by reason and redirected towards virtue'.[12] Hence, the heart of Christianity was a pragmatic programme of love in action which sprang from a scriptural understanding of the human condition and the virtues and vices pertaining to it.[13]

Yet Cranmer respected Erasmus not only for his humanist appeal to the importance of Scripture in the life of *viator* but also for his humanist analysis of the biblical text itself. Seeking to reform the Church by repristinating the learning of the patristic era, Erasmus sought to combine 'a pure, elegant, classical style and knowledge of antiquity with a clear understanding of the Bible and the pious life'.[14] As a

[10] 'Man is a marvellous creature composed of two or three very diverse parts, a soul which is like a divinity and a body which like a brute beast . . . [T]he soul, remembering its heavenly origin, strives upwards with all its might and struggles against its earthly burden . . . And it was not the fabled Prometheus who implanted this discord . . . but sin corrupted that which had been well put together, sowing the poison of dissension between two harmonious entities. Previously the mind commanded the body without any trouble, and the body obeyed the mind freely and willingly. Now on the contrary, with the natural order of things disturbed, the passions of the body strive to have dominion over reason, and reason is forced to accede to the wishes of the body', Erasmus, *Enchiridion*, 41–2.

[11] Erasmus, *Enchiridion*, 47.

[12] Erasmus, *Enchiridion*, 44; cf. Melanchthon's observation in the first edition of his landmark *Loci communes theologici* (1521): Scotists taught that 'the will (*voluntas*) can conform itself to every recommendation of right reason, that is that the will (*voluntas*) is able to will (*velle*) whatever reason and proper counsel of the intellect prescribe', *Melanchthon and Bucer*, ed. Wilhelm Pauck (London: SCM Press, 1969), 40.

[13] For Erasmus's anthropology, see John B. Payne, *Erasmus: His Theology of the Sacraments* ([Richmond, Va.:] John Knox Press, 1970), 35–43.

[14] Payne, *Erasmus*, 19. In this respect, Cranmer's motto is once again truly Erasmian, combining the ancient adage 'Γνωθι σεαυτον' ('Know yourself') with the

result, his scholarship championed a new exegetical emphasis on philology and historical development as exemplified in his fresh translation of the Latin New Testament and its accompanying notes, known as the *Novum Testamentum* and its *Annotationes*. As a don at Cambridge, Cranmer appears to have required candidates for the BD to exhibit knowledge of its philological and historical exegesis. According to Foxe, Cranmer put these students through such a 'seuere examination' on 'the story of the Bible', that members of religious orders 'were commonly reiected by hym'.[15] Since all those seeking the BD were required to give lectures on the Bible,[16] for Cranmer to require biblical knowledge *per se* would not have been exceptional, rather it would have been expected. The key issue in contention was most likely, as Foxe phrased it, that the religious had been trained 'with out regard had to the autority of scriptures', i.e. Cranmer demanded that candidates expound Scripture according to Erasmian principles of exegesis instead of the tenets of scholastic theology. As Erasmus's scholarship amply demonstrated, these humanist methods of biblical criticism raised serious questions about the scholastic doctrine of penance.[17]

On philological grounds, Erasmus challenged the traditional use of certain texts of Scripture to support the necessity of good works for the forgiveness of sins. In the important verses of Matthew 3: 2 and 4: 17, the Vulgate translated μετανοεῖτε as *poenitentiam agite*, 'Do penance'. Erasmus felt this rendering obscured the sense of the

---

traditional Christian teaching that the end of humankind is to know their Maker. For the classical usage of 'Γνωθι σεαυτον', see Erasmus, *Adages: I vi 1 to 1 x 100*, *Collected Works of Erasmus*, 32, trans. R. A. B. Mynors (Toronto: University of Toronto Press, 1989), 62–3.

[15] Foxe, *Actes and Monumentes*, 2033.

[16] Leader, *Cambridge*, 174.

[17] For a full account of Erasmus on penance, see Payne, *Erasmus*, 181–216; Jean-Pierre Massaut, 'La Position "Oecuménique" d'Érasme sur la pénitence', in *Reforme et Humanisme* (Montpellier, Centre D'Histoire de la Reforme et du Protestantisme, 1977), 241–81; Thomas N. Tentler, 'Forgiveness and Consolation in the Religious Thought of Erasmus', *Studies in the Renaissance* 12 (1965), 110–33, at 110–19. For his biblical criticism see C. A. L. Jarrott, 'Biblical Humanism', *Studies in the Renaissance* 17 (1970), 119–52, at 125–8; Erika Rummel, *Erasmus' Annotations on the New Testament: From Philologist to Theologian* (Toronto: University of Toronto Press, 1986), 152–6.

Greek and led to a stress on satisfaction instead of on contrition. He preferred to translate μετανοεῖτε as *resipiscite*, 'to come to one's senses', adding that to connect *poenitentiam agere* with doing satisfaction was a barbarous solecism.[18] On historical grounds, Erasmus also questioned the divine institution of sacramental penance. According to his note on Acts 19: 18, the practice of auricular confession had developed over time:

There was of old some form of confessing a life of evil-doing, but it was a public confession, in my opinion, and a general one, and we do not read that it was compulsory. The secret, aural form of confession practised now seems to have originated in consultations with bishops, if some scruple burdened the soul.[19]

Since its institution was *de iure humano* (by human law), Erasmus denied that auricular confession was 'utterly necessary'.[20] Luther was quick to note the significance of the new translation of μετανοεῖτε for his opposition of faith to works.[21] Consistent with the moralism of his *philosophia Christi*, however, Erasmus was concerned to distinguish between true inner piety and the mere outward performance of empty ceremonies.[22] His writings sought to demonstrate that forgiveness of sins was based on contrition and love in

[18] 'Caeterum, poenitentiam agere, pro affici ducique poenitudine, ut nolim pronunciare barbarum ac soloecum, ita non memini legere apud probos auctores', Erasmus, *Opera omnia Desiderii Erasmi Roterodami*, ed. J. Leclerc (Leyden: Vander, 1703–6) [henceforth *LB*], vi. 17F; Rummel, *Annotations*, 152–3; Payne, *Erasmus*, 182–3; Jarrott, 'Biblical Humanism', 125–7.

[19] 'Vel hinc colligi potest fuisse et antiquitus nonnullam confessionem male actae vitae, sed apertam, ut opinor, et in genere, quam nec ipsam legimus exactam abs quoquam. Caeterum quae nunc recepta est clancularia et in aurem fit, videtur ex consultationibus privatis esse nata, quae solent apud episcopos fieri, si qui scrupulus urgeret animum', *LB* vi. 507F–508E; English translation, Rummel, *Annotations*, 154.

[20] 'Confessionem, quae fit homini, non esse simpliciter necessariam', *LB* v. 152F.

[21] In a letter to Staupitz in 1518, Luther wrote, 'I learned that this word (*poenitentia*) means μετάνοια in Greek which is derived from μετά and νοῦν, i.e., 'afterwards' and 'mind', so that *poenitentia* or μετάνοια means a coming to one's senses . . . The emphasis on works of penance had come from the misleading [Vulgate] translation, which indicates an action rather than a change of heart and in no way corresponds to the Greek μετάνοια'; translated from *WA* 1¹. 525 by Rummel, *Annotations*, 153.

[22] See Richard L. DeMolen, *The Spirituality of Erasmus of Rotterdam* (Nieuwkoop: De Graaf Publishers, 1987), 46–54.

the penitent's heart rather than external works of satisfaction or sacramental action *ex opere operato*.[23]

Thus, Erasmus's most extensive work on contrition and confession, *Exomologesis sive modus confitendi* (1524),[24] presented a demanding description of the personal piety which led to pardon. While contemplating the wages of sin produced a regret for sin from fear of punishment, attrition was insufficient for pardon. Those whose sorrow was so shallow that they would continue to sin if they could do so without suffering the consequences were destined for hell.[25] Instead, the contrition required for divine forgiveness was a detestation of sin proceeding from the love of God with a firm intention not to sin again.[26] People often had to return to the remedy of penance because of human frailty. Nevertheless, they were to come determined to die ten times rather than once commit the same offence again.[27] Love for God was the key motivation for keeping such a vow.[28] Though he were to receive no punishment at all, a son who deeply loved his parents would still not want to do anything

---

[23] 'Huc [i.e. spiritum hunc senserit, quem Paulus vocat filiorum] ubi profecit homo, jam redditus est ecclesiae, jam ex servo diaboli factus est filius Dei, jam liber est a peccato, atque etiam ut sperandum est a poena, si dolor et amor fuerit vehemens', *Exomologesis*, *LB* v. 157E.

[24] *Exomologesis*, *LB* v. 145–70; an English translation, *A lytle treatise of the maner and forme of confession* (London: Iohn Byddell for Wyllyam Marshall) appeared *c.*1535–6, perhaps the work of Cromwell's agent William Marshall; E. J. Devereux, *Renaissance English Translations of Erasmus: A Bibliography to 1700* (Toronto: University of Toronto Press, 1983), 128. For a description of its argument, see Payne, *Erasmus*, 199–208; DeMolen, *Spirituality of Erasmus*, 58–63.

[25] 'Hujus illud est caput, ut homo penitus concipiat odium peccatorum, non hujus aut illius, sed omnium quae Deum offendunt, idque jam non tantum ex formidine vindictae divinae aut humanae, sed amore libero quo rapitur in Deum. Etenim qui hactenus detestatur peccata, ut ea repetiturus sit, si liceret impune, is non effugiet Gehennam', *LB* v. 157B–C.

[26] 'Nulla fit remissio peccati, nisi adsit idonea detestatio commissorum ex amore Dei proficiscens, ac serium certumque propositum in posterum abstinendi ab omnibus quae Deum offendunt', *LB* v. 151F.

[27] 'Ita quamquam ob imbecillitatem humanae naturae non rejiciuntur, qui saepius relapsi redeunt ad poenitentiae remedium: tamen qui poenitentiam suscipit, hoc animo votoque debet esse, ut decies mortem obire malit, quam iterum admittere quae deflet', *LB* v. 157A; 'magnitudo doloris ex peccatorum consideratione concepta, impetrat Dei misericordiam ad relaxanda commissa', *LB* v. 152C.

[28] 'Jam votum illud mutandae vitae, nec firmum est, nec frugiferum, nisi proficiscatur ex amore Dei', *LB* v. 157C.

to displease them. How much more careful not to sin again were they to be who loved God.[29]

Penitents could not obtain this level of sorrow and love in their own power, but God granted contrition as a divine gift to those who persistently sought to have their servile fear turned into filial fear.[30] They were to hate their sins but also to trust in the mercy of God. For consideration of the consequences of sin would lead to desperation, if it did not advance to the hope of forgiveness through *fiducia* (a sure confidence) in Jesus Christ as having paid once for the sins of all.[31] In fact, the chief aim of penitence was that the sinner might develop *fiducia* in Christ's promises so that he might love rather than fear.[32] As penitents expressed their desire for contrition with tears, prayers, alms deeds, and other godly works, they were always to remember that when true sorrow arose in their hearts, it was God's work, not their accomplishment.[33] If true contrition tarried, they were to be steadfast in their efforts, for God 'gyueth his graces & benefites freely: but he gyueth them not to ydle & recheles folke'.[34]

Such cultivation of inner godly sorrow and love was to be preferred to reliance on externals: 'I do thynke it the more surer way, to hope full remission and forgyuenes of synnes | of charite, and of the mercy of Christ | than of any bulles, or wrytinges made by any man'; 'Agayne, euyn this thynge also shall be very profitable herunto: yf we do put the chiefe and

---

[29] 'Etenim si filius ex animo diligens parentes suos, etiam si nullus sit metus poene, tamen nolit sciens admittere, quod offendat animos illorum: quanto magis qui Deum amat . . . cavet ne quid in posterum simile committat?', *LB* v. 152B.

[30] 'Porro, non est in potestate peccatoris, ut ipse sibi largiatur hunc affectum. Dei donum est gratuitum, ab illo tamen lacrymis, precibus, eleemosynis, aliisque piis studiis ambiendum', *LB* v. 157C.

[31] 'Ex harum rerum attenta consideratione nascitur horror peccatorum, qui nonnumquam ducit originem ex metu supplicii, gignitque desperationem, nisi proficiat usque ad spem veniae per contemplationem misericordiae divinae, perque fiduciam erga Dominum Jesum, qui semel dependit pro peccatis omnium', *LB* v. 152A.

[32] 'Quum id potissimum sit agendum, ut peccator sumat fiduciam in Christi promissis, et amet potius quam metuat', *LB* v. 155D.

[33] 'Caveat ne quid hinc sibi tribuat, agnoscat gratuitum Dei donum, et abjectus ad pedes illius, gratias agat ejus benignitati', *LB* v. 157D.

[34] 'Est ille benignus, et gratis largitur suas dotes, sed non largitur oscitantibus', *LB* v. 157D; *A lytle treatise*, sig. [G8]v.

principall truste of helthe and saluation | in charite, and in the mercy of god | rather than in the rehersynge or reckenynge vppe of our synnes | namely, whan deathe is nere at hande.'[35] Erasmus thought that confession was abused by those who came without earnest sorrow and serious intention to change.[36] While he claimed to reserve comment on the Scotist principle that the keys could change attrition into contrition, in practice he instructed penitents not to go to confession until they had cultivated true contrition in their hearts.[37]

Although Erasmus liked to discourage an *ex opere operato* understanding of auricular confession, he still thought that its practice had many worthwhile benefits. Confessing sins to a fellow man promoted humility and meekness in the penitent,[38] and the shame involved in admitting sin discouraged recidivism.[39] By focusing the penitent's thoughts on his offences and Christ's sacrifice, the confessor fostered regret for sin out of love for God.[40] 'It was not rare' that during confession God granted true contrition to a penitent who had before been 'coldly' repentant.[41] By his training, the confessor could identify for the penitent sins that he might have overlooked in his blindness or that he might have exaggerated because of his inexperience. If the penitent

---

[35] 'Ita tutius, arbitror, plenam delictorum remissionem a caritate et a Christi misericordia sperare, quam a diplomatibus humanis', *LB* v. 167E; *A lytle treatise*, sig. [N7]r; 'Huc confert et illud, si praecipuam salutis fiduciam magis in caritate Deique misericordia reponamus, quam in enumerandis criminibus, praesertim imminente morte', *LB* v. 169C–D; *A lytle treatise*, sig. [O7]r.

[36] 'Octavum [malum confitendi]. Sunt alii nimium confidentes, qui quum aut nihil, aut leviter cogitarint de mutanda vita, nec animo conceperint seriam detestationem vitae superioris: hoc sibi satis esse ducunt, si sacerdoti recensuerint quid egerint, et si ille pronunciet absolutionem', *LB* v. 155E.

[37] 'Nam quid sit attritio et an ex attritione per confessionem fiat contritio: et an confessio efficiat, ut in primo statim instanti remittatur peccatum, Scotistis disputandum relinquo', *LB* v. 152E; 'Proinde qui ex consideratione vitae turpiter actae, et ex metu Gehennae concipit aliquam detestationem criminum suorum, non statim accurrat ad sacerdotem, sed perseveret in lacrymis, ac precibus quaerat, petat, pulset, donec senserit aliud timoris genus cum voto certo mutandae vitae, cumque amore bene sperante conjunctum', *LB* v. 157D.

[38] *LB* v. 147C–150A.

[39] *LB* v. 152C.

[40] *LB* v. 151F–152B.

[41] 'Nec id raro accidit, ut qui frigide poenitens accedit ad sacerdotem, inter confitendum accipiat legitimum criminum odium', *LB* v. 170C.

were unaware of some sins, the priest would teach him the proper remedy so he could avoid them in the future. If the penitent were too scrupulous, the confessor would reassure him of the certain hope in God's mercy and promises.[42] As for those who had a pernicious security or boasted in their sins, the priest was able to induce a salutary shame and grief.[43] Sacramental penance also reconciled the sinner to the church, and his submission to the accepted policy prevented any rupture of the established peace.[44] For these very practical reasons, Erasmus argued that auricular confession was expedient, although not necessary for salvation, a beneficial custom that was to be retained in the church.

In the end, Erasmus's concern to encourage inner godliness rather than bare observance of religious ceremonies led him to attempt to hold together two competing truths. Technically, the charity and mercy necessary for forgiveness were solely in the unconstrained gift of God. Practically, this gift came about after the penitent had shown himself worthy by his industry. Emphasizing the former, Jean-Pierre Massaut argues that 'one could never demand pardon, neither *de congruo*, nor *ex pacto Dei*, nor *de potentia ordinata*—it was only given because of the mercy of God.'[45] Emphasizing the latter, John Payne argues that 'although he does not use the term here, Erasmus thus seems to insist on a *meritum de congruo* in order to receive the gift of contrition, which is the indispensable prerequisite for forgiveness'.[46] As recent studies on the Augustinian revival of the sixteenth century have shown, Erasmus seems to have reconciled

---

[42] *LB* v. 150A–D.

[43] *LB* v. 150D–151A.

[44] 'Contemtus publicae ac jam olim receptae consuetudinis, et adversus ecclesiasticam traditionem contumacia offendit Deum, ac laedit Christianae reipublicae tranquillitatem', *LB* v. 152F–153A.

[45] 'Le pardon ne peut jamais être exigé . . . ni *de congruo*, ni *ex pacto Dei*, ni *de potentia ordinata*—il est seulement donné *ex misericordia Dei*', Massaut, 'Pénitence', 247. Although recognizing that contrition is itself a gift, Massaut goes as far as to deny any causality between its presence in the penitent and God's act of pardoning: 'La contrition cependant ne mérite pas et elle ne produit pas le pardon, la rémission des péchés. Elle l'accompagne plutôt. C'est Dieu et lui seul qui pardonne. Son pardon est promis au pécheur contrit, mais il est toujours gratuit', ibid., 247.

[46] Payne, *Erasmus*, 195.

these positions somewhat by leaning towards an Augustinian-influenced soteriology,[47] which was not unlike Fisher's
extra-sacramental way of forgiveness. Against the scholastic
teaching *ex naturalibus*, Erasmus suggested as 'probable
enough' that a special supernatural assistance had to initiate
and sustain the process which led to justification.[48] Against
Luther, he argued that human effort exhibited in good
works played an integral role in the forgiveness of sin.[49] It
appears that at some time Cranmer endorsed Erasmus's dual
emphasis on divine grace and human effort in the forgiveness of sin. In *De libero arbitrio* Erasmus wrote:

If we are entangled in sins, let us strive with all our might and
have recourse to the remedy of penance that by all means we may
entreat the mercy of the Lord without which no human will or
endeavour is effective; and what is evil in us, let us impute to
ourselves, and what is good, let us ascribe wholly to divine
benevolence, to which we owe our very being . . . This, I say,
was in my judgement sufficient for Christian godliness.[50]

Beside this passage in his 1524 copy Cranmer wrote, 'The
standard for the Christian mind on free will'.[51]

[47] Kaufman, *Augustinian Piety*, 133–41; Oberman, *Masters of the Reformation*,
107–9; cf. *Luther and Erasmus: Free Will and Salvation*, ed. Gordon Rupp and
Philip S. Watson (Philadelphia, Pa.: Westminster, 1969), 15.

[48] 'Ergo qui longissime fugiunt a Pelagio, plurimum tribuunt gratiae, libero
arbitrio pene nihil, nec tamen in totum tollunt: negant hominem posse velle bonum
sine gratia peculiari, negant posse incipere, negant posse progredi, negant posse
perficere sine principali perpetuoque gratiae divinae praesidio. Horum sententia
satis videtur probabilis, quod relinquat homini studium et conatus, et tamen non
relinquit, quod suis adscribat viribus', *LB* ix. 1224B–C; Rupp and Watson, *Luther
and Erasmus*, 53; cf. 'Hoc mihi videtur praestare illorum sententia, qui tractum,
quo primum exstimulatur animus, totum tribuunt gratiae: tantum in cursu
tribuunt nonnihil hominis voluntati, quae se non subduxerit gratiae Dei', *LB* ix.
1244B; Rupp and Watson, *Luther and Erasmus*, 90.

[49] 'Non tamen consequitur ex hoc, quod ante gratiam gratum facientem non
possit homo, adjutus auxilio Dei, per opera moraliter bona, sese praeparare favori
divino, quemadmodum legimus de Cornelio Centurione nondum baptizato, ac
nondum afflato Spiritu Sancto: Precationes et eleemosynae tuae adscenderunt in
memoriam apud Deum', *LB* ix. 1235F; Rupp and Watson, *Luther and Erasmus*, 75.

[50] 'Si peccatis involuti, ut totis viribus enitamur, adeamus remedium poenitentiae, ac Domini misericordiam modis omnibus ambiamus, sine qua nec voluntas
humana est efficax, nec conatus: et si quid mali est, nobis imputemus: si quid boni,
totum adscribamus divinae benignitati, cui debemus et hoc ipsum quod sumus . . .
Haec, inquam, tenere, meo judicio, satis erat ad Christianam pietatem', *LB* ix. 1216E;
based on the English translation in Rupp and Watson, *Luther and Erasmus*, 39.

[51] 'Formula c[hri]stianae ment[is] de libero arbitrio', Cranmer's *De libero*

CRANMER AND THE PAPACY

Fisher taught a twofold means of pardon: extra-sacramentally through the right use of prevenient grace; and through the sacrament of penance, *ex opere operato*, with the latter being the more certain means to forgiveness. Erasmus, however, taught only one sure means of forgiveness, through the cultivation of love and *fiducia* in the penitent's heart, and all penitential activities, including receiving the sacrament, were beneficial only if they furthered this inner piety. Erasmus's *ex opere operantis* view of sacramental penance undoubtedly became even more attractive to Cranmer as he became disillusioned with papal authority. As if taking literally Innocent III's imagery of the pope exercising discipline over every Christian in the Western church through an army of confessors,[52] Cranmer came to see the traditional priestly power of the keys as but an extension of the papacy's pretended authority. In 1550, he characterized the medieval practice of sacramental penance as captivity to the rapacious power of the Roman Antichrist:

But the Romish antichrist . . . hath [taught] . . . that christian people cannot apply to themselves the benefits of Christ's passion, but that the same is in the distribution of the bishop of Rome; or else that by Christ we have no full remission, but be delivered only from sin, and yet remaineth temporal pain in purgatory due for the same, to be remitted after this life by the Romish antichrist and his ministers . . . For what is this else, but to be against Christ . . . that the full perfection [of the remission of sins] must be had at the hands of antichrist of Rome and his ministers?[53]

However, Diarmaid MacCulloch has recently shown that there is little evidence for Cranmer having such strongly anti-papal leanings during the mid-1520s.[54] He appears to

arbitrio, sig. A4r. Hence, it is unlikely that *De libero arbitrio* was the probable turning-point after which Cranmer moved away from Erasmus towards Luther; cf. Hall, in Ayris and Selwyn, *Churchman and Scholar*, 16–17.

[52] *Patrologiae cursus completus, Series Latina*, ed. J. P. Migne (Paris: 1878–90) [henceforth *PL*], ccxvii. 677–9.   [53] Cox I, 5.

[54] MacCulloch, 'Cranmer and Gardiner', 7–13.

have agreed with Erasmus that it was wrong to bring the authority of the current church into disrepute. In *De libero arbitrio* Erasmus said that he would refrain from making public any shortcomings in the official positions of the church which his scholarship might uncover. Cranmer echoed his words in a marginal comment: 'Some things are of this kind so that even if they were true and able to be known, it would not be useful at that time to prostitute them before common ears. Thus, it is not useful to speak the truth to just anyone in every place and time.'[55] Judging by his black-ink *marginalia* in his copy of Fisher's *Confutatio*,[56] Cranmer seems to have been a conciliarist at the time. He was prepared to disparage Luther's vitriolic outbursts against the pope: 'Luther rails against the pope', 'He impudently assails the pope', 'Luther mocks', and 'He raves against the pope.' But he also objected to Fisher's depiction of the papacy as able to act apart from a council. When Fisher argued that Christ would not have left his church without a leader to whom Christians could turn during times of controversy, Cranmer wrote: 'By this response, [Fisher] seems to make the pope able on his own to establish whatever he chooses, even without a council.' Similarly, when Fisher argued against Luther's request for a council, Cranmer wrote: 'It is astounding what Fisher means here.'[57] Cranmer during his years as a fellow of Jesus College was respectful of designated religious authority, but he expected that authority to be shared.

Nevertheless, after that fateful meeting at Waltham

---

[55] For Erasmus's comments, see *LB* ix. 1217C–E; 'Quaedam eius [gene]ris sunt, ut [etiam] si vera essent et [sciri] possent non [expe]diret tum ea [prosti]tuere promiscui[s] auribus[.] S[ic] non expedit [apud] quoslibet, q[uovis] loco et tempor[e] verum dicere', Cranmer's *De libero arbitrio*, sig. A5r.

[56] Cranmer's *Confutatio* (BL C. 81.f. 2) has two sets of *marginalia*, those written in red ink from fol. 130v to halfway on fol. 132v, and those written in black ink from fols. 132v to 160r. On folio 132v one black-ink annotation (non Petrum sed Christum intelligit Cyprianus) has been crossed out in red, as if Cranmer had a second later look at Fisher. Such is the view of MacCulloch, 'Cranmer and Gardiner', 10.

[57] 'Convicatur lutherus in pontificem', Cranmer's *Confutatio*, fol. 155v; 'Petulanter incessit pontificem', ibid., fol. 156v; 'Cavillatur lutherus', ibid., fol. 156v; 'Debacchatur in pontificem', ibid., fol. 157r; 'hac responsione [ratione?] videtur facere solum papam statuere posse quicquid libuerit, etiam sine consilio', ibid., fol. 158v; 'mirum quid hic sibi velit roffensis', ibid., fol. 158r.

Abbey on 2 August 1529, Cranmer was soon to be involved in Henry's 'privy matter' as one of the king's scholars who gathered learned opinions against the papacy in support of the royal position.[58] That his growing antipathy towards papal authority was an integral factor in his eventual Protestant conversion is only logical and would seem to be the import of a portion of the more obscure iconography of Flicke's portrait. One curious feature of the painting has always been the grotesque carvings beside the window-jamb—a nude female figure underneath a horn-headed mask. Recently, however, Anthony Wells-Cole has convincingly shown that these features most likely derive from two contemporary prints by Jean Mignon of the Fontainebleau School, the mask coming from the frame of Mignon's *Metamorphosis of Actaeon*, the female figure from the frame of his *The Creation of Eve*.[59] Although the inclusion of these elements no doubt demonstrated the painter's knowledge of the current 'most fashionable' French artistic productions,[60] MacCulloch is surely correct that in a painting as programmatic as this, these curious elements were also meant to convey information about the sitter.[61]

In the case of the mask, the intent may well have been the proper extent of royal power. The *Metamorphosis* depicts Actaeon being turned into a stag as he is spying on the bathing Artemis, a transformation which will subsequently result in him being torn apart by his own hounds as punishment. Although such a myth would seem to be less than promising for a referent in Cranmer's life, the print has a most interesting legend: 'DOMINVM COGNOSCITE

[58] Following the lead of Stephen Ryle, MacCulloch establishes that when Foxe and Gardiner discussed the king's 'divorce' with Cranmer, he was, in fact, by 1527 a veteran of a previous diplomatic mission; *Cranmer*, 33–6, 45–6.

[59] Anthony Wells-Cole, *Art and Decoration in Elizabethan and Jacobean England: The Influence of Continental Prints, 1558–1625* (New Haven: Yale University Press, 1997), 34–7; cf. Henri Zerner, *The School of Fontainebleau: Etchings and Engravings* (London: Thames and Hudson, 1969), 26–30, as well as plates J.M. 56 and J.M. 60.

[60] Catharine MacLeod, 'Archbishop Thomas Cranmer', in *Dynasties: Painting in Tudor and Jacobean England, 1530 –1630*, ed. Karen Hearn (London: Tate Publishing, 1995), 48–9, at 49.

[61] '[T]his carving may be simply there to convey an air of modish magnificence appropriate to a member of Henry VIII's Privy Council: but there is surely more to it than that', MacCulloch, *Cranmer*, 341.

VESTRVM' ('Know your lord'). This precept was at the very heart of Cranmer's Protestant doctrine of the Godly Prince and the reason for his secret repudiation of papal authority prior to his consecration as archbishop. Consequently, the mask would seem a subtle allusion to the importance Cranmer's Erastian views on church government had for his Protestant convictions.[62]

The first substantive evidence that Cranmer had come to associate sacerdotal authority in sacramental penance with the rapacious tentacles of papal power occurs in a manuscript which resulted from the scholars' efforts on Henry's behalf, the 'Collectanea satis copiosa'.[63] As a part of a general pattern to diminish clerical authority, the compilers noted that, according to a quotation from Jerome on Matthew 16: 19, a sinner was not loosed or bound by the sentence of a parish priest, nor even by the pope's, but only by his own guilt or innocence.[64] The notion that neither the pope nor a parish priest had the power to forgive sins intrigued Henry. He had previously been so advised when preparing the *Assertio septem sacramentorum* as to advance the opposite interpretation of the same verse. Accordingly, Henry had argued that by common agreement Matthew 16: 19 meant that a priest had the power to absolve men from mortal sins and take away eternal punishment; consequently, it would be absurd to deny that 'prince of all priests' had no jurisdiction in matters of temporal punishment.[65] Now, the compilers of the 'Collectanea' suggested

---

[62] Whether the artist expected viewers to perceive such a message without explanation is impossible to say without further research. I am indebted to Catharine MacLeod, Sixteenth-Century Curator at the National Portrait Gallery, London, for acquainting me with the work of Anthony Wells-Cole.

[63] For Cranmer's involvement, see Alistair Fox and John Guy, *Reassessing the Henrician Age: Humanism, Politics and Reform, 1500–1550* (Oxford: Basil Blackwell, 1986), 153–7; For the 'Collectanea' itself, see Graham Nicholson, 'The Act of Appeals and the English Reformation', in *Law and Government under the Tudors: Essays presented to Sir Geoffrey Elton*, ed. C. Cross, D. Loades, and J. J. Scarisbrick (Cambridge: Cambridge University Press, 1988), 19–30.

[64] 'Hieronimis ergo existemat reum sacerdotis sententia nec solvi nec alligari, sed sola sua ipsius vel innocentia vel culpa. Item non maiorem esse hac in re pontificis authoritatem quam cuiuscunque sacerdotis', 'Collectanea satis copiosa', BL Cotton MS Cleop. E.VI., fol. 69v.

[65] 'Quibus verbis (i.e., Mt. 16: 19 et Jo. 20: 23), si satis constat sacerdotem quemlibet, habere potestatem a mortalibus absolvendi criminibus: et aeternitatem

that auricular confession was efficacious *ex opere operantis*, not *ex opere operato*. Beside their texts, Henry wrote: 'Note and to be carefully investigated.'[66] Cranmer, no doubt, had already done so and knew that Erasmus was in agreement.

THE LURE OF LUTHERANISM

Despite Erasmus's significant modifications of scholastic theology, two key issues separated him from Luther, the nature of justification and its preparation. For Erasmus, co-operation with grace was a pre-condition for salvation, for Luther such co-operation was the result of salvation. For Erasmus, justification was to be made righteous, for Luther to be considered righteous. Thus, as in Fisher's extra-sacramental way, Erasmus taught that a Christian could become inherently 'good' by prevenient grace enabling him to call forth sanctifying grace through performing good works. For Luther, because of saving faith God reckoned a person 'good', and as a result his subsequent works were considered good as well.[67]

These disagreements over justification were only the logical consequences of an even more fundamental divergence in anthropology caused by Luther's radical reassessment of concupiscence. In keeping with the broad scholastic consensus, Erasmus thought that the human soul naturally sought to do good but, burdened by the legacy of original sin, had to fight against disordered passions which sought to rebel against reason. Luther, however, became convinced by

poenae tollendi: cui non videatur absurdum, sacerdotum omnium principem, nihil habere iuris in poenam temporariam?', Henry VIII, *Assertio septem sacramentorum*, sig. [B2]v. The king assembled the text of the *Assertio*, but was wholly dependent on the *sententiae* and arguments provided for him by experts. Moreover, Thomas More had a hand in revising the final draft. See J. J. Scarisbrick, *Henry VIII* (London: Methuen, 1968), 112–13. The scholars responsible for assisting the king were those eminent theologians from Oxford and Cambridge whom Wolsey convened in London, May 1521. See Rex, 'English Campaign against Luther', 88–9.

[66] 'Nota et perquiri', BL Cotton MS Cleop. E.vi. fol. 69r.

[67] Cf. Rupp and Watson, *Luther and Erasmus*, 19–20. For a good summary of the salient points of Luther's soteriology, see Carl R. Trueman, *Luther's Legacy: Salvation and English Reformers 1525–1556* (Oxford: Clarendon Press, 1994), 54–72.

reading Paul's Epistles that Adam and Eve's disobedience had caused a far greater corruption of human beings, namely, that every aspect of human nature had become thoroughly twisted by sin, including reason and the will.[68] Entirely enslaved to self-centredness, all of human nature was 'flesh' in the Pauline sense. Nothing good remained, nothing which still sought reunion with God.[69] Consequently, concupiscence was 'much more than sensuality lusting against reason'; rather it was 'the opposition of the entire man to God'.[70] This enslaving power shackled the reasoning will into a sinful attitude of rebellion against God and his commandments. To Luther all human aspirations arising from this addiction to self-love were obviously intrinsically sinful to God.

Philip Melanchthon systematically explained the anthropological implications of Luther's view of concupiscence in his first edition of the *Loci communes theologici* (1521), a manual of theology which Luther described as 'an unanswerable little book which in my judgment deserves not only to be immortalized but even canonized'.[71] Conflating the scholastic lower sensitive soul with the higher rational soul, Melanchthon divided human nature into only two

---

[68] 'All, [Paul] says [in Romans 3: 9], all Jews and Greeks are under sin . . . When he says "all" he excepts none, and declares that they are under sin, or in other words, are slaves of sin, he leaves nothing of good in them . . . Nor can you get away from this saying that although they are under sin, yet what is best in them, such as their reason and will, has a bias toward the good. For if a good tendency remains, it is false when he says that they are under sin . . . But the wrath that is revealed from heaven against them is going to damn their whole being, unless they are justified through the Spirit; and that would not be the case if they were not with their whole being under sin', Rupp and Watson, *Luther and Erasmus*, 297–8.

[69] Ibid., 299. 'How, then can they strive after the good, when they are totally ignorant of God and neither seek after God nor pay any regard to him? How can they have a power worth anything as a means to the good when they have all turned aside from the good and are altogether worthless? . . . What can the will choose that is good when it is itself evil and worthless? Or rather, what choice has the will when reason dictates to it only the darkness of its own blind ignorance? With reason in error, then, and the will misdirected, what can man do or attempt that is good?', ibid., 299–300.

[70] Althaus, *Theology of Luther*, 155.

[71] Rupp and Watson, *Luther and Erasmus*, 102. I am grateful to Dr Ronald N. Frost for drawing my attention to Melanchthon's teaching on the affections in the *Loci communes* of 1521; see his Ph.D. thesis, 'Richard Sibbes: Theology of Grace and the Division of English Reformed Theology' (King's College, London, 1997).

parts: a cognitive faculty and a faculty subjected to the affections (*affectus*), that is, 'love, hate, hope, fear, and the like'. By the first, people were able to discern and to deduce from information received through the senses. By the second, people either followed or fled the things they had come to know.[72] Unlike the scholastic model where the will acting in accordance with right reason in the rational soul was supposed to constrain the passions in the lower sensitive soul, Melanchthon argued that the affections were inextricably joined to the will in the same faculty. As a result, these inner attitudes of the human heart determined the will's direction which then had power over the other faculty of reasoning as well.[73]

Since neither knowledge as in Thomist Intellectualism, nor the will as in Scotist Voluntarism, but the passions of the heart ultimately determined human conduct, an affection could only be 'overcome by a more vehement affection'. Paris had been able to put away his love for Oenone only because he became overcome by a more vehement affection for Helen of Troy.[74] Yet because of original sin's thoroughly corrupting legacy, humankind had one overarching affection that twisted every other affection into its service—the affection of self-love.[75] With reason and will both captive to the concupiscence of the flesh, only the intervention of an outside force, the Holy Spirit, could give humanity a new set of godly affections.[76] The Spirit working through God's

---

[72] Philip Melanchthon, *Loci communes theologici* (1521), in Pauck, *Melanchthon and Bucer*, 23–4.

[73] 'For the will (*voluntas*) in man corresponds to the place of a despot in a republic. Just as the senate is subject to the despot, so is knowledge to the will (*voluntas*), with the consequence that although knowledge gives good warning, yet the will (*voluntas*) casts knowledge out and is borne along by its own affection . . . [F]or by experience and habit we find that will (*voluntas*) cannot in itself control love, hate, or similar affections . . . For what is will (*voluntas*) if it is not the fount of the affections? And why do we not use the word "heart" instead of "will"? For the Scriptures call the most powerful part of man the "heart," especially that part in which the affections arise. But the Schools are in error when they image that the will (*voluntas*) by its very nature opposes the affections, or that it is able to lay an affection aside whenever the intellect so advises or warns', Pauck, *Melanchthon and Bucer*, 23–4, 27.

[74] Ibid., 27–9.

[75] Ibid., 31–2.

[76] Melanchthon insisted that the Spirit was not to be identified with an aspect of innate human nature like reason: 'For by the word "flesh" the Scripture means not

Word assured believers of his promised salvation, engendering in them a faith which justified them before God and transformed their conduct. For confidence in God's gracious goodwill towards them reoriented the affections of the justified, calming their turbulent hearts and inflaming in them a grateful love in return. This new Spirit-inspired love for God empowered believers to serve God 'gladly and willingly'.[77] These new godly affections would continually have to fight to restrain the ever-present concupiscence of the flesh. Nevertheless, because of the renewing work of the Holy Spirit believers now had the necessary desire and ability to do so.[78]

Thus, in the light of the Lutheran doctrine of the affections, 'goodness' in the eyes of God was a straightforward issue of the heart, whether desires arose from the flesh's love of self and sin or from the Spirit's love of God and godliness. How could there be good works before justification, for a bad tree only produced bad fruit?[79] How could there be intrinsic righteousness in justification, since concupiscence remained at work—twisting, turning, and assaulting Christians until their release from their physical body through death?[80] How could there be truly good works after justification, since the flesh would always succeed in tainting even the best intentions of believers?[81] For Luther and his fellow Protestants, the justified in this life would always be *simul justus et peccator* (both a sinner and a saint).[82] When Cranmer came

---

just the body as a part of man, but it means the whole man, soul as well as body. And whenever flesh is compared with Spirit, it signifies the best and most excellent powers of human nature apart from the Holy Spirit. "Spirit" means the Holy Spirit himself and his activity and his workings in us', ibid., 37. Cf. ibid., 131–2.

[77] Ibid., 54, 92, 109.

[78] Ibid., 123, 130.

[79] Rupp and Watson, *Luther and Erasmus*, 317. Cf. 'Let it be granted that in Socrates there was a certain constancy, that Xenocrates was chaste, and Zeno temperate. Nevertheless, because these characteristics were in impure minds, and further, because these simulated virtues arose from love of self and love of praise, they ought not to be considered real virtues but vices', Pauck, *Melanchthon and Bucer*, 34.

[80] Pauck, *Melanchthon and Bucer*, 33; cf. Martin Luther, *Defense and Explanation of All the Articles*, in *Luther's Works*, vol. xxxii, ed. George W. Forell (Philadelphia, Pa.: Muhlenberg Press, 1958), 20–2.

[81] Pauck, *Melanchthon and Bucer*, 106.

[82] See Althaus, *Theology of Luther*, 240–5.

to the conclusion that any human goodness followed rather than preceded justification, he crossed the Rubicon, with Rome behind and Germany ahead.

Stephen Gardiner considered the Lutherans extremists for their denial of good works before justification.[83] Dr Cranmer, the careful humanist scholar of Jesus College, gave no indication prior to his enthronement as archbishop that he disagreed with Gardiner, the same fellow Cambridge don who first brought Cranmer's views on the divorce to the king's attention.[84] How then did Cranmer as Primate of All England come to side with the Lutherans rather than the Erasmian humanists? Once again, Flicke's portrait offers a clue. A second book, Augustine's *De fide et operibus*, lies immediately behind the first and directly in front of Cranmer. This work is a significant indication of Cranmer's theological evolution.[85] A product of Augustine's later affective theology, *De fide et operibus* outlined his mature understanding of the relationship between faith and works, as 'Cranmer's Great Commonplaces' would later duly note.[86] On the one hand, he clearly stated that Paul's teaching on justification by faith meant that good works did not precede justification, but followed it, because only those with the Holy Spirit could perform works out of a love for righteousness.[87] On the other hand, once Christ dwelt in

---

[83] 'And in this dreame was Barnes, that folowynge the newe scoole of extremites, he denied all degrees of grace, as you do, and said: A man could do nothyng good or acceptable before the grace of iustification', Gardiner, *Declaration of true articles*, fol. 20r; cf. Gardiner's later comment on this same issue: 'your fonde stoicall scoole of extremities, which admitteth no meane', ibid., fol. 85v.

[84] MacCulloch has usefully traced the contacts Cranmer had with Simon Grynaeus, a Swiss Protestant, over matters pertaining to the divorce in 1531–2. Yet, he concluded that 'Cranmer and Gardiner were apparently both conservative-minded Cambridge humanists' and that the overall picture of Cranmer on the eve of his appointment as archbishop was 'of a conservative don who was becoming cautiously interested in some varieties of Continental reform, but who was not yet definitely associated with it', *Cranmer*, 60–9.

[85] For a contrary opinion, see MacCulloch, *Cranmer*, 341–2.

[86] For the role of *De fide et operibus* in the development of the material on justification in 'Cranmer's Great Commonplaces', see the Appendix.

[87] 'Quicquid enim homo veluti recte fecerit, nisi ad pietatem quae ad deum est referatur, rectum dici non oportet', Augustine, *De fide et operibus*, ca. 7, CGC II, 98v; 'Ut sciat se quisque per fidem posse iustificari etiamsi legis opera non praecesserunt. Sequuntur enim iustificatum non praecedunt iustificandum', Augustine, ibid., ca. 14, *marginalium*: 'opera bona sequuntur iustificationem, non

the believer's heart by faith, this living faith necessarily produced good works performed out of love for God.[88] In short, a good life was inseparable from faith, because a life could not be good without faith, and true faith could not but bear the fruit of a good life.[89] Cranmer would later incorporate both tenets in his description of justifying faith as a 'lively faith'.[90] If Erasmus awoke Cranmer to the authority of the Scriptures over the tenets of scholastic theology, the Flicke portrait suggests that his reading of Augustine, rather than Erasmus, led him to what he considered to be a true appreciation of the Pauline doctrine of justification by faith.[91] As McGrath has noted, the Reformation was certainly a debate over the authority of Scripture but equally a debate over the interpretation of Augustine; for the Lutherans believed that 'the *vera theologia* [true theology] was essentially Scripture as interpreted in the anti-Pelagian writings of Augustine'.[92] When did Cranmer decide to interpret Paul through Augustine, as understood by the Protestants, rather than Erasmus? The decisive moment cannot be ascertained with absolute certainty, but Cranmer's time at Nuremberg in 1532 appears the most likely occasion.[93]

Cranmer would have been confronted by Protestant Augustinianism during his stay in Nuremberg. When Stephen Gardiner passed through the city as ambassador

praecedunt', CGC II, 98v–99r; 'Per diffusa charitate in cordibus nostris [a spiritu sancto] lex non timore poenae, sed iustitiae amore complet', Augustine, ibid., ca. 21, CGC II, 99v.

[88] 'Per fidem quippe habitat Christus in cordibus nostris', Augustine, *De fide et operibus*, ca. 16, CGC II, 99r; 'Sicut etiam ipse Paulus non quamlibet fidem qua in deum creditur, sed eam salubrem, planeque evanglicam definivit [?], cuius opera ex dilectione procedunt, et fides, inquit, quae per dilectionem operatur', Augustine, ibid., ca. 14, CGC II, 99r; 'Recte dici posset ad solam fidem pertinere dei mandata, si non mortua, sed viva illa intelligatur fides quae per dilectionem operatur', Augustine, ibid., ca. 22, CGC II, 99v.

[89] 'Inseparabilis est quippe bona vita a fide', Augustine, *De fide et operibus*, ca. 23, CGC II, 99v; 'In homine ipso nisi praecedat fides, vita bona sequi non poterit', Augustine, ibid., ca. 7, CGC II, 98v; 'Fides itaque Christi, fides gratiae Christianae, id est, ea fides quae per dilectionem operatur', Augustine, ibid., ca. 16, CGC II, 99r.

[90] See Chapter 6.

[91] For further evidence that the mature Cranmer claimed to follow Scripture as interpreted by Augustine, see Chapter 5.

[92] McGrath, *Intellectual Origins*, 186.

[93] On Cranmer in Nuremberg, see MacCulloch, 'Cranmer and Gardiner', 20–1.

to the Imperial court in 1541, Osiander argued with him for nearly three hours over justification by faith.[94] While they both could agree that God was the one who justified and that the righteousness involved was Christ's, they disagreed on how this gift was received, Osiander arguing that faith was the hand that grasped justification, Gardiner insisting that charity as a second hand was needed as well.[95] Osiander defended his position by insisting on a Protestant understanding of the order of justification (*ordo iustificationis*). By faith sinners became sons of God; then because they were sons, they were filled with the Holy Spirit; and only finally was love then kindled in their hearts by the Spirit's presence. Osiander considered it impious to say that they were not yet justified who had become sons of God and received the Holy Spirit, and he thought it absurd to deny that a tree was good before it bore good fruit.[96]

Osiander's account of his conversation with Gardiner outlines the difference between the Erasmian humanism that Cranmer espoused in the 1520s and the Protestant Augustinianism that he would come to adopt in the 1530s. Whereas, like Erasmus, Gardiner wanted to make the penitent's efforts in faith and love to be integral to the process of justification,[97] like Augustine, Osiander wanted good works to be the result of having been justified, not its

---

[94] Letter of Osiander to Justus Jonas, *Philippi Melanchthonis opera, quae supersunt omnia, Corpus Reformatorum* [henceforth *CR*], ed. C. G. Bretschneider and H. E. Bindseil, i–xxviii (Brunswick, 1834–60), iv. 140–2; pertinent sections translated into English in *LP* xvi. 667.

[95] 'Cum concederemus Deum iustificare, et Christum esse iustitiam, et fide eatenus nos iustificari, quatenus fides tanquam manus donum Dei per evangelium oblatum apprehenderet, voluit charitatem, tanquam alteram manum in apprehendo, adiungere', *CR* iv. 140–1.

[96] 'Nos prius fide fieri filios Dei deinde quia filii, effundi in nos spiritum sanctum, ac tandem diffuso spiritu sancto accendi caritatem, ut iam impium esset dicere nondum iustificatos, quos esse filios Dei et accipere spiritum sanctum confiteri oporteret, et ineptum negare arborem bonam antequam bonum fructum attulisset', *CR* iv. 141.

[97] 'As soone as man beleueth, God procedethe to the fulfillyuge [*sic*] of his promise, for his parte, and giueth vs a newe spirite, and a newe hart, and so iustifieth vs, if we receiue it, and assente by oure free choyce vnto it, and worke with it, whiche is the effectuall receiuinge, and the worthynes on our part, whereby we be iustified . . . it is necessarie, we be put in remembraunce, that the promises of god, require the condition of worthines on our befalfe, wherein is required oure endeuour', Gardiner, *Declaration of true articles*, fols. 68r–9r; cf. ibid., fol. 65.

prerequisite. Unlike Augustine, however, but in common with his fellow Lutherans, Osiander also distinguished between reconciliation with God and the interior renovation of the penitent.[98] Although Augustine would not have recognized this distinction,[99] and neither did Gardiner,[100] the Lutherans differentiated between extrinsic justification and intrinsic renovation to make clear without compromise that any human goodness was the result of God's saving action and not its basis.[101] Not only did all good works follow justification, but all human goodness in the eyes of God did as well. A sinner was considered sufficiently 'good' to be a son of God only because God first imputed Christ's goodness to him, not because God made him sufficiently 'good' in his own right beforehand. Thus, by faith in Christ's redeeming work a sinner was justified, and because he was in right-standing with God he was then granted the gift of the Holy Spirit in his heart which brought forth good works in his life. Cranmer would have had similar discussions with Osiander during his stay; for the arguments presented to Gardiner parallel Osiander's description of salvation in his *Catechism*, which was in preparation during the period of Cranmer's visits, and was subsequently translated into English and published under Cranmer's name in 1548.[102]

[98] Osiander presented his understanding of the *ordo iustificationis* logically, not temporally, for Protestants held that justification and regeneration of the will were inseparable in time but distinct in function; McGrath, *Iustitia Dei*, 188–90.

[99] For Augustine's doctrine of justification in the light of sixteenth-century debate, see McGrath, *Iustitia Dei*, 28–33, and G. R. Evans, 'Augustine on Justification', in *Congresso Internazionale su S. Agostino nel XVI Centenario della Conversione*, Studia Ephemeridis 'Augustinianum', 26 (Rome: Institutum Patristicum 'Augustinianum', 1987), 275–84.

[100] '[W]e be called by participacion, by the names attributed to god, and for so muche as we do participate, haue also the thing in dede. And therefore as god is goodnes it selfe, we by participation from him, be good,' Gardiner, *Declaration of true articles*, fol. 13r.

[101] McGrath, *Iustitia Dei*, 188–90.

[102] Cf. the following passage in Justus Jonas's Latin translation of Osiander's *Catechism*: 'Per fidem enim efficimur filii Dei, et ipse donat nobis spiritum sanctum, ille illuminat et accendit corda nostra', *A Short Instruction into Christian Religion, being a Catechism set forth by Archbishop Cranmer in 1548 together with the same in Latin, translated from the German by Justus Jonas in 1539*, ed. Edward Burton (Oxford: Oxford University Press, 1829), 82. On Cranmer's possible familiarity with the *Catechism* at the time of its preparation, see Selwyn, *Catechism*, 'Introduction', 30.

If Osiander was able to persuade Cranmer that justification by faith was closer to Augustine's understanding of Pauline soteriology than either Fisher or Erasmus, the strict civil discipline of Nuremberg would have provided Cranmer with ample first-hand evidence to dispel any lingering concerns which he may have had about its effect on the moral life of a community. Even as an opponent of Luther in the 1520s, Cranmer was not convinced that justification by faith inevitably led to antinomianism. When Fisher accused solifidianism of being a licence to sin so that no one had to submit to any of the other laws of the church which had been handed down in the Gospels and apostolic writings, Cranmer wrote in the margin of his *Confutatio*: 'Luther does not seem to think so evilly.'[103] Cranmer's stay in Nuremberg could only have reinforced his perception that Lutheran soteriology did not necessarily lead to evil living. According to Sir Thomas Elyot, Cranmer's predecessor as ambassador and 'temporary companion',[104] Nuremberg was 'the most proper town and best-ordered public weal that ever I beheld'.[105] The city had a centuries-old tradition of a strong hereditary ruling council which regulated most aspects of daily life within its jurisdiction.[106] The open adoption of Lutheran theology in 1525 did not sweep away this totality of regulation which Henri Pirenne characterized as being 'as logical in its principles, as coherent in its part and as rich in its details, as the finest monuments of Gothic architecture, or as the great *Summae* of the scholastic philosophers'.[107]

That Osiander was more successful in persuading Cran-

[103] 'Non tam male videtur sentire lutherus', Cranmer's *Confutatio*, fol. 156v.

[104] MacCulloch, 'Cranmer and Gardiner', 20. For Elyot's ambassadorship, see Stanford E. Lehmberg, *Sir Thomas Elyot: Tudor Humanist* (Austin, Texas: University of Texas Press, 1960), 95–114.

[105] Elyot to the Duke of Norfolk, BL Cotton MS Vitellius B.xxi, fols. 58–9; cited as reprinted by Nicholas Pocock, *Records of the Reformation* (Oxford: Oxford University Press, 1870), ii. 228–31, at 229; cf. *LP* v. 869.

[106] For a full account of city life in Nuremberg, see Gerald Strauss, *Nuremberg in the Sixteenth Century* (New York, N.Y.: Wiley, 1966), esp. 106–15, 154–69; and Gerald Strauss, 'Protestant Dogma and City Government: The Case of Nuremberg', *Past and Present* 36 (1967), 38–58.

[107] As quoted by Strauss, *Nuremberg*, 107; Henri Pirenne, *Early Democracies in the Low Countries: Urban Society and Political Conflict in the Middle Ages and the Renaissance*, trans. J. V. Saunders (New York, N.Y.: Harper, 1963), 86.

mer than Gardiner seems to be a reasonable conclusion to draw from Cranmer's decision to marry the niece of Osiander's wife.[108] Although an earlier generation of historians has explained Cranmer's marriage as simply a rejection of an unscriptural canon law, Ridley is most likely correct in his analysis that this marriage was 'a gesture by which Cranmer secretly but unequivocally committed himself to Lutheranism'.[109] Firstly, it is highly unlikely that Osiander would have permitted Cranmer to marry into his extended family had not the Englishman's views been compatible with his own Protestant theology.[110] Secondly, for a priest in Henrician England to have sexual relations under any arrangement was to defy a deeply ingrained community expectation.[111] According to one recent study, celibacy was considered so 'absolutely necessary to the priesthood that an unchaste priest by definition was failing in the duties of his office'.[112] Despite Erasmus's apparent willingness to relax the ban on clerical marriage,[113] Thomas More, his influential English humanist friend, firmly disagreed. According to Erasmus, More drew back from the priesthood precisely because of his fear of failure to remain chaste.[114] For

[108] Although the evidence for Cranmer's marriage at this time is not as substantive as would be desirable, being based on two brief accusations at his trial in 1555, it is commonly accepted; MacCulloch, 'Cranmer and Gardiner', 21 n. 85.

[109] Mason, *Cranmer*, 24–5; Pollard, *Cranmer*, 50; Ridley, *Cranmer*, 47; MacCulloch, *Cranmer*, 69–72.

[110] Packer, in Duffield, *Work of Cranmer*, xv; Hall, in Ayris and Selwyn, *Churchman and Scholar*, 19.   [111] See Marshall, *Catholic Priesthood*, 142–73.

[112] Marshall further remarks that to the author of *Dives and Pauper* (a fifteenth-century work printed in 1534) 'unchastity in a priest was a form of sacrilege, a misuse of something consecrated to God', *Catholic Priesthood*, 159.

[113] 'Suerly me thynke, he shulde be nat the worste counsellour for the commune weale (consyderyng the fashyons and manners of men) whych wolde graunt also the prestes and relygyous persons lycence to mary, namely sythe ther is euery where so greate a multytude of prestes, of which (alas) how few lyue a chast lyfe? . . . And this (I trow) the officyals of byshops shulde haue procured long ago, but that greater gaynes aryse by the concubyns, then shuld by the wyues', Erasmus, *Encomium matrimonii* (1518), quoted from *A ryght frutefull Epystle . . . in laude and prayse of matrymony*, trans. Richard Taverner (London: Robert Redman, 1532), sig. C2. No doubt Erasmus's view that sexual desire *per se* was part of God's created order and not a result of the Fall contributed to his divergence from More and Fisher on clerical marriage. See Erasmus, *A ryght frutefull Epystle*, sig. [B8] and Payne, *Erasmus*, 281 n. 36–282.

[114] 'Maluit . . . maritus esse castus quam sacerdos impurus', Erasmus, *Epistolarum*, iv. 18.

although he acknowledged that 'wedlok and prestehed' were 'not repugnaunt but compatyble of theyr nature', More argued that since celibacy was more acceptable to God 'then the worke of wedlokke in matrymony', the church took none to be priests 'but suche as promyse and professe neuer to be maryed, but kepe perpetuall chastyte'.[115] Consequently, in his polemical writings, More repeatedly linked Protestant error with the unbridled licentiousness of clerical marriage, since both heresy and lust were mad passions which overthrew the obedience necessary for the stability of the social order.[116] In *The Confutation of Tyndale's Answer*, published during Cranmer's ambassadorship in Germany, More saved his most savage language for the 'flesshyely felyng fayth' of Martin Luther and the former nun Katherine von Bora which permitted them boldely to 'breke theyr vowes, and wedde theym selfe to gyther' so that they could 'fele' themselves to 'be two specyall electes predestynate by god byfore the worlde was wrought to go to gether in this world and brynge forth holy frute to serue the deuyll at hys dyner'.[117] Fisher was no less harsh. In a sermon delivered at the recantation of Robert Barnes in 1526,[118] Fisher argued that Luther's new promise to his wife could not supersede his previous religious vows:

For <u>that</u> promise | whiche he made before was to kepe his chastitie . . . that promyse was for the weale of his soule: this promyse is made for the carnall pleasure of his body . . . that promise was made solemly <u>and</u> with a great deliberation: this promyse was made in a corner | and of some shorte aduisement . . . That promyse was made accordyng to the rules of holy religion | whiche was deuised by the holy fathers | and inspired by the

---

[115] Thomas More, *The Confutation of Tyndale's Answer*, ed. Louis A. Schuster et al., *The Complete Works of St. Thomas More*, vol. viii in 3 parts (New Haven, Conn.: Yale University Press, 1973), iii. 307. However, before the Reformation controversy, More had suggested otherwise in 1516: 'Sacerdotibus . . . uxores sunt popularium selectissimae', *Utopia*, ed. Edward Surtz and J. H. Hexter, *The Complete Works of St. Thomas More*, vol. iv (New Haven, Conn.: Yale University Press, 1964), 228–9.

[116] See Richard C. Marius, 'Thomas More's View of the Church', in More, *Confutation of Tyndale's Answer*, iii. 1340–1. Cf. Alistair Fox, *Thomas More: History and Providence* (Oxford: Basil Blackwell, 1982), 140–4.

[117] More, *Confutation of Tyndale's Answer*, ii. 926. The work was originally published in 1532–3.

[118] Rex, *Fisher*, 32.

spirite of god: this promise is made agaynst all good rulis | and by the carnall misordre of the wretchednes of the flesshe. That promise was made accordyng to the counsailes of our sauiour Christ | saint Paule | and of the other apostles: this promise was made by the counsaile of Satanas | and of all the deuylles of hell. Finally. that promise was made vnto god . . . But here one wyll say: Sir | Luther sawe that it was impossible for hym to conteyne hym selfe. But I say agayne | that Luther shulde haue loked at that poynt | before that he made this promyse to god | and before he entred holy religion.[119]

Fisher's assessment of those priests who followed Luther's example was equally negative: 'The prestis of his sect | which shulde kepe theyr handes and hartes clene for to mynister the blessed sacrament | followe the luste and canalite of their flesshe.'[120] In the eyes of these two leading Henrician humanists, Cranmer's clerical marriage would have meant that he had endorsed the antinomianism typical of Protestant heresy. Thirdly, Cranmer's own annotations in his *Confutatio* show him opposed to the lawlessness of individuals forming private judgements in theological matters. When Fisher quoted Luther as saying that the pope or even a general council should not be a precedent for anyone, but rather everyone was to abound in his own understanding in things not necessary for salvation, Cranmer noted in the margin: 'He opens the window to heretics.' Fisher went on to quote a further such passage from Luther: 'For we have been called in freedom so that it is not necessary to believe to be true what another man thinks or says, being content to believe in those things which we have been taught in the Scriptures.' Cranmer again disapproved: 'He does the same here.'[121] It seems unlikely that a man as cautious as Cranmer would have felt free to adopt such a controversial course of action, unless he had in fact also first adopted as authoritative the theological consensus which approved of such behaviour—Protestantism.

The appearance of an integral connection between Cranmer's marriage and his adoption of the Protestant faith

---

[119] Fisher, *Sermon had at Paulis*, sigs. [G4]r–H1r.   [120] Ibid., sig. G2.
[121] 'Aperit fenestram haereticis', Cranmer's *Confutatio*, fol. 159v; 'Idem et hic agit', ibid.

would seem to be reinforced once again by the 1545 portrait. While the nude female figure might look like too obvious a reference to Cranmer's wife to be accurate,[122] an examination of Mignon's *The Creation of Eve* suggests such was indeed the case.[123] For the female figure certainly appears to have been based on the border design of this print. Here Eve is depicted as coming to life beside a sleeping Adam while several of God's other creatures are paired with their mates—a scene aptly conveying the sentiment of God's statement in Genesis 2: 18 that it was not good for man to be alone. In a painting designed to indicate the Protestant faith of this archbishop of Canterbury, referring to his marriage in this manner was, at the least, clever and sophisticated. In the light of Margaret Cranmer's enforced absence from her husband's side for a time after The Six Articles, it was also pointed and poignant.

Therefore, the painting indicates that Thomas Cranmer was a typical Protestant cleric in that he was married. But does it tell us more? Did Cranmer's marriage, like his view of royal supremacy, the importance of Paul's Epistles, and Augustine's teaching on works, actually contribute to his decision to convert from the broad Catholicism of Erasmian humanism to Protestant Augustinianism? Cranmer's previous willingness to risk his professional career as an academic for marriage may indicate both that he found celibacy a struggle and that he felt compelled to follow Paul's instruction for the only morally upright alternative—marriage.[124] Only after the painful end of his first marriage, losing both his wife and child in childbirth, did Cranmer undertake to become a priest with the requisite vow of sexual abstinence. That Cranmer concluded afterwards that he lacked the gift of continency perhaps is not an unjust inference from the defensive remark he made at his trial in 1555: 'it was better for him to have his own, than to do like other priests, holding and keeping other men's

---

[122] MacCulloch, *Cranmer*, 341.

[123] Wells-Cole, *Art and Decoration*, 34–7; Zerner, *School of Fontainbleau*, plate J.M. 56.

[124] Cranmer had to resign his fellowship at Jesus College in order to marry. For Cranmer's first marriage, see MacCulloch, *Cranmer*, 21–2. For Paul's view, see 1 Cor. 7: 8–9.

wives'.[125] If Cranmer did indeed find celibacy difficult in the years that followed his ordination, converting to Protestantism would have offered him the theological permission necessary for him as a cleric to apply Paul's remedy once again. As Gardiner wryly noted to the English Protestant George Joye, 'Ye offer priestes wyues to wytte and they can wynne them to you.'[126]

Yet Protestantism would have offered Cranmer more than just theological permission to end a struggle with celibacy. Equally important, the new faith would have provided him a coherent theological explanation for why he might have found continency a struggle in the first place.[127] The Lutheran teaching on the on-going power of concupiscence in the life of the baptized would have given Cranmer a Pauline context in which to understand why even as an ordained man he might have continued to lack contentment in celibacy.[128] The Lutheran doctrine of justification by faith would have enabled him to reject celibacy as a good work efficacious towards his salvation. Moreover, the Lutheran commitment to the priesthood of all believers would have removed the need for Cranmer to have maintained his priestly celibacy as a godly manner of living which was separate from and morally superior to the less spiritually demanding lives of the married laity.[129] In the light of these teachings Cranmer could have come to see any struggle with sexual frustration not as a sign of his feebleness in following God but rather as the inevitable failure that came from trying to adhere to a fundamentally flawed theology.

---

[125] Cox II, 219. Such a response, however, was typical of early Protestant apologetics which defended clerical marriage primarily as a remedy for sexual sin. See Marshall, *Catholic Priesthood*, 164–5.

[126] Gardiner, *Declaration of true articles*, fol. 82v. Steve Ozment has argued that many clerics became Protestant precisely for this reason; *The Reformation in the Cities* (New Haven, Conn.: Yale University Press, 1975), 61.

[127] For a discussion of the Protestant defence of clerical marriage, see Steve Ozment, 'Marriage and the Ministry in the Protestant Churches', *Concilium: Theology in the Age of Renewal* 8/8 (October, 1972), 39–55; John K. Yost, 'The Reformation Defense of Clerical Marriage in the Reigns of Henry VIII and Edward VI', *Church History* 50 (1981), 152–65.

[128] Ozment, 'Marriage and Ministry', 40–6.

[129] Althaus, *Theology of Luther*, 313–18.

Nevertheless, to suppose that relief from celibacy in itself was the primary factor in Cranmer's conversion is in some measure to adopt the partisan cynicism of his critics, namely, that Cranmer cut his theology to suit his own sinful desires. Nicholas Harpsfield, the source for the famous tale of the Archbishop's 'fox in the box',[130] sought to discredit Cranmer and his 'lewd lying divinity' by character assassination; and in Harpsfield's eyes the measure of the man could be clearly seen in his addiction to sexual relations: 'This pernicious pestilent prelate, as in Cambridge he began with the flesh, so afterward also (being once inured) he still smelt of the smock.'[131] Yet, according to Cranmer's own prayer books, marriage was more than just a means 'to satisfy men's carnal lusts and appetites, like brute beasts that have no understanding'. The 1549 and 1552 liturgies did specify that matrimony was 'a remedy against sin, and to avoid fornication' for 'such persons as have not the gift of continence'. Nevertheless, for the first time in an official marriage service Cranmer added that the institution had also been ordained 'for the mutual society, help and comfort, that the one ought to have of the other'.[132] One further possibility must be considered as to why Cranmer's marriage influenced his decision to become a Protestant. Perhaps Thomas's 'mutual society' with Margaret contributed to his re-evaluation of the nature of the affections.

As we have seen, Osiander summarized his differences with Gardiner as a dispute over the role of love in justification. Was godly love something which penitents had to make themselves worthy to receive from God and then use

---

[130] '[T]he Archbishop of Canterbury was married in King Henry his days, but kept his woman very close, and sometime carried her about with him in a great chest full of holes, that his pretty nobsey might take breath in it. In the meanwhile it so chanced that his palaee [*sic*] at Canterbury was set on fire; but lord what a stir and care was there for this pretty nobsey and for this chest; all other care in a manner was set aside. He caused that chest with all speed to be conveyed out of danger, and gave great charge of it, crying out that his evidences and other writings which he esteemed above any worldly treasure were in that chest; and this I heard out of the mouth of a gentleman that was there present, and knew of this holy mystery', Harpsfield, *Pretended Divorce*, 275.

[131] Harpsfield, *Pretended Divorce*, 290, 292.

[132] *The Book of Common Prayer* [henceforth *BCP*], *The Two Liturgies . . . in the Reign of King Edward VI*, ed. Joseph Ketley (Cambridge: Parker Society, 1844) [henceforth *Lit. Ed. VI*], 127, 302; MacCulloch, *Cranmer*, 421.

worthily to be right with him, as Gardiner had argued?[133] Or was godly love something Christians received because God had already made them right with him, as Osiander argued? In part, this divergence reflected a fundamental difference about the nature of salvation. For Gardiner, Christians were to spend their lives seeking to fulfil the scriptural conditions necessary so that they might be saved.[134] For Lutherans, the Christian life was lived as a grateful response to the assurance of the free gift of salvation. With his usual acute insight, Gardiner understood this basic premise of Protestant theology. He made this point in a sermon preached at St Paul's Cross in Lent 1540:

There is no forward in the newe teaching, but al backwarde ... in so moch as he must lerne to say his Pater noster backward, and where we sayd, forgiue vs our debtes, as we forgyue our debters, now it is, as thou forgiuest our debtes, so I wyll forgyue my debters, and so God must forgyue fyrst, and al I sayd is turned backewarde.[135]

Yet, this basic disagreement was once again the inevitable result of their more fundamental differences over anthropology. According to the medieval consensus, the will needed to restrain the passions so as to be able to act in accordance with right reason. As Erasmus had advised his Christian knight, 'the only road to happiness is first to know yourself and then not to act in anything according to the passions but in all things according to the judgment of reason'.[136] Hence, for Gardiner love for God was a free choice of the will as aided by knowledge and grace.[137] For Lutherans, however, the will was the invincible expression

---

[133] 'He is worthy loue [*sic*] and fauour, that wil seke for it, and do his dutie to atteyne it', Gardiner, *Declaration of true articles*, fol. 12v; cf. ibid., fol. 68.

[134] Ibid., fol. 49.

[135] Ibid., fol. 5v. Cf. Stephen Baron's pre-Reformation comments on the Lord's Prayer: 'Math. 6. Si non dimiseritis hominibus peccata eorum: nec pater vester caelestis dimittet vobis peccata. Ubi in Augustino in sermone. In manibus enim nostris et arbitrio posuit deus vt saluemur aut damnemur. Dimitte et dimittetur tibi', *Sermones Declamatio*, sig. [F7]v.

[136] Erasmus, *Enchiridion*, 46.

[137] 'God choseth to geue vnto vs his gyftes, and in that parte we haue no choyce, and then we choose, whether we wyll vse the gyftes or no, and in this parte we haue free choyce ... For in oure inclynatyon to good or euyll, there is neyther necessytye nor compulsyon', Gardiner, *Declaration of true articles*, fol. 74r.

of the affections of the heart. Consequently, godly love was an affection naturally arising from a heart renewed by the divine gift of justifying faith.[138] In short, for Gardiner, like Scotus, love was a chosen act of obedience which assisted in salvation. For Lutherans, love was necessarily an innate response to the certainty of salvation. Gardiner grasped this fundamental divide between English religious conservatives like himself and their Protestant counterparts. He rightly asserted that his opponents taught that human beings did not have the ability to love God or their enemy until they were first assured of God's eternally certain saving love for them.[139]

Was love a conscious choice or an innate response? A theologian as thorough as Cranmer would not have adopted the doctrine of justification by faith without first carefully considering this fundamental question. Since he was also notoriously private about his own feelings, it is impossible to say whether his relationship with Margaret, or any of his other relationships for that matter, significantly influenced his conclusion. Certainly his scholarly appreciation for Augustine played a critical role in his deliberations. Still, Thomas Cranmer would not have been the first person to discover that head followed heart in matrimonial matters. If so, Protestant Augustinianism and its doctrine of deep-seated affections could easily have seemed as patently obvious as a man's indisputable need for a wife. In the end, Cranmer undoubtedly adopted not only a new wife but also a new theology of love, whatever the exact relationship

---

[138] In Gardiner's view, the Protestant approach taught 'fre wyll, as thou it signfied no choyce at all but only a desirouse appetite, they haue graunted that man hath fre wyl to his saluacion, whiche they call a wyll newe create of god, to be desyrouse of saluacion, and therewith defende styll their mere necessitie, and therwithall say this also, that a good man, doth necessarilye well, and also frely well, and an euyll man, doth necessarily euyll, and frely nought. They saye also, that god doth compell no man, for compulsion (saye they) is contrary to free wyll, But not necessite', ibid., fol. 75r.

[139] '[T]hey wold perswade to the world, that we can do no maner of good dedes tyll we haue no nede of them for our saluacion, that is to say, tyl we be iustified, and clerely in gods perfit fauour, and assured by our owne belefe of life euer lastynge, and as though we shulde say to god: Gyue me my wages aforehand, and make me sure that I shall haue heauen, and then I professe I will forgeue my neyghbour. Then I wil fast the true fast from synne. Then I wyl pray. then [*sic*] I wyll do almose. Then I wyll loue myne enemye. For then I can do it', ibid., fol. 21r.

between the two. For once he became a Protestant, he always insisted that true love for God arose solely as a grateful response to the assurance of eternal salvation. In Cranmer's mature view, only the good news of justification by faith empowered Christians to love God, their neighbour, and their enemies from the bottom of their heart.[140]

'By little and little' Cranmer put away his 'former ignorance',[141] and by September 1532 when Henry called him home to be archbishop, it seems likely that Cranmer had moved beyond Erasmus, as well as Fisher, and embraced justification by faith as defined by the Protestant interpretation of Augustine. Cranmer owned a copy of the banned Protestant collection of patristic proof-texts known as the *Unio dissidentium*.[142] As a sign of things to come, that autumn he might well have purchased his copy from the recent Venice edition while on his way home through northern Italy in order to begin quietly to gather scholarly support for his recently acquired views. For, as Cranmer knew well, that was not the time and England was not the place for speaking openly about either his new wife or his new-found understanding of justification by faith.

---

[140] For a perceptive analysis of Cranmer's language of the heart, see Stephen Sykes, 'Cranmer on the Open Heart', in *This Sacred History: Anglican Reflections for John Booty*, ed. Donald S. Armentrout (Cambridge, Mass.: Cowley Publications, 1990), 1–20.

[141] Cox I, 374.

[142] See the Appendix.

4

Cranmer's Doctrine of Repentance *circa* 1537: Lutheran Sacramental Penance

> De numero, usu, et efficacia, sacramentorum, magna est controversia in ecclesia. Scholastici contendunt septem esse, et per haec conferri gratiam, ex opere operato. Alii affirmant tria tantum esse necessaria, quae oporteat etiam cum fide accipi . . . In tanta dissentione plures videas qui frigidam suffundant, qui student concordiae paucissimos.[1]

With its concomitant repudiation of papal supremacy, the 'divorce' of Henry VIII in May 1533 raised hopes and aroused fears that the Reformation taking place on the Continent might soon come to England as well. In matters of authority, the church's new direction was swiftly clarified. The Act in Restraint of Appeals in that year had permitted the divorce by restricting all such appeals to the courts and convocation of the English church. In the year following, two acts of Parliament assigned previous papal prerogatives to the king. The Act in Restraint of Annates required the election and consecration of bishops on royal nomination and forbade the customary practice of seeking papal institution. The Act of Supremacy recognized the king as the supreme spiritual authority of the realm, able to conduct a visitation of the clergy and to decide disputed doctrinal matters.[2] The king having assumed all ecclesiastical power in his person, his court and country awaited some indication of his intentions for matters of faith and practice.

Despite his interest in theology, Henry's exposition of

---

[1] 'Of the number, use and efficacy of the sacraments, there is great controversy in the church. The Scholastics contend that there are seven and that grace is conferred through them *ex opere operato*. Others affirm only three necessary sacraments which must also be received with faith . . . In this dissension, you see many who spread coolness, very few who strive for concord', 'De sacramentis', Lambeth Palace Library MS 1107, fol. 84r.

[2] See G. R. Elton, *Reform and Reformation* (London: Arnold, 1977), 174–200.

doctrine was dependent on the scholarship of his divines, and the future of the English church was to be influenced as much by the men with whom Henry surrounded himself as by the king's personal preferences and political necessities. In matters ecclesiastical, Henry followed a strategy of divide and conquer. He permitted at his court both religious conservatives who accepted his supremacy while opposing further doctrinal innovation and also Protestant sympathizers who encouraged Henry to use his spiritual authority to make reforms in faith and practice. Stephen Gardiner, Bishop of Winchester, and Thomas Howard, Duke of Norfolk, were the foremost representatives of the conservatives at court. The two most highly placed doubters of the old religion were Thomas Cromwell, vicegerent in spirituals, and Thomas Cranmer, archbishop of Canterbury. With Henry as the ultimate but still somewhat amenable arbiter of ecclesiastical matters, both groups sought to persuade the king to endorse their programmes.[3]

Consequently, clarifying Cranmer's theological orientation during the Henrician years is crucial for a proper understanding of the political dynamics of the English Reformation. However, the nature of Cranmer's personal theology under Henry VIII has been much disputed. On the one hand, A. J. Mason, A. F. Pollard, and Theodore Maynard were certain that Cranmer was not a Lutheran at the time of his appointment to the see of Canterbury. In the words of Pollard, 'the pressing need in Cranmer's eyes . . . was not a change of doctrine so much as a change of conduct'.[4] Patrick Collinson, on the other hand, has argued that 'Cranmer's understanding of salvation moved within essentially Lutheran parameters no later than his German embassy of 1532', a position with which, as we have seen, Jasper Ridley, Basil Hall, and Diarmaid MacCulloch concur.[5] Because of the evolving nature of Cranmer's

---

[3] Cranmer wrote to Wolfgang Capito that the king gave disputed books both to a conservative and to a Reformer for assessment. After comparing their conclusions, the king came to his own decision; Cox II, 341.

[4] Mason, *Cranmer*, 87–9; Pollard, *Cranmer*, 94; Theodore Maynard, *The Life of Thomas Cranmer* (London: Staples, 1956), 100.

[5] Collinson, 'Cranmer', 91; Hall, in Ayris and Selwyn, *Churchman and Scholar*, 18–20; Ridley, *Cranmer*, 45–7; MacCulloch, *Cranmer*, 173.

theology, Gordon Rupp, G. W. Bromiley, and Peter Newman Brooks were reluctant to make any definitive judgement.[6] Yet that very development has left a legacy of often overlooked manuscript sources that upon careful examination clarify his soteriology. Indeed, by the late 1530s Cranmer had adopted a Protestant Augustinian understanding of justification, i.e. the imputation of forensic righteousness *sola fide* concomitant with the imparting of the internal presence of the Holy Spirit. Despite the pressures of the Henrician era, and, in fact, probably because of them, Cranmer was able to advance the cause of solifidianism by redefining in Lutheran terms the official description of the traditional forum for post-baptismal justification—the sacrament of penance.

Despite the differing scholastic explanations of how God justified a penitent who had lapsed into mortal sin after baptism, the authorities agreed that the forgiveness of sin required meritorious sorrow and/or absolution made effective by the power of the keys *ex opere operato*. Although historians have tended to treat Henrician evangelicals and Erasmian humanists as being identical,[7] this approach has blurred their differing views on justification. Like the compilers of the 'Collectanea', both groups presented an *ex opere operantis* understanding of sacramental penance as a logical parallel to rejecting papal authority. They disagreed, however, on whether imputed or inherent merit was the basis for forgiveness, as we have seen in Osiander's conversation with Gardiner. Those who held to forgiveness through personal merit remained within the wide parameters of late medieval Catholic teaching, those who embraced justification by the imputation of the alien righteousness of Christ (*reputatio iustitiae Christi alienae*) had crossed over to Protestantism.

Refusing to make a complete break with Catholic soteriology, some Henrician reformers promoted a general

[6] Bromiley, *Cranmer, Archbishop and Martyr*, 37. Cf. Rupp, *Studies*, 129–30; Brooks, *Cranmer in Context*, 20–8.

[7] See Maria Dowling's discussion of this point in 'The Gospel and the Court: Reformation under Henry VIII', in *Protestantism and the National Church in Sixteenth Century England*, ed. Peter Lake and Maria Dowling (London: Croom Helm, 1987), 36–9.

contritionism compatible with Erasmian principles.[8] Hat-field House MS 47 is an anonymous Henrician tract which was written *circa* 1537 to argue against papal authority in preparation for the general council to be convened at Mantua.[9] According to this treatise, auricular confession was required only by 'the lawe of man', but 'it may some-tyme do good and be occasyon to bringe in contrition'. As for satisfaction, 'if it be taken as a parte of penance, gyuen by iniunction of the confessour, in such maner as hath benne used in tyme past after confessions', such teaching was also by 'the lawe of man'.[10] If, however, satisfaction was taken to mean such scriptural activities as prayer, fasting and alms-giving, 'through grace and through the free gyfte of god', it may increase the penitent's merit and reward in heaven. Nevertheless, 'whiche way so euer it be taken, it neuer putteth away synne'.[11] A reformist questionnaire, *circa* 1537 and attributed to the hand of Simon Haynes, dean of Exeter, also suggested support for a general contritionism that denied both the necessity of auricular confession and the power of the keys as concomitant with the repudiation of papal authority.[12] The first question asked what reasons someone could have for wanting the bishop of Rome's

---

[8] NB, however, that the Lollard movement's anti-clericalism had parallel tenets, namely, maintaining contritionism while rejecting the necessity of oral confession and sacerdotal authority to pardon sin. See Anne Hudson, *The Premature Reformation: Wycliffite Texts and Lollard History* (Oxford: Clarendon Press, 1988), 294–301.

[9] See P. A. Sawada, 'Two Anonymous Tudor Treatises on the General Council', *Journal of Ecclesiastical History* 12 (1961), 197–214. This manuscript was printed with only minor changes the next year as *A Treatise concernynge generall councilles, the Byshoppes of Rome and the Clergy* (London: Berthelet, 1538). Since the manuscript has no foliation, the printed version will be cited. Although Burbidge suggested certain affinities between Cranmer's writings and this manu-script, there is no evidence for any direct connection; 'Cranmer's Library', in Duffield, *Cranmer*, 341–65, at 347.

[10] *A Treatise concernynge generall councilles*, sig. [A8]r; cf. Hatfield House MS 47, ch. 3.

[11] *A Treatise concernynge generall councilles*, sig. [A8]v; cf. Hatfield House MS 47, ch. 3. Sawada suggested that Alexander Alesius was the author of this manuscript; 'Two Treatises', 210–11. This suggestion seems unlikely for two reasons: (i) the hand is not his; MacCulloch, 'Cranmer and Gardiner', 9 n. 34; (ii) this section's emphasis on meritorious contrition rather than saving faith is incompatible with Alesius's Lutheran views.

[12] BL Cotton MS Cleop. E.v, fol. 48; quoted from the printed version in Cox II, 465–6. The attribution to Haynes is found in *LP* xii(ii). 409.

authority restored in England. The next question enquired whether someone who had committed mortal sin after his baptism was able to 'obtain remission of his sins by any other way than by contrition, through grace?' The third question queried whether it was wrong for priests to permit people to think that they could remit or retain sins 'at their pleasure'. The fourth question concerned the sufficiency of contrition to remit the pains of purgatory. If someone were contrite for his sins at the time of death would he have a place in heaven 'as if he had never offended'? The fifth question asked if the eternal fate of a man dying contrite but without priestly absolution was any different from another dying contrite and absolved. While both Hatfield House MS 47 and Haynes's questionnaire sought to limit clerical authority in matters of forgiveness, their promotion of contritionism fell short of evangelical principles of justification.

CRANMER'S MATURE THEOLOGY

In a letter dated 28 January 1537, Cranmer clearly indicated his own fundamental agreement with those who would link an *ex opere operato* concept of sacramental penance with the 'pretensions' of papal authority. Writing to Cromwell, Cranmer characterized the preaching of Hugh Payne, sometime curate of the archbishop's peculiar of Hadleigh, as 'erroneous and seditious' because Payne 'taught openly in the pulpit there, that one paternoster, said by the injunction of a priest, was worth a thousand paternosters said of a man's mere voluntary mind.'[13] In fact, his former curate was actually less expansive in his description of the power of the keys than the *Manipulus curatorum* on whose teaching his claim was based.[14] Cranmer's harsh characterization of once

---

[13] Cox II, 333. Although Cox actually transcribed the number of paternosters as 'a million', this is an error in interpreting the abbreviation 'mᶦᶦ' as standing for 'million', when in fact it represents 'mille', one thousand; Public Record Office, State Papers [henceforth PRO SP], 1/115, fol. 89. I am very grateful to Prof. Diarmaid MacCulloch for alerting me to his find; *Cranmer*, 143 n. 24.

[14] 'Unde credo quod unum Pater noster impositum in poenitentia a sacerdote efficacius est ad satisfaciendum pro peccatis quam si aliquis diceret centum milia

common teaching on auricular confession indicates how threatening to the Henrician regime was the notion that priests made the benefits of Christ's passion available to the people, and how far he himself had moved away from Fisher's sacramentalism.[15]

Although some Henrician reformers promoted Erasmian contritionism as the Catholic alternative to scholastic sacramentalism, by the date of this letter Cranmer was no longer among them. As we have noted, his evangelical convictions probably date from his stay in Nuremberg in 1532. Nevertheless, the first direct evidence for Cranmer's own repudiation of Catholic soteriology is his annotations to Henry's corrections of the *Bishops' Book*, the first official theological manual for the Henrician church. A compromise product from a committee of leading ecclesiastical figures, the text was worked over again in writing by the king shortly after its publication in late 1537. When Cranmer responded to Henry's criticisms in January 1538, he left a written record of his views during the English theological debates of 1537 and 1538.[16] Breaking with the entire medieval tradition, Cranmer denied that personal merit had any role in justification. Human effort did not bring about an imperfect but necessary penitential disposition which merited *de congruo* the infusion of *gratia gratum faciens*. Nor did God act to infuse true contrition and love in the penitent's heart so as to make him inherently worthy of divine forgiveness. Nor was the penitent so renovated by divine grace that he was sufficiently free from sinful impurity as to be able to perform works meritoriously good *de condigno* to contribute to his final justification at death.

Cranmer regarded as Pelagian the Scotist doctrine of

per semetipsum; quia illud habet meritum a passione Christi', *Manipulus curatorum*, Pars 2, tract. 3, cap. 10, fol. 98r. See Chapter 1.

[15] That by the late 1530s conservative clerics were reported to be using the opportunity of annual auricular confession to undermine the new religious sensibilities would have only reinforced the connection between papal authority and priestly absolution in the view of the authorities; Marshall, *Catholic Priesthood*, 28.

[16] Officially known as *The Institution of a Christian Man*, the text of the *Bishops' Book* is reprinted in Lloyd's *Formularies of Faith*. Cranmer acknowledged receipt of the king's corrections from Cromwell on 14 January 1538 and sent back his annotations to the Lord Privy Seal on 25 January 1538; Cox II, 358–60.

preparation 'that by the common influence of grace given generally we have inclination to obey the will and precepts of God'.[17] As for Fisher's and Erasmus's teaching that the *auxilium Dei speciale* enabled penitents to perform good works toward justification, true to the Protestant interpretation of Augustine, Cranmer denied that any work was good unless its worker was so already:

But the works which we do before our justification, be not allowed and accepted before God, although they appear never so good and glorious in the sight of man. For after justification only begin we to work as the law of God requireth.[18]

As for justification itself, Cranmer also rejected its traditional factitive understanding; for he now fundamentally repudiated the notion that Christians in this life could ever be fully pleasing to God in their own person. Rather, justification consisted solely in appropriating the 'righteousness of Christ' so as to be 'reputed righteous' for Christ's sake. Even works done after justification were not done 'exactly as the law requireth, by mean of infirmity of the flesh'. Like the penitent himself, his works needed to be reckoned more worthy than they inherently were. Only through the 'merit and benefit of Christ' would they 'be accepted and taken of God, as most exquisite, pure and perfect'.[19] Clearly, such language is congruent with Melanchthon's doctrine of justification by *reputatio iustitiae Christi alienae*.

Cranmer offered Henry three reasons for these radical departures from accepted doctrine. Firstly, he considered any talk of human merit as contrary to St Paul's teaching on grace. As we have seen, the Schoolmen made careful distinctions so as to emphasize human choice while safeguarding the gratuitous nature of salvation. They distinguished between the lesser personal merit which men earned before justification and the true personal merit which God gave in justification; between the imperfect nature of works done before justification and the worthy works which were possible only because of the grace of justification; and between the necessary co-operation of the justified in the pursuit of

[17] Cox II, 108.   [18] Ibid., 114.   [19] Ibid.

personal merit through good works and God's grace as the ultimate source of all such personal merit thus accrued. Cranmer, however, eschewed all such distinctions. He simply equated any form of personal merit that had a role in justification with the 'works-righteousness' against which St Paul had fought.[20]

Broadly accepting the medieval framework on merit, Henry wanted to insert 'only' and 'chiefly' into the text of the *Bishops' Book* so that the description of penance would have read:

The penitent must conceive certain hope and faith that God will forgive him his sins, and repute him justified and of the number of his elect children, not *only* for the worthiness of any merit or work done by the penitent, but *chiefly* for the only merits of the blood and passion of our Saviour Jesus Christ.[21]

Cranmer fought these additions as being wholly unacceptable, citing St Paul as his authority that God's grace and human merit were mutually exclusive:

These two words may not be put in this place in any wise: for they signify that our election and justification cometh partly of our merits, though chiefly it cometh of the goodness of God. But certain it is, that our election cometh only and wholly of the benefit and grace of God, for the merits of Christ's passion, and for no part of our merits and good works: as St. Paul disputeth and proveth at length in the epistle to the Romans and Galatians, and divers other places, saying, *Si ex operibus, non ex gratia; si ex gratia, non ex operibus.*[22]

In the final paragraph of his annotations Cranmer returned to this theme, arguing that those who would seek the 'by-path' of their own merit as the way to God's favour 'go from Christ' and 'they renounce his grace: *Evacuati estis a Christo*, saith St Paul, Gal. v., *quicunque in lege justificamini, a gratia excidistis*'. Striving to advance their own righteousness, they never would have the righteousness which

[20] 'Now they that think they may come to justification by performance of the law by their own deeds and merits, or by any other mean than is above rehearsed, they go from Christ, they renounce his grace', ibid.

[21] Ibid., 95.

[22] The Latin translates as, 'If by works, not by grace; if by grace, then not by works', ibid.

came from God, the righteousness of Christ, 'by whom only all the saints in heaven, and all other that have been saved, have been reputed righteous, and justified'.[23]

Cranmer's second reason for opposing any role for human merit in justification was that such teaching undermined true faith. On the one hand, any inclusion of works in the process of justification led to people putting their faith for God's favour in their efforts for him instead of his promise to redeem them. To believe that a person did all his duty toward God left no need to have faith for the remission of sins. On the other hand, those who had learned from experience that human effort was the weak link in the chain of actions which led to justification found *faciens quod in se est* 'the ready way to desperation'.[24]

Lastly, Cranmer believed that any meritorious role for human effort in justification was demeaning to the glory of Christ. Henry wanted to add that those whom Jesus had redeemed were those 'willing to return to him'. Cranmer rejected this insertion as not in keeping with the Word of God; for Scripture described salvation as the result of Christ's action on behalf of the world in order 'to set forth only the glory of our redemption by Christ'. Since all the saved depended on Christ's righteousness for their justification, all the glory of salvation belonged only to Christ. Therefore, Cranmer wanted Christians to direct their faith towards God's promise of salvation in Christ alone.[25]

Having repudiated personal merit as the basis for forgiveness, Cranmer continued to describe the process of justification in traditional terms, rearranging, however, the order and function of its constituent parts in accordance with the affective theology of solifidianism. At its most basic, justification came about through the fear of punishment for sin and the hope of forgiveness for Christ's sake which the teaching of Scripture inspired. The purpose of servile fear was to direct the sinner away from looking to any personal merit as the basis of forgiveness. Instead, the truly penitent

[23] Cox II, 114.
[24] Ibid., 89, 94.
[25] Ibid., 88, 96, 114. For Gardiner's counter-argument, see *Declaration of true articles*, fols. 16r–17r.

had to 'knowledge himself a miserable sinner not worthy to be called [God's] son'.[26] Such a definition of contrition was closer to the late medieval teaching on attrition: instead of arising from love, it arose from fear; instead of being the basis for justification, it was a necessary disposition which prepared the way for something else as the immediate cause of the forgiveness of sin; and, in its most important departure from the traditional understanding—in fact, the exact opposite of scholastic teaching—instead of being a meritorious sorrow, Cranmer's doctrine of contrition was an acknowledgement of the hopelessness of ever having any personal merit.[27]

Cranmer anchored hope for forgiveness in the promise of God's Word, rather than the depth of human penitence. In Scripture God said he would justify penitent sinners who put their trust in him to forgive their sins for Christ's sake. Those who pondered the benefits of this promise developed 'a firm trust and feeling of God's mercy'.[28] Whoever believed that God forgave sinners but was not convinced that God had forgiven him had faith no better than the demons.[29] True faith included the assurance that the penitents' own sins 'by Christ's redemption be pardoned and forgiven, that themselves by Christ be delivered from God's wrath, and be made his beloved children and heirs of his kingdom to come'. And this hope included not only assurance of the forgiveness of a particular sin at any given moment but also of the Christian's continuing to be in God's favour throughout his life. For 'if by fragility and weakness he fall again, God will not suffer him so to lie still, but put his hand to him and help him up again, and so at the

[26] Cox II, 113. Cf. Melanchthon's description of contrition: '[Mens] nullum invenit opus, quod possit opponere irae Dei, quo possit placare iram Dei. Agnoscit indignitatem suam, agnoscit se ream esse', Philip Melanchthon, *Loci communes theologici* [henceforth *LCT*] (1535), *CR* xxi. 424.

[27] Cox II, 113. NB that Cranmer did not actually use the word 'contrition' in this particular description of justification, but the description corresponds to the definition of contrition in the *Bishops' Book* itself; Charles Lloyd (ed.), *Formularies of Faith* (Oxford: Oxford University Press, 1825), 97.

[28] Cox II, 114.

[29] Ibid., 84–5; cf. 'Ut igitur certa consolatio teneatur, sic sentient pii: Quod persona sit reconciliata et accepta ad vitam aeternam, propter Christum tantum per misericordiam', *LCT* (1535), *CR* xxi. 430.

last he will take him up from death unto the life of glory everlasting'.[30] As we have seen, late medieval teaching sought to instil fear and hope simultaneously so as to keep the *viator* from both despair and presumption. As a result, a Catholic was always to have a degree of uncertainty about the next life. Cranmer, however, like his fellow Protestants, described fear and hope as successive stages whose end result was the opposite effect, a firm confidence in the believer concerning his eternal salvation.[31]

Scholasticism had taught that the infusion of charity brought about true contrition and perfect faith in the penitent, and thereby made forgiveness possible. Despite his misgivings about scholastic theology, Erasmus also insisted that the penitent's faith and love was the basis of justification. Like Osiander, however, Cranmer considered love a fruit of justification by faith rather than an integral participant in the process leading to pardon. Rejecting the scholastic *fides charitate formata*, Cranmer defined perfect faith as 'nothing else but assured hope and confidence in Christ's mercy'.[32] In keeping with the Protestant doctrine of the affections, he argued that faith came first, bringing forth an inner assurance of pardon and personal salvation. This confidence in having been freely forgiven then kindled a new love in the penitent's heart so that he sought to do God's will.[33] While this love for

---

[30] Cox II, 85, 93; cf. 'Continuance is comprehended in faith; for if I believe not that I shall continue in the holy catholic church, I cannot believe that I shall have any benefit by Christ', ibid., 92; see also, ibid., 89, 91, 113–14.

[31] Cf. the Augsburg Confession, Pt. I, art. 12: 'Constat autem poenitentia proprie his duabus partibus: Altera est contritio seu terrores incussi conscientiae agnito peccato; altera est fides, quae concipitur ex evangelio seu absolutione, et credit propter Christum remitti peccata, et consolatur conscientiam, ex terroribus liberat', B. J. Kidd (ed.), *Documents Illustrative of the Continental Reformation* (Oxford: Clarendon Press, 1911) [henceforth referred to as AC, first or second part, article number and page number in Kidd], p. 265; 'Experientia piorum testatur in hac sententia proponi non otiosas κενοφωνίας sed necessariam, veram et firmam consolationem, quae quidem et illustrat Christi beneficia, et veros Dei cultus monstrat et christianorum proprios', *LCT* (1535), *CR* xxi. 420–1.

[32] Cox II, 113. According to the scholastics, in the souls of the justified love infused by *gratia gratum faciens* joined to faith and caused it to carry out meritorious works; hence, the faith of the justified was known as *fides charitate formata*, i.e. faith informed by love. Concerning Cranmer's view, cf. 'Fides significat haud dubie in hac causa apud Paulum fiduciam misericordiae promissae propter Christum', *LCT* (1535), *CR* xxi. 422.

[33] 'But, if the profession of our faith of the remission of our own sins enter

God brought about a deep regret for sins, such sorrow served as a sign that the believer had right faith and strengthened his determination to lead a new life congruent with the forgiveness he had received. As a son was glad to please his father, the justified now laboured to please God in all that they did, crucifying the lusts of the flesh and performing acts of charity as described by St James. '*In summa*', assurance brought about, 'a firm intent and purpose to do all that is good, and leave all that is evil'.[34]

This conversion of the affections served as the standard by which to judge between the general faith which even demons possessed from 'the very right, pure, perfect, lively, christian, hearty, and justifying faith' which Cranmer wanted penitents to verify in themselves. Those who lacked a renewed will to serve God did not have justifying faith and would not inherit the kingdom of God; for 'Christ utterly refuseth them for his, which have faith and love only in their mouth, and have not the same engraven in their hearts, and expressed in their acts and deeds.'[35] Whenever Henry wanted to insert a clause specifying the necessity of good works for justification or eternal life, Cranmer argued against the addition as unnecessary since this was included in justifying faith.[36] Ultimately, Cranmer thought that the

within us into the deepness of our hearts, then it must needs kindle a warm fire of love in our hearts towards God, and towards all other for the love of God', Cox II, 86.

[34] Ibid., 85–6; cf. 'Si quis volet addere tertiam, quae tamen effectus est, videlicet totam novitatem vitae ac morum, non repugno', *LCT* (1535), *CR* xxi. 489.

[35] Cox II, 85. Cf. Cranmer's comment about Anne Boleyn to Henry VIII in 1536: 'if she be found culpable . . . then there was never creature in our time that so much slandered the gospel; and God hath sent her this punishment, for that she feignedly hath professed his gospel in her mouth, and not in heart and deed', ibid., 324. Cf. 'Qui non agunt poenitentiam, sed indulgent vitiosis cupiditatibus, non retinent fidem; fides quaerit remissionem peccatorum, non delectatur peccatis. Nec manet Spiritus sanctus in his, qui obtemperant vitiosis affectibus; iuxta illud Iohannis: Qui facit peccatum, ex diabolo est. Hae tot causae necessitatis concurrunt, quae merito diligentiam bene operandi in nobis acuere debent, ut beneficium Dei retineamus', *LCT* (1535), *CR* xxi. 432.

[36] 'He that hath the true faith in heart is christian, and in will to follow his precepts'; 'His heart is not replenished with a right faith, which in will and heart rejecteth not the devil and his works'; 'He that hath the pure faith is not only willing, but also indeed returneth to Christ', Cox II, 88. 'He hath not the right faith in his heart, that hath not a good heart and will to do his duty', ibid., 89; 'right faith cannot be without following of Christ's precepts, and repentance after falling', ibid., 92.

assurance of justification depended on the penitent being able to see in himself the fruit of justifying faith.[37]

While such an emphasis on works in the life of the justified might seem to indicate that human effort was, at that point, the *sine qua non* of eternal salvation, Cranmer refused to make assurance contingent on human co-operation with grace. He reasoned that since many times good people acted contrary to the will of God, to require them to trust in their justification because they applied their will to his motions was 'the ready way unto desperation'.[38] Instead, Cranmer based the certainty of perseverance on the doctrine of election: 'the elect shall not wilfully and obstinately withstand God's calling'; they 'will follow Christ's precepts, and rise again when they fall'; and 'they shall perpetually continue and endure'.[39]

Who were the elect? Cranmer did not develop his description of election in the annotations beyond *ad hoc* comments. However, one highly significant annotation indicates that Cranmer believed that the elect and the justified were coterminous. Commenting on a correction of Henry's, Cranmer wrote: 'These two words . . . signify that our election and justification cometh partly of our merits, though chiefly it cometh of the goodness of God.'[40] Note that Cranmer rendered the phrase 'election and justification' as singular, using it as the subject of the third-person singular verb 'cometh' and as the antecedent of the singular neuter pronoun 'it'. He then proceeded in the next sentence

---

[37] 'Therefore, let no man deceive his own mind; for no man surely can have the right faith and sure trust of God's favour towards him, and persuade with himself that God is his benign and loving Father, and taketh him for his well-beloved son and heir, except he love God in his heart, and have a willing and glad mind, and a delight to do all things that may please God, and a very great repentance and sorrow that ever he did any thing that should offend and displease so loving a Father, whose goodness he can never account', Cox II, 86.

[38] Ibid., 94.

[39] Ibid., 91–2. Stephen Gardiner found a similar emphasis on divine election rather than on-going human choice in the *Bishops' Book* itself. He noted that the section on the Creed encouraged Christians to trust themselves to be 'predestinates' because of their faith rather than instructing them that they had to keep God's conditions in order to receive his promise of salvation; James Arthur Muller (ed.), *The Letters of Stephen Gardiner* (Cambridge: Cambridge University Press, 1933), 345.

[40] Cox II, 95.

to defend gratuitous pardon by appealing to election, with no further reference to justification: 'But certain it is, that our election cometh only and wholly of the benefit and grace of God'.[41] That one so sensitive to language should write in such a manner can only mean that he considered election and justification to be part of a unitary process, each equally rooted in divine action and both always occurring in the same human lives.

Cranmer's linking of the elect and the justified has three important implications. Firstly, Cranmer believed that since election was not based on personal merit, neither was justification. Hence, it seems only reasonable to infer that since he did not believe that justification was based on human response to God's 'motions',[42] neither did he think that election was dependent on individual receptivity to grace, as Melanchthon suggested from 1535.[43] Secondly, for Cranmer to believe that only the elect were ever justified was to follow Bucer's Reformed interpretation of Augustinianism, rather than Augustine himself.[44] Thirdly, since the justified were always elect and only the elect were ever justified, Cranmer could base the assured perseverance of the justified on their prior divine election. Consequently, even though he did make some straightforward statements about the necessary role of the human will in producing the fruits of true faith,[45] these are best understood as descriptive of what the supernatural gift of justifying faith would inevitably cause to happen in the elect, rather than prescriptive of what the justified had to do to have true faith in order to become elect.

[41] Ibid.

[42] Ibid., 94.

[43] For Melanchthon on predestination, see McGrath, *Iustitia Dei*, 215; Clyde L. Manschreck, *Melanchthon: The Quiet Reformer* (New York, N.Y.: Abingdon, 1958), 293–302; Trueman, *Luther's Legacy*, 73–4.

[44] W. P. Stephens, *The Holy Spirit in the Theology of Martin Bucer* (Cambridge: Cambridge University Press, 1970), 37–41; J. Patout Burns, *The Development of Augustine's Doctrine of Operative Grace* (Paris: Études Augustiniennes, 1980), 175–8.

[45] 'Whensoever we convert in heart and mind [to Jesus Christ], we have the triumph and victory of the Devil', 'the true faithful man endeavoureth himself to conform his will to God's will in all things, and to walk right forth in all his precepts', Cox II, 93; 'whensoever we be repentant, and return fully to God in our hearts', ibid., 113.

Working by the love which arose from assurance, true
faith engendered hatred of sin, purified the heart from all
poison of sin and made 'the sinner clean a new man'.[46] At
first consideration, Cranmer's description of renovation in
the penitent can seem to imply a strongly factitive concept of
justification, as if Cranmer continued to believe that inherent righteousness was imparted to penitents, but by faith
rather than by works. Cranmer's Reformed Augustinianism
did envisage a true change of affections in the justified, but
his Protestant view 'of the infirmity of the flesh' meant that
the elect would only have no fault in them 'finally',[47] that is,
at the end of their life when death released them from the
power of sin at work in their members.[48] Hence, Cranmer's
language of renovation should be understood as referring to
the new will in the justified, not to a restored meritorious
righteousness: 'we, which be renovate by the same Spirit,
and do convert our lives from following our own carnal wills
and pleasures, and repenting us that we have followed the
same, and now apply our minds to follow the will of that
Holy Spirit, be in the favour of God'. While one could argue
that 'renovate' in this statement should be interpreted as a
prior act of regeneration to inherent righteousness that made
the subsequent conversion of the will possible, such an
interpretation is at odds with Cranmer's insistence on
humanity's need to be 'reputed' just. It is more in keeping
with the tenor of his other annotations to interpret the
description of the will's new direction as an appositional
definition of 'renovate' consistent with Melanchthon's
description of the imparting of the Holy Spirit concomitant
with justification.[49] In short, by 1538, like his probable
mentor in Protestant theology, Osiander, and like the
leading Protestant apologist, Melanchthon, Cranmer held

[46] Cox II, 86.

[47] Ibid., 91, 114.

[48] 'And moreover when [we] have received the special grace and singular
inspiration of God, and even the Holy Ghost himself, yet our own carnal
inclination is still unto evil, as St. Paul saith . . . habeo autem legem in membris
meis repugnatem legi mentis meae, et captivantem me in lege peccati, quae est in
membris meis', ibid., 108.

[49] 'Et quia spiritus sanctus affert . . . illa consolatione novam vitam, novos
motus, ideo haec renovatio vocatur regeneratio, et sequi debet nova obedientia',
LCT (1535), *CR* xxi. 428.

to justification by forensic imputation concomitant with the renovation of the will through the imparting of the Holy Spirit, the Protestant interpretation of Augustine's soteriology of grace.

Thus, in his forties Cranmer had at last arrived at his mature understanding of salvation. Embracing the 'extremism' which Gardiner deplored, he accepted the Lutheran teaching on concupiscence with its pessimistic view of both human nature and human potential. Consequently, Cranmer taught that all true goodness resided in God alone, and all grace was utterly gratuitous, so that the work of salvation was Christ's alone, and all religious affections were only reflexive responses to God's good news of election, thereby ensuring that in the end all glory belonged to Christ alone. Yet despite this clear rejection of the standard merit-based soteriology of medieval Catholicism, Cranmer's new-found solifidianism had three fundamental principles in common with the scholastic education he had received at Cambridge.

Like Scotus, Cranmer taught an extrinsic basis for justification. The Subtle Doctor had argued that the divine acceptance of the infusion of sanctifying grace *de potentia Dei ordinata* was the primary basis for justification, although God could have willed otherwise. Cranmer's approach was equally extrinsic, although radically different in nature; for he felt that God had in fact willed a system of salvation other than the one scholasticism had taught. Following the novel Protestant approach which denied any truly meritorious change in the justified at all, Cranmer based justification on the imputation of the alien righteousness of Christ appropriated through the gift of faith.

Also like Scotus, Cranmer held that salvation ultimately depended upon God's prior eternal predestination of the individual *ante praevisa merita*, though here too there was a significant difference. That Cranmer grounded salvation in God's decision to predestine only some to life was not in itself a radical departure from traditional doctrine, but his Protestant teaching that all the justified were also all elect certainly was. Unlike Scotus and the entire medieval tradition, Cranmer insisted that individuals were able to be certain that they would receive final salvation, if they simply trusted God's promise to forgive their sins freely because of Christ's passion. As this assurance of election gave rise to a new-found love for God in their heart, they would feel the stirrings of these new, Spirit-inspired affections, enabling them to certify in themselves their justification and hence that heaven would be their eternal home.

Finally, like Scotus, Cranmer insisted that the principle activity of the Christian life was practising love, hence his habitual leniency towards his personal enemies.[50] In fact, Cranmer had remained committed to this goal throughout his theological development, only his understanding of the means had changed. According to Scotus, to act with selfless love was simply a matter of exercising the native power of the human will to choose to follow right reason. Fisher and Erasmus had agreed to the primacy of love, but they were much less positive about the ease with which human beings could do so. They taught that the human will was frail and fickle and needed the constant strengthening of special grace. Such assistance, however, came only in conditional instalments, the reception of more grace being dependent on right use of previous impartations as demonstrated by the performance of good works. In the light of Protestant thought, however, Cranmer finally came to what he believed was the definitive answer to how a human being found the power to love as God loved.

He concluded that the medieval Catholic doctrine of salvation by increments did not spur a sinner to cling to God's grace even as he climbed the ladder of good works to heaven. Rather, conditional salvation based on human performance promoted self-righteous pride or self-damning despair; and either one led straight to hell. For what but hubris came from teaching that human beings and their works could be considered sufficiently worthy in God's sight, not only after justification but even beforehand as well? For what but hopelessness came from honestly striving to be consistently good enough to meet enough of God's conditions to merit salvation? In the end, Cranmer decided that neither pride nor fear inspired true love for God. The

[50] See the Introduction.

Protestants, however, had the proper measure of both humanity and God, the shallowness of its holiness and the unspeakable depths of his unconditional love. Their doctrine of justification by imputation of the extrinsic righteousness of Christ clearly showed that it was the glory of God to love sinners even though they remained unworthy. And in the face of humanity's just condemnation to everlasting hell, Scripture's assurance of unmerited salvation could but turn the wayward heart back to God, unless a person be a desperate reprobate.[51] Only this promise of free salvation made possible by God's utterly gracious love inspired a lasting grateful human love. Only this certainty of being eternally knit to God by his love could empower human beings to love him and one another in return. This simple premise is the key to understanding Cranmer's mature thought.

CRANMER'S INITIAL STRATEGY

If Cranmer argued for a Protestant understanding of justification in his defence of the *Bishops' Book* to Henry VIII, surely he took the same position in the debates which led to its publication in September 1537. At least as reported by the partisan Protestant Alexander Alesius, Cranmer's speech to a vicegerential synod used Protestant language to call for clarity on how penitents could have personal assurance of forgiveness:

There be waighty controversis now moved & put forth | not of ceremonis & light things but of the tru vnderstanding and of the right difference of the lawe and of the gospel | of the maner and way how synnes be forgeuen | of cowmforting doutful and wauering consciences by what meanes thei may be certifyed that thei please god seing thei fele the strength of the lawe accusing them of sinne.[52]

---

[51] Cf. Cox I, 134.

[52] Alexander Alesius, *Of the auctorite of the word of god agaynst the bisshop of London* (n.p., n.d.), sig. [A7]v. Concerning the date of this meeting, Rupp and Ridley have argued convincingly that this gathering was part of the debate which led to the *Bishops' Book*. They suggested a two-stage process in which the teaching on the sacraments was settled first and then a summer meeting finalized articles on

'De sacramentis' and 'Cranmer's Great Commonplaces' bear out Alesius's depiction of Cranmer as a Protestant sympathizer during the debates which led to the *Bishops' Book*. They suggest that one of the tactics of Cranmer and the evangelical party was to try to redefine in Lutheran terms the traditional Catholic instrument for justification after mortal sin—the sacrament of penance.

Reflecting the evangelical negotiating strategy, 'De sacramentis' clearly expounded the Lutheran approach to penitence.[53] *Poenitentia* had two constitutive parts, contrition and faith.[54] Contrition was defined as a crushing struggle in the conscience, not merely external punishments as 'the hypocrites' thought. Faith brought the assurance of a gratuitous mercy freely promised; and only this confidence in free pardon conquered the desperation which arose from true contrition, because no human merits or satisfactions could withstand the judgement of God.[55] In the context of

the Pater Noster, Ave Maria, the Creed and the Ten Commandments. Rupp thought that February 1537 was the probable *terminus ad quem* for the sacramental discussion, whereas Ridley considered it to be the *terminus a quo* with a final date no later than May 1537; *Studies*, 135–8, *Cranmer*, 119. However, a more precise date is possible by combining the evidence presented by both scholars. Ridley cited *LP* xii(i). 457 to indicate a *terminus a quo*: Husee to Lisle, 18 February 1537 (First Sunday of Lent), 'Most part of the bishops have come, but nobody knows what is to be done'. Rupp cited *LP* xii(i). 789, namely, a statement made by John Dakyn that 'on coming to London in the second week of Lent' he learned from the archbishop of York that 'these four sacraments that were omitted be found again now, and we be concluded upon them yesternight'. At the very least, it seems highly likely that the meeting described by Alesius took place during the first week of Lent 1537 and that the participants agreed to write descriptions of the other four sacraments. Although further meetings in March and beyond might have been necessary to come to agreement on the individual descriptions, Rupp may well be right in interpreting Lee's comment to mean that all the matters pertaining to the sacramental debate had been resolved by the time Dakyn arrived in London. P. J. Holmes has shown how this vicegerential synod followed shortly after the conclusion of a great council convened in response to the Pilgrimage of Grace; 'The Last Tudor Great Councils', *The Historical Journal* 33 (1990), 1–22, at 9–12.

[53] For a detailed discussion of 'De sacramentis' and its association with Cranmer, see the Appendix.

[54] 'Christus iussit praedicari poenitentiam et remissionem peccatorum in ipsius nomine quare haec duo semper coniungenda sunt scilicet contritio et fides,' LPL MS 1107, fol. 86v. Cf. 'Nos docendi caussa partes duas poenitentiae facimus, contritionem et fidem', *LCT* (1535), *CR* xxi. 489; 'Constat autem *poenitentia* proprie his duabus partibus: Altera est contritio . . . altera est fides', AC, Pt. I, art. 12, p. 265.

[55] 'Estque contritio vera, tanta tristitia ut hominem extinguere possit vel ad

auricular confession, however, *poenitentia* was specifically a sacrament, for absolution pronounced on the truly penitent had the promise of Christ to his disciples that 'whatsoever you loose on earth, will be loosed in heaven' (Matthew 18: 18).[56] 'De sacramentis' does not detail how that promise was made effective for the penitent. Nevertheless, the manuscript's emphasis on faith rather than ritual suggests the Lutheran view that absolution was efficacious because the Holy Spirit worked through the ministerial pronouncement of the gospel promise to inspire the penitent with saving faith.[57]

Citing Erasmus's *Modus confitendi* for support, 'De sacramentis' argued that some practices associated with sacramental penance were helpful but that others were inappropriate.[58] The sacrament was useful for examining those about to receive communion to see 'if they be in faith'[59]

laqueum adigere nisi consolatio misericordiae eam mitigaret', LPL MS 1107, fol. 87r; 'Hanc hypocritae non habent, qui putant poenitentiam, in externis tantum castigationibus, iuxta humanas traditiones, positam esse, et non in illo certamine conscientiae cum desperatione, quam tantum vincere potest, fiducia misericordiae gratuitae et gratis promissae. Nam necesse est hominem desperare si nolit sibi ignosci nisi propter propriam satisfactionem, et meritum', ibid.; 'Nostra merita et satisfactiones non posse consistere in iudicio dei', ibid., fol. 87v. Cf. 'Quare non est poenitentia in securis hypocritis, qui nullo dolore afficiuntur, et sibi interim blandiuntur, quasi nihil habeant vitii', *LCT* (1535), *CR* xxi. 490. Cf. Cranmer's concern about people trusting 'in the very bare observation of [ceremonies]', Cox II, 326–7.

[56] 'Absolutio habet promissionem Christi quaecumque solveritis super terram Mathei 18. Constat christum isthic loqui non de baptismo ut quidam negantes poenitentiam esse speciale sacramentum, imaginantur; sed de, confessione peccatorum', LPL MS 1107, fol. 86v. Cf. Cranmer's comment in his 'Annotations' that God's promise for healing and the forgiveness of sin 'chiefly ought to be known' in the anointing of the sick; Cox II, 99.

[57] 'Quare sicut verbum est instrumentum, per quod Spiritus sanctus efficax est; sicut Paulus inquit: Evangelium est potentia Dei ad salutem omni credenti; item: fides ex auditu est etc.; ita per Sacramenta Spiritus sanctus est efficax, cum videlicet fide accipiuntur; admonent enim et movent ad credendum sicut verbum', *LCT* (1535), *CR* xxi. 468; 'Quod requirat Deus fidem, ut illi absolutioni tamquam voci de coelo sonanti credamus, et quod illa fides vere consequatur et accipiat remissionem peccatorum', AC, Pt. ii, art. 4, p. 275.

[58] 'Bonae memoriae erasmus collegit utilitates et incommoda quae sequuntur privatam confessionem', LPL MS 1107, fols. 87v–88r.

[59] 'Concordia . . . quod indecorum sit inexploratos admittere ad communionem et paulus iubet communicantes seipsos probare utrum sint in fide', LPL MS 1107, fol. 87v. Cf. 'Et indecorum est prorsus, inexploratos accedere ad Communionem', *LCT* (1535), *CR* xxi. 494; 'Non enim solet porrigi corpus Domini nisi antea exploratis et absolutis', AC, Pt. ii, art. 4, p. 275.

and for instructing those found deficient;[60] but its chief attribute was providing comfort through absolution.[61] Among its abuses was the enumeration of all hidden sins. This obligation was a scholastic excess; for Peter the Lombard supported private confession of flagrant crimes, and the only confession the fathers knew was the public admission of offence by the excommunicated that they eventually permitted to be done privately to ease embarrassment.[62] As for those who argued that as a judge needed to learn the facts of the case before rendering a verdict so also a priest could not absolve without the listing of sins, John Chrysostom offered the best reply: penance was 'a place for healing, not judgement, granting not punishments but the remission of sins'.[63]

In error as well were the teachings that the power of the keys changed eternal punishment into the punishment of

---

[60] 'Concordia . . . quod commodiss[im]e fit in confessione, ubi rudes, interrogantur, et docentur quid debent credere', LPL MS 1107, fol. 87v. Cf. 'Deinde etiam propter disciplinam, quia per eam occasionem indocti audiri et commodius instituti de tota doctrina possunt', *LCT* (1535), *CR* xxi. 494; 'Et docetur populus diligentissime de fide absolutionis', AC, Pt. II, art. 4, p. 275. In his Visitation Injunctions for Hereford in 1538, Cranmer made use of auricular confession's teaching role by specifying that 'ye, both in your preaching and secret confession, and all other works and doings, shall excite and move your parishioners unto such works as are commanded expressly of God', Cox II, 81.

[61] 'Concordia quod retinenda sit in ecclesia cum propter multas alias causas tum propter absolutionem', LPL MS 1107, fol. 87v. Cf. 'Verum confessio, quum propter maximum absolutionis beneficium, tum propter alias conscientiarum utilitates apud nos retinetur', AC, Pt. II, art. 4, p. 276; 'Retinemus igitur confessionem arcanam, quae fit ministris ecclesiae, ut petatur absolutio propter consolationem uberrimam', *Die Wittenberger Artikel von 1536*, ed. Georg Mentz (Darmstadt: Wissenschaftliche Buchgesellschaft, 1968), 50.

[62] '[Scholastici] exigunt a confitente enumerationem oc[c]ultorum peccatorum et allegant pro hoc dogmate testimonia quaedam ex patribus et quae citat magister xvii distinctione quarti pro privata confessione manifestorum criminum, sed constat eos iniuriam facere magistro, qui praecessit innocentium annis plus minus quinquaginta, et patres tantum loquuntur de excom[m]unicatis ab ecclesia et palam facinorosis, qui principio fatebantur sua peccata coram tota multitudine. Postea eorum verecundiae consultum est ut privatim confiterentur', LPL MS 1107, fol. 88r. Cf. 'Enumeratio delictorum non sit necessaria, nec sint onerandae conscientiae cura enumerandi omnia delicta, quia impossibile est omnia delicta recitare', AC, Pt. II, art. 4, pp. 275–6.

[63] 'Ad consequentiae (?) argumentum, iudex non pronuntiat nisi cognita causa ergo sacerdos non potest absolvere sine enumeratione peccatorum respondit [Chrysostomus] tomo 7 homelia [*sic*] 9 de poenitentia medicinae inquit locus est non iudicii, non poenas sed remissionem peccatorum tribuens,' LPL MS 1107, fol. 88v.

purgatory, that some of this punishment needed to be redeemed by satisfactions, and that papal indulgences could free souls from purgatory. Such doctrine was incompatible with Scripture and was also unknown both to the fathers and to the Lombard.[64] God forgave punishment owed for sin because of his mercy.[65] Satisfaction was owed toward the offended and the church, not God.[66] However, in the case of public scandal and its injury to others, God did threaten sinners with punishments during this life even after the forgiveness of a sin's eternal punishment, as was the case when Nathan told David that his murderous adultery was pardoned, but that his son by Bathsheba would still die (2 Samuel 12: 13–14). Although human satisfactions had no effect on these judgements, sometimes God would lessen them or completely forgo them when people demonstrated true repentance. Since such penitence would manifest itself in external indications, that was the meaning of the scripture, 'Redeem your sins by alms'.[67] Nevertheless, no matter

---

[64] 'Ista doctrina quae dicit sacerdotem potestate clavium commutare poenam aeternam in poenam purgatorii, et huius, partem remitti eadem authoritate, reliquum redimendum esse satisfactionibus, quae docent esse opera indebita suscepta sine verbo dei, et posse praestari in peccato mortali, et pontificem posse liberare animas de purgatorio per indulgentias, haec doctrina quia pugnat cum scriptura, et est ignota patribus atque ipso longobardo', LPL MS 1107, fol. 88v. Cf. 'Sic enim dicunt Scholastici: Deum, cum sit misericors, remittere culpam, sed cum sit etiam iustus et vindex, mutare poenam aeternam in temporalem purgatorii. Deinde addunt partem illarum poenarum remitti potestate clavium, partem redimendam esse satisfactionibus', *LCT* (1535), *CR* xxi. 496. Although the power of the keys to commute eternal pains into temporal ones developed after the Lombard, he taught the importance of satisfaction to avoid purgatory, see *Sententiae*, li. 4, dist. 20, ca. 2.

[65] 'Ideo alii sic docent de satisfactione, sicut irasci dei, est aeterna voluntas puniendi peccatum, ita miserere dei est, remittere poenam debitam peccato', LPL MS 1107, 88v–89r.

[66] 'Confessio peccatorum ibi [i.e. Matt. 18] praecipitur si non audierit ecclesiam sit tibi velut ethnicus et publicanus. Satisfactio quae sit ecclesiae et offensis, eodem loco iubetur, nam hoc significat audire ecclesiam obsequi mandato ecclesiae, hinc ortae sunt poenitentiae et satisfactiones publicae sicut ex Corinthiis apparet et primitiva ecclesia', LPL MS 1107, fols. 86v–87r.

[67] 'Minatur autem deus peccatis praesentes poenas . . . propter schandalum et iniuriam factam fratribus, sic nathan interpretatur afflictionem davidis post poenitentiam, de adulterio et homicidio . . . istas temporales poenas, non possunt tollere humanae satisfactiones, sed interdum propter veram resipiscentiam quam mundo testamur externis indiciis, dominus comminatas poenas propter schandalum, mitigat aut ex toto remittit . . . sic accipiendi sunt loci illi peccata tua eleemosinis redime', LPL MS 1107, fol. 89r. Cf. 'Non solum consequamur vitam

how much people might mitigate present punishments through right living, eternal punishments due for sin were of an entirely different order. In God's righteous judgement, humanity owed a debt of punishment beyond satisfaction to the world and mortification of the flesh; and these punishments he remitted only because of the satisfaction of Christ.[68] Finally, they erred who insisted that private confession was necessary. According to the manuscript, the fathers never thought thus, otherwise how could Bishop Nectarius have been able to abolish the practice at Constantinople in 391? Therefore, it was the conclusion of 'De sacramentis' that because of its positive benefits the sacrament was expedient to be retained but not necessary. This last point, however, was the crux of the debate.[69] The final version of the article on justification referred the reader back to sacramental penance to learn how justification could be attained.[70] Although citing Erasmus as an ally and agreeing with his position on necessity, the exposition of *poenitentia* in 'De sacramentis' clearly sought to rework the constitutive elements of sacramental penance in accordance with solifidianism. The conservative bishops most likely were willing to tolerate a Lutheran definition of the *processus*

aeternam, cum agimus poenitentiam, sed etiam quod remissionem aut mitigationem praesentium poenarum, et calamitatum poenitentia et bona opera nostra mereantur, sicut Paulus inquit: Si nos ipsi iudicaremus . . . Et de hac remissione poenarum vere intelligi potest: Eleemosina liberat a morte, hoc est, meretur remissionem praesentium poenarum', Mentz, *Wittenberger Artikel*, 52.

[68] 'Interim hoc semper statuendum est quod omnem aliam poenam quae neque mundo satisfacit neque est mortificatio praesentis peccati in carne sed quae in iudicio dei quod nobis cum ipso coram suis angelis est ex ipsius iustitia debetur, remittat propter satisfactionem Christi sicut tota scriptura testatur', LPL MS 1107, fol. 89v.

[69] 'Sed non est contentio utrum expediat retinere [confessionem] in ecclesia. Omnis controversia oritur, ex lege quam tulit innocentius tertius Omnes [*sic*] utriusque sexus semel in anno confiteantur omnia sua peccata proprio sacerdoti . . . patres non iudicabant illam privatam confessionem esse necessar[i]am alioqui quomodo potuisset nectareus [*sic*] episcopus, han[c] constantinopoli abrogare', LPL MS 1107, fol. 88r. On Nectarius, see Poschmann, *Penance*, 98–9; McNeill, *Cure of Souls*, 98.

[70] 'Item, That sinners attain this justification by contrition and faith, joined with charity, after such sort and manner as is before mentioned and declared *in the sacrament of penance*', (italicized words added in the *Bishops' Book*) Lloyd, *Formularies*, pp. xxvi, 209.

iustificationis as long as the necessity of the sacrament as the forum for this process was maintained. To remove this requirement, however, would have left in place a description of sacramental penance wholly in agreement with the Lutheran description of justification, and this was a goal towards which Cranmer would consistently work.

CRANMER'S INITIAL SCHOLARSHIP

As 'De sacramentis' offers insight into Cranmer's shared strategy of negotiation with the religious conservatives, the section labelled 'De poenitentia I' in 'Cranmer's Great Commonplaces' records the mostly patristic material gathered to support his Lutheran understanding of sacramental penance.[71] Immediately under the title of the *locus*, the copyist inscribed the Lutheran definition: 'In penance, contrition and faith come together.'[72] Quotations were gathered that described contrition as an inner struggle of self-accusation[73] and forgiveness and new life as coming through faith.[74] Congruent with the Protestant teaching on

[71] For further details on the penitential material in 'Cranmer's Great Commonplaces', see the Appendix. It is important to bear in mind the significance of underlinings in the passages which follow. Although it is impossible to prove conclusively, it is generally accepted that the underlinings are Cranmer's own, 'indicating passages of which the Archbishop wished to make special note', Ayris and Selwyn, *Churchman and Scholar*, 312.

[72] 'Agite poenitentiam, et credite Evangelio' (Mark 1: 15), CGC I, 133v; 'In poenitentia occurrunt, Contritio et fides', CGC I, 133r. The copyist also included Matt. 11: 28 and 1 Sam. 2: 6; CGC I, 133r. Melanchthon used all three as scriptural proof that repentance consisted of contrition and faith in his *Apologia confessionis augustanae*, *CR* xxvii. 543–4.

[73] 'Nec ulla hora fere est cui compunctio districta occurrit . . . cum iudicis et tortoris vices non parcens peccator assumit, semetipsum persequens, dum confessionem confusione honorat: holocausti huius incensio in conspectu dei veniam impetrat . . . poenitentes vero quia seipsos suscipit iudicatos absolvit', 'Cyprian', *Sermo de passione de Christi*, CGC I, 134v; 'Nunquam sine poenitentia obvenire peccatorum remissionem quod nulli nisi afflicti, et peccatorum conscientia vulnerati, dei misericordiam sincere implorare possunt . . . Quo excluderentur et Pharisaei, qui sua iustitia saturi, paupertatem suam non agnoscunt, et contemptores, qui securi irae dei, malo suo remedium non quaerunt. Tales enim nec laborant, nec onerati sunt, nec contriti corde, nec vincti, nec captivi, nec lugent', John Calvin, *Institutio religionis christianae* (1536), CGC I, 143v; *Institutio Christianae Religionis, Corpus Reformatorum*, ed. C. G. Bretschneider and H. E. Bindseil, vol. xxix (Brunswick, 1853) [henceforth *CR* xxix], 152.

[74] 'Ergo et agendam poenitentiam esse et tribuendam veniam credere nos

the impossibility of inherent righteousness, Jerome was quoted as saying that since the just person fell seven times a day, Christians were always sinning, and therefore needed always to be repenting.[75] Confession *coram Deo* was therefore commended, for acknowledging sin was the way to forgiveness, and by confession the heart was sanctified and the penitent made whole.[76] This confession could even be silent, spoken directly to God by the heart.[77] Those reluctant to confess were to remember three things: God already knew;[78] God waited for the penitent to admit his need;[79] and when someone confessed, God was ready at hand to help.[80]

As for confession to men, however, most extracts in 'De poenitentia I' discouraged the practice. Among these negative quotations were the same patristic passages given by

oportet, ut veniam tanquam ex fide speremus, quam tanquam ex singrapha impetrat fides', Ambrose, [unattributed], CGC I, 139r; 'Renovatio vitae inchoatur a fide qua creditur in eum qui iustificat impium', Augustine, *De trinitate*, li. 4, ca. 3, CGC I, 140v.

[75] 'Septies in die cadit iustus . . . Ergo quia semper peccamus, semper poenitere et resipiscere debeamus', Jerome, [unattributed], CGC I, 138r.

[76] 'Confusio est enim peccare, non est confusio confiteri peccata', Chrysostom, *Sermo de poenitentia et confessione*, CGC I, 136r; 'Peccata tua dicito ut deleas illa', Chrysostom, *In Psalmum 50*, Homilia 2, CGC I, 136r [Bodius, *Unio Hermani Bodii in unum corpus redacta et diligenter recognita* (Venice, 1532), fol. 136r]; 'Et digna se confessione cum observantia mandatorum dei cunctorum corda sanctificent', Chrysostom, *In Matthaeum*, Homilia 38, CGC I, 136v; 'Si diligenti dei verborum attentione multoque studio, et continua confessione, supernam curam nobis conciliemus', Chrysostom, *In Genesim*, Homilia 5, CGC I, 136v.

[77] 'Confessio itaque mea, deus meus in conspectu tuo tibi tacite fit, et non tacite. Tacet enim strepitu, clamat affectu', Augustine, *Confessiones*, li. 10, ca. 2, CGC I, 139r [Bodius, *Unio* (1532), fol. 135v]; 'Petrus prorupit ad lacrimas nihil voce precatus . . . recte plane petrus flevit et tacuit, quia quod defleri solet non solet excusari. Et quod defendi non potest, ablui potest, lavat enim lachrima delictum, quod voce pudor est confiteri', Ambrose, *Sermo 46*, De poenitentia Petri Apostoli, CGC I, 138v [Bodius, *Unio* (1532), fol. 136v]; 'Ea coram deo confitere, coram iudice confitere peccata tua, deprecans, et si non lingua, saltem memoria', Chrysostom, *Homilia 41*, De poenitentia, CGC I, 137r.

[78] 'Haec enim si non dixeris, ignoret ea deus', Chrysostom, *In Psalmum 50*, Homilia 2, CGC I, 136r [Bodius, *Unio* (1532), fol. 136v]; 'Frustra autem velis occultare, quem nihil fallas', Ambrose, *In Lucam*, li. 7, ca. 66, CGC I, 138v; 'Illi quem latere non possunt confiteri ea, iugi supplicatione non desinas', John Cassian, *Collationum*, Sermo ad Abbatem Pynunfium, Libello [*sic*] de fine poenitentiae, ca. 8, CGC I, 142r.

[79] 'Nunquit a te vult ea cognoscere?' Chrysostom, *In Psalmum 50*, Homilia 2, CGC I, 136r [Bodius, *Unio* (1532), fol. 136v]; 'Sed et si deus novit omnia vocem tamen tuae confessionis exspectat', Ambrose, *In Lucam*, li. 7, ca. 66, CGC I, 138v.

[80] 'Cum faciebas ea praesto erat', Chrysostom, *In Psalmum 50*, Homilia 2, CGC I, 136r [Bodius, *Unio* (1532), fol. 136v].

'De sacramentis' as proof that auricular confession was not required by the fathers, including the account of Nectarius abolishing private confession at Constantinople.[81] Their hostile attitude was aptly summarized by a lengthy quotation from Augustine:

> What are men to me that they should hear my confessions, as if they would heal all my infirmities? They are a curious people who pry into another's life but are lazy in correcting their own. Why do they seek to hear from me what I am, when they do not wish to hear from you what they are? And how do they know, when they hear my confession, that I am telling the truth? For no one knows what goes on inside a person except the spirit of man which is inside him.[82]

Accordingly, any enumeration of sins was to be made to God, not to man.[83] The only patristic text in 'De poenitentia I' that was positive toward auricular confession emphasized the priest as healer rather than judge. An extract from Jerome encouraged a penitent to confess his sins that a

---

[81] 'Lavat enim lachrima delictum, quod voce pudor est confiteri', Ambrose, *Sermo 46*, De poenitentia Petri Apostoli, CGC I, 138v [Bodius, *Unio* (1532), fol. 136v]; 'Solus te deus confitentem videat', Chrysostom, *Sermo de poenitentia et confessione*, CGC I, 136r [Bodius, *Unio* (1532), fol. 138v]; Non dico ut confitearis conservo tuo', Chrysostom, *In Psalmum 50*, Homilia 2, CGC I, 136r [Bodius, *Unio* (1532), fol. 136v]; 'Non tibi dico, ostenta teipsum, nec apud alios accusa, sed . . . ea coram deo confitere', Chrysostom, *Homilia 41*, De poenitentia, CGG I, 137r; 'Tum Nectarius episcopus removet diaconum sceleratum, et quibusdam suadentibus ut singulos ad communicandum, iudicio conscientiae suae relinqueret, etiam presbyterum nequaquam super poenitentes esse praecepit', *Tripartita Historia*, li. 9, ca. 35, CGC I, 136r [Bodius, *Unio* (1532), fol. 142v]; cf. LPL MS 1107, fol. 88; 'Glosa de poenitentia, dist. 5, in principio. Dicit confessionem auricularem institutam non a Christo, sed a traditione ecclesiae', CGC I, 144v, cf. AC, Pt. II, art. 4, p. 276.

[82] 'Quid mihi ergo est cum hominibus? ut audiant confessiones meas, quasi ipsi sanaturi sint omnes languores meos? Curiosum genus ad cognoscendam alienam vitam, desidiosum ad corrigendam suam. Quid a me quaerunt audire, qui sim, qui nolunt audire a te qui sint? Et unde sciunt cum a meipso, de meipso audiunt, an verum dicam, quandoquidem nemo scit hominum, quid agatur in homine, nisi spiritus hominis qui in ipso est?' Augustine, *Confessiones*, li. 10, ca. [3], CGC I, 139v [Bodius, *Unio* (1532), fols. 135v–136r].

[83] 'Nec tantum nos peccatores esse dicamus, sed etiam ipsa peccata specialiter singula computemus. Non dico tibi, ut te prodas in publicum, neque ut te apud alios accuses . . . apud verum iudicem cum oratione delicta tua pronuntia, non lingua, sed conscientiae tuae memoria', Chrysostom, *In epistolam ad Hebraeos*, Homilia 31, CGC I, 136r [Bodius, *Unio* (1532), fol. 136r], cf. 'Non tibi dico, ut te prodas in publicum . . . sed conscientiae tuae memoria', AC, Pt. II, art. 4, p. 276.

teacher who spoke healing words might be able to help him.[84] A second entry also described confession as a place for healing, in fact the same passage from John Chrysostom which was quoted by 'De sacramentis'; but the extract in 'De poenitentia I' included a further clause which made clear that in order for confession to be healing, it was to be made to God alone.[85]

Just as 'De sacramentis' noted the Catholic teaching on auricular confession which it rejected, so also the great notebooks recorded patristic evidence more supportive of the Catholic position on sacramental penance in a brief *locus* entitled, naturally, 'De confessione'.[86] According to these texts, since self-accusation was a sign of contrition, the admission of sin led to healing and the confessor's counsel assisted in this process.[87] Moreover, the penitent confessed to a priest so as to receive instruction for the making of satisfaction and, if necessary, for the offering of public penance when his sin had been a stumbling-block to others.[88] According to Basil, confession to a priest was

[84] 'Si quem serpens diabolus occulte momorderit, et nullo conscio, eum peccati veneno infecerit, si tacuerit qui percussus est, nec vulnus suum, fratri suo et magistro voluerit confiteri, magister qui linguam habet, sed ad curandum, facile ei prodesse non poterit. Si erubescat enim aegrotus, medico vulnus confiteri, quod ignorat medicina non curat', Jerome, *In Ecclesiasticum*, ca. 10, CGC I, 138r.

[85] 'Medicinae locus hic est, non iudicii, non poenas sed peccatorum remissionem tribuens, deo solo dic peccatum tuum', Chrysostom, *Homilia 5*, CGC I, 136v; cf. LPL MS 1107, fol. 88v.

[86] It is perhaps of some significance that unlike the overtly Protestant 'De poenitentia I', 'De confessione' has no underlinings. This observation must be tempered, however, by the fact that in 'De satisfactione' entries from both Calvin and the *Assertio* are underlined.

[87] 'Dum accusat semetipsum et confitetur, simul evomit et delictum, atque omnem morbi digerit causam', Origen, *In Psalmum 37*, Homilia 2, CGC I, 145v; 'Praeveniamus faciem eius in confessione? Antequam ipse attendat ut puniat, tu praeveni confitendo et puni tu', Augustine, *In Psalmum 58*, CGC I, 146v; 'Tristis esto antequam confitearis, confessus exulta, iam sanaberis', Augustine, *In Psalmum 66*, CGC I, 150r; 'Tu ipse facile sanari, multa hoc deliberatione, et satis perito, medici illius, concilio procurandum est', Origen, *In Psalmum 37*, Homilia 2, CGC I, 145v; 'Confessio peccatorum, hanc habet rationem, quam habet vulnus aliquid corporis, vel passio, quae medico demonstranda est. Ita confessio peccatorum fieri debet, apud eos tantummodo qui curare haec praevalent et emendare', Basil, *De regula monachorum*, ca. 98, CGC I, 146r.

[88] 'Tanquam bonus esse incipiens, accipiat a sacrorum propositis, satisfactionis suae modum, nunc id agat quod solum illi prosit ad salutem, sed etiam ceteris ad exemplum, ut si peccatum eius, non solum in gravi eius malo, sed etiam in scandalo est aliorum, atque hoc expedire utilitati ecclesiae videtur antistiti, in notitia

necessary, of even the least sins, and Nicephorus was cited as saying that before his time auricular confession had been required for all.[89] Even so, two other extracts described auricular confession as one way amongst many means for gaining pardon, including cleansing by the word, contrition, giving alms, turning a sinner from his sin, forgiving the sins of others, and love.[90] Two other quotations from Augustine associated sacramental penance exclusively with public repentance of serious crimes by the excommunicated.[91]

On the crucial issue of the power of the keys, 'De confessione' quoted Augustine as saying that while God revived a sinner's soul, the church loosed him from sin's entanglement. Augustine based his comments on the story of Lazarus, who came forth from the tomb alive but still needed

multorum vel totius plebis agere poenitentiam, non recuset', Augustine, *Homilia 50*, CGC I, 148v–149r; 'Si intellexerit et praeviderit, talem esse languorem tuum qui in conventu totius ecclesiae exponi debeat et curari . . . satis perito, medici illius, concilio procurandum est', Origen, *In Psalmum 37*, Homilia 2, CGC I, 145v.

[89] 'Basilius de Regula Monachorum, ca. 21. Necessarium videtur iis quibus dispensatio mysteriorum dei commissa est, confitenda esse peccata. Et ca. 25 exigit ut minima peccata confiteamur', CGC I, 146r; 'Nicephorus. Cartophilax ad Theodosium monachum. Ligandi solvendique provincia ponitificibus ipsis a domino deo nostro demandata est . . . Unde olim omnes oportebat, ad ipsos pontifices accedere, suaque illis occulta prodere, et sui vel reconciliationem vel repudium ferre', CGC I, 150v. Cf. 'Si quis non prius animae suae vitia et peccatorum suorum cognoverit mala, ac proprii oris confessione providerit, purgari is absolvique non poterit', Origen, *Periarchon*, li. 3, ca. 1, CGC I, 145v.

[90] 'Audi nunc quantae sunt remissiones peccatorum in evangeliis. Est ista prima, qua baptizamur in remissionem peccatorum. Secunda remissio est, in passione martyrii. Tertia est, quae pro eleemosina datur. Quarta nobis fit, per hoc quod nos remittimus peccata fratribus nostris. Quinta, cum converterit quis peccatorem, ab errore viae suae . . . Sexta, quoque fit per abundantiam charitatis . . . Et adhuc est septima, licet dura et laboriosa, per poenitentiam, remissio peccatorum', Origen, *Super Leviticum*, Homilia 2, GCG I, 145r ; cf. CGC I, 151; 'Mundantur et verbo veritatis . . . Mundantur et sacrificio contriti cordis . . . Mundantur et eleemosinis . . . Mundantur ipsa quae supereminet omnibus charitate', Augustine, *Contra Cresconium grammaticum*, li. 2, CGC I, 149v.

[91] 'Est poenitentia gravior et luctuosior, in qua proprie vocantur in ecclesia poenitentes, remoti etiam a sacramentis altaris participandis . . . Grave vulnus adulterium forte commissum est. Forte homicidium, forte aliquid sacrilegum', Augustine, *Homilia 27*, CGC I, 148r; 'Qui post uxores vestras, vos illicito concubitu maculastis, si propter uxores vestras, cum aliqua concubuistis, agite poenitentiam qualis agitur in ecclesia, ut oret pro vobis ecclesia. Nemo sibi dicat, occulte ago, apud deum ago, novit deus qui mihi ignoscit, quia in corde ago . . . Ergo sine causa sunt claves datae ecclesiae dei? Frustramus evangelium dei, frustramus verba Christi?', Augustine, *Homilia 49*, CGC I, 148v.

the disciples to loose him from his burial wrappings.[92] One of these extracts was useful to the conservatives, suggesting that the penitent's guilt was removed by the priest's absolution. Another mentioned belief in association with confession and so could be construed as supportive of Lutheran doctrine.[93] A third could have been claimed by either side, that although the priest pronounced forgiveness, the effect in the penitent was brought about by God: 'We speak to your ears, how do we know what may be happening in your hearts? But what is happening within is not our doing, but his.'[94]

'De poenitentia I', however, was consistently clear about the nature of priestly binding and loosing. In keeping with this section's overtly Protestant orientation, the entries plainly denied sacerdotal power to remit sin. According to Theophylact, Jewish priests, being slaves to sin themselves, did not have 'the power to forgive the sins of others'. John Chrysostom offered a similar judgement on human mediators: 'No one has the power to forgive sin except God.'[95] Quoting the Lombard and the same passage from Jerome cited by the 'Collectanea',[96] 'De poenitentia I'

---

[92] 'Quid prodest ecclesia confitenti . . . Ipsum Lazarum attende cum vinculis prodit. Iam vivebat confitendo, sed non dum liber ambulabat, vinculis irretitus', Augustine, *De verbis domini*, Sermo 8, CGC I, 147r; 'Elevatus est Lazarus, processit tumulo, et ligatus erat, sicut sunt homines in confessione peccati agentes poenitentiam. Iam processerunt a morte. Nam non confiterentur, nisi procederent . . . Sed quid dominus, ecclesiae suae inquit? Quae solveritis in terra, soluta erunt in caelo', Augustine, *Homilia 27*, CGC I, 148r.

[93] 'Quando confiteris procedis . . . Sed ut confitearis, deus facit, magna voce clamando, id est, magna, gratia vocando: ideo cum processisset mortuus, adhuc ligatus, confitens et adhuc reus, ut solverentur peccata eius, ministris hoc dixit dominus, Solvite illum et sinite abire', Augustine, *In Johannem*, tract. 49, CGC I, 149v–150r; 'Mortuus in corde tuo tanquam in sepulchro iacebas . . . Surge et procede, et crede, et confitere . . . tunc dicitur. Solvite illum et sinite abire', Augustine, *In Johannem*, tract. 22, CGC I, 150v.

[94] 'Merito per ecclesiam dari solutionem peccatorum potest. Suscitari autem ipse mortuus, non nisi intus clamante domino potest. Haec enim deus interius agit. Loquimur ad aures vestras, unde scimus quid agatur in cordibus vestris. Quod autem intus agitur, non a nobis sed ab illo agitur', Augustine, *In Psalmum 101*, CGC I, 147r.

[95] 'Et sacerdotes vestri, cum et ipsi servi sint, non habent potestatem, aliis dimittendi peccata', Theophylact, *In Johannem*, ca. 8, CGC I, 141r [Bodius, *Unio* (1532), fol. 140v]; 'Dimittendi peccatum potestatem nemo habet praeter deum', Chrysostom, *In Johannem*, Homilia 53, CGC I, 141r.

[96] 'Deus solus dimittit peccata, et retinet, et tamen ecclesiae contulit potestatem ligandi et solvendi . . . Ipse enim per se tantum dimittit peccatum. Sacerdotibus

presented the priest's role as to declare what God had made clean and linked forgiveness of sin to the priestly declaration of God's Word.[97] A quotation from Chrysostom aptly summarized this Protestant approach to the priestly power of the keys:

For the Scriptures are said to be the kingdom of heaven, because in them is contained the kingdom of heaven. Understanding them is the door . . . Now the priests are the keepers of the keys, to whom the word of teaching and interpreting the Scriptures has been entrusted. The key is the word of knowledge of the Scriptures through which the door of truth is opened to men.[98]

Concomitant with the rejection of the priest as judge, 'De poenitentia I' defined the fruit of repentance as amendment of life rather than performing penances assigned to remit the pains of purgatory. At its root meaning, *poenitentia* was a change of mind that led to a change of behaviour.[99] Hence,

---

potestatem solvendi et ligandi, id est, ostendendi homines ligatos vel solutos', Peter the Lombard, *Sententiae*, li. 4, dist. 18, [ca. 5–6], CGC I, 144v; 'Legimus in levitico de leprosis, ubi iubentur ut ostendant se sacerdotibus, et si lepram habuerint, tunc a sacerdote immundi fiant, non quo sacerdotes leprosos faciant et immundos, sed quo habeant notitiam leprosi, et non leprosi, et possint discernere qui mundus quive immundus sit. Quomodo ergo ibi leprosum sacerdos mundum vel immundum facit, sic et hic alligat, vel soluit episcopus, et presbyter', Jerome, *In Matthaeum*, ca. 16, CGC I, 137v [Bodius, *Unio* (1532), fols. 137v–138r], cf. 'Collectanea', Cotton MS Cleop. E.v. fol. 69.

[97] 'Remittuntur peccata per dei verbum cuius levites interpres, et quidam exsecutor est', Ambrose, *De Cain et Abel*, CGC I, 138v [Bodius, *Unio* (1532), fol. 138v]; 'Verbum dei dimittit peccata, sacerdos est iudex. Sacerdos quidem officium suum exhibet, sed nullius potestatis iura exercet', Peter the Lombard, *Sententiae*, li. 4, dist. [18, ca. 4], CGC I, 144v.

[98] 'Regnum enim caelorum dicuntur Scripturae, quia in illis insertum regnum caelorum. Ianua intellectus earum . . . Clavicularii autem sunt sacerdotes, quibus creditum est verbum docendi et interpretandi scripturas. Clavis autem est verbum scientiae scripturarum per quam aperitur hominibus ianua veritatis', Chrysostom, *In opere imperfecto*, ca. 23, CGC I, 136v [Bodius, *Unio* (1532), fol. 140r]; cf. 'Quos clavis scientiae erudierit ad salutem', a summary of Ambrose, *Sermo de Petro et Paulo*, CGC I, 139r.

[99] 'In graeco sane, poenitentiae nomen, non ex delicti confessione, sed ex animi demutatione compositum est,' Tertullian, *Adversus Marcionem*, li. 3, CGC I, 134r; 'Quem enim facti sui poenitet, errorem suum pristinum intelligit. Ideoque graeci melius et significantius μετανοιαν dicunt, quam nos latine possumus dicere, resipiscentiam', Lactantius, [*Divinae institutiones*], li. 6, ca. 24, CGC I, 134v. 'Quando sic poenites, ut tibi amarum sapiat in animo, quod ante dulce fuit in vita, et quod te prius oblectabat in corpore, ipsum te cruciat in mente', Augustine, *Sermo 3*, De nativitate domini, CGC I, 139r [Bodius, *Unio* (1532), fol. 135v];

true repentance was simply to desist from sin.[100] According
to a gloss on Acts 20: 26 recorded in 'De poenitentia I', since
St Paul demanded works of repentance from the newly
baptized or converted, these works were not those works
'which the scholastics call *satisfactoria'*.[101]

An extract from the *Assertio septem sacramentorum*
recorded in 'De satisfactione' noted the difference between
the Protestant and Catholic approaches to satisfaction.
According to the *King's Book* (i.e. the *Assertio*), Luther
believed that satisfaction was simply amendment of life.
Augustine, however, taught that the penitent needed to
make satisfaction to God through the sacrifice of a contrite
heart, co-operating with alms and fasts. He was to place
himself under the judgement of the priest to do what he was
told in order to recover the life of his soul. For the penitent
was bound by the power of the keys to perform the
satisfactions which the priest had assigned.[102] Consistent
with the Protestant theological agenda of the great notebooks, 'De satisfactione' attempted to gather patristic evidence in support of Luther's view on satisfaction while
accounting for other quotations to the contrary like that
cited by the *Assertio*.

Some time after the compilation of 'De satisfactione', a

'Crucifixio quippe interioris hominis, poenitentiae dolores intelliguntur . . . Et ideo
per talem crucem evacuatur corpus peccati, ut iam non exhibeamus membra nostra
iniquitatis peccato', Augustine, *De trinitate*, li. 4, ca. 3, CGC I, 140v.

[100] 'Vera poenitentia est, iam cessare a peccato', Anselm, *In epistolam ad
Corinthios secundam*, ca. 2, CGC I, 144r; 'Agere poenitentiam nihil aliud est
quam profiteri et affirmare se, ulterius non peccaturum', Lactantius, [*Divinae
institutiones*], li. 6, ca. 13, CGC I, 134v; 'Sufficit enim ei ob magnam misericordiam
suam, ut desistamus a peccatis', Chrysostom, *In Genesim*, Homilia 5, CGC I, 136v.

[101] 'In omni regione Iudaea et gentibus annuntiabam, ut poenitentiam agerent et
converterentur ad deum, digna poenitentiae opera facientes. Ecce Paulus a
baptizatis sive conversis exigit opera poenitentiae, ergo opera poenitentiae non
sunt illa opera, quae scholastici vocant satisfactoria', CGC I, 133v.

[102] 'Quia videtur Lutherus eo urgere, ut poenitens tantum ingrediatur novam
vitam, ac negligat a sacerdote pro commissorum satisfactione suscipere poenitentiam, audiamus quid . . . scribat sanctissimus Augustinus. 'Non sufficit (inquit)
mores in melius commutare . . . nisi etiam . . . satisfaciat domino . . . per contriti
cordis sacrificium, cooperantibus eleemosinis et ieiuniis. Et mox. ponat se
poenitens (inquit) omnino in iudicio sacerdotis . . . ut omnia eo iubente, paratus
sit facere, pro recipienda vita animae . . . Et mox. Ligant quoque (inquit)
sacerdotes, dum satisfactionem poenitentiae confitentibus imponunt, solvunt',
'*Liber regis*' [*Assertio septem sacramentorum*], De satisfactione, CGC I, 166r.

lengthy excerpt on satisfaction from the *Antididagma* (1544) was appended to the collection. Like the effect of chiaroscuro, this text's greater definition of sixteenth-century Catholic teaching makes the contrasting Protestant orientation of most of the remaining quotations more clearly visible. According to this final entry, the Catholic church had 'at all times' taught two kinds of satisfaction: propitiation by which *culpa* was blotted out and eternal punishment was taken away, and this satisfaction Christ alone was able to perform; and ecclesiastical discipline which was imposed by those with the cure of souls in sacramental penance. The latter had efficacy only because of the former, for no human work was acceptable in God's sight on its own merit, but solely on account of the merit of Christ made available to his people through contrition. Satisfactions imposed by the priest had three purposes: (i) to pluck out the roots of sin; (ii) to remove or at least diminish temporal punishments owed for sin through the power of Christ's blood and by the merit of his passion, since God did not always remit both the *culpa* and *poena* owed for sin simultaneously; (iii) to satisfy the injury done to the church by public crimes.[103]

Despite the inclusion of this trenchant presentation of Catholic teaching, the bulk of quotations in 'De satisfactione' expounded in greater detail the Protestant position already briefly presented in 'De poenitentia I'. Only God

---

[103] 'Docuit omni tempore in ecclesia catholica, duplicem esse satisfactionem. Unam propitiatoriam et reconciliatoriam, qua et culpa deleatur, et poena auferetur aeterna. Hanc soli Christo acceptam referre oportet . . . Aliam canonicam et disciplinarem, quae ab hiis qui curam gerunt animarum . . . imponatur . . . De hac semper docuerunt patres. Primo quod evellat radices peccatorum sanetque infirmitates post peccatum in carne haerentes. Deinde quod virtute sanguinis et merito passionis Christi auferat, aut saltem minuat, poenam temporalem peccatis nostris debitam. Ac denique utendum ea esse ad satisfaciendum matri ecclesiae, publicis criminibus laesae et iniuriam passae . . . Constat praeterea non semper cum peccati remissione simul remitti et poenam peccatis debitam . . . Quapropter sancti patres frequenter hoc modo loquuntur, peccata et poenas peccatis ipsis debitas compensari, purificari, operiri, et reconciliari, operibus satisfactionis. Non quidem quod sua dignitate remissionem peccatorum mereantur, sed ideo quia, deo placent: ut quae fiant ab illis, quos deus in gratiam propter contritionem de peccatis recepit. Et hoc merito Christi, a quo istiusmodi opera omnia meritum suum mutuantur', 'Capitulum Coloniense', [*Antididagma*], CGC I, 166v–167r.

could know what sort of punishment each sin deserved;[104] and he sought out the sinner to restore him, not to punish him, to find him not so as to beat him but to bear him on his shoulders back to the flock.[105] As a result, divine forgiveness was total, with no scar or vestige of sin's guilt remaining; for the blood of Jesus availed for a complete deliverance.[106] God promised to remember the sins of the forgiven no more. How could he continue to exact a punishment for them afterwards?[107] Since the execution of God's wrath made sin to cease, God's just demand for punishment was fully met in the repentance of the truly penitent.[108] According to Calvin, no distinction existed between mortal and venial sins. Consequently, if works of satisfaction were required to remit temporal punishments, no one could have a quiet conscience, for even in the most righteous sins multiplied much faster than satisfactions could be performed for them.[109] Rather, God justified the ungodly by his Word

---

[104] 'Qualis autem et quanta poena cuique culpae debeatur, divini iudicii est, non humani', Augustine, *De natura boni contra Manichaeos*, ca. 9, CGC I, 159v.

[105] 'Cernis vero quod reduxit, quod non flagellavit, sed ferens in humeris, rursus gregi reddidit . . . Quod non modo poenas non exigit, sed ad errantium inquisitionem proficiscitur', Chrysostom, *Homilia 10*, CGC I, 156r.

[106] 'Deus autem cum delet peccata, neque cicatricem relinquit neque promittit remanere vestigium, sed cum sanitate, pulchritudinem quoque restituit, cum liberatione a poena dat et iustitiam, et praevaricatum, non praevaricato similem reddit', Chrysostom, *Sermo ad populum de poenitentia*, Homilia Ultima, CGC I, 154v; 'Sic enim delet peccata deus, ut neque eorum vestigium maneat', Chrysostom, *De poenitentia*, Homilia 3, CGC I, 155r; 'Valeat mihi ad perfectionem liberationis tantum pretium sanguinis domini mei', Augustine, *In Psalmum 25*, CGC I, 161r.

[107] 'Quis confunditur confiteri peccata, ut solvat peccata? Num propter hoc iubet confiteri te ut puniat? Non ut puniat, sed ut ignoscat . . . Ecce ego sum deus, qui deleo iniquitates tuas, et numquam memorabor. Vides? Ego numquam memorabor, inquit, hoc misericordiae fuerit', Chrysostom, *Sermo de poenitentia et satisfactione*, CGC I, 153; 'Peccatorum non recordari, est, ea non postulare ad poenam . . . Certe si punit Deus peccata, imputat, si vindicat, recordatur', Calvin, *Institutio* (1536), CGC I, 163r, *CR* xxix. 170.

[108] 'Necesse est ut vindicetur in impium, vindicetur in iniustum, sive convertat se, sive se non convertat. Si enim se converterit, hoc ipsum in illo vindicatur quod periit iniquitas', Augustine, *In Psalmum 36*, Concio 2, CGC I, 161r.

[109] 'Cum tamen assidue peccatum veniale, et mortale, in ore habeant, nondum alterum ab altero discernere potuerunt', Calvin, *Institutio* (1536), CGC I, 162v, *CR* xxix. 169; 'Quae istaec [erit] pacificatio, si audiat peccata redimi satisfactionibus? Quando tandem illi satisfactionis modus constare poterit?' ibid., CGC I, 162r; 'Si unius d[i]ei est, satisfactio peccati unius, dum illam meditantur, septies peccant (loquor de iustissimis) si ad septem satisfactiones se accingunt, cumulabunt 49 peccata', ibid., CGC I, 162v, *CR* xxix. 170.

alone, without inflicting punishment. On that basis Christians could approach the throne of glory with all assurance.[110] Full pardon required only confessing in faith[111] and repenting of sin.[112] Afterwards followed works indicative of a changed life, the fruit of repentance, chief among these being love out of gratitude for free pardon.[113] For, according to Calvin, 'by faith we gain pardon, and we give thanks and

[110] 'Sed tu fortasse timeas eam, quam facere venit delictorum purgationem . . . Audi, agnus [i.e. agnus dei qui tollit peccata mundi] est in mansuetudine, venit cum lana et lacte, verbo solo iustificans impium . . . Ut quid ergo deinceps haesitemus fratres et non omni fiducia ad thronum gloriae ascendamus', Bernard, *Sermo natalis Johannis Baptistae*, CGC I, 161v. Cf. 'Quid est remissio, merae liberalitatis domini [recte, donum]?', Calvin, *Institutio* (1536), CGC I, 161v, *CR* xxix. 168.

[111] 'Dic peccavi, et solvisti peccatum, ut in Davide', Chrysostom, *Homilia 9*, CGC I, 156r; 'Sola opus sit voluntate ac fide, non laboribus ac sudoribus', Chrysostom, [*In Matthaeum*], Homilia 11, CGC I, 157v; 'Ostendit difficultatem legis, fidei facilitate mutandam. Non iam (inquit) ad iustificationem merendam, sudores peccatoris imminentes et labores, sed gratia omnibus occurrit, ac venia plurimo salutis plena compendio', Chrysostom, *In Matthaeum*, Homilia 10, CGC I, 157r; 'Ideo et in eo qui debebat decem milia talenta ut procideret, et in eo qui patrimonium consumperat, solo reditu, et in ove sola, ut portaretur, voluntate contentus fuit', Chrysostom, *In epistolam primam ad Corinthios*, Homilia 23, CGC I, 157r. 'Peccato meo quod multum est, (quia et in via non deest offencio) sacrificio contribulati spiritus propitiaberis', Augustine, *In Psalmum 24*, CGC I, 161r.

[112] 'Num aliud quaero quam ut quiescat a peccato tantum, et sistat mala? Num pro praeteritis rationem exigo? Si videam resipiscentes? Num si videam convertentes differo? . . . Unum enim tantum requiro, nempe ut confiteantur peccata, et ab eis abstineant, et non ultro inferam poenam peccatis', Chrysostom, *In Genesim*, Homilia 44, CGC I, 156v; 'Recedens a pristinis malis, ex animo, vereque promittat deo, se postea numquam ad illa rediturum, nihil aliud deus requirat ad satisfactionem ulteriorem', Chrysostom, *Oratio de Beato Philogomo*, CGC I, 156v; 'Incipe tantummodo orare, atque ad ipsum redire, et recipies profecto cuncta, et confestim omnem iram poenamque restingues', Chrysostom, *In Matthaeum*, Homilia 23, CGC I, 157r; 'Habemus advocatum . . . pro peccatis nostris . . . si modo . . . intelligentes delicta nostra . . . nos ambulare in viis eius, et praecepta eius metuere spondemus', Cyprian, li. 4, *Epistola 4*, CGC I, 152v.

[113] 'Non enim pristinis tantum malis desistere, sed etiam meliora sequi officia, dicitur poenitentia. Dicitur enim, declina a malo et fac bonum', Chrysostom, *Sermo ad populum de poenitentia*, Homila Ultima, CGC I, 155r; 'Facite fructus dignos poenitentiae. Quo autem modo fructificare poterimus? Si utique peccatis adversa faciamus', Chrysostom, *In Matthaeum*, ca. 3, CGC I, 157v; 'Subjicit Dominus: Hinc agnosce, remissa esse huic mulieri peccata, quia dilexit multum. Quibus verbis (ut vides) eius dilectionem non facit causam remissionis peccatorum, sed probationem, sunt enim sumpta a simili eius debitoris, cui remissa erant quingenta, cui non dixit, ideo remissa, quia multum dilexisset, sed ideo multum diligere, quia remissa sunt', Calvin, *Institutio* (1536), CGC I, 165r, *CR* xxix. 173–4. Cf. 'Dicit flagitiosos sola resipiscentia, sive solo reditu expiari. Charitate operante peccatorum multitudine[m]', a summary of Augustine, *Contra Cresconium grammaticum*, li. 3, ca. 19, 23, 24, li. 4, ca. 11 and *Contra secundam Gaudentii epistolam*, ca. 4, CGC I, 160v.

testify to the Lord's kindness by love'.[114] As we have seen, such was Cranmer's description of the relationship between faith and love in his annotations to Henry.[115]

Catholic teaching, however, was not without support from Scripture and tradition. Therefore, 'De satisfactione' also included extracts which offered a Protestant explanation for two of the most prominent examples: Scripture's story of the death of David's son by Bathsheba as evidence for God's loosing of *culpa* but inflicting of *poena*, and the substantial patristic testimony to the necessity of satisfaction for gaining forgiveness of sin after baptism. In the first case, any temporal pains sent by God on the forgiven were merely exercises to strengthen faith and prevent relapsing into past errors.[116] Although forgiven, David suffered the death of his child with Bathsheba 'so that the man's piety might be exercised and approved in that humble condition'.[117] In the second case, as Calvin essentially admitted,[118] Catholics could find support for the necessity of satisfaction for the forgiveness of both venial and mortal sins in many patristic writers, and 'De satisfactione' included several such examples.[119]

---

[114] 'Fides, inquit, tua te salvam fecit, fide igitur remissionem assequimur, charitate gratias agimus et Domini beneficentiam testamur', Calvin, *Institutio* (1536), CGC I, 165r, *CR* xxix. 174.

[115] See earlier in this chapter.

[116] 'Res quarum reatum (ne post hanc vitam obsint) deus soluit, tamen eas certamen fidei sinit manere . . . Ante remissionem esse illa supplicia peccatorum, post remissionem autem certamina, exercitationesque iustorum', Augustine, *De peccatorum meritis et remissione*, li. 2, ca. 33–4, CGC I, 158v; 'Imponit poenam, non exigens supplicium de peccatis, sed ad futura nos corrigens', Chrysostom, *Sermo de poenitentia et satisfactione*, CGC I, 154r; 'Hoc est, dum nos filii dei, manu coelestis patris affligimur, non haec poena est, qua confundamur, sed castigatio, qua erudiamur', Calvin, *Institutio* (1536), CGC I, 163v, *CR* xxix. 172.

[117] 'Ut pietas hominis in illa humilitate exerceretur atque probaretur', Augustine, *De peccatorum meritis et remissione*, li. 2, ca. 34, CGC I, 159r. Cf. 'Nam peccati quidem noxam Davidi, gratis remisit, sed quia tam ad publicum omnium saeculorum exemplum, tam ad Davidis quoque humiliationem pertinebat, tale facinus non impunitum manere, ipsum flagello suo asperrime castigavit', Calvin, *Institutio* (1536), CGC I, 164r, *CR* xxix. 172.

[118] 'Parum autem me movent, quae in veterum scriptis de satisfactione passim occurrunt. Video quidem eorum nonnullos (dicam simpliciter, omnes fere, quorum libri extant) hac in parte lapsos esse', Calvin, *Institutio* (1536), CGC I, 165r, *CR* xxix. 174.

[119] 'Quia quomodo nullus dies est, in quo homo possit esse, sine peccato, sic nullo die debet esse sine satisfactionis remedio', Augustine, *In Apocalypsim*,

Since the call for satisfaction by the fathers could not be denied, other quotations were recorded that offered an alternative explanation of the practice. Augustine had described two kinds of *poenitentia* in the church: private repentance for daily sins of human frailty, and public penance by those excommunicated for serious offences so that they might be worthy of reconciliation to the community.[120] The purpose of alms, fasting, and prayer in the case of private repentance was to heal the sin. A further quotation suggested that satisfactions promoted this healing by rooting out the causes of sin and strengthening the penitent's resistance to sinful suggestions.[121] In the case of public penance, satisfactions imposed on the excommunicated had an additional role, to assure the church that the offender was truly penitent.[122] Calvin cited the second role

Homilia 2, CGC I, 160v; 'Sordes postmodum quascumque contrahimus, eleemosinis abluamus . . . Et quia semel in baptismo remissio peccatorum datur, assidua et iugis operatio, baptisma instar imitata, dei rursus indulgentiam largitur', Cyprian, *De eleemosina*, CGC I, 152r; 'Oportet satisfactionibus et lamentationibus iustis delicta redimere, et vulnera lachrimis abluere', Cyprian, *Epistola 3*, li. 1, CGC I, 153r; 'Possunt agentes poenitentiam veram, deo patri ad misericordiam precibus et operibus suis satisfacere', Cyprian, *Epistola 14*, li. 3, CGC I, 153r; 'Sed et maculas ex peccato, per sedulam orationem, et voluntatum dei meditationem perseverantem exterere poterimus', Basil, *Li. quest. 6*, CGC I, 153r; 'Et quia post acceptam gratuitam misericordiam peccaverunt, non iam gratis, sed interveniente gemitu et fletu, possint ad indulgentiam pervenire', Augustine, *Quaestiones de utroque testamentis mixtis*, q. 102, CGC I, 158r; 'Per eleemosinas de peccatis praeteritis est propitiandus deus . . . miserando deleat iam facta, si non satisfactio congrua, negligatur', Augustine, *Enchiridion*, ca. 69, CGC I, 159v; 'Quicquid autem post eam quae fit in baptismo ablutionem peccatorum, in hac vita manendo peccamus . . . misericordiae sacrificiis expietur', Augustine, *Epistola 54* (Modern Order [henceforth MO]: 153), CGC I, 160r.

[120] 'Agunt etiam homines poenitentiam, si post baptismum ita peccaverint, ut excommunicari, et postea reconciliari mereantur. Sicut agunt in omnibus ecclesiis, illi qui proprie poenitentes appellantur . . . Est etiam poenitentia bonorum et humilium fidelium poena quotidiana', Augustine, *Epistola 108* (MO: 265), CGC I, 160.

[121] 'Dimitte nobis debita nostra sicut et nos dimittimus . . . dicitur . . . de hiis quae quotidie de saeculi amarissimis fructibus humanae vitae infirmitas contrahit. Quibus curandis, adhibentur medicamenta eleemosinarum, ieiuniorum, et orationum', Augustine, *Contra epistolam parmeniani*, li. 2, ca. 10, CGC I, 151v; 'Satisfactio poenitentiae, est causas peccatorum excidere, nec earum suggestionibus aditum indulgere', Augustine (recte, Gennadius of Marseilles), *De ecclesiasticis dogmatibus*, ca. 54, CGC I, 159v. For a discussion of Gennadius, see Chapter 5.

[122] 'Verum quia plerumque dolor alterius cordis, occultus est alteri . . . recte constituuntur ab hiis qui ecclesiae praesunt, tempora poenitentiae, ut fiat etiam satis ecclesiae', Augustine, *Enchiridion*, ca. 65, CGC I, 160r.

as evidence that the fathers 'for the most part called satisfaction not a payment to be rendered to God but a public testimony' for the benefit of the church.[123] Therefore, 'De satisfactione' included two traditional definitions of satisfaction: (i) 'a punishment voluntarily assumed to placate divine animosity'; and (ii) 'a voluntary restitution of an equivalent owed to others'.[124] However, a preponderance of its quotations would suggest that only the second applied to Christians, as the first was accomplished by Christ alone.

When taken together, Cranmer's 'Annotations', his 'Great Commonplaces' and 'De sacramentis' offer a clear picture of his contribution to the theological debate in the Henrician court. The 'Annotations' detailed his soteriology: (i) justification by imputed righteousness through faith; (ii) concomitant regeneration through the imparting of the Holy Spirit; (iii) a renewed will to love producing an amended life as a consequence of the Spirit's indwelling presence; (iv) assurance of perseverance because those who were justified were also the elect. His 'Great Commonplaces' recorded the patristic scholarship he employed in defence of his Protestant doctrine, while noting some of the views of his opponents. Lastly, 'De sacramentis' outlined his shared strategy for incorporating solifidianism into the formularies of the Church of England *circa* 1537.

In the end, however, the divines decided to maintain the Henrician *status quo* and to carry over to the *Bishops' Book* essentially the same description of penance agreed upon in The Ten Articles.[125] By including what was important to

---

[123] 'Vocarunt enim, ut plurimum, satisfactionem, non compensationem quae deo redderetur, sed publicam testificationem, qua qui excommunicatione mulctati fuerant . . . se prioris vitae, vere et ex animo, pertaesos esse approbarent, vel potius priorum memoriam obliterarent, atque ita dicebantur, non deo, sed ecclesiae satisfacere', Calvin, *Institutio* (1536), CGC I, 165v, *CR* xxix. 174.

[124] 'Satisfactio est poena, voluntarie assumpta, ad placandam divinam offensam. Satisfactio est redditio voluntaria aequivalentis, alias indebiti', CGC I, 166r.

[125] All references appropriate to the royal promulgation of The Ten Articles were modified to be suitable for the episcopal origin of the *Bishops' Book*, the Latin Bible quotations were deleted so as to leave their English translations standing alone, and three brief phrases inserted (bracketed words being deleted and italicized words added): (i) 'in like manner you *be* now *bound, and* must give and apply yourselves wholly to justice'; (ii) 'and *God by his prophet Zacharye* [Zacharias the prophet] saith'; (iii) 'and by the selfsame good works to exercise and confirm their faith and hope, and [look for] *to ascertain them, that they shall for the same good*

both conservatives and Reformers, this compromise formula became, as Gardiner said, 'a common storehouse, where every man layd uppe in store suche ware as he lyked, and could tell wheare to fynde to serve his purpose'.[126] The conservatives made sure that sacramental penance was instituted by Christ and necessary for salvation, that works of charity besides faith were necessary for salvation and that penance would lessen earthly punishments from God. Yet, the Reformers had managed to redefine the traditional tripartite division of penance. Justification by faith replaced forgiveness based on meritorious contrition, and amendment of life replaced satisfactions for avoiding purgatory. In keeping with the doctrinal discussions with the Germans, the article's use of clearly Lutheran language is striking. Contrition was defined as a sense of desperation in the penitent at being under God's judgement with 'no works or merits of his own, which he may worthily lay before God, as sufficient for his sins'. 'Certain faith' needed to join with this contrition so that God would 'repute him justified' solely for the merits of the blood and passion of Jesus the Saviour, and this faith came from hearing Christ's promises in Scripture. The purpose of confession was to apply the promises of God's grace and favour to the penitent, not to judge him. Lastly, the penitent was to believe that the words of absolution spoken by the ministers were the 'very words and voice of God', as in the Augsburg Confession.[127]

Although the debate surrounding the *Bishops' Book* had failed to modify the official Henrician description of sacramental penance further toward the Lutheran line, Cranmer

---

works [to] receive at God's hand mitigation and remission of the miseries, calamities, and grevious punishments'; Lloyd, *Formularies*, pp. xx–xxv, 96–100. The article on justification had only two brief insertions as well: (i) 'That sinners attain this justification by contrition and faith, joined with charity, after such sort and manner as is before mentioned and declared *in the sacrament of penance*'; (ii) 'Wherefore [we will that all bishops and preachers shall instruct and teach our people committed by us unto their spiritual charge] *all good Christian people must understand and believe certainly*, that God necessarily requireth of us to do good works', ibid., pp. xxvi–xxvii, 209–10.

[126] Muller, *Letters of Gardiner*, 351.

[127] 'Docentur homines, ut absolutionem plurimi faciant, quia sit vox Dei et mandato Dei pronuntietur', AC, Pt. II, art. 4, p. 275.

continued to work against the remaining precepts of the old order. During the second round of Lutheran negotiations in 1538 which produced The Thirteen Articles, Cranmer's annotations to the article on penance consistently replaced 'necessary' and 'most necessary' with 'beneficial' and 'most beneficial'. He added that 'the person whose conscience is afflicted by one or more sins should seek consolation, counsel, and absolution individually from a priest and not neglect something so healing'.[128] Hence, 'although it is not commanded in the Scriptures, nevertheless, [it ought to be retained] for the aforementioned reasons'.[129]

Cranmer's policy would not bear any meaningful fruit, however, until the most unlikely of circumstances. During the debate on The Six Articles in 1539, Norfolk put the following question to the House of Lords, 'Whether auricular confession be necessary by divine law'.[130] No doubt drawing upon the patristic scholarship recorded in his great notebooks, Cranmer argued for three days in Convocation that auricular confession was not necessary by scriptural injunction for salvation but very requisite and expedient nonetheless to be observed and used for encouraging the spiritual health of God's people.[131] On this point, at least, Cranmer carried the day, for nothing could make the Henrician regime's rejection of the priestly power of the keys more clear than to deny the necessity of auricular confession for the remission of sin. Not surprisingly, the

---

[128] 'Ut cujus conscientia de peccato uno aut pluribus affligitur, is consolationem, consilium, et absolutionem singulatim a sacerdote petere, et rem tam salutarem non negligere debeat', Cox II, 477.

[129] 'Necessaria', 'summe necessaria', 'commoda', 'commodissima', ibid., 476–7; e.g. 'verum etiam valde utilem ac summe necessariam [Cranmer: commodissimam] esse dicimus peccatorum confessionem, quae auricularis dicitur, et privatim fit ministris ecclesiae', ibid., 476; 'Licet non sit praecepta in scripturis tamen praedictis de causis', ibid., 477. Cf. 'A penitent man can have no remission of his sins, but by supplication of the priest', a comment in Cranmer's collection of errors in canon law; ibid., 75. For the dating of this collection to 1533–5, see Ayris, 'Canon Law Studies', in Ayris and Selwyn, *Churchman and Scholar*, 316–22, at 316–17.

[130] 'Utrum Auricularis Confessio sit necessaria, de Jure Divino', *Journals of the House of Lords*, i. 109 [House of Lords Records Office MS LJ i. 321]; Glyn Redworth, 'A Study in the Formulation of Policy: The Genesis and Evolution of the Act of Six Articles', *Journal of Ecclesiastical History* 37 (1986), 42–67, at 53.

[131] *LP* xiv(i). 1065(3); for a fine description of the debate and its consequences, see Redworth, 'Six Articles', 58–63.

king was convinced. In the end, the actual statute read, 'that auricular confession is expedient and necessarie to be retayned and contynued, used and frequented in the Churche of God'.[132] In Henry's realm confession to a priest was no longer to be considered the divinely ordained means of forgiveness, but rather simply a helpful spiritual practice required for the well-ordering of his church. After losing the debate, Cuthbert Tunstall sent Henry a brief in an attempt to change his mind.[133] The king wrote a stinging rebuke, peevishly remarking that Tunstall's position had already been shown to be inadequate 'by the bishope of Cantorbury and me'.[134] Henry noted that none of the authorities quoted by Tunstall required confession, each only commended the practice: 'exemplum dicit, non praeceptum'.[135] Although the change of wording may appear to be of 'small practical importance',[136] in the context of the Henrician church this departure from Catholic orthodoxy removed a significant barrier to justification by faith.

Even as Cranmer's gradual redefinition of sacramental penance came the closest to success in The Six Articles, an entry in 'De poenitentia I' indicates that Cranmer was already studying Calvin's rejection of penance as a sacrament. By defining *poenitentia* as contrition and faith and then applying this definition to the sacrament, Cranmer had been able to make auricular confession the context for the Protestant process of justification. Calvin, however, denied the Lutheran definition of *poenitentia*, cutting the crucial link between the sacrament and solifidianism as a result:

[Paul] lists repentance and faith as two different things . . . Although repentance and faith are held together by a permanent bond, they are to be yoked together rather than confused. And so,

[132] 31 Hen. VIII. c. 14, *Statutes of the Realm*, ed. Alexander Luders et al. (London: 1810–28), iii. 740; Redworth, 'Six Articles', 61–3.

[133] BL Cotton MS Cleop. E.v. fols. 134–7; reprinted in Gilbert Burnet, *The History of the Reformation of the Church of England*, ed. Nicholas Pocock (Oxford: Clarendon Press, 1865) [henceforth referred to as Burnet], iv. 400–4.

[134] BL Cotton MS Cleop. E.v. fol. 131r; Burnet iv. 405.

[135] 'He says example, not precept'; Henry's annotation to Tunstall's brief; BL Cotton MS Cleop. E.v. fol. 134v; Burnet iv. 400 n. 54.

[136] Charles Sturge, *Cuthbert Tunstal: Churchman, Scholar, Statesman, Administrator* (London: Longmans Green, 1938), 217.

in my judgement, repentance is mortification of our flesh and of the old man, which true and pure fear of God brings about in us.[137]

That Cranmer eventually adopted this Reformed approach and decided to seek to free justification entirely from sacramental penance can be inferred from the 1540 survey on the sacraments. When asked whether John 20: 23 required a man 'to confess his secret deadly sins to a priest', Cranmer maintained his previous position that a man might but he did not have to do so. However, when asked to discuss the sacraments, he failed to describe penance in Lutheran terms of contrition, faith, and the promise of absolution. Instead, Cranmer replied:

Of penaunce also I finde in the scripture, Whereby synners after baptisme returnyng holly vnto god be accepted againe vnto goddes favour and mercye, But the scripture speaketh not of penaunce as we call yt a sacrament, consistyng in iii partes | Contrition | Confession | and Satisfaction, but the scripture taketh penaunce for a pure Conversion of a synner in harte and mynde frome his synnes vnto god, makyng no mention of priuate Confession of all deadly synnes to a preiste, nor of ecclesiasticall satisfaction to be enioyned by hym[138]

Thus, in the same year as the Henrician court became notably more conservative with the fall of Cromwell, Cranmer seems to have grown more Reformed, a combination that would make his final years under Henry a continuing battle to preserve the early gains toward Protestantism—a fight fraught often with failure and more often with fear.

---

[137] '[Paulus] tanquam duo diversa, poenitentiam et fidem enumerat . . . Ita poenitentia et fides quanquam perpetuo inter se vinculo cohaerent magis tamen coniungendae sunt, quam confundendae. Est itaque meo quidem iudicio poenitentia, carnis nostrae, veterisque hominis mortificatio, quam in nobis efficit, verus ac sincerus timor dei', Calvin, *Institutio* (1536), CGC I, 142, *CR* xxix. 149.

[138] LPL MS 1108, fol. 71v.

5

Being Made 'Right-Willed' by Faith: Justification in 'Cranmer's Great Commonplaces' *circa* 1544

Qui iam conversus ad deum, peccavisse ex animo dolet, et correctionem vitae melioris firmam in animo habet, omnem peccandi voluntatem abiecit, cur non iam iustus sit? Cum quicquid vitii adhuc supersit, ex infirmitate habeat, non ex animi malitia?[1]

The events of 1543 proved a severe reversal for Cranmer's modest progress towards incorporating justification by faith into the formularies of the Henrician church. The conspiracy against him by the prebendaries of his own cathedral, and then his arrest in the Privy Council, clearly conveyed the insecurity of Cranmer's position. He was utterly dependent for survival on the good will of a king who was reluctant to advance as far in the new religion as had his archbishop.[2] While Henry was openly supportive of Cranmer as a person, the new formulary issued that spring in the king's name explicitly repudiated his solifidian position. Instead, the *King's Book* taught a doctrine of preparation for sanctifying grace through good works inspired by prevenient grace in a manner reminiscent of Fisher's Augustinian-influenced *via attritionis formatae*, albeit without scholastic terminology.[3] Fisher's approach to justification proved persuasive for two reasons. Firstly, divine sanction

---

[1] 'He who now has turned to God, grieves from his heart to have sinned, and he has in his heart a firm amendment of a better life—he has rejected all will to sin. Why is he not already just? For whatever of fault still remains, he has from infirmity, not from the wickedness of his heart', CGC II, 225v.

[2] MacCulloch, *Cranmer*, 296–322; Ridley, *Cranmer*, 229–45; Bromiley, *Cranmer, Archbishop and Martyr*, 54–7.

[3] According to Gardiner, the members of the committee that drew up the *King's Book* were Day, Heath, Thirlby, Cox, Robinson, and Redman; Muller, *Letters of Gardiner*, 365. For Redman's association with St John's College, Cambridge, and Fisher, see Leader, *Cambridge*, 331 n. 42, 341–2.

for the necessity of obedience to authority was the doctrinal touchstone of the Henrician Reformation.[4] In a system of justification *ex merito de congruo* acts of obedience and spiritual merit leading to eternal salvation were inseparably intertwined. Secondly, because these good works arose from prevenient grace, the conservatives were able to provide a credible alternative to Cranmer's insistence that only salvation *sola fide* was salvation *sola gratia*. John Redman's *De iustificatione* summed up the conservatives' understanding of justification through grace and human responsibility:

This is how we understand 'we are justified by grace' or 'everything ought [to be attributed] to grace alone': Justification does not happen in us without the movement of our own will, but that God by grace alone coming before and preparing our will through penance and living faith, that is, joined to charity, effects justification in us.[5]

Thus, unlike the *Bishops' Book*, the *King's Book* taught an Augustinian-influenced scholastic system of two graces, two faiths, and two merits; the first, lesser set operating prior to justification; the second, fully pleasing set working in the justified. Having failed to persuade Henry otherwise, Cranmer subscribed.[6]

Ever the scholar, however, Cranmer responded to this defeat by continuing to gather evidence to discredit the soteriology of the conservatives and to defend his own.[7] Recording extracts from the Bible and Augustine, Cranmer used his great notebooks to delineate in more detail the arguments for solifidianism he had previously outlined to Henry in his 'Annotations'. Firstly, works done before justification had neither saving grace nor saving faith to make them pleasing in God's eyes. Secondly, in justification God pardoned sin by imputing Christ's alien righteousness

---

[4] Rex, *Henry and the Reformation*, 25–6; Rex, 'Crisis of Obedience', 863–94.

[5] 'Gratiam autem nos iustificare aut soli gratiae omnia deberi, sic intelligimus, non quod sine nostrae voluntatis motu et assensu, iustificatio in nobis fiat Sed quod deus ex sola gratia voluntatem nostram praeveniens et praeparans per poenitentiam et fidem vivam, id est charitati coniunctam iustificationem in nobis efficiat', John Redman, *De iustificatione*, LPL MS 1107, fols. 137–59, at 144v. For the relationship between *De iustificatione* and Cranmer, see the Appendix.

[6] Muller, *Letters of Gardiner*, 329, 336.

[7] See the Appendix.

to the ungodly, not by infusing in them an inherent personal merit. Concomitant with this externally based justification was an intrinsic renovation of the will and its affections by the indwelling of the Holy Spirit. Nevertheless, the Spirit's presence and the love he stirred in the believer's heart did not constitute a personal righteousness meritorious *de condigno*. When used in a broader sense to refer to both pardon and renewal, justification could be said to make the ungodly 'right-willed' but never inherently righteous. Lastly, justification could never be contingent on either human preparation or personal merit because salvation was ultimately by unconditional predestination of God's elect.

SAVING GRACE

The linchpin by which the conservatives joined merit and grace in justification was the doctrine of the *auxilium Dei speciale*. According to the *King's Book*, human beings 'cannot eschew sin, except they be illumined and made free by an especial grace, that is to say, by a supernatural help and working of the Holy Ghost'. Because of his goodness, God offers this prevenient grace 'to all men, yet they only enjoy it which by their freewill do accept and embrace the same'. By this special assistance any sinner was able to turn back to God through doing works of penance. Although he was not yet 'to be accounted a justified man', by using the grace he had available to him, the penitent put himself 'in a good way'. If he continued to 'seek for further grace' eventually he would 'attain his justification'.[8]

In the commentary on folios 225–6 Cranmer recognized that the nature of salvific grace was the root issue of the soteriological debates:

According to the writer Augustine, Scripture speaks only of justifying grace which is spread in our hearts through the Holy Spirit. The Pelagians invented another grace, indeed, the grace of free will or nature. The Scholastics fashioned a third middle grace, which, although (like nature) it is equally common to the

---

[8] *The King's Book*, ed. T. A. Lacey (London: SPCK, 1932), 148, 159.

good and the wicked, to the just and the unjust, nevertheless it designates a certain special aid above [nature] which still is not justifying grace, but another grace whereby the ungodly person is able to turn and do good works before justification by which at length he gains justification.[9]

Cranmer considered the scholastic teaching on *ex puris naturalibus cum communi influentia* to be Pelagian,[10] and to label what was essentially Fisher's Augustinian-influenced *via attritionis formatae* as the '*Scholastici*' confirms the extent of Fisher's influence in conservative circles. Because his opponents appealed to the *auxilium Dei speciale*, Cranmer had to demonstrate that the '*via Scripturarum Augustiniana*' knew no 'middle grace', if he were going to prove that only solifidianism ensured salvation *sola gratia*.

In his dispute with Pelagianism, Augustine differentiated between the general grace of creation that Pelagius talked about and that was common to all humanity, and the grace of conversion whereby God 'made sheep out of wolves' and freed the fallen who had expected damnation. According to the accompanying *marginalia* in the great notebooks, these were the two kinds of grace, the former was common to everyone, but only the latter was 'Christian grace'.[11] In the propositional heading of folio 82 *recto*, Cranmer directly

---

[9] 'Scriptura, authore Augustino, loquitur dumtaxat de gratia iustificante quae diffusa est in corda nostra per spiritum sanctum. Pelagiani aliam gratiam reppererunt, nempe, gratiam liberi arbitrii, sive naturae. Scolastici [*sic*] tertiam confinxerunt gratiam mediam, quae licet (quemadmodum natura) communis sit bonis pariter ac malis, iustis et iniustis, designet tamen supra adiutorium quoddam speciale, nec tamen sit gratia iustificans, sed alia gratia qua possit impius converti, et bona opera facere ante iustificationem, quibus tandem consequatur iustificationem', CGC II, 225v–226r.

[10] Cf. 'And if these words be added to signify, that by the common influence of grace given generally we have inclination to obey the will and precepts of God; so much the Pelagians will grant us', Cranmer's 'Annotations', Cox II, 108.

[11] 'Communis est omnibus natura, non gratia. Natura non putetur gratia', *marginalium*: 'Non omnium est gratia'; 'fecit oves de lupis. Haec est gratia. Excepta illa communi gratia naturae, qua homines facti sumus . . . est maior gratia, qua facti sumus populus eius et oves pascuae eius, per Jesum Christum dominum nostrum', *marginalium*: 'gratia duplex', Augustine, *Sermo 11*, CGC II, 289v; 'illam generalem gratiam praedicent, qua creatus est homo, qua homines sumus, et utique et cum impiis homines sumus, sed non cum impiis Christiani sumus, hanc ergo gratiam qua Christiani sumus, ipsam volumus praedicent', *marginalium*: 'Gratia duplex', ibid., fol. 290; 'lapsus autem, damnationem expectabat, et liberatus est, haec est gratia per Jesum Christum dominum nostrum', *marginalium*: 'Gratia Christiana', ibid., fol. 291r.

attacked the scholastic twofold understanding of saving grace by identifying the *auxilium Dei speciale* with the inner renovation associated with *gratia gratum faciens*: 'To receive divine help is to receive the Holy Spirit and charity, through which a delight in the highest good is formed in man'.[12] Thus, Augustine knew only one salvific grace, the justifying grace Cranmer described on folio 225 *verso*. According to the Protestants, concomitant with imparting faith for pardon through imputation, this grace renovated the will and its affections through the indwelling presence of the Holy Spirit.[13]

Because works before justification did not arise from saving grace, they lacked the proper motivation to be acceptable in God's eyes. In his 'Annotations' Cranmer had argued that only works done after justification pleased God because only then were they executed with 'pure faith and love to God'.[14] In his great notebooks, he looked to Augustine's writings to support his claim. A person could fulfil the open requirements of the law but still be a lawbreaker in his heart because he acted out of dread of punishment rather than a delight in righteousness.[15] This love for God was not the result of free choice but was imparted by the indwelling Holy Spirit.[16] In fact, apart from the Holy Spirit's inner presence, the law, however good in itself, only increased evil desire by forbidding it.[17]

---

[12] 'Accipere divinum adiutorium est accipere spiritum sanctum et charitatem, per quae fit in homine delectatio summi boni', CGC II, 82r.

[13] 'Nos autem dicimus humanam voluntatem sic <u>divinitus adiuvari ad faciendam</u> iustitiam, ut . . . <u>accipiat spiritum sanctum, quo fiat in animo eius delectatio,</u> <u>dilectioque summi illius atque incommutabilis boni, quod deus est</u>', Augustine, *De spiritu et littera*, ca. 3, CGC II, 82r.

[14] Cox II, 114.

[15] 'Potuit enim esse intus in affectionibus pravis <u>praevaricator legis</u>, et tamen conspicua <u>opera legis implere</u>, vel timore hominum, vel ipsius dei. Sed poenae formidine non dilectione et delectatione iustitiae', Augustine, *Contra duas epistolas pelagianorum*, li. 1, ca. 9, CGC II, 239v.

[16] 'Namque <u>neque liberum arbitrium, quicquid nisi ad peccandum valet</u>, si lateat veritatis via. Et cum id quod agendum et quo intendum est coeperit non latere, nisi etiam delectet et ametur, non agitur, non suscipitur, non bene vivitur, <u>ut autem</u> <u>diligatur, charitas dei diffunditur in cordibus nostris</u>, non per arbitrium liberum quod surgit ex nobis, <u>sed per spiritum sanctum qui datus est nobis</u>', Augustine, *De spiritu et littera*, ca. 3, CGC II, 239r.

[17] 'Ubi sanctus non adiuvat spiritus, <u>inspirans pro concupiscentia mala, con-</u> <u>cupiscentiam bonam, id est, charitatem diffundens in cordibus nostris</u>, profecto lex

Without the Holy Spirit within, people delighted to sin.[18] Since before justification no one was able 'to have a just will', no one was able 'to do justly'.[19] As Cranmer succinctly stated his point in the commentary on folio 225 *verso*: 'He who lacks a good will does not have good works.'[20]

In folios 213–15, Cranmer gathered texts of Scripture which he interpreted to support this conclusion: 'John 3: [6], "What is born of the flesh is flesh, and what is born of the Spirit is Spirit"—Therefore, before the Spirit, there are flesh and sins, and through them we do not merit justification'; 'Romans 8: [5–9] . . . "Truly they who live according to the flesh are not able to please God" . . . Therefore, before the reception of the Holy Spirit, we are still under the flesh, under death, enemies to God, we are not able to please God, we are not his'.[21] Cranmer summarized this point in his propositional heading for folio 239 *recto*: 'We are held guilty by works [done] before [the reception of] the Holy Spirit, rather than the opposite.'[22] According to Cranmer, good

quamvis bona, auget prohibendo desiderium malum', Augustine, *De spiritu et littera*, ca. 4, CGC II, 239r.

[18] 'Ubi spiritus domini, ibi libertas, hic autem spiritus domini cuius dono iustificamur, quo fit in nobis ut non peccare delectet, ubi libertas est, sicut praeter hunc spiritum peccare delectat, ubi servitus est', Augustine, *De spiritu et littera*, ca. 16, CGC II, 82r.

[19] 'Nemo potest habere voluntatem iustam, nisi nullis praecedentibus meritis acceperit veram, hoc est, gratuitam desuper gratiam', Augustine, *Contra duas epistolas pelagianorum*, li. 1, ca. 3, CGC II, 83r; 'Ad iuste faciendum [homo] liber non erit, nisi a peccato liberatus, esse iustitiae coeperit servus', Augustine, *Enchiridion*, ca. 30, CGC II, 232v; 'Recto enim corde, recta sunt opera. Cum autem cor rectum non est, opera recta non sunt, etiamsi recta videantur', Augustine, *In Psalmum 77, marginalium*: 'Non potest opus esse rectum, nisi sit cor rectum', CGC II, 253r.

[20] 'Bona opera non habet, cui deest voluntas bona', CGC II, 225v.

[21] 'Johannis 3, Quod natum est ex carne, caro est, et quod natum est ex spiritu spiritus est. Ergo ante spiritum, sunt caro et peccata ac per ea non meremur iustificationem', CGC II, 213v; 'Romanos 8 . . . Qui vero in carne sunt, deo placere non possunt . . . Ergo ante acceptum spiritum sanctum, adhuc sub carne sumus, sub morte inimici deo, nec possumus deo placere non sumus illius', CGC II, 214.

[22] 'Ex operibus, ante spiritum sanctum, rei potius tenemur quam contra', CGC II, 239r; cf. 'Hominis quippe meritum superna gratia non ut veniat invenit . . . veniens deus . . . hoc solum invenerat quod puniret', Gregory, *Moralium*, li. 18, ca. 25, *marginalium*: 'Nihil invenit gratia non puniendum', CGC II, 227v; 'Nihil praecesserat in meritis nostris, nisi unde damnari deberemus', Augustine, *In Psalmum 18, marginalium*: 'Nihil boni ante gratiam', CGC II, 229r; 'In quo non invenit salvator quod coronet, sed quod damnet, non invenit merita bonorum, sed invenit merita suppliciorum', Augustine, *In Psalmum 30*, Concio 1, *marginalium*:

works could not restore a penitent to a state of grace because only in a state of grace could works pleasing to God be performed.[23]

The *King's Book* argued that justification was said to be conferred '*gratis*' because the works of penance which eventually obtained forgiveness could be performed only with the aid of grace.[24] Cranmer gathered material from Augustine to support the contrary definition that he used as a propositional heading: '*Gratis*, that is, without any merits preceding'.[25] This definition of '*gratis*' was the logical implication of his understanding of good works. Since works of the law 'follow being justified, they do not precede justification', grace 'is given not because we have done good things, but so that we may be able to do them, that is, not because we have fulfilled the law, but so that we may be able to fulfil the law'.[26] As a person was created freely by God, so also was he justified freely.[27] While both the *King's Book* and

'Nihil boni ante gratiam', CGC II, 229v; 'Non solum nullis bonis, verumetiam multis malis meritis praecedentibus', Augustine, *De gratia et libero arbitrio*, ca. 6, *marginalium*: 'Nihil boni ante gratiam, sed mali plurimum', CGC II, 233v; 'Noli ergo putare, te aliquid operari, nisi in quantum malus es', Augustine, *In Psalmum 142, marginalium*: 'Quicquid ex nobis est, malum est', CGC II, 255r; *marginalium*: 'Nihil est, unde salvemur, plurima vero unde damnemur', CGC II, 267v; 'Qui nihil invenis unde salves, et tamen multum invenis unde damnes', Augustine, *De verbis Apostoli*, Sermo 14, CGC II, 295v.

[23] Cf. 'non [opera bona] gratiam pariant, sed quae gratia pariantur', Augustine, *Ad Simplicianum*, li. 1, q. 2, CGC II, 249r.

[24] 'And although such works of penance be required in us towards the attaining of remission of sins and justification, yet the same justification and remission of sins is the free gift of God, and conferred unto us gratis, that is to say, of the grace of God, whereby we doing such things, and having such motions and works of penance, be prepared and made more apt to receive further grace of remission of our sins and justification', Lacey, *King's Book*, 160.

[25] 'Gratis, id est, nullis praecedentibus meritis', CGC II, 83r; 'Quippe iustificatur gratis, id est nullis suorum operum praecedentibus meritis, alioqui gratia non est gratia', Augustine, *De spiritu et littera*, ca. 10, CGC II, 83r; 'Quare [gratia] gratis datur? Quia merita tua non praecesserunt, sed beneficia dei te praevenerunt', Augustine, *In Psalmum 30*, Concio 1, CGC II, 83v; 'Nihil aliud velit intelligi in eo quod dicit, gratis, nisi quia iustificationem, opera non praecedunt', Augustine, *De spiritu et littera*, ca. 26, CGC II, 83r.

[26] 'Legis opera . . . sequuntur enim iustificatum, non praecedunt iustificandum', Augustine, *De fide et operibus*, ca. 14, CGC II, 83r; 'Ideo datur non quia bona fecimus, sed ut ea facere valeamus, id est, non quia legem implevimus, sed ut legem implere possimus', Augustine, *De spiritu et littera*, ca. 10, CGC II, 83r.

[27] 'Dedisti forte aliquid ut salvus esses? Quid dedisti ut homo esses?', Augustine, *In Psalmum 142, marginalium*: 'Gratis creati, gratis et iustificati sumus', CGC II, 255r.

'Cranmer's Great Commonplaces' cited Jeremiah 17: 14, 'Heal me and I shall be made whole', Cranmer recorded this verse under the propositional heading which characterized all works before justification as sinful to demonstrate humanity's need to be healed before they could do anything good.[28]

SAVING FAITH

The *King's Book* taught that God worked two kinds of faith in a Christian's heart, one before justification, the other after, and each requiring the assent of the individual. The faith possible for the unjustified was the understanding one gained by accepting the teachings of Scripture and the church as true: 'wherein man leaneth not to his own natural knowledge, which is by reason, but leaneth to the knowledge attained by faith'.[29] Known among scholastics as *fides assensus* or *informis*, faith as assent to propositional truth continued to be possible even in a state of mortal sin, for a person who did penitential works to avoid damnation obviously believed the teachings of the church to be true.[30] The faith of the justified, however, was *fides charitate formata*. As justification required prevenient grace eventually to be superseded by sanctifying grace, so too knowledge of God's truth had eventually to be joined with hope of obtaining his promises and charity as exhibited in obedience to his commands. Faith was considered to be 'lively' when it 'worketh in man a ready submission of his will to God's will'. If the faith of knowledge failed to be infused with hope and charity and, thus, failed to exhibit the obedience to divine law that needed to follow, the *King's Book* recognized that Scripture considered such faith to be dead 'because it is void and destitute of the life and efficacy of charity'.[31] Yet works executed in the light of this lesser faith and aided by prevenient grace were still useful for the

---

[28] Lacey, *King's Book*, 149; CGC II, 240r.
[29] Lacey, *King's Book*, 9.
[30] For *fides informis* as 'the faith of knowledge', see ibid., 12.
[31] Ibid., 10.

recovery of justification;[32] for *fides informis* was 'the necessary beginning of all righteousness'.[33]

Cranmer, however, had argued in his 'Annotations' that for works to be acceptable in God's sight they had to proceed from 'pure faith' as well as from a love for God.[34] Gathering evidence drawn from Augustine and the Bible, Cranmer made the same argument in his great notebooks. 'Pure' faith was lively faith, i.e. faith that was grounded in both *fiducia* and fruitful living. Concerning *fiducia*, Cranmer recorded extracts which distinguished between propositional knowledge about God and faith as an interior divine gift by which the believer was joined to God. Faith was not identical with the beliefs to which it held.[35] Faith was individual and discernible in the believer's own heart.[36] Believing in God's existence was not the same as believing in God.[37] Many wicked people were able to believe what was said to be true, although they remained reluctant to want to make this truth their own.[38] True faith was different from such mere propositional apprehension, for this divine gift stirred the believer to seek after the living God.[39] After drawing a person to God, true faith expressed itself as

---

[32] 'Wherefore a transgressor of the law of Almighty God, after baptism, keepeth still a remorse of conscience, and the light of knowledge by faith, whereby he seeth the remedies how to attain remission of sin, and by a special gift of further grace is moved to use the same remedies, and so by faith walketh the ways ordained to attain remission of sins, as in the sacrament of penance shall be declared', ibid., 12.

[33] Ibid., 10.

[34] Cox II, 114.

[35] 'Sed aliud sunt ea quae creduntur, aliud fides qua creduntur', Augustine, *De trinitate*, li. 13, ca. 2, *marginalium*: 'aliud est fides, aliud res quae creditur', CGC II, 245r.

[36] 'Qui credit, propria quaedam fides est', Augustine, *In epistolam Johannis*, tract. 10, CGC II, 256r; 'Ipsam tamen fidem quam inest in nobis videmus in nobis', Augustine, *De trinitate*, li. 13, ca. 1, CGC II, 244v; 'Suam igitur quisque fidem, apud seipsum videt', Augustine, *De trinitate*, li. 13, ca. 2, CGC II, 244v.

[37] 'Hoc est enim credere in deum, qui utique plus est quam credere deo', Augustine, *In Psalmum 77*, *marginalium*: 'Credere deo et in deum', CGC II, 252v; 'Aliud credere illum. Aliud credere in illum', Augustine, *Sermo 181*, CGC II, 259r.

[38] 'Credere vera esse quae loquitur, multi et mali possunt. Credunt enim esse vera, et nolunt ea facere sua, quia ad hoc pedum pigri sunt', Augustine, *Sermo 181*, CGC II, 259v.

[39] 'Quaerentes enim invenient eum . . . . Quaeram te domine invocans te, et invocem te credens in te . . . Invocat te deus, fides mea, quam dedisti mihi', Augustine, *Confessiones*, li. 1, ca. 1, CGC II, 242r.

complete trust in the deity, so that the believer endeavoured to commit himself as fully as he was able to the mercy and power of his Lord.[40] This *fiducia* was based on the hope of salvation to those with saving faith.[41] As Hebrews 11: 1 stated, faith was the substance of things unseen for which the believer hoped.[42] This hope included a confidence that God would fulfil his pledge to bring the believer to eternal life, since by his promise God had made himself a debtor to do so.[43] To be a Christian meant to long for the future life in the divine presence.[44]

According to Augustine, faith was the first means which joined the soul to God.[45] Cranmer recorded several verses of Scripture which stressed belief as the means to eternal life: John 1: 12, 'He gave to them the power to become sons of God, to those who believed in his name'; John 3: 25, 'Everyone that believes on [the Son of Man] will not perish'; John 3: 18, 'He who believes in him is not judged'; Acts 10: 43, 'All the prophets testify to him that all who believe in him receive the remission of sins through his name'; Acts 13: 39, 'Through him everyone who believes is justified'.[46]

---

[40] 'Quae fides praeveniente et vocante misericordia dei, per obedientiam suscitat et applicare incipit ad deum cor, ut dirigatur', Augustine, *In Psalmum* 77, CGC II, 253v; 'Constanter deo crede, eique te totum committe quantum potes. Noli esse velle quasi proprius et in tua potestate, sed eius clementissimi et utilissimi domini te servum esse profitere. Ita enim te ad se sublevare non desinet', Augustine, *Soliloquia*, li. 1, ca. 30, CGC II, 242v.

[41] '[Gratia] non solum magnitudo futurae gloriae promittitur, verumetiam creditur et speratur . . . quorum autem sit fides', summary of Augustine, *De gratia Christi contra Pelagium et Coelestinum*, li. 1, ca. 10, CGC II, 82.

[42] 'Quid est enim fides, nisi credere quod non vides?' Augustine, *In Johannem*, tract. 40, CGC II, 94r; 'Est autem fides, credere quod nondum vides', Augustine, *De verbis Apostoli*, Sermo 27, CGC II, 94r; 'Et nescio utrum credere dicendus est quisque quod videt, nam ipsa fides quae in epistola quae scribitur ad hebreos, ita est definita. Est autem fides, sperantium substantia, et coniunctio rerum quae non videntur', Augustine, *In Johannem*, tract. 79, CGC II, 255v.

[43] 'In hiis ergo quattuor rebus [i.e. praedestinatione, vocatione, iustificatione, et glorificatione] considerare debemus quid iam habeamus et quid iam expectemus. In hiis enim quae iam habemus, laudemus deum largitorem, in his quae nondum habemus, tenemus debitorem. Debitor enim factus est, non aliquid a nobis accipiendo, sed quod ei placuit promittendo', Augustine, *De verbis Apostoli*, Sermo 16, CGC II, 257r.

[44] 'Desiderium ergo nostrum crescat, Christiani non sumus nisi propter futurum saeculum', Augustine, *In Psalmum* 91, CGC II, 254v.

[45] 'Fides est prima quae subiungat animam deo', *De agone christiana*, ca. 13, *marginalium*: 'Fides iungit animam deo', CGC II, 245r.

[46] CGC II, 85v.

Grounded in *fiducia*, true faith worked by love, not by fear.[47] Although faith was the first means to unite the soul to God, it was immediately joined by hope and love, for the other two flowed from *fiducia* so that in the justified all three were present.[48] In fact, according to a *marginalium*, faith, hope, and love were inseparable because, as Augustine said, there was 'no love without hope, no hope without love, and neither love nor hope without faith'.[49] The hope of eternal life based on faith in God's promises inspired a love for God in the heart of the believer which necessarily expressed itself in good works. So close was the identification between faith and the good works which were its fruit that true belief itself could be defined as cleaving to the God who did good in order to work well with him.[50]

Therefore, faith could be defective in two ways, either by being associated with fear instead of loving trust or by lacking the fruit of that love. Any faith which inspired fear was not saving faith but dead faith because fear was the mark of slavery not sonship.[51] Faith without an interior love for God was simply the propositional faith of demons, for devils believed in but trembled at what Christians embraced

[47] 'Haec est fides [qua salvi fiunt], quae per dilectionem operatur, non per timorem, non formidando poenam, sed amando iustificiam', Augustine, *De spiritu et littera*, ca. 32, CGC II, fol 247.

[48] '[Fides] prima datur, ex qua impetrentur cetera', Augustine, *De praedestinatione sanctorum*, ca. 7, CGC II, 251v; 'Pia fides, sine spe, et sine charitate esse non potest', Augustine, *Epistola 85* (MO: 120), CGC II, 242v.

[49] 'Proinde nec amor sine spe est, nec sine amore spes, nec utrumque sine fide', Augustine, *Enchiridion*, ca. [8], *marginalium*: 'fides, spes, charitas, inseparabilia sunt', CGC II, 243r; cf. 'Qui vero non amat, inaniter credit, etiamsi sunt vera quae credit, inaniter sperat, etiam si ad veram felicitatem doceantur pertinere quae speravit', Augustine, *Enchiridion*, ca. 117, CGC 244r.

[50] 'Hoc est ergo credere in deum, credendo adhaerere ad bene operandum, bona operanti deo', Augustine, *In Psalmum 77*, *marginalium*: 'Credere in deum, quid', CGC II, 252v, 284r.

[51] 'Et illi [qui sub lege sunt, et timore poenae iustitiam suam facere conantur] ergo credunt deo. Nam si omnino non crederent, nec poenam legis utique formidarent. Sed non hanc fidem commendat Apostolus qui dicit. Non enim accepistis spiritum servitutis iterum in timore, sed accepistis spiritum adoptionis filiorum dei in quo clamamus Abba pater. Timor ergo ille servilis est, et ideo, quamvis in illo, domino credatur, non tamen iustitia diligitur, sed damnatio timetur', Augustine, *De spiritu et littera*, ca. 32, CGC 247r; *marginalium*: 'Qui timore agit, nondum est inter filios dei', CGC II, 293r; cf. the following *locus*: 'Quod timore poenae fit, non fit', CGC II, 223r–224v.

with hope and love.[52] By scholastic definition, fear, rather than loving trust, was predominant in *fides informis*, since the root of charity came into the penitent only with the infusion of *gratia gratum faciens*. As a result, the faith of knowledge was, by Cranmer's definition, a dead faith, thus providing him with a second reason to deny the possibility of good works before justification:

Romans 14: [23], 'Everything that is not of faith is sin'. Hebrews 11: [6], 'Without faith, it is impossible to please God'—Therefore we do not gain justification through works before faith, since they do not please God, but are sins.[53]

John 3[: 17–18], 'God did not send his Son into the world to judge the world but to save it through him. He who believes in him will not be judged, truly, he who does not believe is already judged because he does not believe in the name of the only-begotten Son of God'—Therefore, before justifying faith, [a person] does not have works through which he may gain justification.[54]

This Augustinian emphasis on a strict dichotomy of either love or fear as the source of all human response to the Law was the implicit rationale behind Cranmer's insistence that true faith included confidence in personal salvation. As long as the believer's eternal destiny depended on the reliability of his own feeble will to be obedient, he could never be completely free from fear and, thus, never fully freed to love God. By relying exclusively on God's faithfulness to keep his promise, *fiducia* in God's mercy certified the conscience of justification and engendered the new affection of love for God which then rooted out all fear from the believer's

---

[52] 'Denique ut ait Apostolus Jacobus, et demones credunt et contremiscunt, nec tamen sperant vel amant, sed potius quod speramus et amamus credendo venturum esse formidant', Augustine, *Enchiridion*, ca. [8], CGC II, 243r; 'Credere autem ipsum esse deum, et demones possunt', Augustine, *Sermo 181*, CGC II, 259v; 'Cum dilectione, fides Christiani, sine dilectione, fides demonis', Augustine, *In epistolam Johannis*, tract, 10, *marginalium*: 'fides duplex', CGC II, 256r; 'Cum dilectione fides Christiani, sine dilectione, fides demonis', Augustine, *Sermo 181*, *marginalium*: 'fides duplex', CGC II, 259v.

[53] 'Ergo non assequimur iustificationem per opera ante fidem, cum non placeant deo, sed sunt peccata', CGC II, 214v; cf. 'Nemo enim bene operatur, nisi fides praecesserit, sicut dicit Apostolus. Sine fide impossibile est placere deo', Augustine, *Sermo 95*, *marginalium*: 'fides praecedit omnia opera bona', CGC II, 259r.

[54] 'Ergo ante fidem iustificantem non habet opera per quae assequatur iustificationem', CGC II, 214r.

heart.[55] Cranmer's adherence to this interpretation of Augustine meant that, by his definition, even the description of *fides formata* offered by the *King's Book* continued to be a fearful faith. For the conservative formulary followed medieval teaching and specifically denied the possibility of personal confidence in eventual salvation apart from a direct revelation from God:

> But whether there be any special particular knowledge which man by faith hath certainly of himself, whereby he may testify to himself that he is of the predestinates, which shall to the end persevere in their calling, we have not spoken, ne cannot in scripture ne doctors find that any such faith can be taught or preached.[56]

Since true faith necessarily was joined by love, any faith lacking fruitful works was also defective. As Cranmer stated in the propositional heading of folio 241 *verso*, 'Faith is not without works, neither the opposite, as the love of God is not without the love of neighbour, neither the reverse.'[57] Cranmer gathered numerous quotations to show that true faith and godly morality were 'mutually linked'.[58] They erred who thought that an evil life was compatible with true faith.[59] Instead, true belief in God was properly characterized as a love for God which the Christian's life

---

[55] 'Dei autem promissio non pendet ex te, sed ex illo', Augustine, *Homila 17*, *marginalium*: 'Promissio dei ex ipso solo pendet', CGC II, 268v; 'Quis enim sic praesumat de conscientia sua, ut certus sit eam sibi in iudicio dei posse sufficere, nisi misericors misericorditer iudicet', Augustine, *Epistola 120* (MO: 140), *marginalium*: 'Conscientia non potest esse certa nisi per misericordiam dei', CGC II, 273v.

[56] Lacey, *King's Book*, 12.

[57] 'Fides non est sine operibus, nec contra, sicut nec dilectio dei, sine dilectioni [*sic*] proximi nec e converso', CGC II, 241v.

[58] '[Fides et mores] utraque enim mutuo connexa sunt', Augustine, *De fide et operibus*, ca. 13, CGC II, 241v.

[59] 'Homines autem non intelligentes quod ait ipse Apostolus, arbitramur iustificari hominem per fidem, sine operibus legis, putaverunt eum dicere, sufficere homini fidem, etiamsi male vivat, et bona opera non habeat. Quod absit ut [Paulus eum] sentiret vas electionis', Augustine, *De gratia et libero arbitrio*, ca. 7, CGC II, 252; 'Errat autem quisquis putat veritatem se posse cognoscere, cum adhuc nequiter vivat', Augustine, *De agone christiana*, ca. 13, CGC II, 245r. Cf. CGC II, 243v; 'Omnis qui credit quod Jesus sit Christus, ex deo natus est. Quis est qui credit quod Jesus sit Christus, qui non sic vivit quomodo praecepit Christus, multi enim dicunt, Credo, sed fides sine operibus non salvat', Augustine, *In epistolam Johannis*, tract. 10, CGC II, 255v.

expressed in deeds.[60] Fruitful faith distinguished God's faithful from unclean demons; consequently, the presence of love and good works was the individual's test for whether his faith was saving or not.[61] Since obedience was the doctrinal touchstone of the Henrician church, Cranmer was no less determined than the *King's Book* to make godly living a necessity for the Christian, although his explanation was radically different. Whereas the conservative formulary taught that any hope of salvation was possible only after the right response of human obedience to grace, Cranmer insisted that true obedience to God's laws was possible only after the assurance of gratuitous salvation.

Whether fearful or fruitless, defective faith was dead faith. Again and again Cranmer recorded passages from Augustine which contrasted dead faith with true and living faith, eventually gathering prime examples of *duplex fides* on folio 261 *verso*: 'Thus, Paul himself, has not defined just any faith as believing in God but the faith which is wholesome and clearly evangelical, the faith which he says works by love'; 'if they rightly understand what it is to believe in Christ, for it is not this, to have the faith of demons, which is rightly called dead faith, but the faith which works by love'; 'it is rightly able to be said that the commandments of God pertain only to faith, provided that the faith which is meant is not a dead faith, but that living faith which works through love'.[62] For Cranmer the two kinds of faith described in the

---

[60] 'Credere vero in deum, soli noverunt qui diligunt illum, qui non solum nomine Christiani sunt, sed et factis et vita, quia sine dilectione, fides inanis est', Augustine, *Sermo 181*, *marginalium*: 'Credere in deum, quid?', CGC II, 259v; 'Dicis, credo, fac quod dicis, et fides est', Augustine, *Sermo 237*, *marginalium*: 'fides, id est, fac quod dicis', CGC II, 260v.

[61] '[Fides quae per dilectionem operatur] est fides quae fideles dei separat ab immundis demonibus', Augustine, *De gratia et libero arbitrio*, ca. [7], CGC II, 252v; cf. 'Fides autem sic est in anima ut radix bona quae pluviam in fructu ducit. Perfidia vero et error diabolicus, et cupiditas mala, radix omnium malorum, sicut radix spinarum, etiam dulcem pluviam ad punctiones convertit', Augustine, *In Psalmum 139*, CGC II, 254v; 'Prius ergo discerne fidem tuam, a fide demonis. Unde eam discernis? Demones hoc dixerunt timendo, Petrus amando . . . . Discernite ergo fidem vestram. Iam estis de praedestinatis, vocatis, iustificatis', Augustine, *De verbis Apostoli*, Sermo 16, CGC II, 258r; 'Suam igitur quisque fidem, apud seipsum videt . . . et tanto firmius credit, quanto fructus eius magis novit, quos operari solet fides per dilectionem', Augustine, *De trinitate*, li. 13, ca. 2, CGC II, 244v–245r.

[62] 'Sicut etiam ipse Paulus, non quamlibet fidem, qua in deum creditur, sed eam

King's Book were both defective and dead, whereas solifidianism taught a fruitful *fiducia* which was living and offered
eternal life.

CORNELIUS: TWO GRACES VERSUS ONE FAITH

The most serious scriptural challenge to Cranmer's denial
that good works could prepare for justification was the story
of Cornelius the centurion in Acts 10. Because God took
notice of the centurion's prayers and almsgiving, Cornelius
was sent an angel who instructed him to ask for Peter to
come to his house. Upon hearing the apostle's preaching,
Cornelius was filled with the Holy Spirit, and the Jewish
Christians felt compelled to baptize him, even though he
was a gentile. Fisher appealed to the centurion's works
before baptism as evidence of the *prima gratia* which
enabled a penitent to do good works, but these were of an
insufficient quantity of grace to merit salvation. For eternal
life, the penitent needed the *secunda gratia*, that is, *gratia
gratum faciens*. In support of his interpretation, Fisher cited
Augustine's explanation that Cornelius' works were good
because they preceded from the grace of faith, although not
of a sufficient quantity to receive eternal life.[63] Adapting
Augustine's simile, Fisher likened first grace to a conception
which needed to come to birth through second grace.[64]

---

salubrem, planeque Evangelicam, definivit, quae, inquit, per dilectionem operatur',
Augustine, *De fide et operibus*, ca. 14, CGC II, 261v; 'Si recte intelligerent quid sit
credere in Christum, neque enim hoc est, habere demonum fidem, quae recte
mortua perhibetur, sed fidem quae per dilectionem operatur', ibid., ca. 17, CGC
II, 261v; 'Recte dici posset [*sic*], ad solam fidem pertinere dei mandata, si non
mortua, sed viva illa intelligitur [*sic*] fides, quae per dilectionem operatur', ibid., ca.
22, CGC II, 261v.

[63] 'In quibusdam est tanta gratia fidei, quanta non sufficit ad obtinendum
regnum caelorum, sicut in catechumenis, sicut in ipso Cornelio, antequam
Sacramentorum participatione incorporaretur Ecclesiae', Fisher, *ALC*, Art. 36,
cols. 713–14; Augustine, *De diversis quaestionibus ad Simplicianum*, li. 1, q. 2; *PL* xl.
112.

[64] 'Per illam gratiam (uti paulo post illic Augustinus asserit) fit inchoatio
quaedam conceptioni similis, quae conceptio non sufficit Christiano, sed oportet
eum etiam nasci, quod fit per secundam gratiam, qua quis dignus aeterna vita
redditur', Fisher, *ALC*, Art. 36, col. 714; cf. Rex, *Fisher*, 126–7.

Because Augustine had referred to the 'grace of faith' not being sufficient for salvation, Fisher argued that Peter had to come to Cornelius because the centurion lacked a fullness of grace. In fact, it was equally possible, and perhaps more accurate, to read Augustine as arguing that what Cornelius lacked was a fullness of faith.[65] While not appealing to this specific passage, Cranmer recorded passages which suggest that Cornelius' two-step process of coming into the church resulted from his need to have a more knowledgeable faith, not his need for a second kind of grace. Firstly, Cornelius had been justified by his great faith and that lively faith had expressed itself in doing good works prior to the centurion's baptism.[66] His works were pleasing to God because of this faith.[67] And yet, while Cornelius had the same faith as other ancient godly people in the Old Testament, the coming of Christ into the world had now made such faith insufficient for salvation; consequently, Cornelius needed Peter to inform him that the Incarnation had taken place and to baptize him, so that his faith would be in unity with apostolic teaching and the sacraments.[68] By arguing that

---

[65] 'Fiunt ergo inchoationes quaedam fidei, conceptionibus similes: non tamen solum concipi, sed etiam nasci opus est, ut ad vitam perveniatur aeternam', Augustine, *De diversis quaestionibus ad Simplicianum*, li. 1, q. 2; *PL* xl. 112.

[66] 'Ambrosius super 3 cap. ad Romanos dicit Cornelium iustificatum', CGC II, 209v; 'De illo scriptum est, quod iustus erat', Peter the Lombard, *Sententiae*, li. 3, dist. 25, CGC II, 211r; 'Et Cornelio iam iustificato, dicit Angelus', Durand of Saint-Pourçain, *In quattuor sententiarum libros quaestionum resolutiones*, li. 4, dist. 4, CGC II, 225v; 'De hac re prolixe disputat, ac tandem hunc in modum concludit. Sola (inquit) fides, et mentis ad deum conversio, sine sanguinis effusione, et sine profusione aquae, salutem sine dubio operatur, volenti, sed non valenti, prohibente articulo, baptizari', Bernard, *Epistola 77*, Ad Hugonem de Sancto Victore, CGC II, 212r; 'Vide quanta fides, quanta pietas', Chrysostom, *In Actus*, Homilia 23, CGC II, 208r; 'Conversio cordis potest inesse non percepto baptismo, sed contempto baptismo non potest', Augustine, *De baptismo contra Donatistas*, li. 4, ca. 25, CGC II, 209r; 'In omni opere bono non nos incipimus, et postea per dei misericordiam adiuvamur, sed ipsis nullis praecedentibus bonis meritis, et fidem et amorem sui prius inspirat, unde manifestissime credendum, quod . . . Cornelii centurionis . . . illa tam admirabilis fides, non fuerit de natura, sed divinae gratiae largitate donata', Augustine (recte, Gennadius), *De ecclesiasticis dogmatibus*, ca. 51, *marginalium*: 'Fides et charitas ante omnia opera bona gratis inspirantur', CGC II, 208.

[67] 'Fidem ergo habuit, cuius operationes et eleemosinae placere potuerunt', Gregory, *Super Ezechiel*, Homilia 19, CGC II, 210r; 'Fidem habuit, cuius orationes et elemosinae placere potuerunt', Bede, *In Actus*, ca. 10, CGC II, 210v; 'Per fidem placuerunt deo opera eius', Peter the Lombard, *Sententiae*, li. 3, dist. 25, CGC II, 211v.

[68] 'Sed si posset sine fide Christi esse salvus, nec ad eum mitteretur Petrus. Ex

Cornelius lacked full knowledge, not full justification, Cranmer was able to deny the traditional two-tier understanding of saving grace and the good works before justification which it supported.

In sum, Cranmer considered it human pride to attribute the beginning of justification to human effort,[69] and he fought against any meritorious preparation for justification. The *King's Book* taught that works of penance performed in a state of mortal sin could be considered good because they proceeded from a measure of faith and grace. Cranmer, however, considered the doctrine of *meritum de congruo* a scholastic invention which more sound theologians denied.[70] Drawing upon Augustine and the Bible, he denied the validity of a lower grade of faith and grace which effectively eliminated any possibility of a lower grade of merit.

quo apparet, quod licet crederet hoc idem quod antiqui simplices, tamen propter temporis qualitatem iam non sufficiebat', Hugo de Sancto Victore, Pars 3, fol. 251P, CGC II, 212r; 'Sed incarnatum iam esse dei filium ignoravisse, et ideo missus est ad eum Petrus, ut iam natum dei filium, ei annuntiaret, et sacramentum regenerationis ei conferret', Peter the Lombard, *Sententiae*, li. 3, dist. 25, CGC II, 211r; 'Propter doctrinae tamen sacramentorumque unitatem, ad Petrum iubetur mittere', Augustine, *Quaestiones evangelicae*, li. 2, ca. 40, CGC II, 209v; cf. this quotation from a later section: 'Dicitur baptismus flaminis inquantum cor hominis monetur a spiritu sancto ad credendum et diligendum deum, et poenitendum pro peccatis . . . Ideo iustificatus baptismo flaminis, adhuc tenetur baptizari baptismo fluminis, non propter remedium quo non indiget, sed propter praeceptum divinum', Durand of Saint-Pourçain, *In quattuor sententiarum libros quaestionum resolutiones*, li. 4, dist. 4, *marginalium*: 'Totum hoc pertinet ad titulum de Cornelio', CGC II, 224v–225r.

[69] *Marginalium*: 'Superbia est, hominem sibi tribuere iustificationis initium', commenting on Augustine, *De spiritu et littera*, ca. 7, CGC II, 100v.

[70] 'Scholastici invenerunt ad hoc dicendum terminos de condigno et congruo'; 'Quid hoc iam ut sic mereamur de congruo? Reputo igitur saniorem theologum, fideliorem catholicum, et scripturis sanctis magis concordem, qui tale meritum simpliciter abnegat, et cum modificatione Apostoli et Scripturarum concedit, quia simpliciter quis non merebitur regnum caelorum, sed ex gratia dei, aut voluntatem largitoris'; 'meritum nostrum, in articulo minime deus attendit, sive rationem congrui, vel condigni sed gratiam suam, aut voluntatem suam, aut misericordiam suam', Thomas Netter, *Contra Wycliffe*, titulum 1, ca. 7, CGC II, 264v–265r, 300r.

JUSTIFICATION

Although Cranmer and the conservatives disagreed about the role of works in preparation for justification, that issue must not be confused with the related but separate dispute over the nature of justification itself. For the conservatives, the manner in which the meritorious basis for justification came about was not nearly as important as that the basis was inherent. Although Erasmus stressed *fiducia* in God's promise to pardon, he remained in the broad medieval Catholic tradition because he taught that the divine infusion of love was the means by which God pardoned. As long as the forgiveness of sins was based on an inherent righteousness, the decisive role of personal merit in salvation would remain. Cranmer promoted solifidianism because the Protestant doctrine of *sola fide* based justification on the extrinsic righteousness of Christ, rather than on the intrinsic merit of the justified.[71]

Cranmer gathered numerous quotations to support justification by faith only: 'He says that a man is justified by faith and not by works, because faith itself is first given, whereby the rest may be obtained by asking'; 'A man will not be justified by the works of the law, but only through faith in Jesus Christ'; 'He who trusts in faith only will be blessed'; 'The Ebionites were condemned, because, among other errors, they denied that only faith in Christ was sufficient for salvation'; 'A man is justified through faith. The works of the law confer nothing towards his justification'; 'No one may think that he comes to the gift of justification by the merits of prior good works, this gift is in faith'; 'By faith only they are justified by a gift of God'; Without labour or any observance, by faith only they be justified with God', 'Still, belief only ought to suffice for the remission of sins'; 'He says that Paul now plainly shows that faith itself, even only faith, has in itself the power of justifying'.[72]

---

[71] 'Iustitia autem dei per fidem Jesu Christi, non per ullum sudorem aut dolorem', Chrysostom, *In oratione 4 contra Judeos*, CGC II, 86r.

[72] 'Ex fide autem ideo dicit iustificari hominem non ex operibus, quia ipsa prima datur, ex qua impetrentur cetera', Augustine, *De praedestinatione sanctorum*, ca. 7,

Although a gift from God,[73] faith itself was not the basis for justification.[74] Rather, faith was the means for appropriating Christ's death for the forgiveness of sins. Under the propositional heading—'By faith in Christ, that is, we are justified by the merit of the passion of Christ, not by our works'—Cranmer recorded passages from Cajetan's comments on Romans 3 that explained the manner in which faith justified.[75] Justification consisted of three parts, the grace of God, the righteousness of Christ's passion, and the believer's faith in the blood of Jesus. Grace was the cause both of redemption and of the believer's faith, but the believer's faith was the means by which God's grace and Christ's passion were joined to him. Faith as human work

CGC II, 251v; 'Non iustificabitur homo ex operibus legis, sed tantum per fidem Jesu Christi', Chrysostom, *In epistolam ad Galatas*, ca. 2, CGC II, 86r; 'Hic . . . demonstrat, qui sola fide nititur eum benedictum esse', ibid., ca. 3, CGC II, 86r; 'Eubeonii condemnati sunt, quod inter ceteros errores, negarent solam Christi fidem ad salutem sufficere', Eusebius, *Ecclesiastica Historia*, li. 3, ca. 27, CGC II, 88r; 'Iustificatur homo per fidem, cui ad iustificandum nihil conferunt opera legis', Origen, *Super 3 ca. ad Romanos*, CGC II, 88v; 'Nemo meritis priorum bonorum operum, arbitretur se pervenire ad donum iustificationis, quae est in fide', Augustine, *Octoginta trium quaestionum*, q. 76, CGC II, 248r; 'Sola fide iustificati sunt dono dei', Ambrose, *Super 3 ca. ad Romanos*, CGC II, 89r; 'Sine labore et aliqua observatione, sola fide iustificentur apud deum', Ambrose, *Super 4 ca. ad Romanos*, CGC II, 89r; 'Verum de remissione peccatorum sufficere deberet sola credulitas', Cyprian, *In expositionem symboli Apostolorum*, CGC II, 88v, cf. CGC II, 215r; 'Nunc plane (inquit) monstrat Paulus fidem ipsam vel solam iustificandi in se habere virtutem', Theophilact, *Super ca. 3 ad Galatas*, CGC II, 89v. For further quotations, see the following *loci*, 'Sola fides', CGC II, 86r–89v, and 'Ex sola fide iustificamur', CGC II, 90r–91r.

[73] 'Quae est fides plena et perfecta? Quae credit ex deo esse omnia bona nostra et ipsam fidem', Augustine, *Homilia 17*, *marginalium*: 'fides plena, quae sit', CGC II, 268v–269r; 'Et quod dixi per fidem, non ex vobis, sed dei donum est', Augustine, *De praedestinatione sanctorum*, ca. 7, CGC II, 251v; 'Cum similiter errarem, putans fidem, qua in deum credimus, non esse donum dei, sed a nobis esse in nobis', Augustine, *De praedestinatione sanctorum*, ca. 3, *marginalium*: 'Erravit quondam Augustinus putans gratiam non praecedere fidem', CGC II, 251v; 'Possent enim dicere, ideo accepimus gratiam, quia credimus, tanquam sibi fidem tribuentes, gratiam deo, propter hoc Apostolus cum dixisset per fidem, et hoc, inquit, non ex vobis, sed dei donum est', Augustine, *De gratia et libero arbitrio*, ca. 7, CGC II, 252r.

[74] *Marginalium*: 'fides non est meritum gratiae', CGC II, 249v; 'Cum dixerit ut merear iustificationem habeo fidem, respondetur ei, quid enim habes quod non accepisti?', Augustine, *Epistola 106* (MO: 186), *marginalium*: 'fides non est meritum iustificationis', CGC II, 232r.

[75] 'Fide in Christum, hoc est, merito passionis Christi, non nostris operibus iustificamur', CGC II, 91v.

did not justify; for 'believing in him who justifies the ungodly is to trust in another's righteousness, that is, God's through Christ'. While good works were to be performed by the just, such activity did not make them just.[76]

The difference between Cranmer and his opponents can be seen in the following extract and its marginal comment. According to Augustine, God extended his righteousness to the ungodly so that they might have an upright heart.[77] Cranmer's opponents would have understood Augustine as saying that God extended his righteousness to the ungodly by infusing in them the love which made them inherently righteous *de condigno*. However, according to the marginal comment in the great notebooks, 'Justification precedes a right heart.' Since Cranmer claimed on the basis of this text that justification preceded renovation, he must have understood the application of God's righteousness to the ungodly as being an external act, namely, through imputation rather than infusion. Justification may have resulted in a right heart, but a right heart was not the basis for justification. Pardon for sin was based on God's mercy not on personal merit,[78] on the extrinsic righteousness of Christ appro-

---

[76] 'Credere in eum qui iustificat impios, innititur iustitiae alienae, scilicet dei, per Christum', CGC II, 93r; for all the excerpts from Cajetan's *Commentary on Romans*, CGC II, 91v–93v; for a comparison of pertinent quotations from Cajetan in the great notebooks and Cranmer's *Homily on Salvation*, see Chapter 6.

[77] 'Nec quia recti sunt corde, sed etiam ut recti sint corde praetendit iustitiam suam qua iustificat impium, haec cogitatio non affert superbiam, quod vitium oritur, cum sibi quisque praefidit', Augustine, *De spiritu et littera*, ca. 7, *marginalium*: 'iustificatio praecedit rectum cor', CGC II, 227r.

[78] 'De Iustificatione, Hieronimus, Adversus Pelagianos, li. 1, Tunc iusti sumus, quoniam nos peccatores fatemur, et iustitia nostra non ex proprio merito, sed ex dei consistit misericordia, dicente sancta scriptura, Iustus accusator sui est, in principio sermonis', CGC II, 106v; 'Non per nostram iustitiam, sed per eum cuius fide, nobis peccata dimittuntur', Jerome, *Super 3 ca. ad Ephesios*, CGC II, 263r; 'Homines autem sic benedicit deus, ut donum gratiae eis suae impartiat, non secundum opera vel merita eorum, sed secundum suam misericordiam', Ambrose, *Super 1 ca. ad Ephesios*, CGC II, 263r; *marginalium*: 'In remissione peccati, nulla merita nostra respicit deus', CGC II, 265r; 'Nemo glorietur in operibus quia nemo factis suis iustificatur, sed qui iustus est, donatum habet, quia post lavachrum iustificatus est. Fides ergo est, quae liberat per sanguinem Christi, quia Beatus ille cui peccatum remittitur, et venia donatur', Ambrose, *In epistolam ad Ireneaum*, CGC II, 89v; 'Itaque ibi misericors auxilium est, quia nullum habet meritum peccator', Augustine, *In Psalmum 7, marginalium*: 'Misericordia datur impio ut sanetur', CGC II, 228v.

priated by faith, not on an intrinsic righteousness infused by grace.[79]

Thus, justification in its proper sense was the remission of sin understood to be based on a divine act of imputation.[80] Cranmer adhered to the classic Protestant forensic definition of justification in his propositional heading for folio 84 *recto*: 'Henceforth, "to justify" signifies "to pronounce, declare or demonstrate just".'[81] Under this heading, he recorded verses of Scripture which used the word 'iustificare' in a forensic sense.[82] Two examples will suffice: Ecclesiasticus 18: 1—'God will be justified' (obviously, God could not be made just, his justice could only be declared); Ezekiel 16: 52—'[Judea] bear your shame, since you have surpassed your sisters by your sins, by your acting more wickedly than them, they have been justified by you.'[83] Under this same heading Cranmer also recorded key Pauline passages on justification, indicating that he understood these important texts to be speaking of forensic justification: Romans 3: 24–6—'They have been justified freely through his grace, through the redemption which is in Christ Jesus whom God made a perfect offering through faith in his blood to demonstrate his righteousness in this time, so that he himself may be just and be the one justifying him who has faith in Jesus Christ'; Romans 9: 30—'The Gentiles who did not pursue righteousness have gained righteousness, a righteousness,

---

[79] 'In [gratia] nos sua, non nostra iustitia, iustos facit, ut ea sit vera nostra iustitia, quae nobis ab illo est', Augustine, *De gratia Christi*, li. 1, ca. 47, *marginalium*: 'Adiutorium gratiae est, quomodo nos, sua iustitia, iustos facit', CGC II, 282r; 'Quis sed novit se quidem inopem esse omnis verae iustitiae, fide autem sola in Christum coniecta, esse iustificatum', Basil, *In sermone de humilitate*, CGC II, 91r.

[80] 'De abundantia bonitatis eius accipimus. Quid? Remissionem peccatorum, ut iustificaremur ex fide', Augustine, *In Johannem*, tract. 3, *marginalium*: 'Iustificatio, remissio peccatorum', CGC II, 235r; 'Uniusquisque vestrum iam in ipsa iustificatione constitutus, accepta, scilicet, remissione peccatorum', Augustine, *De verbis Apostoli*, Sermo 16, *marginalium*: 'Iustificatio est remissio peccatorum', CGC II, 257v.

[81] 'Iustificare subinde significat, iustum pronuntiare, declarare, aut ostendere', CGC II, 84r. For a discussion of 'iustum . . . ostendere', see later in this chapter.

[82] See, e.g., 1 Kings 8: 31–2; Job 9: 20; 40: 3; Psalms 18: 10; 50: 6; 81: 3; Ecclesiasticus 7: 5; 14: 15–16; 18: 1; Isaiah 43: 25; Jeremiah 3: 11; Ezekiel 16: 46–52; Romans 3: 20–6, 28, 30–1; 4: 16; 9: 30–2; 10: 3–6, 11; 11: 5; Ephesians 2: 9–10; Galatians 2: 16; 3: 21–2, 26; CGC II, 84r–85v.

[83] CGC II, 84.

however, which is by faith'; Galatians 2: 16—'We believe in Jesus Christ so that we are justified by the faith of Christ, and not by works of the law.'[84]

Although few, patristic quotations scattered elsewhere in the great notebooks are also suggestive of imputed righteousness: 'Our righteousness is only by faith. Angels alone have perfect righteousness, and only just when compared to God'; 'If righteousness is the work of God, as I have said, how will it be the work of God which the Lord said was to believe in him, except that righteousness be to believe in him'; 'Your faith is your righteousness'; 'For there is a righteousness of God, which becomes ours also when it is given to us . . . . lest man think that he has righteousness from himself. As Paul says, for the one believing in him who justifies the ungodly . . . his faith is reckoned as righteousness.'[85] In his 'Annotations' Cranmer had said that a sinner needed to be reckoned righteous.[86] In the 'Great Commonplaces', he gathered evidence from Scripture, Augustine, several other patristic authorities, and Cajetan to demonstrate that forgiveness based on the extrinsic righteousness of Christ appropriated by faith was, in fact, the *vera theologia*.

RENOVATION

Although Cranmer believed that faith only justified, he did not believe that faith was the only virtue present in the justified. In the moment of justification, saving grace simultaneously brought about faith, love, and the remission of sins.[87] Although both faith and love were present, they

---

[84] CGC II, 85.

[85] 'Iustitia modo nostra ex fide. Iustitia perfecta non est nisi in angelis, et vix in angelis, si deo comparentur', Augustine, *In epistolam Johannis*, tract. 4, CGC II, 207v; 'Si iustitia est opus dei, sicut ego dixi quomodo erit opus dei, quod dixit dominus, ut credatur in eum nisi ipsa sit iustitia credere in eum', Augustine, *Sermo 237*, CGC II, 260r; 'Fides tua, Iustitia tua', Augustine, *In Psalmum 32*, Concio 1, CGC II, 241v; 'Est enim iustitia dei, quae et nostra fit cum donatur nobis . . . ne homo se putet a seipso habere iustitiam. Sic enim dicit Apostolus Paulus, "Credenti in eum qui iustificat impium" . . . deputatur fides eius ad iustitiam', Augustine, *In Psalmum 30*, Concio 1, CGC II, 229v.   [86] Cox II, 114.

[87] 'Quattuor enumerantur quae requiruntur ad iustificationem impii, scilicet,

had separate functions. Through the gift of saving faith, the ungodly received pardon. However, concomitant with pardon, the justified received a renewed will to love which enabled them to lead a new life pleasing to God.[88] Paul's teaching that justification came by faith without works did not contradict James's insistence that faith without works was dead faith, for Paul was describing works before faith, whereas James was talking about the works which necessarily came after justification.[89] Logically, if not chronologically speaking, grace first remitted sin and then healed the will and its affections so that the believer was able to lead a life of love.[90] In fact, Cranmer found a passage in Augustine that supported Osiander's claim that the Holy Spirit was given after forgiveness.[91] Thus, pardon through an extrinsic act of imputation was always associated with an intrinsic

gratiae infusio, motus liberi arbitrii in deum per fidem, et motus liberi arbitrii in peccatum, et remissio culpae . . . praedicta quattuor quae requiruntur ad iustificationem impii, tempere quidem sunt simul, quia iustificatio impii non est successiva', Thomas Aquinas, *Summa Theologiae*, 1ae2ae. q. 113, art. 6, 8, CGC II, 222v; *marginalium*: 'fides et charitas donantur, nullis praecedentibus nisi malis meritis', CGC II, 233r.

[88] 'Novus (inquit) homo ex veteri nascitur, quoniam spiritalis regeneratio mutatione vitae veteranae atque saecularis, inchoatur', Augustine, *In Psalmum 8*, *marginalium*: 'Inchoatio novae gratum deo facit hominem', CGC II, 206v.

[89] 'Quapropter non sunt sibi contrariae duorum apostolorum sententiae, Pauli et Jacobi, cum dicit unus iustificari hominem per fidem sine operibus, et alius dicit, inanem esse fidem sine operibus. Quia ille dicit de operibus quae fidem praecedunt, iste, quae fidem sequuntur, sicut ipse Paulus multis locis ostendit', Augustine, *Octoginta trium quaestionum*, q. 76, CGC II, 106r; for the *locus*, 'Conciliatio Pauli et Jacobi', see CGC II, 106.

[90] 'Per legem cognitio peccati, per fidem impetratio gratiae contra peccatum, per gratiam sanatio animae a vitio peccati, per animae sanitatem libertas arbitrii, per liberum arbitrium iustitiae dilectio, per iustitia dilectionem, legis operatio', Augustine, *De spiritu et littera*, ca. 30, *marginalium*: 'Ordo iustificationis', CGC II, 240v; cf. ibid., fols. 227r, 246r; 'Ita prima curatio est, causam languoris removere, quod per omnium indulgentiam fit peccatorum, secunda, ipsum sanare languorem, quod fit paulatim proficiendo in renovatione huius imaginis', Augustine, *De trinitate*, li. 14, ca. 17, CGC II, 218r; 'Quique fiunt filii dei, quoniam esse incipiunt in novitate spiritus, et renovari in interiorem hominem, secundum imaginem eius qui creavit eos. Non enim ex qua hora quisque baptizatur, omnis vetus infirmitas eius absumitur, sed renovatio incipit a remissione peccatorum', Augustine, *De peccatorum meritis et remissione*, li. 2, ca. 7, *marginalium*: 'Adoptio incipit a renovatione, renovatio, a remissione peccatorum', CGC II, 207v.

[91] 'Donum autem maximum ipse Spiritus Sanctus est . . . Ideo gratis datur, quia non quasi merces redditur post discussionem meritorum, sed donum datur post delictorum veniam', Augustine, *De verbis domini*, Sermo 61, CGC II, 287r.

imparting of the Holy Spirit. Through saving faith the believer was joined to Christ so that Christ dwelled in him, and he was now a member of Christ's body.[92]

Despite the Spirit's intrinsic presence, however, the justified still lacked an inherent righteousness which could have been considered meritorious *de condigno*. The infirmity of the flesh remained. In his 'Annotations' Cranmer had noted that despite the gift of the Spirit, 'our own carnal inclination is still unto evil'.[93] Scholastic theologians taught that the presence of the *fomes peccati* did not effect personal merit unless consent was given to its motions, and then they differentiated between mortal and venial sins which arose from such consent. Cranmer rejected these distinctions. He recorded in his notebooks several extracts from Augustine which characterized the infirmity of the flesh as a serious impediment to inherent righteousness: its presence was a disease of evil character, its motions became the mother of many sins, and its desire for disobedience Paul called sin.[94] While it was possible for the just to have lives free from sin in the sense of not allowing sin to reign in their conduct,[95] it was impossible for them to be entirely free from sin in their lives.[96] The concupiscence of the flesh was always at war

---

[92] 'Qui ergo in Christum credit, credendo in Christum veniet in eum Christus et quoquomodo in eum unitur, et membrum in corpore eius efficitur', Augustine, *De verbis domini*, Sermo 61, CGC II, 287v; 'Quis sed novit se quidem inopem esse omnis verae iustitiae, <u>fide autem sola in Christum coniecta</u>, esse iustificatum', Basil, *In sermone de humilitate*, CGC II, 911.

[93] Cox II, 108.

[94] 'Quamvis autem reatu suo iam soluto, manet tamen . . . affectio est quaedam malae qualitatis sicut languor', Augustine, *Ad Valerium*, li. 1, CGC II, 313r; 'Ex hac inquam concupiscentia carnis, tanquam filia peccati, et quando illi ad turpia consentitur, etiam peccatorum matre multorum', Augustine, *Ad Valerium*, li. 1, CGC II, 312v; '[Paulus] sciebat quippe inesse peccati delectationem, quam peccatum vocat, depravata, scilicet, ex prima transgressione natura', Augustine, *De Genesi ad litteram*, li. 10, ca. 12, CGC II, 314r; 'Ita concupiscentia carnis, adversus quam, bonus concupiscit spiritus, et peccatum est, quia inest illi inobedientia contra dominatum mentis, et poena peccati est, quia reddita est meritis inobedientis, et causa peccati est, defectione consentientis, vel contagione nascentis', Augustine, *Contra Julianum*, li. 5, ca. 4, CGC II, 313v.

[95] 'Verum ecce iam talem constituamus animam humanam in hoc corruptibili corpore . . . ad illicitum aliquid operandum, eidem libidini nulla inclinatione consentiat . . . Non regnet peccatum in vestro mortali corpore ad obediendum desideriis eius', Augustine, *De spiritu et littera*, ca. 36, CGC II, 314v–315r.

[96] 'Sed dici potest quaedam iustitia minor, huic vitae competens qua iustus ex fide vivit . . . non absurde dicitur, etiam ad istam pertinere ne peccet'; 'Quam

with the rule of the Spirit in the justified so that they did not always do what they wanted.[97] As Cranmer noted in his commentary on folio 225 *verso*, although the justified no longer had wickedness in their heart because of the renewal of their will and affections, they continued to have some kind of fault through the infirmity of their nature.[98]

Cranmer recorded several references to the continuing sins of the justified. The apostle James was holy and just, and he had said, 'We all offend in many things.'[99] The just had to acknowledge themselves as sinners, for God had designed justification so that his saints would still need to ask for forgiveness.[100] In fact, the purpose of the commandment against concupiscence was to convince people of their infirmity so that they would not rely on their own efforts but seek God's grace by faith.[101] On folio 202 *verso*, Cranmer noted that while Daniel was himself already just, he still prayed for the forgiveness of his offences and sought gratuitous remission.[102] According to Jerome, out of fear of human frailty and the dread of their own consciences,

obrem debet homo . . . nihil . . . appetere illicitum'; 'nullus in [hac vita] sit hominum, qui nullum habeat omnino peccatum', Augustine, *De spiritu et littera*, ca. 36, CGC II, 314v–315r; cf. CGC II, 247v.

[97] 'Caro (inquit) concupiscit adversus spiritum, spiritus autem adversus carnem, ut non ea quae vultis facitis', Augustine, *Ad Simplicianum*, li. 1, q. 2, CGC II, 280v.

[98] 'Cum quicquid vitii adhuc supersit, [iustus] ex infirmitate habeat, non ex animi malitia', CGC II, 225v.

[99] 'Sanctus enim et iustus erat Apostolus Iacobus cum dicebat, "In multis offendimus omnes" ', Augustine (recte, Gennadius), *De ecclesiasticis dogmatibus*, ca. 36, CGC II, 203r, 276v; cf. CGC II, 297r.

[100] 'Nullus sanctus et iustus caret peccato . . . Et ideo veraciter se e[sse] sancti pronuntiant peccatores, qui in veritate habent, quod plangant, et si non reprehensione conscientiae, certe mobilitate, et mutabilitate praevaricatricis naturae', Augustine (recte, Gennadius), *De ecclesiasticis dogmatibus*, ca. 186, CGC II, 313v–314r; 'Qui sic operatur iustificationem in sanctis suis . . . ut tamen sit, et quod petentibus largiter adjiciat, et quod confitentibus clementer ignoscat', Augustine, *De spiritu et littera*, ca. 36, CGC II, 315r; cf. CGC II, 247v.

[101] 'Hoc enim lex posuit dicendo, "Non concupisces". Non quod hic valeamus, sed ad quod proficiendo tendamus. Verum hoc fit non lege quae hoc imperat, sed fide quae hoc impetrat, non littera qua iubetur, sed spiritum quo sanatur. Non ergo meritis operantis hominis, sed largientis gratia salvatoris. Utilitas itaque legis est, ut hominem de sua infirmitate convincat, et gratiae medicinam quae in Christo est, implorare compellat', Augustine, *Epistola 200* (MO: 196), Ad Asellicum, CGC II, 312r.

[102] 'Daniel iam iustus, orat tamen pro venia commissorum, et gratuitam petit remissionem, per circumcisionem ante iustificatus', CGC II, 202v; CGC II, 297r.

even the newly baptized immediately turning to receive Communion were commanded first to confess their sins.[103]

In his 'Annotations', Cranmer stated: 'after our justification only begin we to work as the law of God requireth. Then we shall do all good works willingly, although not so exactly as the law requireth, by mean of infirmity of the flesh'.[104] In his great notebooks, Cranmer gathered evidence to support this description of renovation as an immediate freeing of the will from servitude to wickedness but only a gradual strengthening of inner rectitude against the flesh's daily urgings to disobedience. Since the Holy Spirit was at work in the lives of the justified, they naturally had some inherent merit.[105] Nevertheless, justification imparted in this life only the beginnings of a personal righteousness. To prove this point Cranmer recorded a number of patristic quotations under a heading entitled *'Incipit'*: 'Baptism takes away whatever sins there be, at which point the regeneration of man <u>begins</u>, in which every guilt, both original and actual is forgiven'; 'For it is not from the hour someone is baptised that all his old infirmity is destroyed, but <u>renovation begins</u> <u>with the remission of all his sins</u>'; '<u>love begun therefore is</u> <u>righteousness begun</u>'; 'The new man . . . is born from the old, since spiritual regeneration <u>begins</u> by a change of the old and worldly life'; 'We believe in him, when <u>we begin to</u>

---

[103] 'De baptismatis fonte surgentes, et regenerati in dominum salvatorem, impleto illo quod de se scriptum est, Beati quorum remissae sunt iniquitates, et cetera, statim in prima corporis Christi communione dicunt, Et dimitte nobis debita nostra, quae illis fuerant in Christi confessione dimissa . . . Et tamen iubentur dicere, Dimitte nobis et cetera, non humilitatis mendatio, ut tu interpretaris, sed pavore fragilitatis humanae, suam conscientiam formidantes', Jerome, *Adversus Pelagianos*, li. 3, CGC II, 204r.

[104] Cox II, 114.

[105] 'Nulla ne igitur sunt merita iustorum? Sunt plane, quia iusti sunt, sed ut iusti fierent, merita non fuerunt', Augustine, *Epistola 105* (MO: 194), CGC II, 83v. On two occasions the great notebooks even acknowledged that eternal life could be described as a reward for merits accrued through grace in the present: *marginalium*: 'Gratia est qua dimittuntur peccata, et ipsa nullis datur meritis, quamvis vita aeterna possit dici dari meritis', CGC II, 252r; *marginalium*: 'Sed coronae aliquo modo est meritum', CGC II, 232r. This 'aliquo modo' would seem to be what Cranmer was describing to Henry in his 'Annotations': 'Then we shall do all good works willingly, although not so exactly as the law requireth, by mean of infirmity of the flesh. Nevertheless, by the merit and benefit of Christ, we being sorry that we cannot do all things no more exquisitely and duly, all our works shall be accepted and taken of God, as most exquisite, pure and perfect', Cox II, 114.

enter into a good life.'[106] Several of these quotations mentioned faith as the means for this beginning: 'by faith [our righteousness] has begun to be in us according to the Spirit'; 'If the faith which works through love is present, the inner man begins to delight in the law of God'; 'A man begins to be changed from evil to good by the beginning of faith only because the free mercy of God which was not his due effects this in him'; 'Therefore you begin to be in faith through forgiveness. Now this faith, with hope and love added, begins to work well.'[107]

If Cranmer at times could emphasize the on-going struggle with sin in the justified, at other times he could describe the intrinsic renovation of the justified in language more suggestive of inherent than incipient righteousness. In his 'Annotations' Cranmer said that lively faith 'suffereth no venom or poison of sin to remain within the heart . . . but gendereth in the heart an hatred to sin, and maketh the sinner clean a new man'.[108] In his great notebooks, Cranmer recorded similar references to purity and righteousness associated with the justified.[109] Yet, in the light of his

---

[106] *Locus* heading 'Incipit', CGC II, 204r; 'Baptismus quaecumque peccata tollit, unde incipit hominis renovatio in qua soluitur omnis reatus et ingeneratus et additus', Augustine, *Enchiridion*, ca. 64, CGC II, 204r; 'Non enim ex qua hora quisque baptizatur, omnis vetus infirmitas eius absumitur, sed renovatio incipit a remissione peccatorum', Augustine, *De peccatorum meritis*, li. 2, ca. 7, *marginalium*: 'adoptio incipit a renovatione, renovatio, a remissione peccatorum', CGC II, 207v; 'Charitas ergo inchoata, inchoata iustitia est', Augustine, *De natura et gratia*, ca. 70, CGC II, 205r; 'Novus . . . homo ex veteri nascitur, quoniam spiritalis regeneratio mutatione vitae veteranae atque saecularis, inchoatur', Augustine, *In Psalmum 8*, CGC II, 206v; 'Illi credimus, quando incipimus vitam bonam ingredi', Augustine, *In Psalmum 13*, CGC II, 207r.

[107] 'In nobis autem [iustitia nostra] ex fide coepit esse secundum spiritum', Augustine, *In epistolam Johannis*, tract. 4, CGC II, 207v; 'Si adsit fides quae per dilectionem operatur incipit condelectare legi dei secundum interiorem hominem', Augustine, *De spiritu et littera*, ca. 14, CGC II, 204v; 'Nec omnino incipit homo ex malo in bonum per initium fidei commutari, nisi hoc illo agat indebita et gratuita misericordia dei', Augustine, *Contra duas epistolas pelagianonum*, li. 2, ca. 10, CGC II, 205v; 'Incipis ergo esse in fide per indulgentiam. Iam fides illa assumpta spe, et dilectione, incipit bene operari', Augustine, *In Psalmum 31*, CGC II, 207r.

[108] Cox II, 86.

[109] See, e.g., 'Anima iusta est et innocens', Augustine, *In Psalmum 7*, CGC II, 228v; '[Homo] accepit ergo iustitiam, propter quam beatitudinem accipere mereretur', Augustine, *De trinitate*, li. 14, ca. 15, CGC II, 238r; 'iustificetur impius, id est, ex impio fiat iustus', Augustine, *De gratia et libero arbitrio*, ca. 6, CGC II, 233v; 'Illa ergo fides, inquam, mundat cor, quae per dilectionem operatur', Augustine, *De sanctis*, Sermo 14, CGC II, 261r; 'Haec est benedictio (inquit) gloriari a deo, et

belief in the infirmity of the flesh and the incipient nature of internal renovation, such language would best be understood as referring to either the extrinsic righteousness imputed to the believer by God or the intrinsic renewal of the will and its affections concomitant with the forgiveness of sin.[110] For Cranmer, no matter how pure the newly inspired love for God made the hearts of the justified, the law of sin continued to be at work in their carnal members.[111] Consequently, justification made the ungodly 'right-willed', not inherently righteous.

REPENTANCE: THE HALLMARK OF THE LOVING RIGHT-WILL

According to the *King's Book*,

Men may not think that we be justified by faith, as it is a several virtue separated from hope and charity, fear of God and repentance; but by it is meant faith neither only ne alone, but with the aforesaid virtues coupled together, containing, as it is aforesaid, the obedience to the whole doctrine and religion of Christ.[112]

Gardiner's letters make clear that the phrase 'faith neither only ne alone' was directed specifically against Cranmer's argument that faith was not alone in the justified—love and other virtues being present—but only faith justified.[113] At best, conservatives would have understood 'faith only' as an attempt to avoid the necessity of making satisfaction for sin, a position doctrinally unacceptable. The *King's Book* con-

inhabitari a deo. Ista sanctificatio conceditur iustis', Augustine, *In Psalmum* 5, CGC II, 228r; 'Gratia sanat voluntatem, praeceditque meritum, et Iustificatio cor rectum', propositional heading, CGC II, 227r.

[110] As we have seen, Cranmer argued that even the works of the justified, because of the infirmity of the flesh, needed to be reputed more 'exquisite, pure and perfect' than they actually were; Cox II, 114.

[111] Ibid., 108.

[112] Lacey, *King's Book*, 11.

[113] Gardiner to Cranmer: 'And ther your Grace could have bene content to have fayth alone reproved, but not fayth only; wheruppon your Grace sayd you woold sheew your mynde to the King, who, to make the matter clere, would have yt termed so as "only faith" were as well denyed as "fayth alone"', Muller, *Letters of Gardiner*, 336.

tinued to teach the need for works of penance.[114] At worst, by eliminating personal merit from the basis of salvation, 'faith only' seemed to deny the regime of its ultimate sanction, the promise of eternal salvation to those who obeyed and the threat of eternal damnation to those who refused; this forfeiture of power was politically unacceptable. To defend solifidianism Cranmer had to prove that faith justified without works and that this justification necessarily led to a godly, obedient life. Cranmer found his answer to both questions in his doctrine of repentance.

According to Gardiner and the conservatives, repentance was fundamentally a matter of human choice, of whether or not people wished to obey the conditions necessary for gaining divine favour so as to receive eternal salvation at the end of their lives. For Cranmer, however, true repentance was the reflexive response to the good news of what God had already done for humankind in offering the free gift of salvation. In his 'Annotations', Cranmer made the argument that God's utterly gracious love inspired grateful human love, and this new affection naturally expressed itself in repentance and amendment of life:

But if the profession of our faith of the remission of our own sins enter within us into the deepness of our hearts, then it must kindle a warm fire of love in our hearts towards God, and towards all other for the love of God,—a fervent mind to seek and procure God's honour, will, and pleasure in all things,—a good will and mind to help every man and to do good unto them, so far as our might, wisdom, learning, counsel, health, strength, and all other gifts which we have received of God and will extend,—and, *in summa*, a firm intent and purpose to do all that is good, and leave all that is evil.[115]

In his commentary on folios 225 *verso*–226 *verso* of the great notebooks, Cranmer applied this principle to the criticisms

---

[114] Satisfaction was an integral part of sacramental penance whereby a penitent 'declareth a desire to please and content God his Father, for the unkindness towards him, in falling from the estate of grace' as well as recompensed 'all hurts and injuries done by him . . . wherein the neighbour ought to be satisfied'. Although no person could satisfy for sin in equivalence, God still required satisfaction and judged the person's efforts according to his will and power, agreeing to accept the penitent's attempts for Christ's sake; Lacey, *King's Book*, 47–8.   [115] Cox II, 86.

of solifidianism. Ignoring the scholastic distinctions between prevenient grace and sanctifying grace and between *culpa* and *poena*, he systematically narrowed the requirements for justification down to having a right will made known by repentance.

Cranmer reasoned that remission of sins could not be tied exclusively to sacramental absolution. If it were a true saying of Cyprian that a penitent was not forgiven by God unless he was first forgiven by the church, then at that time God forgave the lapsed just once, because the early church received the lapsed into penance only once.[116] Neither could remission of sins be dependent on satisfactions. If penitents were not forgiven before fasting, prayer, almsgiving, and other works of penance, then neither were the baptized or those absolved by priests forgiven of sin before satisfaction.[117] The true mark of justification was repentance.

On the one hand, repentance was the initial affective sign of the will made 'right':

> He who now has turned to God, grieves from his heart to have sinned, and he has in his heart a firm amendment of a better life— he has rejected all will to sin. Why is he not already just? For whatever of fault still remains, he has from infirmity, not from the wickedness of his heart.[118]

The one who had a good will was already a 'good man' and 'pleasing' to God, but the one without a good will had no good works.[119] Therefore, all remedies, satisfactions, or rewards for remitting sins were inventions of men which insulted the redeeming power of Christ's blood. These included indulgences, holy water, holy bread, fasts, prayers,

---

[116] 'Si vera est sententia Cypriani, non remitti poenitenti a deo, nisi prius ab ecclesia illi remittatur, ergo olim semel dumtaxat ignovit deus lapsis, quia ecclesia primativa, semel tantum lapsos ad poenitentiam recipiebant [*sic*]', CGC II, 225v.

[117] 'Si poenitenti non condonatur ante ieiunium, orationem, et eleemosinam, et cetera poenitentiae opera. Ergo baptizato, et ab sacerdotibus absoluto, non condonatur peccatum ante satisfactionem', CGC II, 225v.

[118] 'Qui iam conversus ad deum, peccavisse ex animo dolet, et correctionem vitae melioris firmam in animo habet, omnem peccandi voluntatem abiecit, cur non iam iustus sit? Cum quicquid vitii adhuc supersit, ex infirmitate habeat, non ex animi malitia?' CGC II, 225v.

[119] 'Bona opera non habet, cui deest voluntas bona. Quisquis autem bonam habet voluntatem, iam vir bonus est, et deo gratus, ac iustificatus. Ergo qui iustificatus non est, bona opera non habet', CGC II, 225v.

the entering of religion or religious ceremonies and works of supererogation. By narrowing justification to a renewed will and denying that any works were good without a renewed will, Cranmer made a coherent argument for rejecting the scholastic teaching on making satisfaction for sin. If his unstated rejection of scholastic distinctions were accepted, Cranmer's logic offered a compelling defence of solifidianism.[120]

On the other, repentance as the perennial flowering of a loving right-will would naturally manifest itself in a life of right actions. Although good works did not justify, the truly justified were never without good works:

For although God forgives sins because of faith in the blood of Christ, none the less he only forgives those who repent, who forgive sins, who give alms, who are clean in heart, who chastise their body and redirect it into service, who love God and neighbour, who extend themselves in good works, who are earnest to show themselves approved through their good works, not only to God but also to all men, who take off the old man with his works and put on the new man who is created by God, who drive out of their heart the love of sin and bring in the love of God and neighbour, who crucify their flesh with [its] affections and lusts.[121]

This statement helps clarify the propositional heading on folio 84 *recto* which included *ostendere iustum* in the definitions of *iustificare*.[122] For Cranmer, good works were evidence of the loving right-will resulting from divine pardon,

---

[120] 'Sanguis Christi, multis modis contumelia afficitur. Primum, ab iis qui praeter Christi sanguinem, alia excogitant aut supponu[n]t remedia, satisfactiones, aut pretia pro abluendis peccatis, veluti indulgentias, aquam consecratam, panem consecratum, certa ieiunia, certas precationes, ingressum aut ceremonias religionis, opera supererogationis quae aliis vendant, et quicquid ab hominibus inventum est pro abluendis peccatis, et ita erigitur in locum sanguinis Christi', CGC II, 226r.

[121] 'Licet enim propter fidem in sanguinem Christi condonet deus peccata, tamen non nisi resipiscentibus, nisi dimittentibus peccata, nisi eleemosinam facientibus, nisi mundis corde, nisi castigantibus corpus suum et in servitutem redigentibus, nisi deum et proximum diligentibus, nisi in bona opera se extendentibus, nisi intentibus ut per bona opera se probatos exhibeant, non solum deo sed etiam omnibus hominibus, nisi exuentibus veterem hominem cum operibus suis, et induentibus novum hominem qui secundum deum creatur, nisi animo suo expellentibus dilectionem peccati, et admittentibus dilectionem dei et proximi, nisi carnem suam crucifigentibus cum affectibus et concupiscentiis', CGC II, 226r.

[122] 'Iustificare subinde significat, iustum pronuntiare, declarare, aut ostendere', CGC II, 84r.

not its basis. Whereas the *King's Book* described justification as being made truly righteous,[123] Cranmer described justification as being made truly repentant. Consequently, obedience was no less integral in his description of solifidianism than in his opponents' Catholic soteriology, although Gardiner found Cranmer's explanation of how repentance arose 'throughlye . . . backeward'.[124] Thus, by focusing on the loving right-will which accompanied justification, Cranmer was able to present cogent answers to his critics.

Cranmer gathered evidence from Scripture and the Fathers to support these conclusions. With regard to his contention that a right will separated the just from the unjust, Cranmer recorded Luke 16: 13, 'No one is able to serve two masters, for either one he will hate and the other love or he will cling to one and despise the other.'[125] Therefore, he argued, an individual was either under the power of sin or under the power of grace, but never under both at the same time. Hence, those who had turned to God and were performing good works in order to be justified were, in fact, already justified, for if they had the grace necessary to turn to God and do well, they were no longer under sin's dominion.[126] Gregory also described conversion as a change of will whereby the penitent now hated the evil which he had loved and *vice versa*.[127] Cranmer sought to

---

[123] Lacey, *King's Book*, 152.

[124] '[S]cripture preacheth penaunce to obtayne remission of synne, and ye teache remission of synne whereby to come to penaunce. Scripture sayth, and we do not forgiue our neighbour, god wyll not forgiue vs. You teache that god must fyrste forgiue vs, and then we to forgyue our neighbour. Christ calleth vs to him to be vnburdened of our synne, And ye teache that we be vnburdened of our synnne or we come at him. And so throughlye ye teache chryst backeward', Gardiner, *Declaration of true articles*, fol. 87r.   [125] CGC II, 214r.

[126] 'Opponitur gratia peccato, ut appareat non posse quemquam simul esse sub peccato et gratia. Ergo conversus ad deum et bona opera faciens ut iustificetur, si gratiam habet, peccatum non habet', CGC II, 214r; Although perhaps 'si gratia habet, peccatum non habet' could be understood to refer to factitive justification, this phrase serves as an example of the need to interpret specific examples of Cranmer's language in the context of his Protestant understanding of justification and renovation.

[127] 'Conversio autem peccatoris, non est in humilitate confessionis, sed in renovatione interioris hominis, cum peccatori iam divina inspiratione correcto, et malum displicet quod amavit, et bonum placet quod odit', Gregory, *Super I Reg.*, li. 2, ca. 3, *marginalium*: 'Conversio quid', CGC II, 218r.

show that this conversion happened in an instant,[128] so that he could argue in his commentary on 226 *verso*, that 'we be made partakers of the divine mercy through the blood of Christ, <u>as soon as earnestly and with all our heart we turn to God from our evil ways</u>'.[129] Times of penance were established by leaders of the church to satisfy the church, not God.[130] Divine forgiveness required no other satisfaction beyond intending to lead a new life.[131] According to 2 Kings 12: 13, after Nathan had rebuked him for his sin with Bathsheba, David said, 'I have sinned', and the prophet replied, 'The Lord has taken away your sin.' Cranmer recorded this verse and noted that Nathan's announcement of forgiveness was 'before all external

---

[128] '<u>In momento</u> impietas religionem, crudelitas induit pietatem', Cyprian, *De coena domini*, CGC II, 216r; 'Haec conversio voluntatis <u>repente mutavit</u>', Augustine, *Contra Crosconium grammaticum*, li. 2, ca. 9, *marginalium*: 'repente', CGC II, 221r; cf. 'hodie fit confessio . . . <u>hodie dimittatur</u>', Augustine, *De ovibus*, CGC II, 217r.

[129] 'Ita nec diffidere nedum desperare debemus, divinae misericordiae per Christi sanguinem nos factos esse consortes, <u>quum primum serio atque ex toto corde a viis</u> nostris malis ad deum fuerimus conversi. Quippe ut deus omnipotens odit et aversatur omnes impios et aversos, sic idem absque dubio conversos recipit et amplectitur', CGC II, 226v.

[130] 'Tempora poenitentiae constituentur, a praesidibus ecclesiae, non ut satisfiat deo, sed ecclesiae', propositional heading, CGC II, 262v. Cf. 'Recte constitutum ab iis qui ecclesiae praesunt, ut fiat etiam satis ecclesiae in qua remittuntur ipsa peccata', Augustine, *Enchiridion*, ca. 65, CGC II, 262v; '<u>Recte constituuntur ab iis qui ecclesiae praesunt, tempora poenitentiae, ut fiat etiam satis ecclesiae, in qua</u> remittuntur ipsa peccata', ibid., *marginalium*: 'Cur in ecclesia constituuntur tempora poenitentiae', CGC II, 243r.

[131] '<u>Recedens a pristinis malis ex animo, vereque promittat deo</u>, se postea numquam ad illa rediturum, <u>nihil aliud deus requirat ad satisfactionem ulteriorem</u>', Chrysostom, *In oratione de Beato Philogomo*, *marginalium*: 'Sine satisfactione', CGC II, 216v; 'Magna pietas dei, quod <u>ad solam promissionem, peccata dimiserit</u>', Cassiodorus, *In Psalmum 31*, CGC II, 215r; 'Habemus advocatum et depraecatorem pro peccatis nostris Jesum Christum dominum nostrum, <u>si modo nos in praeteritum peccavisse poeniteat</u>, et confitentes atque intelligentes delicta nostra quibus nunc deum offendimus, <u>vel de cetero nos ambulare in viis eius et praecepta eius metuere spondemus</u>', Cyprian, li. 4, *Epistola 4, marginalium*: 'remissio peccatorum promissioni novae vitae deputatur', CGC II, 216r; '<u>Unum enim tantum requiro, nempe, ut confiteantur peccata, et ab eis abstineant. Et non ultro infero poenam peccatis</u>', Chrysostom, *In Genesim*, Homilia 44, *marginalium*: 'Nihil aliud exigit deus quam ut peccare cessemus, et misericordiam non differt', CGC II, 216; 'Dicit <u>flagitiosos sola resipiscentia, sive solo reditu expiari, charitate operiente peccatorum multitudinem</u>', Summary of Augustine, *Contra [secundam] Gaudentii epistolam*, ca. 4 and *Contra Cresconium grammaticum*, li. 3, ca. 19, 23, 24, li. 4, ca. 11, *marginalium*: 'Resipiscentia sola, purgantur peccata', CGC II, 222r.

works of penance'.[132] Summarizing his research, Cranmer aptly entitled the first line of the propositional heading for folio 213 *recto*: 'When the ungodly turn, immediately all their sins are forgiven.'[133] Thus, Cranmer's research and his position in the Henrician court encouraged him to make repentance the focus of soteriology, both as the pastoral description of solifidianism and as the on-going goal of the Christian life.

'De poenitentia II' and 'De poenitentia III' in the great notebooks were completed about the same time as the section on justification and reflect Cranmer's changing approach to repentance.[134] Rather than the Lutheran definition, Cranmer now followed Augustine's twofold description which he had recorded earlier, and referred to again in the section on justification.[135] He gathered extracts which presented *poenitentia* as a public rite of excommunication ('De poenitentia II') and as an individual's decision to turn to God and away from sin ('De poenitentia III'). Cranmer recorded lengthy quotations from Tertullian and Ambrose on the patristic practice of public penance in 'De poenitentia II'. This material highlighted the manner in which early ecclesiastical penance differed from medieval praxis, since *poenitentia* was described as a discipline which could not be repeated rather than as a sacrament which was a yearly duty.[136] The manner in which excommunication in the patristic church eventually evolved into the routine pastoral practice of auricular confession was also suggested by early references to public penances being imposed after private

---

[132] 'Hoc ante omnia poenitentiae opera externa, dixerat propheta', CGC II, 213v.

[133] 'Cum impius convertitur protinus omnia peccata dimittuntur', CGC II, 213r; cf. 'Conversis ad se donat peccata', Augustine, *In Psalmum 32*, Concio 1, CGC II, 221v; 'Quisque se converterit ad fidem ipius, a via sua . . . omnia illi praeterita dimittuntur', Augustine, *De verbis domini*, Sermo 59, *marginalium*: 'Conversis, omnia condonatur', CGC II, 219r.

[134] See the Appendix.

[135] Augustine, *Epistola 108* (MO: 265), CGC I, 160; ibid., CGC II, 262v.

[136] 'Itaque exomologesis . . . disciplina est', Tertullian, *De poenitentia*, ca. [9], CGC II, 128r; 'Hoc enim dico, poenitentiam . . . semel cognitam atque susceptam numquam posthac iteratione delicti resignari oportere', ibid., ca. [5], CGC I, 126v; 'Sicut unum baptisma, ita una poenitentia, quae tamen publice agitur. Nam quotidiani nos debet poenitere peccati, sed haec delictorum leviorum, illa graviorum', Ambrose, *De poenitentia*, li. 2, ca. 10, CGC I, 131r.

confession.[137] The final presentation page for the entire *locus*, the first entry in 'De poenitentia III' was a linguistic definition of *poenitentia*. This description of repentance was at once an indication of Cranmer's probable humanist training in the *tres linguae* and a reminder of his presentation of solifidianism as turning to God and away from sin:

In Scripture, the words 'repentance' and 'to repent' do not signify the execution of a certain work but a coming to one's senses, a turning of the ungodly from ungodliness, a recovery of a sound mind. Therefore, in the prophets where we read, 'If the ungodly will do penance' etc., 'Turn and do penance' etc., the Hebrews read וְהָרָשָׁע כִּי יָשׁוּב מִכָּל־חַטֹּאתָו that is, 'And the ungodly, when he turns away from all his sins' and afterwards, שׁוּבוּ וְהָשִׁיבוּ, that is, "Turn and be converted.' The Hebrew verb transliterated is 'Shabh,' which the Hebrews use here for 'to return,' 'to go back.' In the Septuagint the translators and all the Greeks read 'μετανοεῖτε' because the word signifies 'a change of mind,' 'to discern after the deed,' 'to come to one's senses,' not 'to make satisfaction' or 'to inflict punishment.'[138]

Immediately beneath this definition Cranmer recorded extracts from the Lombard which supported his twofold approach to *poenitentia*, namely, that contrition was sufficient for the forgiveness of sin and serious sins needed to be punished with graver consequences.[139]

[137] 'Sufficit enim illa confessio, quae primum deo offertur, tunc etiam sacerdoti, qui pro delictis poenitentium precator accedit. Tunc enim demum plures ad poenitentiam poterunt provocari, si populi auribus non publicetur conscientia confitentis', Leo the Great, *Epistola 78* (MO: 168), CGC II, 129v; 'Paulinus in vita Ambrosii. Quotienscumque illi aliquis ob percipiendam poenitentiam lapsus suos confitebatur . . . causas autem criminum quas illi confitebantur, nulli, nisi domino soli, apud quem intercedebat, loquebatur . . . Ex hoc loco colligit Capitulum Coloniense, olim in arbitrio et potestate sacerdotis fuisse in ecclesia ut non solum publico, verumetiam occulto peccatori, poenitentiam publicam imponeret', CGC I, 132v.

[138] 'Poenitentia et poenitere in scripturis, non significat operis alicuius executionem, sed recipiscentiam, conversionem impii ab impietate, reditum ad sanam mentem. In locis itaque prophetarum ubi legimus, Si impius egerit poenitentiam ab omnibus peccatis suis et cetera, Convertimini et agite poenitentiam, et cetera, hebraei legunt וְהָרָשָׁע כִּי יָשׁוּב מִכָּל־חַטֹּאתָו id est, impius cum aversus fuerit ab omnibus peccatis suis, et cetera [Ez. 18: 21]. Et postea, שׁוּבוּ וְהָשִׁיבוּ id est, Convertimini et facite converti [Ez. 18: 30], 'Shabh,' quo utuntur hic hebraei, Reverti, Redire. Septuaginta interpretes et Graeci omnes legunt μετανοεῖτε quod verbum significant mentem mutare, post factum sapere, resipiscere, non satisfacere, aut poenam tenere', CGC I, 124r.

[139] See, e.g., 'Facite dignos fructus poenitentiae, scilicet, ut secundum qual-

This connecting of solifidianism as loving repentance with medieval contritionism was the final part of Cranmer's strategy. In the 1530s he had been willing to work within the Catholic tradition of sacramental penance by redefining its constituent parts. Having abandoned penance as a sacrament, in the 1540s he was willing to recast the medieval emphasis on contrition into a Protestant practice of repentance.

In his 'Annotations' Cranmer had outlined the process of justification as beginning with contrition and ending with faith.[140] In his great notebooks, he gathered patristic evidence which described turning to God in sorrow as the first stirrings of saving faith. Prior to justification the penitent found nothing of good within himself.[141] Faced with the terror of being helpless in the face of the righteous judgement of God's law, he could only flee by faith to God's promise of mercy as his sole hope and consolation.[142] Prayer

itatem et quantitatem culpae, sit qualitas et quantitas poenae', 'Non enim sufficiunt graviter delinquentibus, quae sufficiunt minus vel parum peccantibus', Peter the Lombard, *Sententiae*, li. 4, dist. 16, ca. 1, 3, CGC II, 124r; 'Ante confessionem oris et satisfactionem peccatum dimittitur unde propheta [in Ps. 31], Dixi confitebor adversum me iniustitiam meam Domino, et cetera. Sacrificium deo, spiritus contribulatus, et cetera. Quacumque hora peccator, et cetera'; 'Super his sentiendum sit, quid tenendum? Sane dici potest quod sine confessione oris, et solutione poenae exterioris peccata delentur per contritionem et humilitatem cordis', ibid., li. 4, dist. 17, ca. 1, CGC I, 124.

[140] Cox II, 113–14.

[141] 'Ut eum laudes te accuses, quia illius est misericordia ut peccata nostra dimittat. Nam si vellet pro meritis agere, non inveniret, nisi quos damnaret', Augustine, *In Psalmum 94*, CGC II, 263v; 'Nihil invenis unde salves et multum invenis unde damnes', Augustine, *Sermo 15, marginalium*: 'Nihil est, unde salvemur, plurima vero unde damnemur', CGC II, 267v; cf. *marginalia*: 'Gratiae redemptionis, nullam potest homo invenire causam', 'Cum pleni essemus sceleribus, deus nos dilexit et iustificavit', CGC II, 266v.

[142] 'Sub quo timore [ex lege] anima laborans . . . per fidem confugiat ad misericordiam dei', Augustine, *De spiritu et littera*, ca. 29, CGC II, 246r; 'Vide philosophicam mulieris animam dicentis, Miserere mei. Non, inquit, habeo conscientiam bonorum operum, nec rectae vitae fiduciam, ad misericordiam confugio, ad tranquillum portum peccantium, ad misericordiam confugio, ubi cessat iudicium, ad misericordiam confugio, ubi ineffabilis salus est', Chrysostom, *De muliere cananea*, Homilia 12, CGC II, 88r; 'Nusquam bonorum suorum meminit, sed semper ad misericordiam dei confugiat, et in ipsa sola collocat salutem suam', Chrysostom, *De compunctione cordis*, li. 2, CGC II, 88r; 'Miserere mei deus, ad misericordiam, inquit, confugio . . . nec enim confido operibus meis . . . Miserere mei deus, quia misericordia tua inaestimabilis est', Chrysostom, *In Psalmum 50*, Homilia 2, CGC II, 87v.

and confession preceded justification, for admission of sin was the acknowledgement of human helplessness. As such, this humility was the first stirrings of the new life of righteousness and good works.[143] When a penitent was angry with himself for what he had done, he could be assured that he had the Holy Spirit and was united with God in love.[144] A contrite prayer *coram deo*, even just a small one, was all God required for him to forgive entirely a penitent's sins.[145] David confessed his sin as soon as Nathan confronted him, but God responded to the king's admission by granting him forgiveness even more quickly, even though David's transgression had been in deed and his repentance was only in word.[146] So willing was God to forgive a penitent who turned to him in humble prayer that even before his confession had reached his lips, God had heard its cry while still in the heart and granted forgiveness.[147]

---

[143] 'Tamen ut iustificaretur peccator orabat, et peccator confitebatur, et exauditus, iustificatus est', Augustine, *Contra epistola parmeniani*, li. 2, ca. 8, *marginalium*: 'Oratio et confessio ante iustificationem', CGC II, 221r; 'Qui sunt pauperes spiritu? Humiles trementes verbum dei, confitentes peccata sua, non de suis meritis, nec de sua iustitia superbientes', Augustine, *In Psalmum 73*, CGC II, 263r; 'Quid faciemus nos, qui tot malis involuti sumus, et bonorum nobis operum nulla fiducia est quibusque cum abundent delicta nulla satisfactio est, nulla confessio? Ob hoc igitur beatus hic tali utitur confessione', Chrysostom, *De compunctione cordis*, li. 2, CGC II, 87v; 'Audistis cum psalmus legeretur, Incipite domino in confessione. Incipite, inquit, initium iustitiae nostrae, confessio peccatorum. Coepisti non defendere peccatum tuum, iam inchoasti iustitiam, perficietur autem in te, quando nihil aliud facere delectabit, quando absorbebitur mors in victoria', Augustine, *In epistolam Johannis*, tract. 4, *marginalium*: 'Agnitio peccati inchaotio iustitiae', CGC II, 207v; 'Cum coeperit tibi displicere quod fecisti, inde incipiunt bona opera tua, quia accusas mala opera tua. Initium operum bonorum, confessio est operum malorum', Augustine, *In evangelium Johannis*, tract. 12, CGC II, 207v.

[144] 'Cum quisque sibi irascitur, et sibi displicet, sine dono Spiritus Sancti non est. Nec ait Spiritum Sanctum tuum da mihi, sed ne aufera a me', Augustine, *In Psalmum 50*, *marginalium*: 'In confitente sive poenitente, est Spiritus Sanctus', CGC II, 233; 'Est (inquit) spiritus sanctus in confitente', ibid., CGC II, 204r.

[145] 'Solum a nobis deus orationem vel parvam exigit, atque universa nobis dimittet peccata', Chrysostom, *De poenitentia*, Homilia 10, CGC II, 88r.

[146] 'Audistis dicentem regem, Peccavi domino. Et prophetam respondentem, Dominus transtulit peccatum tuum. Velox confessio, velocitior medicina, facto peccavit, verbo poenituit, annuit deus', Chrysostom, *In Psalmum 50*, Homilia 2, CGC II, 87v.

[147] 'Non iam pronuntiat, sed promittit se pronuntiaturum, et deus dimittit et cetera. Confessio vero mea, ad os nondum venerat, verum deus audivit vocem cordis mei. Vox mea in ore nondum erat, et auris dei in corde erat', Augustine, *In Psalmum 31*, CGC II, 215r.

Because God forgave those who asked, and his wrath came upon those who did not, sinners should not put off turning to him.[148]

This identification of Protestant repentance as the successor to medieval contritionism could easily lead to an emphasis on the human initiation of justification. Hence, Cranmer included a brief liturgical section in the great notebooks which placed his solifidianism in a wider theological context of God's sovereignty and glory. According to Cranmer's propositional heading for folio 202 *recto*, 'We pray that those things come to pass which we know are certainly about to happen from the promises of God.' Underneath Cranmer recorded 2 Samuel 7: 26b–29, a passage in which David prayed to God by acknowledging God's faithfulness and asking him to fulfil his promise.[149] What is the first thing to be prayed in conformity to what divine sovereignty will bring about? Above his next entry, Cranmer had recorded: 'We pray so that glory, praise and imperium be given to God forever.'[150] This sentence is followed by Paul's prayer in Ephesians 1: 16 that his readers may be given by revelation knowledge of God, the Father of glory. And what both reveals the glory of God and is the proper response to his glory? According to Cranmer's next heading, 'God ought always to be asked so that he may forgive sins, even those belonging to godly sons which are already all forgiven.'[151] For Cranmer, the only proper response to recognizing God's glory is to acknowledge how much the holiness of the Almighty differs from humanity and, thus, how much humanity continually needs to turn to God for the forgiveness of their sins. According to his 'Annotations', because of the infirmity of the flesh, even the justified need to be sorry that in their works they can not do

---

[148] 'Ne tardes converti ad dominum, neque differas de die in diem. Subito enim veniet ira eius, et in tempore vindictae disperdet te', Augustine, *De verbis domini*, Sermo 59, *marginalium*: 'Non est differenda conversio', CGC II, 220r.

[149] 'Oramus ut eveniant ea quae ex dei promissis certo novimus eventura', CGC II, 202r.

[150] 'Precamur ut deo sit gloria, laus, et imperium, in saecula saeculorum', CGC II, 202r.

[151] 'Semper orandus est deus, ut condonet peccata, etiam piis filiis quibus iam omnia peccata dimissa sunt', CGC II, 202v.

'all things no more exquisitely'.[152] So as children and heirs of God, they are to be displeased to have displeased 'so loving a Father, whose goodness [they] can never account'.[153] Cranmer's final paragraph in his commentary on folio 226 *verso* concluded with a reference to this characteristic concern for God's glory shown in saving sinful humanity:

It is the work and glory of God alone to justify the ungodly, to forgive sins, to give life freely out of his goodness, not from any merits of ours. Satan desires that divine honour be paid to him. Therefore, the one who has attributed either justification's beginning or its pardon to his own works, does he not blaspheme his Creator with satanic wickedness?[154]

Nothing could summarize Cranmer's soteriology any better, or his attitude toward his opponents at the Henrician court.

PREDESTINATION

Emphasizing repentance as the hallmark of justification, Cranmer was able to insist that good works did not justify, but that the justified were never without good works. Such a defence of solifidianism would have suited the particular circumstances of the Henrician court. Nevertheless, this very emphasis on the turning of the human will left Cranmer vulnerable to the charge that salvation remained contingent on the individual, if on a narrower basis. Cranmer addressed this possibility in his commentary on 226 *verso*. He argued that if human action toward salvation *per se* were meritorious, then adult converts were saved by works, since they had to choose to be baptized.[155] Yet Cranmer

---

[152] Cox II, 114.

[153] Ibid., 86.

[154] 'Solius dei opus est et gloria, iustificare impium, remittere peccata, donare vitam ex sua bonitate gratis, non ex ullis nostris meritis. Satan cupit sibi impendi divinum honorem. Qui itaque suis operibus tribuit iustificationis vel initium vel absolutionem, an non satanica impietate creatorem suum blasphemat?', CGC II, 226v.

[155] 'Si iustificationem per opus fieri ideo volunt, quia primo oportet converti ad deum, ergo in prima iustificatione baptismatis, adulti iustificantur per opera, quia eos etiam oportet ad deum converti', CGC II, 226v; cf. *marginalium*: 'Ad baptismi gratiam, nemo venit per liberum arbitrium', CGC II, 277v.

needed more than just syllogisms to safeguard his defence of solifidianism from undermining the utter gratuity of salvation. His liturgical section suggested that divine sovereignty was the necessary theological context in which to set prayers for repentance. According to Gardiner, justification by faith inevitably slipped toward predestination.[156] On this point, he and Thomas Cranmer agreed.

The debate on the relationship between grace and repentance had three central issues: the nature of human potential apart from grace; the nature of the interaction between grace and the human will; and the basis on which saving grace was given. As we have seen, Cranmer associated any notion of free will by natural endowment after Adam to be Pelagian.[157] Although humankind had free choice, this power was insufficient to fulfil God's purposes apart from working together with God's Spirit.[158] In such co-operation, the initiative lay with God, not his creature. Although repentance was an action of the human will, God's grace prompted the desire and brought it into being.[159] On the second issue, Cranmer followed Augustine rather than Luther.[160] Grace

---

[156] For Gardiner, see *Declaration of true articles*, fols. 21r–43v; Muller, *Letters of Gardiner*, 345; and David B. Knox, *The Doctrine of Faith in the Reign of Henry VIII* (London: James Clarke, 1961), 224–5. For predestination in the thought of the early English Reformers, see Dewey D. Wallace, Jr., 'The Doctrine of Predestination in the Early English Reformation', *Church History* 43 (1974), 201–15; O. T. Hargrave, 'The Doctrine of Predestination in the English Reformation', Ph.D. dissertation (Vanderbilt University, 1966), 5–96; Knox, *Doctrine of Faith*, ad passim; Trueman, *Luther's Legacy*, ad passim.

[157] See earlier in this chapter.

[158] 'Voluntatis habetis arbitrium . . . vero vobis non sufficit voluntatis arbitrium ad implendum', Augustine, *De verbis Apostoli*, Sermo 7, *marginalium*: 'liberum arbitrium habemus, sed liberum arbitrium non sufficit', CGC II, 288v; 'Quando enim cum spiritu dei operante, spiritus hominis cooperantur, tunc quod deus iussit impletur', Augustine, *In Psalmum* 77, CGC II, 283v; 'Ubique domini virtus studiis cooperatur humanis, ut nemo possit aedificare sine domino, nemo custodire sine domino, nemo quicquam incipere sine domino', Augustine, *De gratia Christi contra Pelagium et Coelestium*, li. 1, ca. 44, *marginalium*: 'Ambrosius', CGC II, 281v.

[159] 'Ipsam denique poenitentiam, quam procul dubio voluntas agit, domini misericordia et adiutorio fieri', Augustine, *De gratia Christi contra Pelagium et Coelestium*, li. 1, ca. 45, *marginalium*: 'poenitentia fit per gratiam dei', CGC II, 282r; 'Ideo eos vocando et miserando per suam gratiam ipse revocavit, quia per seipsos redire non possent', Augustine, *In Psalmum* 77, CGC II, 284v; *marginalia*: 'petere, quaerere, et pulsare, deus concedit', CGC II, 281r; 'Nemo agit poenitentiam nisi illuminatus Spiritu Sancto', CGC II, 279v.

[160] For a summary of Luther's view, see Trueman, *Luther's Legacy*, 67–72. For Augustine's view, see Burns, *Augustine's Operative Grace*.

did not compel the will by a divine necessity but rather elicited the will's consent, because consent certainly was the property of the will.[161] As a result, Cranmer was able to record as consistent with his understanding of grace the very same quotation that Fisher had used to defend free will against Luther:

And so freedom of choice remains for the seeking of salvation, that is, the reasonable will. But the warning and inviting of God to salvation [comes] first . . . Therefore, the beginning of our salvation we have by God's mercy so that to trust in his saving inspiration is within our power. To receive what we desire by trusting in his warning, [this] is a divine gift.[162]

It is interesting to note that the source of this quotation was not Augustine, as was thought at the time, but Gennadius of Marseilles, a late fifth-century semi-Pelagian, who was hostile to the primacy of grace in salvation.[163]

Accepting his work as genuine Augustinian teaching, both Fisher and Cranmer would have interpreted his *De ecclesiasticis dogmatibus* in the light of their differing understandings of Augustine's teaching. For example, in the passage in question, Gennadius stated that it is in our power *acquiescere* in God's saving inspiration. While Gennadius intended this statement to mean that God permitted humans to initiate the process of salvation, neither Fisher nor Cranmer would have thought that position Augustinian. Fisher's paraphrase made the statement orthodox by defining primary grace as the beginning of salvation which God's mercy granted: 'First is the beginning of our salvation, by which he means the primary grace whereby we are stirred to do good.'[164] Cranmer would also have equated *initium salutis*

---

[161] 'Consentio autem utique volentis est', Augustine, *De spiritu et littera*, ca. 31, CGC II, 246v.

[162] 'Manet itaque ad quaerendam salutem arbitrii libertas, id est rationalis voluntas, sed admonente prius deo, et invitante, ad salutem . . . Initium ergo salutis nostrae, deo miserante habemus, ut acquiescamus salutifere inspirationi nostrae potestatis est, ut adipiscamur quod acquiescendo admonitioni cupimus, divini est muneris', Augustine (recte, Gennadius), *De ecclesiasticis dogmatibus*, ca. 21, CGC II, 274r; cf. Fisher, *ALC*, Art. 36, col. 714.

[163] For the arguments in favour of Gennadian authorship, see Rex, *Fisher*, 249 n. 124.

[164] 'Primum est initium salutis nostrae, per quod intelligit primam gratiam, qua stimulamur ad bene agendum', Fisher, *ALC*, Art. 36, col. 715.

deo miserante with a reference to saving grace. However, Gennadius' use of *acquiescere* permitted Fisher and Cranmer to have different interpretations of the work of that saving grace. *Acquiescere* can mean either 'to obey willingly' or 'to trust in'.[165] In keeping with Fisher's theology, Rex has translated this verb as 'assent', so that, according to 'Augustine', salvation began when grace prompted the human will to assent to its motions.[166] Cranmer's theology, however, would have preferred the alternate definition, rendering the passage as saying that salvation began when grace prompted the human decision to trust in God's inspiration.

In addition to his patristic scholarship, Cranmer found support for these positions in the paraphrases he recorded from Aquinas on the relationship between grace and free will: 'A man however is not able to turn to God, or prepare himself to receive the light of grace, unless through the gratuitous help of God he is moved inwardly'; 'When the will first begins to wish the good, the will has only itself as the motion, but God alone is the mover'; 'He works in us so that we will, but when we will, he co-operates with us so that we can bring our action to completion'; 'a movement for free [choice] and consent to justification is the effect of grace, not the cause'.[167] In sum, the will's granting of consent was an integral part of salvation, but this consent was the effect of grace, not its cause, voluntary, not compelled.

The *King's Book* would have had no quarrel with the necessity of the will to respond to God's motions. As has been noted, the great divide between Cranmer and his

---

[165] *Oxford Latin Dictionary*, 28–9.

[166] Rex, *Fisher*, 127–8.

[167] 'Homo autem non potest ad deum converti, seu praeparare se ad lumen gratiae suscipiendum, nisi per auxilium dei gratuitum, interius moveatur', Thomas Aquinas, *Summa Theologiae*, 1a2ae, q. 109, art. 6, CGC II, 113v; 'Cum voluntas primum incipit bonum velle, voluntas se habet solum ut mota, solus autem deus est movens', ibid., q. 111, art. 2, CGC II, 115r; 'Ut autem velimus in nobis operatur, cum autem volumus, ut proficiamus nobis cooperatur', ibid. 'Motus liberi et consensus ad iustificationem, est effectus gratiae, non causa', ibid. The material from Aquinas is entered under a *locus* entitled 'Distinctio 25, De libero arbitrio', referring to the Lombard's *Sententiae*, li. 2, Dist. 25 and includes summaries from the *Summa* on 1a2ae, q. 109, art. 2, 3, 4, 6, 7, 8, 9, 10; q. 110, art. 1, 2, 3, 4; q. 111, art. 1, 2, 3; q. 112, art. 1, 2; CGC II, 112v–118r. Although these summaries do contain references to the distinctions between actual and habitual graces, only material discussing actual grace has been underlined.

opponents was the nature of salvific grace. Cranmer rejected the conservatives' teaching of a supernatural assistance available to all by which anyone could prepare himself for justification. In the telling words of Cranmer's propositional heading for folio 105 *recto*, justifying grace was what distinguished the good from the wicked, not what was common to both groups.[168] The *King's Book* taught that penitents making good use of God's special assistance, although not yet justified, were still 'in a good way'.[169] For Cranmer, no 'middle' grace meant no middle ground of preparation between the sons of God and the sons of the Devil, as his propositional heading for 213 *recto* stated.[170] In this *locus* he recorded numerous scriptures to prove that all humanity fell under either one or the other category.[171] In his 'Annotations' Cranmer had suggested that election and justification were inseparable and by grace alone.[172] In his great notebooks, Cranmer gathered evidence primarily from Augustine to prove that salvation *sola gratia* meant *ex praedestinatione ante praevisa merita*.[173]

---

[168] 'Gratia, accipitur pro gratia iustificante, sive pro gratia illa quae bonos discernit a malis, non pro illa quae communis est bonis et malis', CGC II, 105r.

[169] Lacey, *King's Book*, 159.

[170] 'Nec medium est ullum inter filios dei et diaboli', propositional heading, CGC II, 213r.

[171] 'He makes his sun to shine upon the bad and the good, and sends rain upon the just and the unjust' (Matthew 5: 45); 'He who is not with me is against me, and he who does not gather with me scatters' (Matthew 12: 30); 'Make a tree good and its fruit will be good, or make a tree bad, and its fruit will be bad' (Matthew 12: 33); 'The kingdom of heaven is like a man who sowed good seed in his field, but while everyone was sleeping, his enemy came and sowed weeds among the wheat' (Matthew 13: 24–5); 'They chose the good fish for the baskets, but threw the bad away' (Matthew 13: 48); 'Two men will be in a field, one will be taken and one will be left' (Matthew 24: 40); 'Indeed, he will put the sheep on his right and the goats on his left' (Matthew 25: 33); translated from the Latin, CGC II, 213r–214v.

[172] Cox II, 95.

[173] It is interesting to note that Gardiner felt obligated to minimize the importance of Augustine's teaching on predestination: 'Mary saynt Austen troubled with the pelagians . . . thought not necessarie to folowe the rest in that poynte, whereby to note the cause of goddes election to be any wyse referred to thendeuour of man but only to be in gods wil, which is most just, and wherein is no acception of persons. And yet saynt Austine doth not so dissent from the other fathers for auoydinge the pelagians as he doth any thynge fauour thopinion of them, who nowe a dayes by vnderstandinge of those actes of election and predestinacion in god wolde establisshe mere necessitie . . . saint Austen in this point dissent frome other, not with contencion but rather therby to exclude the matter of argument that might serue the Pelagians', *Declaration of true articles*, fol. 43r.

Justifying grace was not made available to all.[174] Rather, before the foundations of the world, God chose a set number of people, his elect, to spend eternity with him.[175] He first gave them the grace of conversion to bring about their justification, and then he gave them the grace of perseverance so that they would continue in their justification until they entered the age to come.[176] Augustine taught that God gave justifying grace to more people than he gave the grace of final perseverance, enabling him to teach the regeneration of every baptized child but the assured final salvation by grace of only the elect.[177] Consistent with his earlier characterization of the justified and the elect as being coextensive, Cranmer failed to record any indication of either position in the material on justification. Instead, a quotation was included that presented the linkage of predestination and justification as a source of confidence in eternal salvation.[178] While none of those predestined would be lost, none of those passed over could ever be saved.[179]

God's decision was not based on foreseen works, foreseen

---

[174] 'Scimus [gratiam dei] non omnibus hominibus dari . . . Scimus eis quibus non datur, iusto iudicio dei non dari', Augustine, *Epistola 107* (MO: 217), CGC II, 270r.

[175] 'Ante omnia saecula scire quibus esset per fidem, gratiam largiturus', Augustine, *De fide ad Petrum diaconum*, ca. 34, *marginalium*: 'Deus ante saecula novit quibus esset gratiam largiturus', CGC II, 279v; 'Numerus ergo sanctorum per dei gratiam, dei regno praedestinatus, donata sibi etiam usque in finem perseverantia, illuc integer producetur', Augustine, *De correptione et gratia*, ca. 13, CGC II, 121v.

[176] 'Sicut duo sunt officia medicinae, unum quo sanatur infirmitas, aliud quo custoditur sanitas, Ita duo sunt dona gratiae, unum quod aufert carnis cupiditatem, Aliud quod facit animi perseverare virtutem', Augustine, *In sententiis Prosperi*, ca. 131, CGC II, 105v; cf. CGC II, 282v.

[177] See Burns, *Augustine's Operative Grace*, 175–8.

[178] 'In hiis ergo quattuor rebus [i.e. praedestinatione, vocatione, iustificatione, et glorificatione] considerare debemus quid iam habeamus et quid iam expectemus. In hiis enim quae iam habemus, laudemus deum largitorem, in his quae nondum habemus, tenemus debitorem. Debitor enim factus est, non aliquid a nobis accipiendo, sed quod ei placuit promittendo', Augustine, *De verbis Apostoli*, Sermo 16, CGC II, 257r.

[179] 'Firmissime tene, et nullatenus dubites, omnes quos vasa misericordia gratuita bonitate deus fecit, ante constitutionem mundi in adoptionem filiorum dei praedestinatos a deo neque perire posse aliquem eorum quos deus praedestinavit ad regnum caelorum, neque quemquam eorum quos non praedestinavit, ad vitam, ulla posse ratione salvari', Augustine, *De fide ad Petrum diaconum*, ca. 35, *marginalium*: 'Nemo praedestinatorum potest perire, nec salvari quisquam non praedestinatorum', CGC II, 279v–280r.

merits, or even foreseen faith. All these were, in fact, the results of his decision to grant grace to his elect, not the reverse. Good works sprang from a renewed will, the renewed will arose from saving faith, and faith, while indeed an action of the human will, was the result of God preparing the will of the elect to believe.[180] What merit of will did children have that they should receive salvation through baptism?[181] God gave his justifying grace freely to the elect before considering any future merits and based solely on the hidden judgement of his will.[182] Just as humankind did not merit Christ's Incarnation on their behalf, neither did the elect merit the grace conferred on them.[183] In fact, there was no difference in the situation between those who received grace and those who did not.[184] Like a potter who made from the same lump of clay one vessel for honour and another for disrepute, God simply decided to separate out from the mass of damned humanity some which he chose to

---

[180] 'Praeparavit iustificandos, ut accepta gratia recte credant, et bene vivant . . . quos deus gratis, nullo bonae voluntatis, vel boni operis merito praecedente, salvavit', Augustine, *Ad Petrum diaconum*, ca. 3, *marginalium*: 'praedestinatio', CGC II, 238r; 'Profecto fides in potestate est. Sed sicut Apostolus dicit, Non est potestas nisi a deo . . . Nam ut credamus, deus dedit', Augustine, *De spiritu et littera*, ca. 31, CGC II, 246v; 'Nostrum est enim credere et velle . . . Neque velle possumus nisi vocemur', Augustine, *Retractationes*, li. 1, ca. 23, *marginalium*: 'Et credere et velle, dei est', CGC II, 270r; *marginalia*: 'vel credere, deus operatur in nobis', CGC II, 104v; 'voluntatem praeparat deus', CGC II, 237v; 'voluntas praeparatur a domino', CGC II, 278v; cf. CGC II, 274v–275r.

[181] 'Quomodo voluntatis humanae meritum, sequitur gratia, cum detur et parvulis, qui hoc nondum possunt velle, seu nolle?', Augustine, *Epistola 107* (MO: 217), CGC II, 271r; 'Quibus datur [gratia dei], non solum secundum merita operum non dari, sed nec secundum merita voluntatis eorum quibus datur, quod maxime apparet in parvulis, Scimus eis quibus datur, misericordia dei gratuita dari', ibid., CGC II, 270r.

[182] 'Dedit enim [gratia], non quia digni eramus, sed quia voluit', Augustine, *De trinitate*, li. 4, ca. 1, *marginalium*: 'Gratiam dat deus, non quia digni sumus, sed quia vult', CGC II, 280r; *marginalium*: 'Iustificatio fit occulto dei iudicio', CGC II, 273r; 'Occulta illius iustitia tibi sors est', Augustine, *In Psalmum 30*, Concio 2, CGC II, 230r.

[183] *Marginalium*: 'Natura humana in Christo sine merito adsumpta est, sic et gratia nobis confertur', summarizing Augustine, *De trinitate*, li. 13, ca. 17, CGC II, 280r; *marginalium*: 'Natura humana in Christo gratis assumpta est', CGC II, 286v; cf. the same argument used for the gratuity of justification, CGC II, 233r.

[184] 'Illis quibus gratia ista non datur, nullo plerumque merito, nulla voluntate distantibus, sed similem cum eis quibus datur habentibus causam', Augustine, *Retractationes*, li. 2, ca. 66, *marginalium*: 'Quomodo sequatur gratia voluntatem, cum hii quibus non datur gratia, similem habent caussam cum illis quibus datur?', CGC II, 271r.

save according to his own inscrutable counsel.[185] The utter gratuity of salvation was summed up in the following sequence: 'He predestined us before we were, he called us although we were turned away [from him], he justified us although we were sinners, he glorified us although we were mortals.'[186]

A Christian believed in the Lord by his own will and free choice.[187] Nevertheless, salvation was not determined by human consent because the gift of grace imparted the Holy Spirit which brought about whatever good pertained to salvation, including consent.[188] Like the conversion of Paul on the road to Damascus or Xerxes in the presence of Esther, by his omnipotent power God drew the unwilling to himself, took away their heart of stone, gave them his Spirit and made them willing.[189] In accordance with the

---

[185] 'Habet potestatem figulus luti ex eadem massa facere aliud vas in honorem, aliud in contumeliam, Sed dicis, me quare fecit in honorem, et alium in contumeliam?', Augustine, *De verbis Apostoli*, Sermo 11, *marginalium*: 'Electio dei investigabilis', CGC II, 291r. The section from Aquinas referred the reader to examine Thomas's distinction between love, election, and predestination in his commentary on Romans 9, at the end of the second lection; CGC II, 115v. According to Thomas, 'Unde non propter aliquod bonum quod in homine eligat Deus eum diligit, sed potius eo quod ipsum diligit, praefert eum aliis eligendo. Sicut autem dilectio de qua hic loquitur [i.e. Ad Romanos 9: 13], pertinet ad aeternam Dei praedestinationem, ita etiam odium, de quo hic loquitur, pertinet ad reprobationem qua Deus reprobat peccatores', *Super Epistolas Sancti Pauli Lectura* (Rome: Marietti, 1953), i. 138.

[186] 'Praedestinavit antequam essemus, vocavit cum aversi essemus, iustificavit cum peccatores essemus, glorificavit cum mortales essemus', Augustine, *De verbis Apostoli*, Sermo 16, *marginalium*: 'Iustificavit nos deus cum peccatores essemus', CGC II, 257r.

[187] 'Scimus eos qui corde proprio credunt in dominum, sua id facere voluntate, ac libero arbitrio', Augustine, *Epistola 107* (MO: 217), CGC II, 270; 'Consentire autem vocationi dei, vel ab ea dissentire, sicut dixi, propriae voluntatis est', Augustine, *De spiritu et littera*, ca. 33, *marginalium*: 'Consentire autem vocationi dei propriae voluntatis est', CGC II, 104v.

[188] *Marginalium*: 'Idem, Spiritus Sanctus efficit cogitare, eligere, consentire, cuilibet bono, ad salutem pertinenti', CGC II, 277r.

[189] 'Sed ut volentes ex nolentibus fiant', Augustine, *Contra duas epistolas pelagianorum*, li. 1, ca. 19, *marginalium*: 'Deus quomodo trahat', CGC II, 227v; 'Ezekiel 36[: 26], Dabo eis cor aliud, et spiritum novum dabo illis, et evellam eorum cor lapideum, et dabo eis cor carneum', ibid., ca. 20, CGC II, 227v; 'Qui et praeveniendo dedit eis bonum velle quod noluerunt', Gregory the Great, *Moralium*, li. 22, ca. 10, CGC II, 118r; *marginalium*: 'Deus facit conversionem, quoniam ex nolentibus volentes facit', CGC II, 271v; *marginalium*: 'Gratia aufert lapideum cor, et praeparat hominum voluntates', CGC II, 272r; 'Eosque ad seipsum omnipotentissima facilitate convertit, ac volentes ex nolentibus fecit?'

principle of *lex orandi–lex credendi* this was self-evidently true, for the church prayed for the conversion of un- believers.[190] Although some might want faith to begin as a human initiative to which God then granted saving grace, in fact, without God's calling, no one was able to believe.[191] This inability of the non-elect to believe explained why some hearing the gospel came to faith and others did not.[192] Despite having no alternative, sinners still bore the responsibility for their damnation. While the non-elect could not believe because God had blinded their eyes and hardened their hearts, he did so simply by withdrawing his presence and denying his aid so that unbelievers freely followed their own depraved wills.[193] Summing up the situation of the non-elect, Cranmer maintained that their

Augustine, *Epistola 107* (MO: 217), *marginalium:* 'Et gratia sua convertat eos qui impii sunt, et doctrinae suae persecutores, ac volentes ex nolentibus faciat', CGC II, 271r; conversion of Paul, Acts 9, Esther and Xerxes, Esther 14. Cf. *Contra duas epistolas pelagianorum,* li. 4, ca. 5, 6, cited on CGC II, 105v.

[190] 'Ut legem credendi, lex statuat supplicandi . . . tota secum ecclesia con- gemiscente postulant, et precantur, ut infidelibus donetur fides', Augustine (recte, Gennadius) *Ecclesiasticis dogmatibus,* ca. 30, CGC II, 275r; 'Scimus pro eis qui nolunt credere, nos qui iam credimus recta fide agere, cum deum oramus ut velint', Augustine, *Epistola 107* (MO: 217), CGC II, 270v; 'Cur enim admonemur orare pro inimicis nostris, utique nolentibus pie vivere, nisi ut deus in illis operetur ut velint?', Augustine, *Enchiridion,* ca. 30, CGC II, 278v.

[191] 'Initium fidei ubi est etiam initium bonae, hoc est, piae voluntatis, non vis donum esse dei, sed ex nobis, nos habere contendis, ut credere incipiamus, cetera autem religiosae vitae bona, deus per gratiam suam, iam ex fide petentibus, quaerentibus, pulsantibus, donare consentis', Augustine, *Epistola 107* (MO: 217), *marginalium:* 'Error Vitalis', CGC II, 272v; 'Nemo enim credit qui non vocatur. Misericors autem deus vocat, nullis hoc vel fidei meritis largiens, quia merita fidei sequuntur vocationem potius quam praecedant', Augustine, *Ad Simplicianum,* li. 1, q. 2., CGC II, 249v.

[192] *Marginalia:* 'Frustra audit verbum dei, qui gratia non praevenitur', CGC II, 279v; 'Sine gratia inspirante, frustra audiantur conciones', CGC II, 285v; cf. Augustine, *In Psalmum 87,* CGC II, 253v–254r; 'Praedicato Christo, crucifixo, audiunt duo, unus contemnit, alter ascendit', Augustine, *De verbis Apostoli,* Sermo 2, *marginalium:* 'praedestinatio', CGC II, 266v.

[193] 'Quare autem non poterant, si a me quaeratur, cito respondeo, quia nolebant. Malam quippe eorum voluntatem praevidit deus . . . Sic enim excaecat, sic obdurat deus, deserendo et non adiuvando, quod occulto iudicio facere potest, iniquo non potest', Augustine, *In evangelium Johannis,* tract. 53, commenting on Isaiah 6: 10 as discussed in Romans 11: 7, CGC II, 120r. In this context should the following reference to the human will's ability to decline to give consent to God's general calling be understood: 'Consentire autem vocationi dei, vel ab ea dissentire, sicut dixi, propriae voluntatis est', Augustine, *De spiritu et littera,* ca. 33, CGC II, 104v.

inability to believe needed to be understood in the light of
2 Timothy 2: 11—'If we are unbelieving, he remains
faithful because he cannot deny himself.' 'Since the Lord
is not able to deny himself, praise belongs to the divine
will, since they are not able to believe, the blame belongs
to the human will.'[194] While it was understandable that
such a teaching might be difficult to accept, who was man
to question his Maker, the depths of whose wisdom was
beyond the capacity of the human mind? A beast might as
well have questioned why it was not made human, as a
man to question why God prepared one person for eternal
blessedness and another for eternal damnation.[195] Thus,
Cranmer considered repentance the sure sign of salvation
not because it demonstrated the penitent's good will
towards God, but rather because it was evidence of
God's good will towards the penitent.[196] Only if a sinner
had been chosen by God was he able to repent, only if he
were elect would he be able to say with Jeremiah, 'For
after you turned me, I did penance, and after you showed
me, I struck my thigh.'[197]

---

[194] 'Sic ergo intelligendum est non poterant, quemadmodum dictum est de
Christo, II Tim. 2 . . . Sicut ergo quia dominus negare seipsum non potest, laus est
voluntatis divinae, ita quia illi non poterant credere, culpa est voluntatis humanae',
CGC II, 120r.

[195] 'Sed movet me (inquis) quod ille perit, ille baptizatur, movet me, movet
tanquam hominem . . . O homo, tu quis es, qui respondeas deo? Numquid dicit
figmentum ei qui se finxit, cur me sic fecisti? Si posset loqui pecus, et dicere deo,
Quare istum hominem fecisti, et me pecudem?', Augustine, *De verbis Apostoli*,
Sermo 11, CGC II, 291v–292r; 'Quare ille, deo deserente, excaecatur, ille, deo
adiuvante, illuminatur, non nobis iudicium de iudicio tanti iudicis usurpemus sed
contremiscentes exclamemus cum Apostolo, O altitudo divinitiarum sapientiae et
scientia dei', Augustine, *In evangelium Johannis*, tract. 53, CGC II, 120r; cf.
Augustine, *Sermo 20*, CGC II, 258v.

[196] 'Bona enim voluntas dei, praecedit bonam voluntatem nostram, ut peccatores
vocet in poenitentiam, Augustine, *In Psalmum 5, marginalium*: 'Bona voluntas dei,
praecedit in nos, bonam voluntatem nostram in eum', CGC II, 228r.

[197] 'Per seipsos redire non possent . . . nisi per electionem gratiae', Augustine, *In
Psalmum 77*, CGC II, 284v; 'Sic Hieremias [31: 18–19]. Converte me domine, et
convertar, quia tu dominus deus meus. Postquam enim convertisti me, egi
poenitentiam, et postquam ostendisti mihi, percussi femur meum', Augustine,
De verbis domini, Sermo 50, CGC II, 119v.

CRANMER'S 'NOTES ON JUSTIFICATION'

At about the same time Cranmer was researching Augustine's soteriology, he wrote out in his own hand propositions and patristic quotations which have come to be known as his 'Notes on Justification'.[198] These 'Notes' consist of two different collections of quotations written mostly in Cranmer's hand, but only the second, longer set has propositional headings like the great notebooks, and for that reason they are the natural focus for a comparison with the 'Great Commonplaces'.[199] In his 'Notes' Cranmer included a much wider range of authors than the corresponding section in his great notebooks; consequently only a few scattered quotations are common to both manuscript collections. Naturally, of these, most are from Augustine.[200] The

---

[198] Since 'Notes on Justification' include an integral extract from the *Antididagma* (1544), a final date for their composition must be the mid-1540s. Cf. D. G. Selwyn, 'Thomas Cranmer's Writings: A Bibliographical Survey', in Ayris and Selwyn, *Churchman and Scholar*, 281–302, at 292.

[199] LPL MS 1108, fols. 58r–67v record material relevant to justification, fols. 58–9 with full attribution of sources but with no propositional headings, fols. 60r–67v with propositional headings but usually attributed by author's name only. Both collections were together in the same order prior to their inclusion in LPL MS 1108, having a second set of folio numbers running from 166 to 175. Although both in Cranmer's hand, they were probably drawn up separately, fols. 58–9 having a jester watermark, fols. 60, 64–6 having a hand and star mark instead, in addition to the differences already noted.

[200] Cf. Scriptures: Ephesians 2: 8–9, LPL MS 1108, fol. 60r, CGC II, 85v; Galatians 3: 21–2, LPL MS 1108, fols. 60r, 62v, CGC II, 85v; Romans 3: 20, 31, LPL MS 1108, fol. 62r, CGC II, 85r; Romans 9: 30, LPL MS 1108, fol. 62r, CGC 85r; Romans 4: 16, LPL MS 1108, fols. 61r, 65v, CGC II, 85r; Romans 3: 23–4, 28, LPL MS 1108, fol. 60r, CGC II, 85r; Romans 11: 6, LPL MS 1108, fol. 65r, CGC II, 85r; Revelation 22: 11, LPL MS 1108, fol. 63v, CGC II, 85r; James 2: 21, LPL MS 1108, fol. 63v, CGC II, 85r; Acts 10: 43, LPL MS 1108, fol. 65v, CGC II, 85v; Acts 13: 38, LPL MS 1108, fol. 65v, CGC II, 85v. Authors: Augustine, *Epistola 106* (MO: 186), *marginalium*: 'Fides non meretur iustificationem', LPL MS 1108, fol. 58r, *marginalium*: 'fides non est meritum iustificationis', CGC II, 232; Augustine, *Enchiridion*, ca. 8, LPL MS 1108, fol. 58v, CGC II, 242v–243r; Augustine, *In Psalmum 31*, LPL MS 1108, fol. 60v, CGC II, 231r; Augustine, *De spiritu et littera*, ca. 7, LPL MS 1108, fol. 60v, CGC II, 100v, 227r; Ambrose, *Epistola 41*, LPL MS 1108, fol. 60v, CGC II, 89v; Augustine, *De spiritu et littera*, ca. 10, LPL MS 1108, fol. 61r, CGC II, 101v [note same underlining]; ibid., ca. 26, LPL MS 1108, fol. 61r, CGC II, 102v [note same underlining]; ibid., ca. 30, LPL MS 1108, fol. 61r, CGC II, 103v; Chrysostom, *Contra Iudaeos*, Oratio 4, LPL MS 1108, fol. 61r, CGC II, 86r; Chrysostom, *Homilia 80*, De poenitentia, LPL MS 1108, fol. 61r, CGC II, 87r; Gennadius, *Super 5 ca. ad Romanos*, LPL MS 1108, fol. 61r, CGC II, 90r;

purpose of his 'Notes on Justification' also differed from his great notebooks. 'Cranmer's Great Commonplaces' researched Augustine's soteriology with a polemic in mind. In his 'Notes', however, Cranmer was attempting to outline a pastoral presentation of solifidianism in preparation for his 'Homily on Salvation'.[201] He avoided the technical language of justification. Here Cranmer simply presented forgiveness of sin as the result of turning to God in faith so that he would pardon the believer because of Christ's merits. If his purpose in 'Notes on Justification' was different from that of his great notebooks, Cranmer's Protestant theological approach remained consistent. Any ambiguity in his presentation of solifidianism in his 'Notes' must be interpreted in the light of his great notebooks.

Cranmer wrote out eight English propositional headings under which he recorded Latin quotations from Scripture and a range of authors from Origen to Erasmus. The first proposition advanced Cranmer's customary thesis that sinners were justified by faith only because any human contribution was derogatory to God's glory: 'St. Paul saith that we be justified freely by faith without works, because no man should glory in his works.'[202] The second referred the sinner not to his own merit, but to Christ's alone: 'Meaning thereby to exclude the merit and dignity of all works and virtues, as insufficient to deserve remission of sin, and to ascribe the same only to Christ.'[203] The third proposition clarified that the works excluded by Paul were, in fact, all works commanded by the old covenant, not just those no longer observed by Christians: 'When St. Paul said, "We be justified freely by faith without works", he meant of all manner of works of the law, as well of the Ten Command-

Augustine, *In Psalmum 31*, LPL MS 1108, fol. 61v, CGC II, 230v; the citation of Augustine, *De spiritu et littera*, ca. 8, 13–14, 29 and *Ad Simplicianum*, q. 2, LPL MS 1108, fol. 63r, CGC II, 101, 103, 249r–250r, 280v–281r; *Glossa ordinaria*, Super 2 ca. in epistolam Jacobi, LPL MS 1108, fol. 63v, CGC II, 106v; Augustine, *In libro sententiarum Prosperi*, ca. 131, LPL MS 1108, fol. 64v, CGC II, 105v.

[201] For the relationship between 'Notes on Justification' and the 'Homily of Salvation', see Chapter 6.

[202] LPL MS 1108, fol. 60r; Cox II, 205. All citations from 'Notes on Justification' follow the modernized spelling and unnoted expansion of abbreviations of the printed editions.

[203] LPL MS 1108, fol. 61r; Cox II, 206.

ments, as of ceremonials and judicials.'[204] Cranmer's fourth proposition emphasized that this understanding of Paul was the position of the early undivided church: 'The same meant divers ancient authors, as well Greeks as Latins, when they said, "We be justified by only faith, or faith alone".'[205]

Cranmer's fifth proposition addressed the common objection to claiming ancient authority for justification by faith, the relationship between James and Paul: 'St James meant of justification in another sense, when he said, "A man is justified by works, and not by faith only". For he spake of such a justification which is a declaration, continuation, and increase of that justification which St. Paul spake of before.'[206] Without any specific definition of justification as either forensic or intrinsic in 'Notes', this phrase could be construed as implying factitive righteousness.[207] However, as in his great notebooks, Cranmer merely meant that good works which followed justification served as a testimony to that justification and an indication of the increasing inner rectitude against the infirmity of the flesh.[208] Underneath this proposition, Cranmer recorded quotations which illustrated this point. Abraham was justified by his works in the sense that they demonstrated his faith.[209] Paul excluded human works prior to justification, whereas James excluded the possibility that those so justified did not have to do good deeds.[210] Finally, although

---

[204] LPL MS 1108, fol. 62r; Cox II, 207.

[205] LPL MS 1108, fol. 63r; Cox II, 208.

[206] LPL MS 1108, fol. 63v; Cox II, 208.

[207] McGrath, *Iustitia Dei*, 288, 485 n. 24.

[208] See earlier in this chapter.

[209] 'Jac. 2[: 21] . . . Abraham pater noster nonne ex operibus justificatus est, cum immolaret filium suum super altare. Ecclesiasticus 44: [21] Abraham in tentatione nonne inventus est fidelis', LPL MS 1108, fol. 63v, Cox II, 208, cf. CGC II, 85r; 'Haec oblatio fuit opus et testimonium fidei et justitiae', *Glossa ordinaria*, LPL MS 1108, fol. 63v, Cox II, 209, CGC II, 106v; 'Et suppleta est scriptura dicens, Credidit Abraham Deo, et imputatum est ei ad justitiam. Ex oblatione Isaac scriptura illa dicitur esse suppleta, in quantum per hoc magnitudo fidei Abrahae fuit aliis declarata', Lyra, LPL MS 1108, fol. 64r (not in Cranmer's hand).

[210] 'Cum Jacobus bona opera commemorat Abrahae, quae eius fidem comitata sunt, satis ostendit Paulum apostolum non ita per Abraham docere justificari hominem per fidem sine operibus, ut, si quis crediderit, non ad eum pertineat bene operari, sed ad hoc potius, ut nemo arbitretur meritis priorum bonorum operum se pervenisse ad donum iustificationis, quae est in fide', Beda, LPL MS 1108, fol. 63v, Cox II, 209.

good works augmented justification, they did not do so in the sense of increasing personal righteousness. Rather, good works strengthened the source of a believer's righteousness through Christ, his faith.[211] Cranmer's reconciliation between Paul and James was consistent with Protestant thought.[212]

In his last three propositional headings, Cranmer returned to his central concern for protecting God's glory from humanity's vanity. The purpose of justification by faith was to ensure that Christ's sacrifice and God's benevolence received proper credit: 'This proposition, that we be justified by Christ only and not by our good works, is a very true and necessary doctrine of St. Paul and other the apostles and prophets, taught by them to set forth thereby the glory of Christ, and mercy of God by Christ.'[213] Neither faith nor love as human virtues could serve as a meritorious basis for the remission of sins, since justification was Christ's work alone: 'Although all that be justified must of necessity have charity as well as faith, yet neither faith nor charity be the worthiness and merits of our justification, but that is to be ascribed only to our Saviour Christ, which was offered upon the cross for our sins, and rose again for our justification.'[214] Instead, consistent with his separation of justification and renovation in the great notebooks, Cranmer described faith as the instrumental cause by which the penitent received the freely given benefits of Christ's passion. God forgave the penitent because of Christ's merits appropriated by faith not because of the presence of love in the believer's heart:

---

[211] 'Hic de operibus agitur quae fidem sequuntur, per quae amplius justificatur, cum jam per fidem fuisset justus', *Glossa ordinaria*, LPL MS 1108, fol. 63v, Cox II, 209; 'Abraham per fidem fuit justificatus, opera autem fidem perficiunt, notificant, augmentant, et confirmant', Hugo Cardinalis, LPL MS 1108, fol. 63v, Cox II, 209 (not in Cranmer's hand).

[212] See, e.g., Calvin, *Institutio* (1539/1543): 'Si et reliquis scripturis, et sibi ipsi consentaneum Iacobum facere velis, necessarium est, iustificandi verbum alio significatu accipere, quam apud Paulum . . . certe de iustitiae declaratione, non autem imputatione, ipsum loqui apparet. Ac si diceret: qui vera fide iusti sunt, ii suam iustitiam obedientia bonisque operibus probant, non nuda et imaginaria fidei larva', *CR* xxix. 789.

[213] LPL MS 1108, fol. 65r; Cox II, 209.

[214] LPL MS 1108, fol. 65r; Cox II, 209.

Yet nevertheless, because <u>by faith we know God's mercy</u> and grace promised by his word, (and that freely for Christ's death and passion sake), <u>and believe the same</u>, and, being truly penitent, we by faith <u>receive the same</u>, and so excluding all glory from ourselves, we do by faith <u>transcribe the whole glory of our justification to the merits of Christ only</u>, (which properly is not the nature and office of charity;) therefore to set forth the same, it is said of faith in ancient writers, 'we be justified only by faith', or 'by faith alone', and in St Paul, 'we be justified by faith freely without works'.[215]

Thus, Cranmer presented solifidianism in the 'Notes' in a pastoral manner consistent with his Protestant theology. In keeping with his definition of justification as an extrinsic imputation of righteousness accompanied by an intrinsic renewal of the will, pardon came by turning to God in repentance and faith, trusting God to forgive because of the work of Christ on the cross. However, it must be admitted that in the 'Notes on Justification' Cranmer failed to address the nature of the personal righteousness which resulted from reconciliation with God. While insisting that pardon was based on an alien righteousness, he never stipulated in the 'Notes' that after forgiveness, regeneration remained incomplete in this life. As we have seen, Cranmer could speak of the results of this regeneration both as pleasing to God and requiring God to overlook shortcomings.[216] Only in his emphasis on repentance as the hallmark of the 'right-will' and repentance as the hallmark of the Christian life did Cranmer bring together both aspects of his doctrine of renovation.

The ambiguity of Cranmer's description of renovation has led recent scholars to suggest that he held some form of factitive justification. While recognizing that Cranmer in these folios excluded love from the basis of pardon, Alister McGrath has been led by proposition five and the use of patristic quotations which described justification as being made righteous to state that Cranmer held to a 'strongly factitive Augustinian concept of justification', a position which he thought the 'Homily of Salvation' also reflected.[217]

---

[215] LPL MS 1108, fol. 65v; Cox II, 210.   [216] Cox II, 114.
[217] McGrath, *Iustitia Dei*, 288, 485 n. 24. It must be noted, however, that

In analysing the 1548 translation of Justus Jonas's *Catechism*, David Selwyn has come to a similar conclusion:

> No doubt some of the instances in the *Catechism* where the believer is said to be 'made holy and righteous' are to be interpreted proleptically, as referring to the inward and moral transformation which is taking place as he is progressively renewed by the sanctifying Spirit, a process completed ultimately only after death. But it seems undeniable that something further than this is also intended, viz., an actual imparting of Christ's righteousness to the believer as well as his regeneration and indwelling by the Spirit, and that this is related, at least in embryo, to Osiander's later doctrine.[218]

These scholars have rightly pointed to Cranmer's willingness to use strong language about the inner rectitude of the justified. Nevertheless, the fuller understanding of Cranmer's soteriology made possible by an examination of his great notebooks demonstrates that his doctrine of sanctification never veered beyond the boundaries of acceptable Protestant thought. In the 'Great Commonplaces' Cranmer outlined his distinction between extrinsic justification and incipient intrinsic renovation, the very point of doctrine to which Calvin appealed in order to refute Osiander's doctrine of essential righteousness.[219]

Within Protestantism, however, Cranmer's emphasis on eternal predestination before justification and holy living afterward had more in common with Bucer and Calvin than Luther and Melanchthon, despite his close work with the Lutherans during the 1530s. Cranmer never accepted Luther's embrace of necessity, and while Melanchthon

McGrath has evidently been misled about the homily itself. The phrase 'make himself righteous' which he cites in support of his interpretation is actually an Elizabethan alteration of 'justify himself'; Bond, *Certain Sermons*, 89 n. 83.

[218] Selwyn, *Catechism*, 'Introduction', 46. For a brief life of Andreas Osiander in English, see David C. Steinmetz, *Reformers in the Wings* (Philadelphia, Pa.: Fortress Press, 1971), 91–9. For Calvin's rejection of Osiander and the relevant passages in Osiander's *Confessio*, see *Calvin: Institutes of the Christian Religion*, ed. John T. McNeill, trans. Ford Lewis Battles (Philadephia, Pa.: Westminster, 1960), Bk. III, ch. 11, 5–12; i. 729–43. See also Wilhelm Niesel, *The Theology of Calvin*, trans. Harold Knight (London: Lutterworth, 1956), 133–4 and Francois Wendel, *Calvin: The Origins and Development of his Religious Thought*, trans. Philip Mairet (London: Collins, 1963), 235–7, 258–60.

[219] Calvin, *Institutes*, Bk. III, ch. 11, 6; i. 732.

shared Cranmer's concern for good works in the life of the justified, from 1535 he moved towards a synergistic understanding of justification and hence predestination based on foreknowledge of individual receptivity to grace.[220] Bucer and Calvin, however, held to unconditional election as well as holiness of life and gratuitous remission of sins.[221] Bucer insisted that assurance of salvation kindled a love for God and customarily spoke of the imparting of righteousness as well as its imputation, although this granting of personal purity was never of a sufficient degree to merit salvation.[222] Calvin described repentance as the on-going mark of regeneration and could also speak of the signs of grace reassuring the believer of his salvation.[223] Although more Reformed than Lutheran in matters of soteriology, Cranmer would attempt in the next reign to gather together all the leading Protestant theologians to devise a standard confession of their faith.

In summation, during the doctrinal disputes surrounding the publication of the *King's Book*, Cranmer undertook to prove that Reformed soteriology was the true heir to Augustine's teaching of salvation *sola fide et gratia*. He acknowledged Augustine's clear teaching that justification involved a truly significant internal change in the believer, but he argued that this inner transformation was insufficient for a truly meritorious basis for the forgiveness of sin. Rather, God pardoned a sinner based on the extrinsic righteousness of Christ which a believer laid hold of through the divine gift of faith. At the same time, however, the Holy Spirit indwelt the believer and reordered his desires by shedding an intrinsic love in his heart. Hence, justification made a believer 'right-willed', not righteous. Therefore, justification could be narrowed to the moment of repentance

---

[220] For Melanchthon on works, see Carl E. Maxcey, *Bona Opera: A Study in the Development of the Doctrine in Philip Melanchthon* (Nieuwkoop: De Graaf, 1980). For Melanchthon on predestination, see McGrath, *Iustitia Dei*, 215; Manschreck, *Melanchthon*, 293–302. For a brief overview of Melanchthon on both, see Trueman, *Luther's Legacy*, 72–4.

[221] See Stephens, *Bucer*, 23–41, 77–98; for Calvin, see Niesel, *Theology of Calvin*, 120–51, 159–81; and Wendel, *Calvin's Thought*, 233–55, 263–84.

[222] Stephens, *Bucer*, 71–4, 81–3.

[223] For regeneration as repentance, see Calvin, *Institutio* (1543), CR xxix. 685–92; for Calvin on assurance from signs of grace, ibid., CR xxix. 767–8, 879–80.

when saving grace changed the will's direction away from sin and towards God. By emphasizing repentance as the hallmark of a loving 'right-will', Cranmer was to able to argue that the repentant were already justified before any works of satisfaction. However, since to be justified meant to be repentant, those pardoned would lead amended lives obedient to both God and his king.

Away from polemics, repentance had distinct pastoral advantages. To a church steeped in medieval contritionism, a solifidian soteriology presented in the language of repentance could seem more familiar than foreign. Encouraging people to bewail the depths of their sin so as to be given personal merit was not too distant from encouraging people to acknowledge the impossibility of personal merit because of the depth of their sinfulness. Moreover, as the mark of renovation, the on-going desire to repent out of love for God offered evidence to believers that they were justified and, thus, would indeed spend eternity with God. Repentance as turning to God (because of his love) to be turned by God (through his love) was Cranmer's pastoral presentation of solifidianism. Yet, to protect God's glory, Cranmer set this pastoral description of justification by faith within the larger theological framework of *praedestinatio ante praevisa merita*. If it can be said that the Continental Reformation was the triumph of Augustine's soteriology over his ecclesiology,[224] then the English Reformation was the eventual triumph of Augustine's doctrine of effectual grace over his doctrine of free will.[225] With the accession of the new Josiah in 1547, Cranmer could at last transfer the doctrine he had carefully delineated in his private papers to the official formularies of the Edwardian church.

---

[224] Benjamin B. Warfield, *Calvin and Augustine* (Philadelphia, Pa.: Presbyterian and Reformed Publishing, 1956), 322.

[225] No doubt Cranmer thought these words could have just as easily been spoken by his opponents as by Augustine's: 'Eo ipso, inquit, non contra gratiam dei disputo, quod liberum arbitrium defendo', Augustine, *De verbis Apostoli*, Sermo 11, CGC II, 290r.

6

The Edwardian Years: Public Protestant Augustinianism

> Who dothe not manifestly perceave that [repentaunce]
> is the only refuge and anker of our helth and salvacion?
> . . . This did Paule commend unto the Corinthians, and
> almost to all other to whome so ever he wrote, and did
> bothe often and diligently beate it into mens heddis.[1]

Six months into Edward's reign, the solifidianism Cranmer
had long delineated in his private papers at last became the
basis for official teaching in the Church of England. On 31
July 1547 Richard Grafton published in the king's name *The
Book of Homilies*, a set of twelve sermons appointed to be
read seriatim by clergy with cure of souls 'until the King's
pleasure should be further known'.[2] Cranmer was dissatis-
fied with the *Legenda Aurea* and Mirk's *Festyuall* as the
standard for parish preaching,[3] and Convocation agreed in
1542 to produce a new homiletic collection, only to have the
project superseded by the publication of the *King's Book* in
1543.[4] In the new reign, Cranmer revived the plan and
contributed himself the homilies 'Of Salvation', 'Of Lively
Faith' and 'Of Good Works'[5]—a trilogy on the nature of

[1] Cranmer, 'Sermon on Rebellion', Parker Library, Corpus Christi College,
Cambridge, MS 102, pp. 487, 493–[4]; reprinted in Cox II, 200, 201.

[2] Ronald B. Bond, 'Cranmer and the Controversy Surrounding Publication of
Certayne Sermons or Homilies (1547)', *Renaissance and Reformation* 12 (1976), 28–
35, at 30; John Griffiths, *The Two Books of Homilies Appointed to be Read in
Churches* (Oxford: Oxford University Press, 1859), vii–viii.

[3] According to Gardiner, in June 1547 Cranmer was 'fully perswaded of the
foolishnesse of *Legenda Aurea* and the *Festivall*', surely an opinion of long-
standing; Muller, *Letters of Gardiner*, 311–12. Customarily, Cranmer's interest
in composing homilies is dated from 1539; e.g. Bond, 'Cranmer and the Controversy', 28–9; Wall, 'Fruitful Lessons', 85; McGrath, *Iustitia Dei*, 485 n. 21.
However, MacCulloch has shown this dating is based on a misunderstanding;
Cranmer, 224.

[4] Bond, 'Cranmer and Controversy', 29; Griffiths, *Homilies*, vii–viii; Wall,
'Fruitful Lessons', 85–7.

[5] Although all the homilies were published anonymously, since the sixteenth

justification which established solifidianism as the official
soteriology of the Edwardian era, much to the objection of
Stephen Gardiner.[6]

The nature of the solifidianism espoused in these homilies
has been a matter of some scholarly dispute. In the nineteenth century, R. C. Jenkins suggested that 'Of Salvation'
derived its doctrine of justification from Cajetan, while
William Fitzgerald thought it indisputably based on the
work of Melanchthon.[7] In the twentieth century, Pollard,
Bromiley, and Packer found Cranmer's homilies to be
clearly Protestant, but Ridley considered them to fall 'a
good way short'.[8] More recently, John Wall has offered the
novel interpretation that the sermons were the capstone of
an Edwardian programme to promote Erasmian humanism.[9]
According to this account, Cranmer promulgated the *Book
of Homilies* because he thought that people could 'be
brought to act better by giving them the right models for
imitation'.[10] Alister McGrath, however, has interpreted the
'Homily of Salvation' as a mixture of both Protestant and
patristic doctrine, the fiduciary basis of justification being
strongly Melanchthonian but its nature conforming to
Augustine's factitive approach.[11] In keeping with their
purpose to be instruction for a popular audience, and
perhaps even as a typical Cranmerian attempt to placate
the opposition through moderation, his homilies lack the
technical theological precision which would have avoided
the later scholarly debate over their interpretation. Once
again, the key to understanding Cranmer's doctrine lies in a
careful examination of his private papers. Although not

century there has been general agreement that these three were from Cranmer's
pen; Bond, *Certain Sermons*, 26–7.

[6] Muller, *Letters of Gardiner*, 296–372; Bond, 'Cranmer and Controversy',
29–30.

[7] Robert C. Jenkins, *Pre-Tridentine Doctrine: A Review of the Commentary on
the Scriptures of . . . Cardinal Cajetan* (London: Nutt, 1891), 70–2; William
Fitzgerald, *Lectures on Ecclesiastical History* (London: Murry, 1885), ii. 214–15.

[8] Pollard, *Cranmer*, 23; G. W. Bromiley, *Thomas Cranmer, Theologian*
(London: Lutterworth, 1956), 36; Packer, in Duffield, *Cranmer*, xxiv; Ridley,
Cranmer, 266.

[9] Wall, 'Fruitful Lessons', 85–125.

[10] Ibid., 110.

[11] McGrath, *Iustitia Dei*, 288.

exclusively, much of the material for these sermons was derived from the 'Notes on Justification' and the 'Great Commonplaces'. Thus, Cranmer's homilies received their final form no earlier than 1543 and represent the mature public expression of his Protestant Augustinianism.

Cranmer organized the 'Homily of Salvation' into three sections, each reflecting different source material from his private papers.[12] He began the sermon by describing justification in terms of forensic imputation, albeit in nontheological terms: (i) justifying righteousness was an alien righteousness: 'Because all men be sinners and offenders against God . . . every man of necessity is constrained to seek another righteousness, or justification to be received at God's own hands'; (ii) justification was pardon for sins because of Christ's merits and received by faith: 'justification . . . that is to say, the remission, pardon, and forgiveness of his sins and trespasses in such things as he hath offended'; 'this justification . . . we so receive by God's mercy and Christ's merits, embraced by faith'; (iii) the righteousness given to the believer through faith because of Christ was not true inherent righteousness but merely reckoned as such by God: 'this justification . . . is taken, accepted, and allowed of God for our perfect and full justification'.[13] Significantly, at no point in this description of justification did Cranmer make any reference to a divine internal act as the basis for the believer's external pardoning by God.

Cranmer then explained the mechanics and consequences of the solifidianism he had just defined. Christ's death satisfied God's justice and expressed his mercy; lively faith in Christ's merits justified the believer, not faith itself; faith only justified, but the presence of such fruit of inner renovation as repentance and love was necessary in every justified person as well.[14] Jenkins was quite perceptive in noting the similarity of thought between Cajetan's exposition of Romans 3 and this portion of Cranmer's 'Homily of

---

[12] In 1549, the homilies were divided into subsections so as to be more suitable for inclusion in the communion service of the new prayer book; Griffiths, *Homilies*, xi; Bond, *Certain Sermons*, 5.

[13] Cox II, 128.

[14] Ibid., 128–30.

Salvation'.[15] Although recent scholars have been understandably sceptical of any direct connection between Cranmer's work and that of Cajetan,[16] the very selections from

[15] See Jenkins's comparison between the two in *Pre-Tridentine Doctrine*, 70–2:

Cajetan in Rom. c. iii v. 24

Adverte quod in hoc quod homines ex peccatoribus fiunt justi concurrunt gratia Dei, et justitia Dei. Ita quod non concurrit sola gratia, quae tunc sola concurreret quando Deus remitteret peccata sine aliquâ solutione. Sed hoc deus nunquam fecit aut facit. Sed gratiae suae inserit justitiam suam quam toties Apostolus nominat Justitiam Dei.

At si contra hoc instetur, quod haec duo sibi invicem adversantur, scilicet quod simus justificati gratis per gratiam Dei, et quod simus justificati per redemptionem quae est in Christo Jesu. Nam si per redemptionem ergo non gratis, et si per gratiam ergo non per justitiam redemptionis. Solutio est, quod scriptura sacra non dicit nos justificari per solam gratiam sed per gratiam simul et justiciam, sed utramque Dei.

Et adverte tria 'PER' attulisse apostolum in hae [*sic*] sententiâ. Primum dicendo *per* gratiam ipsius, secundum *per* redemptionem, et tertium *per* fidem redemptionis; ut intelligamus ad iustificandum nos concurrere, primum ex parte Dei gratiam, deinde ex parte Jesu Christi, justitiam redemptionis, et demum ex parte nostri fidem in sanguine Jesu Christi. Et gratia quidem primum tenet locum, utpote etiam causa secundi et tertii. . . . Fides donum Dei est et non creaturae (in [Rom] c. X).

Arbitramur igitur iustificari hominem per fidem sine operibus legis iustificantibus. Non enim intendit excludere opera legis . . . Non intendit excludere ab executione sed a iustificatione.

Homily on Salvation

In our justification is not only God's mercy and grace, but also His justice. And, although this justification be free to us, yet it cometh not so freely to us that there is no ransom paid for it at all.

But here may man's reason be astonied, reasoning after this fashion. If a ransom be paid for our redemption, then it is not given us freely. For a prisoner that paid his ransom is not let go freely . . . This reason is satisfied by the great wisdom of God in this mystery of our redemption, who hath so tempered his justice and mercy together, and with his mercy hath joined his upright and equal justice (*gratiae suae inserit justitiam suam*, ut supr.).

In these foresaid places the Apostle toucheth specially three things which must go together in our justification. Upon God's part His great mercy and grace, upon Christ's part justice—that is, the satisfaction of God's justice by the offering of his body—and upon our part true and lively faith in the merits of Jesus Christ, which yet is not ours, but God working in us.

The grace of God doth not shut out the justice of God in our justification, but only shutteth out the justice of man—that is to say, the justice of our works . . . Faith doth not shut out repentance, hope, love, dread, &c., but it shutteth them out from the office of justifying.

[16] McGrath attributed the similarity to a mutual Augustinianism; *Iustitia Dei*, 485 n. 21. T. H. L. Parker noted that the homily's three causes of justification were as common to Calvin as they were to Cajetan; *Commentaries on the Epistle to the Romans: 1532–1542* (Edinburgh: T & T Clark, 1986), 159 n. 8.

Cajetan that Jenkins suggested paralleled Cranmer's words were recorded in the great notebooks.[17] Cranmer did not derive his definition of justification from Cajetan as Jenkins inferred,[18] but he did use some of the Cardinal's work as a resource for making his point. Cranmer wanted to convey clearly to the English people that solifidianism was 'opposed not to good works *per se*, but to their merit'.[19] Having established that Christians could not merit pardon by the virtue of either their faith or their good works, Cranmer concluded the first section by referring back to the only remaining possible source for justification, the imputation of an alien righteousness: 'Christ is now the righteousness of all them that truly do believe in him . . . forasmuch as that which their infirmity lacketh, Christ's justice hath supplied.'[20]

In the second section of the 'Homily of Salvation' Cranmer sought to explain the antiquity and utility of solifidianism, deriving his exposition from 'Notes on Justification'.[21] He began by quoting five verses of Scripture, all found in 'Notes'.[22] 'If justice comes of works, then it cometh not of grace; and if it comes of grace, then it cometh not of works', but remission of sin came through belief.[23] Having quoted Scripture, Cranmer turned to the Fathers for support. Claiming that justification by faith was espoused by 'all the old ancient authors, both Greeks and Latins', Cranmer cited Origen, Chrysostom, Cyprian, Augustine, Prosper, Oecumenius, Photius, Bernard, and Anselm as well as quoting from Hilary, Basil, and Ambrose as examples. He had included a similar proposition and range of authors along with the same quotation from Basil in 'Notes'.[24]

---

[17] CGC II, 92v–93r [Note that the Latin text used in CGC differs in a few minor ways from Jenkins's quotations].

[18] Jenkins, *Pre-Tridentine Doctrine*, vii.

[19] Alan C. Clifford, 'Cranmer as Reformer', *The Evangelical Quarterly* 63 (1991), 99–122, at 112.

[20] Cox II, 130.

[21] Since both 'Notes on Justification' and the 'Homily of Salvation' are reprinted in Cox II, all cross-referencing between the two texts will refer to this source.

[22] Galatians 3: 21; 2: 21; 5: 4; Ephesians 2: 8–9; Acts 10: 43; Cox II, 130. Cf. ibid., 205, 208, 210. [23] Ibid., 130.

[24] 'The same meant divers ancient authors, as well Greeks as Latins, when they said, "We be justified by only faith or faith alone"', ibid., 208. All the authors

In the remaining paragraphs, Cranmer described the purpose of justification by faith: to take away 'all merit of our works' in order 'most plainly to express the weakness of man, and the goodness of God; the great infirmity of ourselves, and the might and power of God; the imperfectness of our own works, and the most abundant grace of our Saviour Christ' so that all merit for justification was ascribed to 'Christ only, and his most precious blood-shedding'. In short, solifidianism 'advanceth and setteth forth the true glory of Christ and suppresseth the vain-glory of man'.[25] As we have seen, this was a characteristic theme of Cranmer's teaching, included in his annotations to Henry's corrections,[26] forming two of the propositions in 'Notes on Justification',[27] and provoking a rebuttal from Gardiner in their correspondence over the publication of the homilies.[28] Similar to his comments on folio 226 *verso* in the great notebooks, Cranmer argued that 'man cannot justify himself by his own works, neither in part, nor in the whole; for that were the greatest arrogancy and presumption of man that antichrist could erect against God'.[29]

mentioned have quotations recorded in 'Notes', except Photius and Hilary; ibid., 205–11 ad passim. Photius, however, is quoted in a *locus* entitled 'Ex sola fide iustificamur' in the great notebooks, CGC II, 90r–91r. For the quotation from Basil cf. Cox II, 205 and Cox II, 130. Although the Latin text of Basil in 'Notes on Justification' would appear to be the basis of the homily's English translation, 'Ex sola fide iustificamur' recorded another Latin version: 'Ea demum est perfecta et integra gloriatio in deo, quando neque super iustitia quae sua ipsius sit extollitur quis, sed novit se quidem inopem esse omnis vere iustitiae, fide autem sola in Christum coniecta, esse iustificatum', CGC II, 91r.

[25] Cox II, 131.

[26] Ibid., 88, 96, 114; see Chapter 4.

[27] 'Meaning thereby to exclude the merit and dignity of all works and virtues, as insufficient to deserve remission of sin, and to ascribe the same only to Christ'; 'we by faith receive the same, and so excluding all glory from ourselves, we do by faith transcribe the whole glory of our justification to the merits of Christ only', Cox II, 206, 210.

[28] 'In all this dyscussyon no man could have cause to saye, "Alas, good poore people, what meaneth men to teach you justyficacion by workes, to the diminution of Godes glory?" Their is no cause to crye oute so', Gardiner to Cranmer, shortly after 1 July 1547; Muller, *Letters of Gardiner*, 345.

[29] Cox II, 131; cf. 'Solius dei opus est et gloria, iustificare impium, remittere peccata, donare vitam ex sua bonitate gratis, non ex ullis nostris meritis. Satan cupit sibi impendi divinum honorem. Qui itaque suis operibus tribuit iustificationis vel initium vel absolutionem, an non satanica impietate creatorem suum blasphemat?', CGC II, 226v.

[30] Cox II, 131–2.

Cranmer wanted people to understand that justification was 'not a thing which we render unto [God], but which we receive of him; not which we give to him, but which we take of him'. Although it was the individual's part to believe in Christ, a person's faith *per se* offered nothing to God on account of which he could grant pardon, for faith as an inherent virtue was 'far too weak and insufficient and unperfect' to merit justification. Rather, like John the Baptist, faith pointed to Christ as the true extrinsic source for the remission of sins.[30] Cranmer had already covered this ground in the first section, but now he was following his 'Notes on Justification' rather than Cajetan.[31] It is conceivable that Cranmer borrowed from Melanchthon's *Loci communes* (1543) to expound in the homily the seventh proposition found in his 'Notes'—a suggestion first made by Fitzgerald in the light of the similarity between this section of the sermon and the description of grace in *Loci communes*.[32] While scholars have considered either Cajetan

---

[31] 'Although all that be justified must of necessity have charity as well as faith, yet neither faith nor charity be the worthiness and merits of our justification, but that is to be ascribed only to our Saviour Christ, which was offered upon the cross for our sins, and rose again for our justification', ibid., 209; 'Anselm. Rom. 3 . . . Sed si quis dixerit, Ut merear justificationem, habeo fidem; respondetur ei, "Quid habes quod non accepisti?"', ibid.

[32] Fitzgerald, *Ecclesiastical History*, ii. 214–15. The texts cited by Fitzgerald follow in parallel columns:

Homily:	Melanchthon:
This sentence that we be justified by faith only, is not so meant that the said justifying faith is alone in man, without true repentance, hope, charity, dread and the fear of God, at any time and season. But this saying that we be justified by faith only, freely and without works, is spoken for to take away clearly all merit of our works; . . . and therefore wholly to ascribe the merit and deserving of our justification to Christ only. . . . Justification is not the office of man, but of God: for man cannot make himself righteous by his own works, neither in part nor in whole. . . . The true understanding of this doctrine, we be justified freely by faith without works, or that we be	When Paul says that we are justified freely through faith, he does not mean that contrition does not exist in those that are converted, or that the other virtues do not follow, yea rather he means that they are present; but he excludes the condition of merit or worthiness on our part; he denies that contrition or any virtues of ours are the causes of our reconciliation, and he testifies that the cause thereof is the merit of Christ the Mediator. Nor is the meaning of our divines different when we say that we are justified by faith only. Nor does that word 'only' exclude contrition or other virtues from being present in him who is justified, but denies that they are the causes of

or Melanchthon as the source for the homily's doctrine,[33] the examples cited in support of each candidate actually refer to different portions of the homily. Evidently, in his homilies as in his liturgical work, Cranmer drew upon a variety of sources to find the best linguistic expression of the doctrine which he wished to promote.

Cranmer began the last section of the homily with a recapitulation of God's office in justification. He then finished with a fuller, final description of humanity's role in the Christian life, namely, to have a faith which bears good fruit. As in his 'Annotations' and great notebooks, Cranmer contrasted lively faith with the dead faith of devils.[34] Since demons also believed the principal truths of Christianity, 'right and true christian faith' was not only assent to Scripture and the articles of faith but also 'a sure trust and confidence in God's merciful promises, to be saved from everlasting damnation'. Characteristically for Cranmer, from this assurance of salvation flowed a love 'to obey his commandments' so that no possessor of true faith could profess God with his mouth but deny him in his deeds. When the benefits of God's merciful grace were considered, unless they were 'desperate persons' with 'hearts harder than stones', people would be moved to

justified by faith in Christ only, is not that this our own act to believe in Christ, or this our faith in Christ which is within us, doth justify us, and deserve our justification unto us (for that were to count ourselves to be justified by some act or virtue that is within ourselves); but the true understanding and meaning thereof is, that although we hear God's word and believe, although we have faith, hope, charity, &c., we must renounce the merit of all such virtues. (Cranmer, Cox II, 131–2)

our reconciliation, and transfers the cause to Christ alone. So that this saying, 'we are justified by faith in Christ', is equivalent to this, that we are justified for the sake of Christ, and not for our own deservings. Faith is itself a work, like love, patience, chastity, and as these are infirm and weak, so is faith; so that we are not said to be justified by faith because faith is a virtue of such dignity as to deserve justification, but because there must needs be some instrument in us by which we lay hold upon the Mediator who intercedes on our behalf. (Melanchthon, in translation by Fitzgerald, based on *CR* xxi. 755–6)

[33] For example, J. T. Tomlinson cited both Jenkins's work and Fitzgerald's, but chose the latter as more probable; *The Prayer Book, Articles, and Homilies: Some forgotten facts in their history which may decide their interpretation* (London: Elliot Stock, 1897), 237–9.   [34] Cox II, 133–4; see Chapters 4 and 5.
[35] Cox II, 134.
[36] Collinson, 'Cranmer', 94.

give themselves wholly unto God and the service of their neighbours.[35]

An example of the rhetorical device of *concessio*,[36] Cranmer's two homilies on 'Faith' and 'Good Works' explained in greater detail the twin tenets of his soteriology first outlined in the 'Homily of Salvation'. In 'Faith', Cranmer taught the necessity of good works in the life of the justified, whereas in 'Good Works' he insisted on the necessity of faith for justification. For the exposition of both sermons, Cranmer drew upon his great notebooks. In the 'Homily of Faith' Cranmer elaborated the theme of the *duplex fides* by citing a quotation from Augustine that justifying faith brought forth a renewed will to serve God: 'Good living cannot be separated from true faith, which worketh by love'.[37] In the 'Homily of Good Works' Cranmer insisted that no work was good unless it flowed from saving faith, quoting three Scriptures, two long passages from Augustine and Chrysostom, and a brief extract from Ambrose.[38] He then went on to define at great length good works as keeping the moral commandments of the Bible rather than the vain imaginations of men, much to the considerable disparagement of many medieval practices. In the light of the extensive research contained in his great notebooks, Cranmer asserted that on the matter of good works 'St. Augustine at large in many books disputeth'.[39] In the 'Homily of Faith' Cranmer challenged Christians to examine themselves for the new life which sprang from faith. Just as good works necessarily followed from having eternal life through faith, the presence of good works in their lives served to certify the consciences of believers and show that their election was sure and stable.[40] In this regard, Cranmer cited several times repentance as the dividing line between

---

[37] Cox II, 137; 'Inseparabilis est quippe bona vita a fide, quae per dilectionem operatur, immo vero ipsa est bona vita', Augustine, *De fide et operibus*, ca. 23, CGC II, 99v.

[38] John 15: 4–5; Hebrews 11: 6; Romans 14: 23: Cox II, 141; under propositional heading 'Ex operibus, ante Spiritum Sanctum, rei potius tenemur quam contra', CGC II, 240r. Augustine, *In Psalmum 31*, Prologus: Cox II, 141–2; CGC II, 106.

[39] Cox II, 142.

[40] Ibid., 138–41.

[41] Cox II, 135–6, 139, 140.   [42] Ibid., 148–9.   [43] Cox I, 94.

[44] Cox II, 133, 135–6.

living and dead faith.[41] If Christians perceived such faith
within themselves, they were to rejoice and be diligent to
maintain it and keep it still in themselves, letting it increase
daily. Cranmer concluded the 'Homily of Good Works' by
giving directions on how to stir up and sustain this lively
faith:

As you have any zeal to the right and pure honouring of God; as
you have any regard to your own souls . . . apply yourselves chiefly
above all things to read and to hear God's word; mark diligently
therein what his will is you shall do, and with all your endeavour
apply yourselves to follow the same.[42]

Thus, in his homilies on 'Salvation', 'Faith', and 'Good
Works' Cranmer gave practical, public expression to the
Protestant interpretation of Augustinian soteriology which
he had outlined in his private papers. By assigning all merit
to Christ's work and not to the Christian's, Cranmer
expressed his solifidianism. He conveyed the sense of
forensic imputation by speaking of justifying righteousness
as extrinsic and the believer's own as merely 'accepted and
allowed'. He expounded the effects of the intrinsic renovation by stressing the necessity for true faith to produce a
renewed love for God and neighbour. He clearly defined
saving faith as assurance of eventual salvation because of
Christ's promises, and repentance from sin for the love of
God as its first fruit. The only serious possible discrepancy
between the Protestant Augustinianism he delineated in his
private papers and the soteriology of his homilies is the
clarity of the doctrine of predestination in the former and
the ambiguity of the origin of new life in the latter.

The crucial issue for Cranmer was the nature of saving
grace, namely, that it was effectual. Since salvation was the
work of God alone, all glory belonged to him, and believers
could have assurance of eternal life. The role of predestination was secondary, namely, to explain why grace was
effectual in the lives of some people but not others, lest
salvation at any point be made contingent on human effort
and, thus, lead to 'desperation'.[43] In his 'Annotations' and
great notebooks, Cranmer presented predestination as both

the basis for assurance and the guarantee of *sola gratia*. In his public preaching, however, Cranmer distinguished between promoting the benefits of saving grace and explaining its mechanics.

On the importance of repentance to the Christian life, Cranmer could sound much like Fisher. He urged people to consider the great and merciful benefits of God, since only those desperate persons (the medieval term for those who were reprobate) with hearts harder than stones would fail to be moved by them. People were to examine their lives and rejoice when they found faith. If they had any zeal for God, they were to use it in obeying his commandments. Cranmer encouraged people to strive to repent, but never publicly preached that only some people would be given effectual grace so that they could repent. On assurance, however, he parted company with Fisher. Cranmer encouraged people to believe that by trusting in Christ's merits rather than their own, they had been saved from everlasting damnation and made a partaker of the heavenly kingdom. For true faith was a 'sure trust and confidence of all good things to be received at God's hand', a 'certificate and sure expectation of them, although they yet sensibly appear not unto us'.[44] Fisher would have considered such preaching as promoting presumption. Cranmer did not discuss unconditional election in his sermons, but he did preach its benefits. More a pastor than a systematizer, Cranmer wanted to convey to the English people the hope that effectual grace made possible, without encumbering the message with difficult and secondary theological truths.

In general, then, Cranmer's preaching is compatible with a pastoral presentation of the Reformed understanding of predestination outlined in the great notebooks. However, one specific passage in the 'Homily of Good Works' requires special attention. As Professor Collinson has noted, Cranmer included a quotation from Chrysostom which reads: 'If [the thief on the cross] had lived, and not regarded faith and the works thereof, he should have lost his salvation again.'[45] There are four possible interpretations of this statement. Firstly, Cranmer believed that justification could be lost finally through human failure to make right use of saving grace. Although the thief was justified, it was possible that he was not of the elect, election being contingent on human response to God's motions. Secondly, Cranmer thought that justification could be lost finally, but the reason was the divine withholding of the grace of perseverance. Hence, although the thief had received sufficient grace to be justified, it was possible that he would have not been given that which would have enabled him to continue in a life of good works. Thirdly, for illustrative purposes, Cranmer was, in effect, speaking loosely, proposing a hypothetical situation which, in fact, would never have occurred. If Cranmer believed that only the elect were ever justified and that they never lost their justification, the thief would never have actually lost justifying faith and so would have performed the good works which inevitably flowed from its presence in the life of the justified. Fourthly, Cranmer thought that only the elect were ever justified but acknowledged that it was possible for them at times to fall from a state of sonship and grace, although never finally. Since the justified thief had to be of the elect, any fall from grace would have only been temporary. Being effectual, saving grace would have worked to bring about his repentance, restoration, and final perseverance. Each possible interpretation will be considered in turn.

As for final perseverance being ultimately contingent on human obedience, it has already been argued that Cranmer's refusal to base assurance of salvation on the will's response to God's motions constituted a denial of this position.[46] The exposition of 2 Peter 1: 10 in the 'Homily of Faith' would seem consistent with such a rejection, for the *King's Book* cited this verse to prove that good works *made* election sure and stable, whereas the homily quoted the passage to demonstrate that good works *showed* election to be sure and stable.[47]

[45] Cox II, 143; 'Seventy years later, that doctrine would have been called grossly Arminian', Collinson, 'Cranmer', 97.

[46] Cox II, 94. See Chapter 4.

[47] 'And this [persevering in grace and good living] St. Peter exhorteth us to make our vocation and election sure and stable', Lacey, *King's Book*, 155; 'Let us by such

However, the strongest evidence against the first interpretation is found in Cranmer's commentary on Matthew 3, written at Croydon before the end of summer, 1549, and now found in Corpus Christi College, Cambridge, MS 104.[48] In his own hand, Cranmer described the justification, sanctification, and eternal salvation of the elect wholly in terms of divine activity. The elect were 'those given to the [Son] by the Father' whom 'the Son of God liberates from the power of Satan, purges, sanctifies, protects and leads to him through his Holy Spirit until the day in which he will hand this kingdom to God the Father'.[49] Since Cranmer believed that election arose from the divine will and was brought to completion in eternal salvation by divine power, he would not have thought that the thief could have been denied final justification because of a failure on his part.

Concerning the second possibility, that God gave justifying grace to more people than he gave the grace of final perseverance, it has already been argued that Cranmer's description of election and justification as a part of a unitary process indicates that he believed the elect and the justified to be co-extensive.[50] That the section on justification in the 'Great Commonplaces' failed to quote Augustine's opinion in the matter was seen as consistent with Cranmer having chosen to depart from his chief patristic source for soteriology on this point.[51] The Croydon commentary on Matthew 3 provides further evidence that Cranmer rejected Augustine's teaching on this issue. Augustine distinguished between the elect and the justified so as to be able to assert both baptismal regeneration of every child and the final perseverance by grace of only the elect. If Cranmer held to the view that only the justified were elect and only the elect were ever justified, he would have had to have

---

virtues [i.e. good works] as ought to spring out of faith shew our election to be sure and stable, as St. Peter teacheth: "Endeavour yourselves to make your calling and election certain by good works" ', Cox II, 140.

[48] For a description of this manuscript source, see the Appendix.

[49] 'Filius dei donatos sibi a patre vindicat potestate Satanae, purgat, sanctificat, tuetur, et ducit per spiritum sanctum suum ad eum usque diem, quo tradet regnum hoc deo patri', written in Cranmer's hand, CCCC MS 104, p. [32].

[50] See Chapter 4.

[51] See Chapter 5.

abandoned belief in universal regeneration in paedobaptism. That Cranmer had done so by the summer, 1549, seems the most reasonable conclusion to draw from the final sentence of the Croydon commentary:

Therefore, God is both the God of our children, and he has among these those chosen to his kingdom. Since it is not ours to discern them from others, we ought, no less than ancient Israel [who practised infant circumcision], reverently to seek and to receive with good faith the grace offered in baptism for all our children. For these also belong to the kingdom of God. Matthew 19.[52]

Thus, according to Cranmer's Reformed theology, the justified thief had to have been of the elect as well.

Since Cranmer equated the elect with the justified, only the last two interpretations remain possible: either Cranmer was speaking hypothetically because he believed the elect never lost their justification or Cranmer was describing a situation which could have occurred but would not have been permanent, because the justified could fall away from God totally but not finally. Naturally, Cranmer recognized that those who were elect and justified still committed sins.[53] That the sins of the justified could be serious enough for them to fall from sonship was the central message of the 'Homily of Declining from God': 'thei shalbe no lenger of his kyngdom; they shalbe no lenger governed by his Holy Spirite; thei shalbe frustrated of the grace and benefites that thei had . . . Thei shalbe, as thei wer once, as men without

[52] 'Est ergo deus, et nostrorum infantium deus, et habet in his electis [recte, electos?] ad regnum suum, quos cum nostrum discernere non sit ab aliis debemus non minus quam veteres omnibus nostris infantibus oblatam gratiam baptismate religiose petere et bona fiducia recipere pertinent enim et hi ad regnum dei. Infra [i.e. caput sequens] 19', CCCC 104, pp. 213–[14]. The Latin is difficult, and I offer a slightly different translation from MacCulloch, *Cranmer*, 428. For 'veteres' as referring to the Israelites and their practice of circumcision, see the immediately preceding discussion of the relationship between circumcision and baptism, especially the sentences, 'Certum est apud nos baptisma successisse circumcisioni Coloso. 2. Certum etiam est gratiam Christi apud nos et verbis et sacramentis debere obsignari, et predicari augustius etiam, quam apud veteres, ut est ea glorificato Christo uberius in omne humanum genus effusa Ro. 3, 5, 8', ibid., 213.

[53] 'The elect shall follow Christ's precepts, or when they fall, they shall repent and rise again', 'Annotations', Cox II, 92; 'Although we through infirmity or temptation of our ghostly enemy, do fall from him by sin . . .', 'Homily of Faith', ibid., 135.

God in this worlde.'[54] Although of unknown authorship, its inclusion in the collection of homilies edited by Cranmer would seem to indicate his general agreement with its teaching. So also would the 'Sermon concerning the time of rebellion' whose composition was overseen by Cranmer.[55] A response to the uprisings of 1549, its text suggested that disobedience could cause God to 'strike us cleane out of his book'.[56] Thus, when all the available evidence is considered, the fourth interpretation is the most likely: the justified thief could have fallen from a state of grace, but only temporarily, because he was necessarily also of the elect.

This doctrine of election and perseverance helps to clarify the difficult question of the relationship between baptismal regeneration and justification by faith in Cranmer's thought. Although he spoke of the sacrament remitting the guilt of original sin from infants,[57] he never directly addressed how justification in paedobaptism could be consistent with solifidianism. According to Brooks, 'the problem is very like that facing the archaeologist who has unearthed an imperfect mosaic pavement of complex design and of no obvious period or influence'.[58] Consider, for example, the *Catechism* of 1548, 'ouersene and corrected' by Cranmer.[59]

[54] Bond, *Certain Sermons*, 142–3.

[55] Peter Martyr wrote two Latin sermons, apparently from an outline supplied by Cranmer. A single English draft was fashioned from the two Latin sources through translation, adaptation, addition, and abridgement. Cranmer then made further changes to the English draft in his own hand. For the 'Notes for a Homily Against Rebellion', see CCCC MS 102, pp. 529–[34], reprinted Cox II, 188–9. For Martyr's two sermons, see CCCC MS 340, pp. 73–95, 115–31. For the English sermon with title and corrections in Cranmer's hand, see CCCC MS 102, pp. 409–99. For the text printed as amended by Cranmer, see Cox II, 190–202. The first Martyr sermon underlies the bulk of the English text, CCCC MS 102, pp. 411–83, Cox II, 190–200. The second Martyr sermon is a source for the final portion of 'On Rebellion', beginning with 'But methinks that I have not doon my office and duetye, untill I have shewed also the remedies', CCCC MS 102, pp. 485–99, Cox II, 200–2.

[56] CCCC MS 102, p. [494], Cox II, 201. Cf. 'Vosque ex albo suorum expungat', Peter Martyr, CCCC 340, p. [120].

[57] 'Insomuch that infants, being baptized, and dying in their infancy, are by this sacrifice washed from their sins, brought to God's favour, and made his children, and inheritors of his kingdom of heaven', 'Homily of Salvation', Cox II, 128.

[58] Peter Newman Brooks, 'Thomas Cranmer's Doctrine of the Sacraments', Ph.D. thesis (University of Cambridge, 1960), 2.

[59] Selwyn, *Catechism*, 1. For a helpful discussion of the degree of Cranmer's involvement in the preparation of this English translation of Jonas's Latin

David Selwyn has observed that 'baptism and justification are so closely related in the *Catechism* as to be practically interchangeable terms',[60] yet 'it has no specific treatment of infant baptism and the theological problems which this raises'.[61] Not surprisingly, Bromiley believed that Cranmer 'had not thought out all the implications' of the interconnection between baptism and justification.[62]

The first unresolved question is Cranmer's understanding of the means of sacramental efficacy in paedobaptism. As we have seen in penance, medieval scholasticism held that a sacrament worked *ex opere operato*, if no obstacle was placed in its path. Infant baptism posed no difficulties for the medieval understanding of sacramental efficacy, for what obstacle of wilful sin could an infant place in the way of grace? To the mature Cranmer, however, as Brooks rightly noted, the sacraments were 'instrumentally connected with the faith which is necessary for the reception of God's grace'.[63] This was as true for Cranmer in baptism as it was in the Eucharist: 'Therefore we must trust only in God's mercy, and in that sacrifice [of Christ] . . . to obtain thereby God's grace and remission, as well of our original sin in baptism, as of all actual sin committed by us after our baptism, if we truly repent, and convert unfeignedly to him again.'[64] Yet, as Cranmer himself admitted, young children presented for baptism 'in deed have no knowledge' of belief and conversion to God.[65] The obvious awkward question, then, is how could infants receive the sacramental effect of pardon from original sin when they were incapable of noetic faith, on which the reception of such grace depended.

Cranmer's doctrine of predestination, in itself, does not provide an answer to the issue of sacramental efficacy. Who

---

translation of the Nuremberg Catechism, see ibid., 'Introduction', 56–65. For an exposition of the English text's teachings on baptism, see ibid., 48–50.

[60] Selwyn, *Catechism*, 50. Cf. 'Our office is, not to pass the time of this present life unfruitfully and idly, after that we are baptised or justified', 'Homily of Salvation', Cox II, 133.

[61] Selwyn, *Catechism*, 'Introduction', 48.

[62] Bromiley, *Cranmer, Theologian*, 65.

[63] Brooks, 'Sacraments', 74.

[64] Cox II, 132.

[65] Cox I, 124–5.

would be given saving grace was a separate issue from how they would receive it. Although Zwingli, Bullinger, and Calvin all believed in the doctrine of election, Gerrish has recently suggested that each had a different sacramental theory.[66] Even among scholars of Calvin, more than one opinion exists on how to interpret his views on sacramental efficacy in paedobaptism.[67] If scholars disagree on how to interpret Calvin's teaching on this issue, what can be said of Cranmer's view on the basis of far less material? It can only be noted that in the Croydon commentary Cranmer described infant baptism as offering saving grace to the elect,[68] without ever actually explaining how the sacrament did so.

The second issue involved is the nature of the sacrament's effect. In the 'Homily of Salvation' Cranmer stated that 'infants, being baptized, and dying in their infancy are by this sacrifice [of Christ] washed from their sins, brought to God's favour, and made his children, and inheritors of his kingdom of heaven'.[69] This brief reference is capable of a number of interpretations. While such language could seem to imply a Catholic understanding of baptismal regeneration to inherent righteousness, this non-imputation of original sin should be interpreted in the light of Cranmer's commitment to forensic justification. For Cranmer, baptismal regeneration meant the infant's receiving the Holy Spirit, not the child's restoration to perfect purity as well.

The 'Homily of Salvation' can also seem to imply that Cranmer held to Luther's position on the extent of this

[66] B. A. Gerrish, *The Old Protestantism and the New: Essays on the Reformation Heritage* (Edinburgh: T & T Clark, 1982), 106–30.

[67] According to Ronald S. Wallace, Calvin's teaching on the possibility of infant regeneration was 'an exception to the rule that men become reconciled to God by faith alone'; *Calvin's Doctrine of the Word and Sacrament* (Edinburgh: Oliver and Boyd, 1953), 196. According to Jill Raitt, however, Calvin managed to maintain a role for faith in the efficacy of infant baptism; 'Three Inter-Related Principles in Calvin's Unique Doctrine of Infant Baptism', *The Sixteenth Century Journal* 11 (1980), 51–61, at 56–60. I am grateful to Dr Sean Hughes for our discussions on these matters.

[68] 'Est ergo deus, et nostrorum infantium deus, et habet in his electis [recte, electos?] ad regnum suum, quos cum nostrum discernere non sit ab aliis debemus . . . omnibus nostris infantibus oblatam gratiam baptismate religiose petere', CCCC 104, pp. 213–[14].

[69] Cox II, 128.

regeneration, namely, that by the virtue of the Word spoken during the sacrament's administration, all baptized infants were considered to be regenerate.[70] Nevertheless, both Cranmer's doctrine of predestination in general and the Croydon commentary specifically seem to suggest otherwise, namely, that Cranmer thought paedobaptism effective only for the elect. The homily's language of baptismal forgiveness and the doctrine of divine election were not mutually exclusive. Bucer also described baptism in terms of justification and regeneration, and, like Calvin and Martyr, he restricted the benefits of baptism to the elect while never insisting on the necessity of baptism for their salvation.[71] According to Peter Martyr, his opponents among the Edwardian church leaders denied that little children were justified or regenerated prior to baptism.[72] Although possible, this would seem an unnecessary position for Cranmer to have to adopt in the light of his doctrine of predestination.[73] Moreover, Cranmer was not averse to describing the sacraments as signs or seals.[74] Hence, there remains no substantial reason why Cranmer should not have agreed with Martyr's description of paedobaptism:

But in the case of children, when they are baptized, since on account of their age they cannot have that assent to the divine promises which is faith, in them the sacrament effects this, that pardon of original sin, reconciliation with God, and the grace of

---

[70] Althaus, *Theology of Luther*, 364–70.

[71] Stephens, *Bucer*, 221–37; Raitt, 'Calvin's Doctrine of Infant Baptism', 56–60; Joseph C. McLelland, *The Visible Words of God: An Exposition of the Sacramental Theology of Peter Martyr Vermigli, A.D. 1500–1562* (Edinburgh: Oliver and Boyd, 1957), 147–59.

[72] *An Unpublished Letter of Peter Martyr, Reg. Div. Prof. Oxford, to Henry Bullinger; written from Oxford just after the completion of the Second Prayer Book of Edward VI*, ed. William Goode (London: Hatchard, 1850), 6 (English translation), 16 (Latin original).

[73] Although Bucer, Calvin, and Martyr did not think baptism necessary for salvation because of their doctrine of election, Augustine reasoned the reverse. One of his favourite arguments in favour of divine election was God's control over human perseverance through death; hence, infants dying unbaptized were damned because God had not granted them the opportunity to live long enough to receive the sacrament of regeneration; Burns, *Augustine's Operative Grace*, 134.

[74] e.g. 'Certum etiam est gratiam Christi apud nos et verbis, et sacramentis debere obsignari, et praedicari', CCCC MS 104, p. 213. Cf. 'Our Lord Jesus Christ hath instituted and annexed to the gospel, thre sacraments or holy seales, of his couenant and lege made with vs', Selwyn, *Catechism*, 'Text', 183.

the Holy Spirit, bestowed on them through Christ, is sealed in them, and that those belonging already to the Church are also visibly implanted in it.[75]

The final issue is how Cranmer understood the connection between conversion from actual sin during the years of discretion and the pardon from original sin associated with paedobaptism. Cranmer clearly wanted to maintain both. Again, according to the 'Homily of Salvation',

Insomuch that infants, being baptized, and dying in their infancy, are by this sacrifice washed from their sins, brought to God's favour, and made his children, and inheritors of his kingdom of heaven. And they which actually do sin after their baptism, when they convert and turn again to God unfeignedly, they are likewise washed by this sacrifice from their sins.[76]

Ascribing to Cranmer 'loosely Lutheran views', Brooks described the relationship between the two as follows: 'Hence those who receive the sacrament as children, and are counted regenerate according to their infant state, recall their Baptism with repentance as they come to years of discretion.'[77] In the light of the heavily Lutheran *Catechism* of 1548, Brooks's assessment is solid enough, but Cranmer's views on election and justification expounded in his private papers suggest a more nuanced explanation as a possibility. Paedobaptism sealed pardon from original sin for the elect. Those who died before growing old enough to commit actual sin never lost divine grace and, thus, were inheritors of heaven at their deaths. As for those of the elect who grew old enough to commit actual sins, they could so persist in declining from God as to fall temporarily from the state of grace in which they had been sealed in baptism. When, however, the sure workings of grace brought forth in them a lively faith, these lapsed elect would repent, receive forgiveness, and be restored to their inheritance in Christ.

The Croydon commentary offers a description of the process by which the elect initially gained justification by noetic faith. Firstly, their human initiative did not precede restoration to divine fellowship:

[75] Martyr, *Unpublished Letter*, 6; for the Latin, see ibid., 15.
[76] Cox II, 128.   [77] Brooks, 'Sacraments', 67.

At this point, turn your mind, you whoever wish to seek God and learn what amount or of [what] capacity there be in us: I will not speak of a preparation to faith in Christ in our nature; Whoever is from Adam, we are born with as much as there is in stones so that they may be sons of Abraham and, consequently, sons of God.[78]

Secondly, their conversion was the result of grace given based on predestination, for 'to know [the kingdom's] secret is given only to the elect'.[79] Thirdly, the marks of this conversion were a sense of humility and an eagerness for the gospel:

This kingdom is seized by the poor in spirit, and they are shut out from it who do not receive it as children nor do the will of the Father. The rich of this age enter into it with difficulty. It is seized violently when the gospel is eagerly heard.[80]

We have already seen Cranmer's conviction that saving grace was certain but not coercive, that God worked by sure and effectual persuasion rather than compulsion when he moved those predestined thus to embrace salvation.[81] The Croydon commentary continued that approach, noting that 'the elect are freely and willingly ruled and led to eternal life by God through his son'.[82]

The belief that the elect could fall from grace is consistent with human choice having a large (if not ultimately definitive) role in the life of God's sons and daughters. This was the theme of the 'Sermon on Rebellion' and its clarion call to

---

[78] 'Hic adverte mentem quisquis quaeris deum, et disce quantum sit in nobis vel capacitatis, taceo preparationis ad fidem Christi in nostra natura: quicumque ex Adam tantum geniti sumus, quantum scilicet est in lapidibus, ad id ut sint filii Abrahae ac proinde filii dei', CCCC MS 104, p. [32].

[79] 'Nosse autem mysteria eius datur tantum electis', CCCC MS 104, p. 33.

[80] 'Capitur hoc regnum a pauperibus spiritu, excluduntur, eo, qui illud non recipiunt ut pueri, nec faciunt voluntatem patris. Divites huius saeculi difficile in illud ingrediuntur; violenter rapitur cum Evangelion cupide auditur', ibid., p. 33.

[81] See Chapter 5. Cf. Peter Martyr's similar position, Joseph C. McLelland, 'The Reformed Doctrine of Predestination According to Peter Martyr', *Scottish Journal of Theology* 8 (1955), 255–71, at 260; Richard A. Muller, *Christ and the Decree: Christology and Predestination in Reformed Theology from Calvin to Perkins* (Grand Rapids, Mich.: Baker Book House, 1988), 65–6; Frank A. James III, *Peter Martyr Vermigli and Predestination: The Augustinian Inheritance of an Italian Reformer* (Oxford: Clarendon Press, 1998), 82–4.

[82] 'Deus electos suos per filium suum liberos et volentes regit et ducit at [recte, ad] vitam coelestem, et divinam', CCCC 104, pp. [32]–3.

repentance.[83] God's punishments were an integral part of the divine economy to provoke the elect to choose repentance. In his patience God deferred punishment to encourage Christians to repent. Yet, if his people persisted in sin to the point that 'peradventure we shuld have forgotten god, and dyed without repentaunce',[84] God effectually persuaded them to desire to return to him by inflicting his judgements. When God did so, if people wished the punishments to cease, they needed to regret their disobedience, to trust that their sins were forgiven for Christ's sake, to intend to amend, and to make restitution. If they hardened their hearts, and did not repent, God would surely strike them 'cleane out of his book'.[85] If they failed to repent before their deaths, then they would hear the 'terrible voyce of damnation: Goo ye wicked into everlasting fyer'.[86] The loss of salvation was only a hypothetical threat to the elect, but not the temporary loss of their state of grace. Since their progress toward eternal salvation was sure but unsteady, repentance was 'the only refuge and anker of our helth and salvation'.[87] Since God granted sufficient freedom of choice to the elect that even they could harden their hearts for a time against God, Paul 'did bothe often and diligently beate [repentaunce] into mens heddis'.[88] And what of the propriety of preaching

[83] Especially the final section, CCCC MS 102, pp. 485–99, Cox II, 200–2.

[84] CCCC MS 102, p. 489, Cox II, 200. This sentence is not found in Martyr's sermon, cf. CCCC MS 340, p. [118].

[85] CCCC MS 102, p. [494], Cox II, 201. Cf. 'Et si obduraveritis corda vestra, illa duritie poteritis eo proficere, ut cum vos non poenituerit admissorum scelerum, deum ipsum poeniteat vestrum, vosque ex albo suorum expungat', Peter Martyr, CCCC MS 340, p. [120].

[86] CCCC MS 102, p. [498], Cox II, 201. This illustration is not found in Martyr's sermon, cf. CCCC MS 340, p. 129.

[87] CCCC MS 102, p. 487, Cox II, 200. Cf. 'Et summam et columen esse nostrae salutis', Peter Martyr, CCCC MS 340, p. 117.

[88] CCCC MS 102, p. [494], Cox II, 200–1. Cf. 'Hanc paulus corinthiis et omnibus ferme ad quos scribit sedulo et frequenter inculcat', Peter Martyr, CCCC MS 340, pp. 119–[20]. Peter Martyr made the same point in his discussion of predestination: 'Cur autem Deus repetere voluit illas promissiones, non est obsurum; ita enim infirmus est animus noster ut nisi repetantur et identidem inculcentur verba Dei, facile resiliat a fide. Neque vero iustificatio semel tantum apprehenditur sed quoties promissionibus divinis vere atque efficaciter assentimur: nam quum assidue labamur et incidamus in peccata, opus habemus subinde repetita iustificatione', *Loci Communes* (1583), 545, as cited by John Patrick

repentance to the non-elect at the same time? Although Cranmer did not quote the passage in the great notebooks, like Calvin, he surely followed Augustine on this point:

Therefore, as much as it pertains to us, who are not worthy to discern the predestined from those who are not predestined, and because of this we ought to wish all people to be saved, a severe rebuke ought to be applied medicinally by us to all people, lest they perish or destroy others. However, it is God's [place] to make the rebuke useful for those whom he foreknew and predestined to be conformed to the image of his Son.[89]

The Forty-Two Articles of 1553 reflect Cranmer's mature soteriology, although the final shape was the result of many hands.[90] According to Article XII, works done before justification, cannot 'make menne mete to receiue Grace, or (as the Schole aucthoures saie) deserue grace of congruitie'. According to Article IX, humanity has no power to do any good works without prevenient grace granting sinners a good will and working in them while they have that will. Article X makes a similar point using scriptural language echoing the analogy in the Croydon commentary: 'The grace of Christ or the holie Ghost by him giueun dothe take awaie the stonie harte, and geueth an harte of flesh', a phrase consistent with the notion that the grace given to the elect brings about regeneration itself, not the choice for regeneration. The article continues on to attribute a changed will in the regenerate to God's action, while denying any compulsion: 'And although, those that have no will to good things, he maketh them to will and those that would evil thinges, he maketh them not to will the same: Yet nevertheless he enforceth not the wil.'

Donnelly, *Calvinism and Scholasticism in Vermigli's Doctrine of Man and Grace* (Leiden: Brill, 1976), 154 n. 91.

[89] 'Proinde, quantum ad nos pertinet, qui praedestinatos a non praedestinatis discernere non valemus, et ob hoc omnes salvos fieri velle debemus; omnibus, ne pereant, vel ne alios perdant, adhibenda est a nobis medicinaliter severa correptio: Dei est autem illis eam facere utilem, quos ipse praescivit et praedestinavit conformes imaginis Filii sui', Augustine, *De correptione et gratia*, ca. 16, *PL* xliv. 946. Cf. Calvin, *Institutes* (1559), Book III, ch. 23, 14; ii. 963–4. See Burns, *Augustine's Operative Grace*, 174–5.

[90] Charles Hardwick, *A History of the Articles of Religion* (London: Bell, 1904), 76. For the text of The Forty-Two Articles, ibid., 290–345.

According to Article XXVI the sacraments were 'effectuall signes of grace and Goddes good will towarde us, by which he dothe worke invisiblie in us' to quicken and to confirm faith. Hence baptism is described by Article XXVIII as 'a signe, and seale of our newe birth, whereby, as by an instrument thei that receive Baptism rightlie' enjoy its benefits. Article XV, however, warns that once the Holy Spirit has been received, its presence may be lost: 'we maie departe from grace geuen, and fall into sinne'. As in Cranmer's own writings, the remedy is repentance, not sacramental penance: 'by the grace of God wee maie rise again, and amende our lives'. Moreover, binding and loosing is associated with excommunication rather than auricular confession. Article XXXII explains that when the church excommunicates an individual, 'the whole multitude of the faithful' ought to shun him until he is officially reconciled. This description of *poenitentia* as either repentance or excommunication reflects Augustine's description which we have seen recorded in 'Cranmer's Great Commonplaces'.

Since the justified can fall, Article XVII outlines the doctrine of predestination as a 'swete, pleasaunte, and unspeakable coumfort to godlie persones' to assure them that any lapse from grace is only temporary. Firstly, God 'hath constantly decreed by his own judgement secret to us' those whom he would bring to everlasting life. Secondly, the end of election is to be made sons by adoption so that the elect might be made like the image of Christ and walk in good works. Thirdly, the purpose of the doctrine is to offer assurance to those who feel the Spirit at work in them so that they may inherit eternal life. As in Cranmer's papers, this work is defined as repentance, i.e. 'mortifying the workes of the flesh, and drawing up their minds to high and heavenly things'. Again as in Cranmer's own writings, this assurance kindles a love in the hearts of the regenerate. Many scholars have argued that Article XVII reflects a moderate Melanchthonian approach, especially its concluding reference to encouraging everyone to believe the promises of Scripture to be true for himself.[91] In fact, the framers of The Forty-Two

[91] The article 'seems to have been framed in perfect conformity with the . . .

Articles have followed Cranmer's practice of separating the discussion of grace and predestination. Since Article X has already established the utter gratuity of election inherent in the description of effectual grace, Article XVII concentrates on how predestination provides assurance. Thus, in the final months of Edward's reign in 1553, Thomas Cranmer was at long last able to gain approval for a Church of England formulary that reflected all the essential points of the soteriology he had outlined in his private papers.

REPENTANCE IN THE LITURGY

Semper orandus est deus, ut condonent peccata, etiam piis filiis quibus iam omnia peccata dimissa sunt.[92]

If The Forty-Two Articles were the fullest public exposition of Cranmer's soteriology, his liturgical work was the most moving expression of his beliefs. In his prayers for the English people Cranmer gradually enshrined turning to God in repentance and faith as the chief effect of saving grace and its chief means. In the process, excommunication came to supersede auricular confession as the normal means for church discipline.

In 1548, the *Catechism* he 'set forth' taught two kinds of ecclesiastical penance. Absolution by the power of the keys was numbered as one of three sacraments, and its purpose was to quiet troubled consciences.[93] Excommunication, however, was an additional function of the power of the

opinions of the Lutherans', Richard Laurence, *An Attempt to Illustrate Those Articles of the Church of England Which the Calvinists Improperly Consider as Calvinistical, in Eight Sermons*, 3rd edn. (Oxford: John Henry Parker, 1838), 170; Hargrave was more cautious: 'Perhaps it is sufficient to say that in its caution and moderation the article was closely akin to the Melanchthonian spirit'; 'Predestination in the English Reformation', 91; Peter White argues that Article XVII was neither Lutheran nor Calvinist but kept 'as closely as possible to the words of Scripture', *Predestination, Policy and Polemic: Conflict and Consensus in the English Church from the Reformation to the Civil War* (Cambridge: Cambridge University Press, 1992), 59.

[92] 'God ought always to be asked to forgive sins, even those belonging to the godly sons which are already all forgiven', CGC II, 202v.

[93] Selwyn, *Catechism*, 'Text', 183, 199; for Selwyn's analysis of the doctrine of the keys in the *Catechism*, see 'Introduction', 50–3.

keys for disciplining doers of 'open synnes'.[94] Although the
Catechism insisted that absolution should not be despised,
two other products of Cranmer's pen from the same year
made it evident that auricular confession was no longer
compulsory.[95] His 'Visitation Articles for the Diocese of
Canterbury' enquired whether clergy with a cure of souls
examined 'such persons as come to confession' during Lent
in the traditional rudiments of the faith, as if receiving
sacramental penance was at the option of parishioners.[96]
Cranmer's wording, however, was consistent with the new
Communion liturgy which he and others had agreed upon at
Windsor and published in March 1548.[97] The opening
exhortation required

such as shall be satisfied with a general Confession, not to be
offended with them that doth use, to their further satisfying, the
auricular and secret Confession to the Priest; nor those also which
think needful or convenient for the quietness of their own
consciences particularly to open their sins to the Priest, to be
offended with them which are satisfied with their humble confession to God, and the general confession to the Church; but in all
these things to follow and keep the rule of charity; and every man
to be satisfied with his own conscience, not judging other men's
minds or acts, where as he hath no warrant of God's word for the
same.[98]

That the new formulary denied any biblical warrant for the
necessity of sacramental penance was, as Dixon noted, 'the
first open stroke that was made by authority against secret or
auricular confession'.[99]

In the following year Cranmer outlined his mature understanding of *poenitentia* in his contribution to the Croydon
commentary on Matthew. Saving penitence was defined as
sorrow for sin for having offended God joined with a hope of
gaining forgiveness through Christ and the intention of
amending one's life with his help.[100] The true and saving

---

[94] Ibid., 'Text', 199–202. [95] Ibid., 203.

[96] Cox II, 155.

[97] Dixon, *History of the Church of England*, ii. 492–7.

[98] *The Order of the Communion* (*Lit. Ed. VI*, 4).

[99] Dixon, *History of the Church of England*, ii. 495; quoted in Brooks,
'Sacraments', 80.

[100] 'Poenitentia peccatorum Evangelice [*sic*] salutaris est dolor de peccatis

confession that always accompanied complete penitence was not the enumeration of sins and the explication of their circumstances but rather a hatred of sin from a true recognition of the heart before God coupled with a fervent prayer for their forgiveness.[101] The fruits worthy of repentance were all kinds of good works done with the zeal that springs from an eager desire for God. This desire was like that of godly children who have offended their parents by a rather grave sin. They strive to declare their repentance, prove their will to amend, and carefully seek to satisfy themselves that they persist in these things, so that whatever they know to be pleasing to their parents, they do as fully and willingly as possible.[102] Dating from 1549, this is the doctrine to which Cranmer sought to conform the prayer book's presentation of confession and penance.

Therefore, all the absolutions in the prayer books of 1549 and 1552 contained a description of forgiveness of sin through justification by faith: 'Almighty God our heavenly Father, who of his great mercy hath promised forgiveness of sins to all them, which with hearty repentance and true faith turn unto him' (the absolution from the Communion); 'Our Lord Jesus Christ, who hath left power to his Church to absolve all sinners, which truly repent and believe in him' (the absolution of the sick); 'Almighty God . . . pardoneth and absolveth all them which truly repent, and unfeignedly believe his holy Gospel' (the absolution added to the Daily Office in 1552). Likewise, the fruit of repentance was described as amendment of life, rather than making satisfaction: 'Forgive us all that is past, and grant that we may every

---

propter offensam dei, cum spe veniae per Christum obtinendae et proposito vitam adiuvante Christo emendandi', CCCC MS 104, p. 29.

[101] 'Confessio autem vera, et salutaris peccatorum, quae ex solida semper poenitentia existit eamque continenter comitatur non est peccatorum enumeratio, et per circumstantias explicatio, sed quam detestanda sint peccata quantoque digna supplicio ex vera cordis cognitione coram deo, deploratio et pro venia eorum ardens supplicatio', CCCC MS 104, p. [30].

[102] 'Fructus digni poenitentiae sunt bona opera omnium generum, sed ardentiore dei studio perfecta[.] Ita enim videas pios in parentes liberos, cum a delicto aliquo graviore quo parentes offenderunt, student illis declarare suam poenitudinem, et constantem approbare, emendationis voluntatem, satagere soliciteque sibi ipsis instare, ut quaecumque novint [*sic*] parentibus placere, faciant quam plenissime et gratissime', CCCC MS 104, p. 31.

hereafter serve and please thee in newness of life, to the honour and glory of thy name' (the general confession prior to the Communion in 1549 and 1552); 'Confirm and strengthen you in all goodness' (the absolution which followed); 'Grant . . . that we may hereafter live a godly, righteous, and sober life, to the glory of thy holy name' (the general confession added to the Daily Office in 1552); and 'Grant us true repentance and his holy Spirit, that those things may please him which we do at this present, and that the rest of our lives hereafter may be pure and holy' (the absolution which followed).[103]

Alongside this fundamental commitment to solifidianism, however, the Edwardian prayer books continued to retain vestiges of the medieval approach to *poenitentia*. The 1549 *Book of Common Prayer* continued to use the exhortation from *The Order of the Communion* which offered confession to those with restless consciences:

And if there be any of you, whose conscience is troubled and grieved in any thing, lacking comfort or counsel, let him come to me, or to some other discreet and learned priest, taught in the law of God, and confess and open his sin and grief secretly, that he may receive such ghostly counsel, advice, and comfort, that his conscience may be relieved, and that of us (as of the ministers of GOD and of the church) he may receive comfort and absolution, to the satisfaction of his mind, and avoiding of all scruple and doubtfulness.[104]

'The Visitation of the Sick' also suggested a private confession if the person who was ill should 'fele his conscience troubled with any weightie matter'. The absolution stipulated in the service not only referred to the power of the keys entrusted to the church but also specified the medieval *ego te absolvo* formula:

Our Lord Jesus Christ, who hath left power to his Church to absolve all sinners, which truly repent and believe in him, of his great mercy forgive thee thine offences: and by his authority committed to me, I absolve thee from all thy sins, in the name of the Father, and of the Son, and of the Holy Ghost. Amen.[105]

---

[103] *BCP* (*Lit. Ed. VI*, 90–1, 138, 218–19, 276, 314).
[104] *BCP* (*Lit. Ed. VI*, 82); cf. *The Order of the Communion* (*Lit. Ed. VI*, 4).
[105] *BCP* (*Lit. Ed. VI*, 138, 314).

The rubric directed the use of this absolution for all other private confessions. Hence, Maskell pointed to the absolution for the sick as proof that through the indicative formula given in individual confession the priest did 'actually absolve the sinner from his sins', and as a consequence restored 'him to the state of justification'.[106] However, since Cranmer made the efficacy of even this absolution dependent on repentance and faith,[107] its language should be understood in a Lutheran fashion: the power that Christ entrusted to his church was his Word;[108] in using the indicative formula the minister was speaking God's words of forgiveness; and the purpose of absolution was to strengthen the penitent's faith on which all forgiveness was based.

In 1552, Cranmer revised the prayer book's presentation of private confession to be more clearly in line with a merely pastoral, rather than sacramental, understanding of the practice. In the second exhortation at Communion, the offer of individual absolution remained, but its description was significantly altered. The minister was no longer described as learned in the 'law of God' which could imply a juridical understanding of confession but rather learned in 'God's word'. The penitent was to open 'his grief' not his 'sin and grief'. Lastly, the comfort and absolution he received was to come not from the priest 'as of the ministers of GOD and of the church' but 'by the ministry of God's word', a change which made explicit that assurance of forgiveness came through trusting the gospel promise.[109] While Cranmer did retain the indicative absolution for 'The Visitation of the Sick', the new absolution added to the Daily Office was precatory: 'Almighty God . . . pardoneth and absolveth all them which truly repent, and unfeignedly believe his holy Gospel. Wherefore we beseech him to grant us true repentance and his Holy Spirit'.[110]

---

[106] Maskell, *Absolution*, 127.

[107] The clause was taken from Archbishop Hermann's *Simplex ac pia Deliberatio* of 1545 (German edition, 1543), to which Melanchthon and Bucer were major contributors. The 'ego te absolvo' formula is derived from Sarum; Brightman, *English Rite*, ii. 828.

[108] Cf., Selwyn, *Catechism*, 'Text', 199–203.

[109] *BCP* (*Lit. Ed. VI*, 82, 274).   [110] *BCP* (*Lit. Ed. VI*, 219, 314).

Cranmer also deleted the sentence which mentioned other private confessions beyond that offered to the ill in the rubrics for 'The Visitation of the Sick'.[111] By restricting the *ego te absolvo* formula to the very ill, Cranmer may have intended to retain the traditional formula of explicit assurance of forgiveness to the dying out of pastoral sensitivity to a flock only recently educated in Protestant thought. We can only conjecture whether Cranmer would have eventually revised this formula as Protestant teaching became normative in the lives of his people.

If Cranmer's liturgy gradually sought to lessen the sacramental connotations of auricular confession, his prayer books also contained the seeds of a rite for public church discipline which his great notebooks suggested was the origin of ecclesiastical penance in the early church. The rubrics for the Communion in 1549 and 1552 required the curate to prevent any 'open and notorious evil liver' from coming to the Lord's Table until he had truly repented and amended his wicked life;[112] and the service for 'The First Day of Lent commonly called Ash Wednesday'—re-titled in 1552 as 'A Commination against Sinners . . . to be used divers times in the year'—described itself as an intermediate form until the restoration of that godly discipline which was in the primitive church whereby notorious sinners were openly punished in this world to save their souls for the next. Like the 'Sermon on Rebellion', this rite promised relief from God's curses to those who repented in time.[113] Although never approved as a formulary of the Edwardian Church, the *Reformatio legum ecclesiasticarum* of 1553 included provisions for excommunication and a service of public reconciliation of the excommunicated after Evening Prayer on Sundays.[114]

The same liturgical revision in 1552 which lessened the

---

[111] *BCP* (*Lit. Ed. VI*, 138, 314).

[112] *BCP* (*Lit. Ed. VI*, 77, 265).

[113] *BCP* (*Lit. Ed. VI*, 150–4, 323–7).

[114] *The Reformation of the Ecclesiastical Laws*, ed. Edward Cardwell (Oxford: Clarendon Press, 1850), 93–4, 167–88. For a useful discussion of Cranmer's understanding of ecclesiastical discipline in the *Reformatio*, including his views on the nature of the church and on the authority of the clergy, see Ayris, 'Cranmer's Register', 313–62.

role of auricular confession also greatly increased the emphasis on repentance. In keeping with the great notebooks' propositional heading, 'God ought always to be asked so that he may forgive sin, even those belonging to godly sons which are already all forgiven',[115] Cranmer added a penitential opening to the Daily Office,[116] and to the end of the Litany he appended prayers which promised repentance in order to mitigate divinely sent punishments.[117] He also inserted a recitation of the Ten Commandments at the beginning of the Lord's Supper which aptly expressed his understanding of repentance as turning to God to be turned by God, for in response to hearing the commandments read, the people were to say: 'Lord, have mercy upon us, and incline our hearts to keep this law.'[118] Yet the most significant change in the 1552 prayer book was Cranmer's complete reordering of the Communion service to fit his Protestant understanding of what made true repentance possible.[119]

Cranmer dropped the explicit epiclesis over the elements and made their reception the immediate response to the words of Institution. As a result, the receiving of the sacramental bread and wine, not their prior consecration, was the liturgy's climax. Now the sacramental miracle was not changing material elements but drawing human hearts to the divine, not increasing personal righteousness but strengthening the communicants' 'right-willedness'. In so doing, Cranmer removed the prayer of oblation from the canon all together, using it as a post-Communion prayer instead. The community now offered nothing themselves to propitiate God but simply responded after the Communion

---

[115] 'Semper orandus est deus, ut condonet peccata, etiam piis filiis quibus iam omnia peccata dimissa sunt', CGC II, 202v.

[116] *BCP (Lit. Ed. VI,* 217–19).

[117] e.g., 'We humbly beseech thee, that although we for our iniquities have worthily deserved this plague of rain and waters, yet upon our true repentance thou wilt send us such weather whereby we may receive the fruits of the earth in due season, and learn both by thy punishment to amend our lives, and for thy clemency to give thee praise and glory', *BCP (Lit. Ed. VI,* 237).

[118] *BCP (Lit. Ed. VI,* 266–7). Gregory Dix attributed this addition to the influence of the *Ritus Ministerii* by the Alsatian Calvinist Pullain which was published in London in 1551; *The Shape of the Liturgy* (Westminster: Dacre, 1945), 659. But G. J. Cuming suggested their inclusion was the result of Hooper's insistence; *A History of Anglican Liturgy* (London: Macmillan, 1969), 106.

[119] See Buchanan, *What did Cranmer Think?*; Brooks, *Eucharist,* 112–62.

with praise, thanksgiving, and a life of service because of the 'full, perfect and sufficient sacrifice, oblation, and satisfaction' of Christ 'once offered' on their behalf.[120] At last grateful love clearly flowed from gracious love.[121] And as if to settle his long-standing dispute with Gardiner over the nature of the human will, Cranmer also moved the Lord's Prayer from before reception to immediately afterwards. Now communicants could pray that they would forgive others because their wills had just been strengthened by receiving afresh God's promised prior forgiveness in Christ.[122] By these changes Cranmer enshrined the responsive nature of the Christian life as taught by the Protestant doctrine of the affections in the very heart of his last Eucharistic liturgy.

Cranmer also removed the prayers for the church and the preparation for reception from their 1549 position following the narrative and placed them between the offertory and the Sursum Corda. Now the Protestant approach to justification was reaffirmed prior to the canon. Participants heard the Law and then the Gospel (both read and preached), prayed for grace to receive God's Word effectually so that they might serve him in holiness, sought forgiveness for where they had not done so, and then heard the comfortable evangelical promises assuring pardon. Consequently, the grounds of grace, both humanity's need and God's promises, were renewed afresh immediately before the hearts of the people were to ascend on high to where Jesus' corporeal body was locally circumscribed at the right hand of God.

Lastly, Cranmer detached the prayer of humble access from the preparation for reception and placed it within the canon so that it immediately followed the Sanctus and preceded the narrative. Now the response to being admitted to the Heavenly Throne Room was the same as Isaiah's.[123]

---

[120] BCP (*Lit. Ed. VI*, 279).

[121] For this theme in Calvin's Eucharistic theology, see B. A. Gerrish, *Grace and Gratitude: The Eucharistic Theology of John Calvin* (Edinburgh: T & T Clark, 1993).

[122] For Gardiner, see Chapter 3. Buchanan notes that such a change was also in keeping with Cranmer's new practice to use the Lord's Prayer to introduce a section of prayers; *What did Cranmer Think?*, 26.

[123] Buchanan, *What did Cranmer Think?*, 27. Cf. both Isaiah 6: 1–8 and 'Semper

Communicants were to acknowledge that their human unworthiness remained even in those so privileged as to come into the very courts of God in this life, but that God's mercy had provided the necessary cleansing so that they may dwell in him and he may dwell in them. And the natural result of their participation in this mutual indwelling, despite their on-going sinfulness, was not only to offer their grateful service (like Isaiah) in the post-Communion prayers but also to offer their praise by singing afterwards the newly-positioned Gloria. This final anthem captured the essence of Cranmer's understanding of the Christian life. Believers were first to give glory to God because of his loving good will towards them which had brought them peace through Jesus Christ. They were also to continue to acknowledge their on-going dependence on his mercy; for only through their gracious union with Christ could they please God and find the power to serve him. For Cranmer, the glory of God was his love of sinners, and the goodness of humanity was gratitude for such grace.

Packer and Leuenberger have stressed that these changes created a threefold 'sin–grace–faith' cycle in the Eucharistic service, namely, the Law–Gospel–Creed, Confession–Absolution–Sanctus, and Prayer of Humble Access-Words of Distribution–Gloria.[124] Although the 'triple-beat' of 'sin–grace–faith' can be detected at many points in the service and in many individual prayers as well,[125] far more important is the solifidian shape of the liturgy as a whole. The new order took participants through the steps which Cranmer believed led to conversion of the will and new life in Christ: fear inspired by the Law; faith springing forth from the Gospel; God's gift of repentance; re-entry into God's presence; and the reception of power for a renewed holiness. Cranmer's second post-Communion prayer appropriately

---

orandus est deus, ut condonet peccata, etiam piis filiis quibus iam omnia peccata dimissa sunt', CGC II, 202v.

[124] Packer, in Duffield, *Cranmer*, xxvi; Samuel Leuenberger, *Archbishop Cranmer's Immortal Bequest—The Book of Common Prayer of the Church of England: An Evangelistic Liturgy* (Grand Rapids, Mich.: Eerdmans, 1990), 105–11.

[125] As Leuenberger's more detailed analysis pointed out when considering the Exhortations, the Consecration Prayer and the Prayer of Humble Access; ibid., 107, 110–11.

summarized his understanding of the aim of the justification:

We most heartily thank thee for . . . that we be very members incorporate in the mystical body which is the blessed company of all faithful people, and be also heirs through hope, of thy everlasting kingdom, by the merits of the most precious death and Passion of thy dear son . . . assist us with thy grace that we may continue in that holy fellowship, and do all such good works as thou hast prepared for us to walk in.[126]

Regular participants in the Communion service would have fulfilled their baptismal pledge to strive continually to 'die from sin and rise again unto righteousness'.[127] Thus, 'the 1552 rite was no accident, no afterthought, and no overreaction'.[128] Cranmer intended his Eucharistic liturgy both to inspire loving repentance in the hearts of the English and to make this new affection possible through Word and Sacrament properly presented. In the words of Dom Gregory Dix, Cranmer's 1552 *Book of Common Prayer* stands as 'the only effective attempt ever made to give liturgical expression to the doctrine of "justification by faith alone"'.[129]

IN SUMMATION

Turn thou us, O good Lord, and so shall we be turned: be favourable (O Lord) be favourable to thy people, which turn to thee in weeping, fasting and praying.[130]

The heart of Cranmer's commitment to solifidianism was his conviction that salvation by any other means exalted man at God's expense. Repentance was turning to God (by confessing one's sins) to be turned by God (through his gift of lively faith), an act which both humbled humankind and glorified God as humanity's only hope. As the practical,

---

[126] *BCP* (*Lit. Ed. VI*, 280).
[127] *BCP* (*Lit. Ed. VI*, 290).
[128] Buchanan, *What did Cranmer Think?*, 21.
[129] Dix, *Shape of the Liturgy*, 672.
[130] 'A Commination Against Sinners', *BCP* (*Lit. Ed. VI*, 327); for the 1549 version, ibid., 154.

pastoral expression of justification *sola fide*, Cranmer made repentance the focus of his theology and liturgy. Yet, he realized that even repentance thus understood could be seen as the human contribution to salvation *sine qua non*. To ensure that justification was also *sola gratia*, he adopted the doctrine of God's predestination of his elect and shaped his public writings accordingly. Repentance as the expression of a loving faith was interpreted as a sign of justification and election which assured the believer of his salvation. Just as important, however, repentance as turning to God and away from sin was presented as a concrete task towards which all sinners were to strive. In this way, repentance was also the pastoral, practical expression of predestination, enabling Cranmer to offer assurance of election to the saints and at the same time to encourage all people to be obedient to the laws of God and the king. Thus, through the promotion of repentance rightly understood Cranmer sought to enshrine salvation *sola fide et gratia* in the formularies of the Edwardian church.

In the end, repentance has come to symbolize Cranmer himself, his life's work being interpreted by his last days. In the eyes of his critics, Cranmer's recantations prove that at best he was weak and vacillating, at worst he was a shallow time-server whose only theology was current expediency. In the hearts of his admirers, however, Cranmer's last-minute renunciation of his recantations proved his true commitment to the Protestant faith. But what of Cranmer himself, how did he interpret his last days and the meaning they gave to his life? According to a contemporary account, having previously been distraught, Cranmer came to the stake with 'a cheerful countenance and willing mind'.

Fire being now put to him, he stretched out his right Hand, and thrust it into the Flame, and held it there a good space, before the Fire came to any other Part of his Body; where his Hand was seen of every Man sensibly burning, crying with a loud Voice, *This Hand hath offended*. As soon as the Fire got up, he was very soon Dead, never stirring or crying all the while.[131]

[131] John Strype, *Memorials of . . . Thomas Cranmer, sometime Lord Archbishop of Canterbury*, 2 vols. in 1 (London: Richard Chiswell, 1694), Book 3, ch. 21, i. 389. Strype has helpfully collated the separate accounts of Cranmer's death written by

His Catholic executioners surely thought Cranmer was making satisfaction to his Protestant God. Yet his doctrine of repentance would have taught him otherwise, for the God he served saved the unworthy.

Having believed in his own justification by faith, Cranmer would have thought he could fall totally, but not finally. As God's child, the burden of all the multitude of his sins was no cause for him to distrust or despair of help at his Father's hand; for the incredible richness of God's merciful love for him would never have shone brighter than on that cloudy day, precisely because he, the chief promoter of the new faith, had fallen so far as to become a declared enemy of the gospel.[132] To Cranmer, his hand in the fire would have been an act of loving service of a heart turned back to God by the power and promise of his immeasurably loving grace. His final resolve would have been a joyous confirmation that he was indeed one of the elect in whom there would be no fault found in the end. His firmness of purpose would have been sustained by the hope he expressed in the Burial Office that was never read for him: 'the souls of them that be elected, after they be delivered from the burden of the flesh, be in joy and felicity'.[133]

eyewitness 'J.A.' (BL Harley MS 422, fols. 48–52, at 49v and 51r) into a single narrative.

[132] Cf. 'And being assured of so good, so loving, and therewith so mighty a governor, mediator, and advocate in heaven as Christ is . . . all the multitude or burden of my sins, shall [never] cause me to distrust or despair of help at his hands', Lloyd, *Formularies*, 45–6.

[133] *BCP* (*Lit. Ed. VI*, 319). A shrewd judge of liturgy, Eamon Duffy has rightly pointed to this prayer as evidence of Cranmer's holding to a doctrine of election; 'Cranmer and Popular Religion', in Ayris and Selwyn, *Churchman and Scholar*, 199–215, at 215. However, Duffy interprets Cranmer's use of the language of election to mean that the Burial Office was envisaged for a very narrow community, for 'of the openly sinful or merely mediocre majority it said nothing at all'. While probably Cranmer would have preferred the openly sinful to have been excluded from the church by excommunication and those dying in that state to have been denied a Christian burial, he would have intended his language of election to be a sign of hope to those who remained in the visible church, that, despite their 'mediocrity', salvation was by grace and if grace stirred them to have sorrow for their shortcomings and to trust in Christ, they had reason to hope for eternal life in the end.

Conclusion

[W]hen do you think is the time to love somebody the
most? When they done good and made things easy for
everybody? Well, then, you ain't through learning—
because that ain't the time at all.[1]

Like his first royal master, Cranmer did not make himself
easy to love. To traditionalists he represented all that was
shoddy, sordid, and squalid in the new religious regime. To
Protestants impatient for evangelical progress he was timid
and tepid, the heart of all that was temporalizing in the old
establishment. In an era noted for the fervent courage of
many martyrs for faith, Cranmer's very survival under a
king as unprincipled, or at least unpredictable, as Henry
VIII has made him suspect. His late vacillation under Mary
has only seemed to confirm the image of a man ruled more
by the grip of fear than the assurance of the faith. Undoubtedly, Cranmer's quiet but consistent attempts to push
the Reformation further than Henry's natural inclinations
meant the Archbishop lived much of the time in a climate of
anxious uncertainty and uncomfortable compromise. Yet
fearful men do not often pass off lightly the criticism of
their inferiors; nor do theologically unprincipled prisoners
defiantly urge royal adherents of Spanish Catholicism to
repudiate the pope as Antichrist.[2] Brooks was right that
Cranmer was 'a very foxy Archbishop' in the sense that he
knew many things, including both the latest trends in
Continental Protestant scholarship and how best to meet
the pastoral needs of Henry VIII.[3] Yet his life and thought

---

[1] Lorraine Hansberry, *A Raisin in the Sun* (New York, N.Y.: Signet, 1987), 145.
[2] For Cranmer's treatment of personal offences, see the Introduction; for his
uncompromising appeal to Philip and Mary, see MacCulloch, *Cranmer*, 579–80.
[3] For Cranmer's keeping current theologically, see Cox II, 342–4. For Cranmer's pastoral sensitivity to Henry's needs, see MacCulloch's discussion of
Cranmer's suggestion that the king's affection for Katherine Howard made her a

also had the kind of inner coherence that Berlin's fox lacked.[4] Fundamentally, Cranmer was an ecclesiastical hedgehog who built a unitary vision of history on one big idea—that God's love for his enemies worked everything to good.

For if divine love had the power to effect the ultimate course of human wills, then divine love must also have had the power to arrange the course of human affairs—not only with regard to the eternal destinies of individuals but also with regard to the social and political histories of nations. Accordingly, Cranmer believed that the sovereign was 'elected by God' to govern all affairs in his kingdom, both temporal and spiritual, as 'God's vice-gerent and Christ's vicar'.[5] Because of his confidence in God's providential governance, the naturally pastoral Cranmer could willingly subordinate himself to Thomas Cromwell as vice-gerent in spirituals, leaving the cut and thrust of court politics to the King's Minister, while he concentrated on developing the theological justifications for their shared evangelical agenda. Consequently, Cranmer's record as archbishop has left 'no sign that power was ever very important to him: what mattered was the furtherance of the Gospel as he conceived it'.[6] Cranmer would have seen his survival under Henry as a vindication of his policy of relying on the power of love rather than the love of power. Indeed, maybe only someone as committed to loving the unworthy as Cranmer could have inspired such loving loyalty from someone so personally unattractive in character as Henry VIII. For most of his life,

---

more suitable wife than Cromwell's candidate, the Protestant Anne of Cleves; *Cranmer*, 258.

[4] 'There is a line among the fragments of the Greek poet Archilochus which says, "The fox knows many things, but the hedgehog knows one big thing" . . . taken figuratively, the words can be made to yield a sense in which they mark one of the deepest differences which divide writers and thinkers . . . For there exists a great chasm between those, on one side, who relate everything to a single central vision . . . a single, universal, organizing principle in terms of which alone all that they are and say has significance—and, on the other side, those who pursue many ends, often unrelated and even contradictry, connected, if at all, only in some *de facto* way . . . related by no moral or aesthetic principle', Berlin, *The Hedgehog and the Fox*, 1.

[5] Cox II, 126–7.

[6] MacCulloch, *Cranmer*, 136.

Cranmer displayed both the courage of his convictions and the obedient adaptability he felt they and their advancement required.

In the light of Cranmer's unitary vision of history, the recantations of his last days seem not so much a sign of fear-inspired theological instability as an indication of his penultimate despair that the course of events in England had apparently failed to vindicate the Gospel he had served. Whereas Edward's ascension appeared to validate Cranmer's cautious and compromising path toward reform under Henry, the boy-king's early death did the exact opposite. This obvious observation could not have been too far from Cranmer's mind during the intense campaign of intellectual pressure and emotional manipulation conducted by the Marian authorities to bring about his complete capitulation in the months leading up to his execution.[7] Eventually, the dissidence between Cranmer's beliefs and his circumstances became too much for him. When a threatened hedgehog finds himself on impenetrable rock, he naturally imitates the strategy of a fox, running to and fro looking for some kind of cover until he can find burrowing-friendly ground once again. Eventually, Cranmer was willing to sign the series of increasingly more self-incriminating statements as the price of admission to a circle of Christian friends who would love him, if only 'for his new-found faith'.[8] Yet, he could find no peace as an unprincipled Romish fox bereft of a unifying vision for his life. In the final hours, he regained his confidence in God's working in history and God's working through both his contributions and compromises, a conclusion soon to be shared by the Elizabethan church. Cranmer went to his death bravely, even joyfully, certain that God's unfailing love would finish the good work he had begun in him and through him.[9]

If Cranmer's belief in the power of divine love at times left his life looking inconsistent, this fundamental tenet gave coherence to the trajectory of his theological development and its eventual doctrinal maturity. For from the beginning of his days in Cambridge, Cranmer was educated among

---

[7] Ibid., 585–99.   [8] Ibid., 596.   [9] Ibid., 600.

theologians who sought to renew the human power to love by restoring the pre-eminence of grace in salvation. By blending the humanist emphasis on Augustine's writings with Scotist penitential theology, Fisher taught two means of forgiveness for renewal: either through the rigorous *via attritionis formatae* as assisted by the *auxilium Dei speciale*; or by the easier, more certain way of sacramental penance. When Cranmer came under the influence of Erasmus's biblical humanism, he gradually abandoned an *ex opere operato* understanding of the sacrament. As a result, he embraced only a single means for forgiveness and new life, namely, the penitent striving to cultivate *fiducia* and love in his heart through good works inspired by grace. In the 1530s, however, Cranmer decided to interpret Paul through the Protestant understanding of Augustine rather than Erasmus; consequently, he accepted that God's love justified the ungodly and that solifidianism and unconditional election were the chief doctrinal means of safeguarding the utter gratuity of this salvation. Nothing a sinner did, nor any quality a sinner had, was acceptable to God until God had imputed Christ's righteousness to him by faith. For only after his rebellious heart had been inflamed with the godly love that came with justification could a person begin to love God and others as he ought. Once Cranmer had come to this decision, he spent the remaining years of his ministry trying to shape the formularies of the Church of England accordingly.

During the doctrinal debates of the 1530s, Cranmer's strategy was to redefine sacramental penance in accordance with Lutheran teaching which stressed solifidianism and the sacrament's optional nature. In the 1540s, however, Cranmer rejected the idea of a sacramental context for justification, while Henry decided to permit an explicit repudiation of solifidianism. With the publication of the *King's Book* in 1543 the Henrician church officially endorsed what was essentially Fisher's Augustinian-influenced *via attritionis formatae*. In response to his conservative opponents, Cranmer engaged in a massive research project to prove that justification *sola fide et gratia ex praedestinatione ante praevisa merita* was the true Augustinian soteriology.

Crucial to Cranmer's argument was the renovation of the will and its affections which justification by imputation effected. In the moment of justification God granted both faith and love. The believer's faith laid hold of the extrinsic righteousness of Christ on which basis his sins were pardoned. At the same time the Holy Spirit indwelt the believer, stirring in him a love for God out of gratitude for the assurance of salvation. Before love had been shed in a Christian's heart, no work which he did could be considered good. Once love had been shed in his heart, before he did any good works he was already a child of God. Hence, works could play no role in justification itself. Rather, striving to please God out of love was the natural response to free pardon and the good works which arose accordingly certified the believer's conscience that he was justified. God's gracious love inspired grateful human love. Thus, justification was being made 'right-willed' by faith, not being made inherently righteous through a preparation of good works. To protect the utter gratuity of this saving faith Cranmer appealed to Augustine's teaching on the unconditional predestination of the elect to eternal life, although like his fellow Reformed theologians, he rejected Augustine's views that not all those who were justified would persevere to final glory.

Developed and defended in the unique situation of the Henrician church, Cranmer's Reformed theology emphasized the 'right-will' concomitant with justification. As a result, he was able to continue the medieval focus on *poenitentia*, albeit significantly redefined by being placed within a solidly Protestant theological context. Repentance was now turning to God (by confessing one's sins) to be turned by God (through his gift of lively faith), an act which both humbled humankind and glorified God as their only hope. When God granted repentance as an on-going fruit of a life of godly love, the believer knew he was elected to eternal salvation. This doctrine of repentance Cranmer sought to make the focal point of his formularies for the Edwardian church. Nevertheless, since Cranmer's larger theological context of predestination was hidden from view in the prayer book, just as Scotus's similar doctrine was not apparent in the penitentials, Cranmer's liturgy remained vulnerable to being understood as stressing salvation contingent on human response. Consequently, much of the subsequent history of Anglican theology can be understood as a struggle to reach agreement on the proper understanding of repentance.

No doubt Cranmer would be disappointed by the disputes of his theological descendants, but he would have understood. As an academic, he knew that different presuppositions often predetermined conflicting conclusions, despite rigorous logic being employed by both sides. As a pastor, he realized that human frailty fought against admitting error, the necessary prelude to anyone switching perspectives. As a sinner, he too struggled with the ever-present human tendency to put his own interests ahead of God's glory and the advancement of the gospel. His final answer was to put his hand in the fire and commit his life and legacy to God's love: its unconditional pardon, its unlimited power, its indwelling presence, its inspiration of reciprocal love, its often invisible purposes, and its ultimately invincible plan to order all things right. Anglicans may not find Cranmer and his prayer book so easy to love today, but his faith still offers much from which they can learn.

APPENDIX

Manuscript Sources for Cranmer's Doctrine of Repentance

This reconstruction of Cranmer's doctrinal development has used three important manuscript sources: his great commonplace books, a description of the debate over the sacraments which led to the *Bishops' Book*, and three chapters of a manuscript commentary on Matthew.

'CRANMER'S GREAT COMMONPLACES'

Cranmer undergirded his defence of the Protestant faith with years of scholarship, the fruit of which was recorded in the many notebooks he maintained. Consisting of extensive quotations from leading theological authorities, these collections were described as 'a rare and precious treasure' in a letter of Queen Elizabeth.[1] By far the largest of Cranmer's commonplaces is the British Library's Royal MSS 7B.XI and 7B.XII.[2] Such was their importance that Matthew Parker enlisted the aid of the Privy Council in gaining possession of them. For after Cranmer's arrest and the dispersal of his library, these notebooks came into the possession of Dr Stephen Nevinson, the son-in-law of Reyner Wolfe, Cranmer's printer; and he was most reluctant to admit his ownership lest they be whisked away, as they indeed were.[3] These volumes are

---

[1] Cox II, 459. Cox suggested that this letter was only a secretary's draft composed in Elizabeth's name which Cecil rejected in favour of a letter from himself passing on the Queen's wishes. Note also that this letter concerned the return of various Cranmer commonplace books in the possession of Mr Herd of Lincoln and not 'Cranmer's Great Commonplaces' specifically; P. M. Black, 'Matthew Parker's Search for Cranmer's "great notable written books"', *The Library*, Fifth Series, 29 (1974), 312–22, at 322.

[2] G. F. Warner and J. P. Gilson, *Catalogue of Western Manuscripts in the Old Royal and King's Collections* (Oxford: Oxford University Press, 1921), i. 172–3.

[3] Parker enlisted Cecil's aid in gaining possession of the notebooks from Nevinson, contributing the red chalk pagination numbers during his custodianship. See Black, 'Parker's Search', 312–22; Cf. J. Strype's more uncertain account; *Memorials of Cranmer*, Book 3, ch. 22, i. 398–9, and ibid., Appendix, no. 90, ii. 217–18. After Parker, it appears from his signature on the last folio of 7B.XII that Andrew Perne, Master of Peterhouse, Cambridge, from 1554 to 1589, had them in his care before they eventually passed to John Theyer (1597–1673) from whose collection they were purchased for the Royal Library in 1678. See

usually styled 'Cranmer's Commonplace Books',[4] although other Cranmer manuscript notebooks have survived. Attempting to distinguish among them, Paul Ayris referred to Lambeth Palace Library MS 1108 as Cranmer's 'legal *Commonplaces*' and BL Royal MSS 7B.XI, 7B.XII, as his 'sacramental *Commonplaces*'.[5] Yet, neither is an entirely apt appellation because both notebooks contain material of more diversity than such a title would suggest. Since Matthew Parker called them 'great notable written books',[6] in this work, BL Royal MSS 7B.XI and 7B.XII have been styled as 'Cranmer's Great Commonplaces', referred to as either the 'Great Commonplaces' or the great notebooks, and abbreviated as CGC.

Bound in two volumes containing between them 558 leaves (for the most part 12¼" × 8½"), the great notebooks are both 'massive' and mostly 'unstudied', as one Cranmer scholar recently noted.[7] Of the limited research published on them, some is of purely antiquarian interest.[8] Others have noted in passing that the wide range of readings in the 'Great Commonplaces' indicates that Cranmer made use of the large library he was known to possess; and David Selwyn has systematically studied them to help reconstruct that library.[9] The most common mention of them is during a discussion of the controversial decision by the seventeenth-century historian John Strype to endorse *A Confutation of Unwritten Verities* as a reliable source for Cranmer's views. The nineteenth-century historian Henry Jenkyns was unpersuaded by

Paul Ayris and D. G. Selwyn, 'Cranmer's Commonplace Books', in *Churchman and Scholar*, 312–15, at 313.

[4] Strype, *Memorials of Cranmer*, Book 3, ch. 22, i. 397. Henry Jenkyns, *Remains of Thomas Cranmer* (Oxford: Oxford University Press, 1833), iv. 144; Mason, *Cranmer*, 84; Warner and Gilson, *Royal Manuscripts*, 172; Brooks, *Eucharist*, xxvii; Paul F. Bradshaw, *The Anglican Ordinal: Its History and Development from the Reformation to the Present Day* (London: SPCK, 1971), 12; Ayris and Selwyn, *Churchman and Scholar*, 312–15; however, F. E. Brightman called them 'Cranmer's *Note Books*', 'Capitulum Coloniense: An Episode in the Reformation', *Church Quarterly Review* 31 (1891), 419–37, at 420.

[5] Paul Ayris, 'Thomas Cranmer's Register: A Record of Archiepiscopal Administration in Diocese and Province', Ph.D. thesis (University of Cambridge, 1984), ad passim.

[6] *Correspondence of Matthew Parker, D. D.*, ed. J. Bruce and T. T. Perowne (Cambridge: Parker Society, 1853), 186.

[7] K. J. Walsh, 'Cranmer and the Fathers, especially in the *Defence*', *Journal of Religious History* 11 (1980), 227–47, at 231.

[8] Warner and Gilson, *Royal Manuscripts*, i. 172–3; Black, 'Parker's Search', 312–22.

[9] Mason, *Cranmer*, 84; Bromiley, *Cranmer, Theologian*, 3; Selwyn, *Library*, 235–46.

the former's arguments.[10] While admitting that its text was clearly based on the collection of authorities compiled by Cranmer in the first section of the great notebooks, Jenkyns was suspicious of the interpretation of the material by the unknown editor, E. P.[11] Nevertheless, those scholars who have used the *Unwritten Verities* in their description of Cranmer's theological views have, in effect, made an indirect evaluation of some of the theological material contained in 'Cranmer's Great Commonplaces'.[12] Their use of a mediated means, however, renders their conclusions somewhat tentative.

The first direct analysis of the theological importance of the 'Great Commonplaces' was an unattributed article by F. E. Brightman. He effectively demonstrated that the entries listed in them as 'Capitulum Coloniense' referred to the *Antididagma*—the response of the conservative Catholic cathedral canons to the reforming work of Archbishop Hermann von Wied of Cologne—although Brightman drew the wrong conclusions from their inclusion.[13] From time to time others have followed suit, mining selections from Cranmer's quotations to assist them in their investigations in other matters.[14] Nevertheless, until now the most systematic theological study of the 'Great Commonplaces' themselves has remained Brooks's use of the sacramental sections to reconstruct Cranmer's theological views at the end of the 1530s, including his landmark study of Cranmer's understanding of Communion in the light of the 'De Eucharistia' section.[15]

The text is mostly written in abbreviated Latin by a single

---

[10] Bromiley and Packer, however, agreed with Strype, making much use of the *Unwritten Verities* in their description of Cranmer's theological views. For a description of the Strype–Jenkins debate, see Cox II, 5. For the text of *Unwritten Verities*, see Cox II, 9–67.

[11] Since 'it was moulded by him, by addition, omission, and transposition, into the shape in which it now appears', Jenkyns felt that 'under these circumstances it cannot be safely quoted as evidence of Cranmer's tenets'; Jenkyns, *Cranmer*, iv. 144. Pollard concurred; *Cranmer*, 243. For MacCulloch's suggestion that Stephen Nevinson was also E.P., see *Cranmer*, 633–6.

[12] Bromiley, *Cranmer, Theologian*, 15–27 and passim, noting, however, the need to ignore the preface and concluding chapter as obvious works of the redactor; Packer, in Duffield, *Cranmer*, xxi–xxiii, xxxvi n. 30 where he added, 'Strype ascribed it to Cranmer; style and content make this likely, though not certain'.

[13] [Brightman], 'Capitulum Coloniense', 421, see below.

[14] The most recent example is Gordon Jeanes's citation of common patristic quotations found in 'De sacramentis' (LPL MS 1107, fols. 84r–93v) and 'Cranmer's Great Commonplaces' to argue for Cranmer's authorship of the former; 'Reformation Treatise', 149–90. For a discussion of this research, see below.

[15] Brooks, 'Sacraments', passim, and Brooks, *Eucharist*, xxii, 11, 21–36.

copyist in Secretary hand, although on occasion the entries are written by others. The chief copyist's handwriting belongs to neither Cranmer nor Ralph Morice, his principal secretary.[16] As is to be expected from its size, the number of authors included and the subjects considered is substantial. Ayris and Selwyn have recently published a description of the contents based on its *tabula repertoria* with foliation references.[17] It should be noted that the manuscript has both page and folio numbers, both of whose numeration is imperfect. The red pagination numbers every odd page in each volume, but in the second tome, page 545 is followed by page 447, creating two sets of red pagination numbered 447–545.[18] The black ink foliation numbers the *recto* side of every inscribed leaf. However, numerous blank folios remain uncounted for in this system, 39 in the first volume, 18 in the second. Although the pagination is more precise in terms of the actual number of leaves, the foliation is less confusing in ordering the material, and for that reason is used in this work.

'Cranmer's Great Commonplaces' is commonly divided into three sections. In general, the first considers the church's lack of authority apart from Scripture (CGC I, 6–49), the second deals with sacraments and contentious issues (CGC I, 50–CGC II, 81 and CGC II, 298–320), and the third with justification by faith and purgatory (CGC II, 82–297). This book includes an analysis of 'De poenitentia', 'De confessione' and 'De satisfactione' from the second section and material associated with justification in the third. Since portions of the third section on justification appear to be an expansion of the *loci* associated with the subject in the last folios of the second section,[19] all *loci* relevant to justification after CGC II, 82 *recto* will be considered together.[20] In general, the second section would seem to be no later than 1538 and the third

---

[16] Warner and Gilson, *Royal Manuscripts*, 172.

[17] *Churchman and Scholar*, 313–15. However, Jenkyns published a more complete listing of folio titles; *Remains*, iv. 147–50, reprinted Cox II, 7–8. For a summary list in English, see Packer, in Duffield, *Cranmer*, xxxvi n. 28.

[18] Consequently, Jenkyns, who referred to the pagination numbers, used the letters 'a' and 'b' to differentiate between the two sets, e.g., 447a versus 447b [recte, 547]; *Remains*, iv. 147–50; Cox II, 7–8.

[19] Cf. 'De gratia et meritis' (CGC II, 300) and 'Contra merita humana' (CGC II, 263r–267v); 'Semper orandus est Deus, etc', (CGC II, 302) and 'Semper orandus est Deus, etc', (CGC II, 202v–204r).

[20] Penitential material: CGC I, 124r–167r; Material on Justification: CGC II, 82r–106v, 112v–121v, 202r–302v, 311r–315r. A separately foliated section on purgatory has been inserted in the middle of the material on justification, fols. 122r–201v, which previously had been numbered 1–80 on the upper right corner of the recto side of each leaf.

section contains material available no earlier than 1543.[21] Since the penitential and soteriological material originate at different times and, in fact, have different organizing principles, they will be considered separately.

According to Warner and Gilson, in general the sacramental section was completed *circa* 1538 with some later additions. The original penitential section consisted of three *loci*: 'De poenitentia' (CGC I, 133r–144v and styled in this book as 'De poenitentia I'), 'De confessione' (CGC I, 145r–150v) and 'De Satisfactione' (CGC I, 151r–166r). Since 'De poenitentia I' and 'De satisfactione' include extracts from Calvin's first edition of the *Institutio*, it is reasonable to follow Warner and Gilson and date this material as compiled prior to 1539.[22] After the publication of the *Antididagma* (1544), an extract was added to 'De satisfactione' (CGC I, 166v–167r). This entire section (CGC I, 133r–167r) was then numbered one to thirty-five on the lower right-hand corner of the *recto* side of each folio. Also following the publication of the *Antididagma*,[23] an additional gathering of lengthy extracts describing the practice of penance in the early church was compiled and given an abbreviated heading 'de pnia' as an apparent afterthought (CGC I, 125r–132v, styled in this book as 'De poenitentia II'). Another folio with a definition of repentance and extracts from the Lombard under a formally written 'De poenitentia' heading was also prepared (CGC I, 124 styled in this book as 'De poenitentia III').[24] Eventually, 'De poenitentia III' was added to the front of 'De poenitentia II' and the combined *locus* numbered one to nine in the lower right-hand corner of the *recto* side of each folio. At the same time, the two separate groups of penitential quotations, 'De poenitentia III'–'De poenitentia II' and 'De poenitentia I'–'De confessione'–'De satisfactione [as appended]', were brought together and incorporated into a larger framework of sacramental *loci*, the letter 'f' prefacing the number one on the first folio of 'De poenitentia III'–'De poenitentia II' and the letter 'g', perhaps written over a previous number one, inscribed on the initial folio of 'De poenitentia I'–etc.

While it may be true that sometimes in 'his notebooks, Cranmer adopted the scholastic approach of opposing a thesis (*propositio*) to

---

[21] Warner and Gilson, *Royal Manuscripts*, 172.

[22] CGC I, 142r–144r, 161v–165v; For a detailed comparison of the extracts in the great notebooks and Calvin's first edition of the *Institutio*, see Brooks, 'Sacraments', 98 n. 1.

[23] CGC I, 132v.

[24] CGC I, 124.

an antithesis (*oppositio*) to secure a synthesis (*solutio*)',[25] that description does not apply to the penitential material. 'De poenitentia', 'De confessione', and 'De satisfactione' are each a *locus* in the traditional sense of a 'commonplace', that is, a 'place' of storage for material gathered together on a single subject for convenient retrieval later, in this case, authoritative *sententiae* on a theological topic.[26] Since a secretary has simply 'stored' these quotations under the subject headings without any comment, two questions confront anyone attempting to use this material as evidence for Cranmer's own theological views. Firstly, since the entries are not in Cranmer's hand, do they represent his own research, or that of an assistant? While it is not possible to say so conclusively, the available evidence would suggest that the selections were the work of Cranmer himself. During his years in Cambridge it was Cranmer's habit to write out passages from what he read as 'a great helpe to hym in debating of matters ever after'.[27] As archbishop, he apparently continued the practice. For when Henry would routinely ask Cranmer to prepare a brief on a given theological controversy, 'being throughlie seene in all kinde of expositors, he coulde incontynentlie laye open xxx^{ti}, xl^{ti}, lx^{ti} or mo sumwhiles of authors'.[28] Ralph Morice attributed Cranmer's feat of scholarship, not to notes made by his secretaries but specifically to Cranmer's normal custom of spending 'iii partes of the daie in studie as effectuallie as he hadd byn at Cambridge'.[29] An example of an assistant's research for Cranmer does survive in Peter Alexander's *Loci communes* based on the writings of Origen, Athanasius, and Epiphanius, but this manuscript is clearly labelled as Alexander's work given to Cranmer.[30] In summary,

---

[25] Ayris and Selwyn, *Churchman and Scholar*, 312.

[26] Joan Marie Lechner, *Renaissance Concepts of the Commonplaces* (New York, N.Y.: Pageant, 1962); Quirinus Breen, 'The Terms "Loci Communes" and "Loci" in Melanchthon', in *Christianity and Humanism*, ed. Nelson Peter Ross (Grand Rapids, Mich.: Eerdmans, 1973), 93–105; Neal W. Gilbert, *Renaissance Concepts of Method* (New York, N.Y.: Columbia University Press, 1960), 107–15.

[27] 'For he was a slowe reader, but a diligent marker of whatsoever he redd, for he seldom redd without pen in hand, and whatsoever made eyther for the one parte or the other, of thinges being in contraversy, he wrote it out yf it were short, or at the least noted the author and the place, that he might fynd it and wryte it out by leysure; which was a great helpe to hym in debating of matters ever after', Nichols, *Narratives*, 219.

[28] Ibid., 249–50.

[29] Ibid., 250.

[30] 'Accipe praesul igitur Reverendus . . . theologiae compendium et hunc nostrum qualemcunque laborem', Peter Alexander to Thomas Cranmer, 'Collectanea ex libris Origenis Adamantii, Athanasii et Epiphanii una', Cambridge University Library MS ᴇᴇ. 2. 8, fol. 1v.

Cranmer had need of theological *sententiae* to answer Henry's questions. He was known to take significant time for theological study despite the pressures of his office. And early on in life he formed the habit of writing out extracts from what he read. These facts suggest that as archbishop, Cranmer continued to read and to mark significant passages, but then left the actual copying to a secretary. As David Selwyn has noted: 'Again and again, it will be found that a passage copied out in one of the "commonplace" collections . . . has been marked and often annotated in [Cranmer's] own edition of the Fathers'.[31]

Since it can be accepted that Cranmer selected the entries for the *loci*, a second question arises: Does his desire to have these passages recorded reflect his agreement with them? Cranmer was known to underline passages of interest,[32] and entries so marked can often be shown to buttress his own position. Nevertheless, the mere inclusion of individual entries does not necessarily imply 'manifest marks of approval'.[33] 'De poenitentia', 'De confessione', and 'De satisfactione' do not have as clear a scholastic apparatus as Brooks has shown was used in the great notebooks' *locus* on the Eucharist.[34] Nevertheless, a careful reading of the material as a whole suggests a similar '*sic et non*' method at work.

'De poenitentia' is consistently Protestant (CGC I, 124r–144v). As has been noted, 'De Poenitentia I' included a lengthy extract from Calvin. Moreover, twenty-five of the sixty-eight quotations were derived directly from the equally Protestant *Unio dissidentium*,[35] a collection of Scripture texts and *sententiae* banned in England quite soon after its publication in 1527.[36] Whereas

---

[31] D. G. Selwyn, 'Cranmer's Library: Its Potential for Reformation Studies', in Ayris and Selwyn, *Churchman and Scholar*, 39–72, at 68.   [32] Ibid., 61.

[33] Contrary to Brightman's suggestion concerning the extracts from the *Antididagma*; 'Capitulum Coloniense', 437.

[34] Brooks, *Eucharist*, 21–34.

[35] Anthony N. S. Lane records over twenty editions of the *Unio* between 1527 and 1562; 'Justification in Sixteenth-Century Patristic Anthologies', in *Auctoritas Patrum: Contributions on the reception of the Church Fathers in the 15th and 16th Century*, ed. Leif Grane, Alfred Schindler, and Markus Wriedt (Mainz: Philipp von Zabern, 1993), 69–95, at 94. Of the various versions, the copyist appears to have used a text similar to the 1532 Venice edition, Hermann Bodius, *Unio Hermani Bodii in unum corpus redacta et diligenter recognita*. This early imprint referred to biblical texts by chapter and letter, a practice followed by the great notebooks as well. Cf. CGC I, 136v, 139v, 141r and *Unio* (1532), fols. 137v, 140. The only discrepancy would seem to be a copyist's error: Hieronimus in Matth. Ca. 16. E. [CGC I, 137v] vs. Hiero. in Mattheum Cap. 16. C. [*Unio* (1532), fol. 137v]. Hence, all references in this work to the text of the *Unio dissidentium* are based on the 1532 Venice edition.

[36] Foxe and Wilkins incorrectly dated its banning to 1526, a year before its publication; Foxe, *Actes and Monumentes*, 1157; *Concilia Magnae Britanniae et*

'Bodius' used quotations from various writers to build an argument, the texts in 'De Poenitentia I' were listed by author.[37] As the secretary encountered a passage to be copied from the *Unio*, he recorded the text under its author in 'Cranmer's Great Commonplaces'. Hence, the initial entries under several writers, and their sequence, depend directly on the *Unio*.[38] The much briefer 'De

Hiberniae, ed. David Wilkins (London: Gosling et al., 1737), iii. 707. For the role of the *Unio* in early English Protestantism, see 'Appendix', concerning page 667, line 39, in John Foxe, *Acts and Monuments*, ed. Josiah Pratt (London: Religious Tract Society, [1877]), iv. 765–6. Since the 1532 Venice edition replaced all Protestant glosses with biblical citations, that particular edition might have been more acceptable to Catholic authorities. In 1602 a text similar to the Venice edition was reprinted at Constance and dedicated to the Catholic bishop, John George Halwiel. Nevertheless, Paul F. Grendler has noted that in 1533 the papal nuncio to Venice expressed his concern about the book's publication; *The Roman Inquisition and the Venetian Press, 1540–1605* (Princeton, N.J.: Princeton University Press, 1977), 75.

[37] For an investigation into the identity of 'Hermannus Bodius', see R. Peters, 'Who Compiled the Sixteenth-Century Patristic Handbook *Unio Dissidentium*?', *Studies in Church History* 2, ed. G. J. Cuming (1965), 237–50. Peters suggested that the *Unio* might have been the work of the Strasbourg Reformers. For the humanist editions of the Fathers employed in *Unio*, see R. Peters, 'The Use of the Fathers in the Reformation Handbook *Unio Dissidentium*', *Studia Patristica* 9, ed. F. L. Cross (1966), 570–7.

[38] For example:

Unio Dissidentium	'Cranmer's Great Commonplaces'
Chrysostom: in epistolam ad Heb. Homi. 31. Cap. 12; in psal. Miserere. Homi. 2 (fol. 136); tomo. 6. sermone de poenitentia et confessione; tomo 7. Homi. 9, de poenitentia (fol. 138v); in opere imperfecto. cap. 23. B. (fol. 140r).	Chrysostom: in Epistolam ad Hebr. Hom. 31 Ca. 12; in psalm. Miserere. Hom. 2; tomo. 6. sermone de poenitentia, et confessione; tomo. 7. Hom. 5; in opere imperfecto. ca. 23 B; (I, 136)
Ambrose: de poenitentia Petri Apostoli, sermone. 46 (fol. 136v); libro de Cain, et Abel; libro de Noe, et Arca (fol. 138v).	Ambrose: de poenitentia petri apostoli. sermone. 46; li. de Cain et Abel; li. de Noe et Archa; (I, 138v)
Augustine: ad Seleucianam. Epi. 105; sermone. 3. de Nativitate domini; libro Decimo confessionum. Cap. 1 [actually quotes from chapter 2] (fols. 135v–136r); De verbis domini super Mattheum sermone. 16. Matthaei. 18. C (fol. 137v); in Epistolam Beati Iohannis Tractatu. 1 (fol. 141v).	Augustine: ad seleucianam. Epistola 105; sermone 3. de nativitate domini; li. 10. confessionum. Ca. 2; de verbis domini. super Matth. Sermone. 16. Matth. 18. C; in Epistolam beati Iohannis tractat. 1; (I, 139r–140r)

However, the great notebooks did not follow the *Unio* slavishly. All the material in a selection from the *Unio* was not always copied, nor indeed all the entries in the *Unio* itself. The copyist corrected the mislabelling of the extract from Augustine's *Confessions* and included an additional two sentences to the transcription of the extract from Chrysostom's *Sermo de poenitentia et confessione*.

confessione' (CGC I, 145r–150v) is more supportive of Catholic teaching, whereas, on the whole, 'De satisfactione' returns to a Protestant orientation (CGC I, 151r–167r). The bulk of the passages (CGC I, 151r–161v) agree in tone with another lengthy extract from Calvin (CGC I, 161v–165v). However, the last two folios (CGC I, 166r–167r) illustrate the Catholic position with a brief entry from Henry's own *Assertio septem sacramentorum* and a passage from the equally Catholic *Antididagma*.

Thus, the dominant theological orientation of the penitential *sententiae* is of a clearly Protestant character, but a minority witness to the contrary has also been included. As the preponderance of the passages would seem to indicate, other evidence from the period demonstrates Cranmer's own commitment to the Protestant approach to justification and penance.[39] If Cranmer ever used his great notebooks to provide Henry with authorities on the nature of sacramental penance, the entries would have enabled him to give a cursory description of Catholic teaching before moving on to a more fulsome account of the evangelical position. Any evaluation of individual entries from the penitential *loci* must take into account this unstated but definite theological agenda.

However, the material associated with justification must be interpreted in an entirely different manner. The bulk of the soteriological quotations was compiled separately from the 'commonplace project'. Most of the titles of its folios are not recorded in the *tabula*,[40] and these headings are more often than not propositional statements rather than general topics. Because the quotations have been arranged under propositions, the entries sustain an argument. In fact, the material on justification has clearly been assembled as a systematic attempt to demonstrate that Protestant Reformed soteriology was the true heir to Augustine's writings and that its doctrine was in agreement with other recognized theological authorities as well. A close examination of the material suggests the procedure by which it was compiled.

The third section of 'Cranmer's Great Commonplaces' contains ten folios devoted exclusively to extensive extracts from the anti-Pelagian works of Augustine: *De peccatorum meritis et remissione* (II, 95r–96r), *De gratia Christi . . . contra Pelagium et Coelestium* (II, 96), *Contra duas epistolas pelagianorum* (II, 97r–98r), *De fide et*

---

[39] For an exposition of these *loci* and the relationship of their opinions to other writings associated with Cranmer from this period, see Chapter 4.

[40] CGC I, 5r; Ayris and Selwyn, *Churchman and Scholar*, 315.

operibus (II, 98v–99v) and *De spiritu et littera* (II, 100r–104v). In addition to the usual citation of book and chapter, the ascriptions of all the entries but one include a reference to the corresponding volume number in Cranmer's copy of Augustine's *Opera*.[41] After this initial culling of material from Augustine, three marginal comments written beside the extracts taken from *De spiritu et littera* were used as propositional headings for new folios.[42] Although not based on prior *marginalia*, two more propositional titles were derived from the earlier study of Augustine's works.[43] Under each of the five headings, quotations or summaries pertinent to the proposition were gathered from the previous Augustinian folios with new similarly supportive extracts from Augustine added.[44] A sixth propositional heading based primarily on a lengthy passage from *De praedestinatione sanctorum* completed the great notebooks' core analysis of Augustine's writings.[45] In addition, however, eight traditional 'topic' *loci* were also compiled that once again consist of predominately Augustinian quotations

[41] *De peccatorum meritis et remissione contra pelagianos*, to. 7 (CGC II, 95r); *Contra duas epistolas pelagianorum*, to. 7 (CGC II, 97r); *De fide et operibus*, to. 4 (CGC II, 98v); *De spiritu et littera*, to. 3 (CGC II, 100r). Cranmer had in his library an annotated copy of Augustine, *Opera*, 5 vols. (Paris, 1531–2), BL C. 79.i.1 [henceforth Cranmer's *Opera Augustini*, and abbreviated as COA].

[42] Cf. the *marginalium* 'Adiutorium dei est per acceptionem spiritus sancti et per charitatem', CGC II, 100r and the folio heading 'Accipere divinum adiutorium est accipere spiritum sanctum et charitatem, per quae fit in homine delectatio summi boni', CGC II, 82r; cf. the *marginalium* 'Gratis, id est, nullis meritis praecedentibus', CGC II, 101v, and the folio heading 'Gratis, id est nullis praecedentibus meritis', CGC II, 83r; cf. the *marginalium* 'Gratia, sanat voluntatem', CGC II, 101r, and the folio heading 'Gratia sanat voluntatem, praeceditque meritum, et iustificatio cor rectum', CGC II, 227r.

[43] 'Ex operibus, ante spiritum sanctum, rei potius tenemur quam contra', CGC II, 239r; 'Fides non est sine operibus, nec contra, sicut nec dilectio dei, sine dilectioni [*sic*] proximi nec e converso', CGC II, 241v.

[44] Folio 82: cf. *De spiritu et littera*, ca. 2, 5, 16, 21, 25, and ibid., CGC II, 100, 102r; the summary of *De gratia Christi*, li. 1, ca. 10, and ibid., CGC II, 96; however, the final entry is a new Augustinian quotation. Folio 83: cf. *De spiritu et littera*, ca. 10, 26 and ibid., CGC II, 101, 102v; *De fide et operibus*, ca. 14, and ibid., CGC II, 98v–99r; however, the next three entries come from *Contra duas epistolas pelagianorum*, but do not correspond to the extracts on folios 97r–98r. Folio 227r: cf. Augustine, *De spiritu et littera*, ca. 7, 9, 30, and ibid., CGC II, 100v, 101r, 103v; however, much new material follows, including two extracts from Gregory the Great, CGC II, 227r–238v. Folio 239: cf. *De spiritu et littera*, ca. 3, 4, 8, 12, 17, 25, and ibid., CGC II, 100r–102v; however, the next three Augustinian quotations are new, including a different extract from *De spiritu et littera*, ca. 28, and the *sententiae* conclude with Scripture verses, CGC II, 239v–240v. Folio 241v: cf. *De fide et operibus*, ca. 13, and ibid., CGC II, 98v; however, the remaining Augustinian material is new, CGC II, 241v–242r.

[45] 'Gratia, accipitur pro gratia iustificante, sive pro gratia illa quae bonos discernit a malis, non pro illa quae communis est bonis et malis', CGC II, 105r.

on aspects of soteriology.[46] So strong was the Augustinian influence in the great notebooks' material on justification that even a propositional heading which began as an examination of a scholastic distinction became *de facto* another Augustinian *locus*.[47]

In addition to this solid foundation in Augustinian thought, other *loci* were added based on authorities whose writings were perceived to agree with the Protestant Reformed interpretation of Augustine: 'Iustificare subinde significant iustum pronuntiare, declarare, aut ostendere' (Holy Scripture),[48] 'Sola fides' (Chrysostom, Origen, Ambrose, et alia),[49] 'Ex sola fide iustificamur' (Greek patristic writers),[50] 'Fide in Christum, hoc est, merito passionis Christi, non nostris operibus iustificamur' (Cajetan and the *Antididagma*),[51] '*Distinctio 25: De libero arbitrio*' (Aquinas)[52] and 'Contra merita humana' (Jerome, Bede, Bernard, Thomas Netter, and Augustine).[53]

The clearest exposition of this effort to demonstrate broad-based support for a Protestant Reformed interpretation of Augustine is found in a separately foliated brief now incorporated into the second volume of the great notebooks as folios 202 *recto*–226 *verso*.[54] Although drawing heavily on Augustine, the brief was actually quite comprehensive in its sources, including quotations from Scripture, early church fathers (Irenaeus, Cyprian, 'Athanasius', Ambrose, Chrysostom, Jerome, Prosper, and Cassiodorus), early medieval writers (Gregory the Great and Bede) scholastics (Peter the Lombard, Hugh of Saint Victor, Thomas Aquinas, Richard of Mediavilla, and Durand of Saint Pourçain) and Bernard. The *loci* are concerned with conversion. The first two propositional headings grounded the Christian life in praising

---

[46] 'Fides, quid sit', CGC II, 94; 'Conciliatio Pauli et Jacobi', CGC II, 106; 'Praedestinatio', CGC II, 121v; 'De fide', CGC II, 242r–261r; 'Duplex fides', CGC II, 261v–262v; 'Gratia et meritum', CGC II, 267v–295v; 'De libero arbitrio', CGC II, 301r; 'Peccatum originale', CGC II, 311r–315r.

[47] 'Distinctio 26: Praevenit gratia dei, bonam voluntatem, non contra', CGC II, 118r. The previous *locus* also had a similar reference to the Lombard, 'Distinctio 25: De libero arbitrio', and is followed exclusively by material from Aquinas's *Summa*; CGC II, 112v–118r. However, this *locus* begins with two quotations from Gregory and ends with a synopsis of a passage in Ambrose, but in between all fifteen extracts are from Augustine; CGC II, 118r–121r.

[48] Ibid., 84r–85v.
[49] Ibid., 86r–89v.
[50] Ibid., 90r–91r.
[51] Ibid., 91v–93v.
[52] Ibid., 112v–118r.
[53] Ibid., 263r–267v.

[54] Although originally separate, the next *locus* beginning on fol. 227r referred to an extract recorded in the brief; consequently, the brief was an integral part of the notebooks' developing analysis of Augustine's soteriology. Cf. '[De spiritu et littera], ca. ultim. ut supra folio 2', CGC II, 227r, and ibid., CGC II, 203r (i.e. folio 2).

God and praying to him for those things which he has promised.[55]
The third *locus* addressed the need of the justified to still ask for
the forgiveness of their sins, for the fourth presented evidence that
regeneration only 'begins' at justification.[56] The last three *loci*
argue against the notion that it is possible to prepare for justification through works meritorious in the eyes of God.[57] Of these, the
middle *locus* entitled 'When the ungodly converts . . .' is of
particular importance, for its numerous quotations from Scripture
are often followed by 'ergo' and a comment supportive of Protestant soteriology. The brief concludes with an untitled series of
propositions which distinguish between Augustine's interpretation of Scripture's understanding of justifying grace and the view
of the scholastics who are described as asserting the existence of a
supernatural grace, which was not justifying grace, 'whereby the
ungodly person is able to turn and do good works before
justification'.[58]

This survey of the soteriological *loci* in the great notebooks
should be sufficient to establish that they were indeed compiled
according to an explicit theological design. Who then was the
architect of the argument? His identity is of particular importance
because the author's position on the key issues associated with
justification is clearly expounded in this section's numerous
marginalia, the propositional headings, the conclusions from
Scripture on folios 213 *verso*–214 *verso* and, above all else, the
commentary on folios 225 *verso*–226 *verso*. If it can be shown that
Cranmer was the architect, the argument expounded by the great
notebooks will greatly augment our limited knowledge of the
details of his soteriology and will at last give historians a solid
theological context for interpreting his writings for the general
public.

In actuality, there is much to suggest that Cranmer was directly
responsible. Firstly, the same arguments for his guiding hand in
the compilation of the sacramental *loci* continue to apply here.

[55] 'Oramus ut eveniant ea quae ex dei promissis certo novimus eventura', CGC
II, 202r; 'Precamur ut deo sit gloria, laus, et imperium, in saecula saeculorum', ibid.
[56] 'Semper orandus est deus, ut condonet peccata, etiam piis filiis quibus iam
omnia peccata dimissa sunt', CGC II, 202v–204r; 'Incipit', CGC II, 204r–207v.
[57] 'Cornelius', CGC II, 208r–212r; 'Cum impius convertitur protinus omnia
peccata dimittuntur nec medium est ullum inter filios dei et diaboli', CGC II,
213r–223r; 'Quod timore poenae sit, non sit', CGC II, 223r–225v.
[58] 'Scriptura, authore Augustino, loquitur dumtaxat de gratia iustificante quae
diffusa est in corda nostra per spiritum sanctum', CGC II, 225v; 'Scolastici [*sic*] . . .
designet tamen supra adiutorium quoddam speciale, nec tamen sit gratia iustificans, sed alia gratia qua possit impius converti, et bona opera facere ante
iustificationem', CGC II, 226r.

Indeed, even more so. For, if Cranmer's own research was responsible for the gathering of passages on general topics, it seems highly unlikely that he would have entrusted to others the development of a defence of solifidianism, the issue at the heart of his reforming efforts. Secondly, as with his other manuscript commonplaces, there is a significant correlation between passages marked in his copy of Augustine's *Opera* and entries in the *loci*.[59] Although the quotations are not in his hand, it seems a reasonable conclusion that Cranmer designated which passages were to be included. Thirdly, an internal piece of evidence suggests that the current manuscript is a copy of a prior work. The *marginalium* on folio 216 *recto* is exactly the same as the *marginalium* scored out on the folio 215 *verso*.[60] It would seem that the secretary was working from a prior draft, wrote the *marginalium* beside the wrong passage, discovered his error and corrected it. Since the extant manuscript is evidently a copy, Cranmer could have easily made the *marginalia* in a previous draft. Fourthly, the 'Notes on Justification', written in his own hand, have a *marginalium* similar to one in the great notebooks and follow the same pattern of organizing quotations under propositional headings.[61] Hence, for example, the brief incorporated as folios 202 *recto*–226 *verso* originally could have been a similar autograph which was discarded once the fair copy had been made.[62] Fifthly, there is a close correlation between the soteriological material contained in the commonplaces and Cranmer's Edwardian writings.[63] Finally, Cranmer had a compelling reason to compose a work arguing that the Reformed interpretation of solifidianism was the true heir to Augustine. It is to this last reason that careful attention must now be given.

LPL MS 1107 contains a treatise on justification with a cover folio inscribed in Cranmer's hand, 'De iustificatione

[59] For example, cf. CGC II, 95r–96r and COA vii. 135v–140v; CGC II, 97r–98r and COA vii. 185v; CGC II, 228 and COA viii. 7r–10r.

[60] 'Remissio peccatorum promissioni novae vitae deputatur', CGC II, 215v, 216r.

[61] LPL MS 1108, fols. 58r–67r; reprinted in Cox II, 203–11. Cf. two *marginalia* on Augustine's *Epistola 106* (MO: 186): 'Fides non meretur iustificationem', LPL MS 1107, fol. 58r (Cox II, 203) and 'fides non est meritum iustificationis', CGC II, 232r.

[62] Cf. Selwyn's assessment, 'The 2 vols. appear to be a "fair copy" from earlier collections of texts and marginalia by T[homas] C[ranmer] or assembled at his direction, the contents of which have probably been rearranged at various times. TC's role in assembling these collections is established by the fact that again and again a passage in the Commonplace Books has been marked and often annotated in his own copies of the editions cited'; *Library*, 172.

[63] See Chapter 6.

D. Redman'.[64] A comparison with the work on justification by John Redman which Cuthbert Tunstall had published in 1555 shows that the treatise among Cranmer's papers is in fact a surviving copy of the same work.[65] According to Tunstall, Redman presented his manuscript on justification to Henry VIII and that it had since come into his hands.[66] Tunstall could have acquired the Redman manuscript by perusing through Cranmer's papers after his arrest. That Cranmer had a work on justification given to Henry VIII would seem to indicate that the king had previously passed the manuscript on to him, for Henry was known to give works on theological controversies to his advisors for comment.[67] Since Redman's exposition of justification clearly attacked solifidianism, it is reasonable to assume that Henry VIII gave the work to Cranmer and asked him for a rebuttal. A product of Fisher's St John's College,[68] Redman described justification in accordance with the Augustinian-influenced scholasticism expounded in the *Confutatio*.[69] Any

[64] LPL MS 1107, fol. 137r.

[65] Cranmer's Copy
Iustificari est ex impio iustum fieri, a peccato liberari in iustitia progredi, et in iudicio absolvi, Ro. 3. act. 13. Ia. 2. Apoc. 22. Ro. 8.
Deus ex sola bonitate et misericordia ineffabili omnes qui ad aeternam salutem et bonitatem perventuri sunt, gratis praedestinat, vocat, iustificat, glorificat, [in margin: Ro. 8.]
Omissa illa archana et inscrutabili praedestinatione, et fidelium [in margin: Ro. 11.], etc. (LPL MS 1107, fol. 138r)

Printed by Tunstall
Iustificari est ex impio iustum fieri, a peccato liberari, in iustitia progredi, & in iudicio absolui. Roma. 3. act. 13. Iac. 2. Apoc. 22. Rom. 8.
Deus ex sola bonitate & misericordia ineffabili, omnes qui ad aeternam salutem & beatitudinem perventuri sunt, gratis praedestinat, vocat, iustificat, glorificat. [in margin: Roma. 8]
Omissa illa archana & inscrutabili praedestinatione, & fidelium [in margin: Roma. 11], etc. (John Redman, *De iustificatione opus* (Antwerp: I. Withagius, 1555), 1)

[66] 'De iustificatione tractatum quem Ioannes Redmanus sacrae Theologiae professor dum viveret absolvit, et celeberrimae memoriae Henrico octavo . . . cuius sacellanus erat, obtulit, proferamus in lucem ad legentium omnium utilitatem. Nam is tractatus integer ad manus nostras pervenit', Cuthbert Tunstall, 'Praefatio', in Redman, *De iustificatione*, sig. A3v.

[67] Cox II, 341.

[68] Redman was part of a college delegation that called on Fisher while in the Tower; Leader, *Cambridge*, 331 n. 42.

[69] e.g., 'Gratiam autem nos iustificare aut soli gratiae omnia deberi, sic intelligimus, non quod sine nostrae voluntatis motu et assensu, iustificatio in nobis fiat Sed quod deus ex sola gratia voluntatem nostram praeveniens et praeparans per poenitentiam et fidem vivam, id est charitati coniunctam iustificationem in nobis efficiat', Redman, *De iustificatione*, LPL MS 1107, fol. 144v; printed edition, 16. For Fisher's soteriology in the *Confutatio*, see Chapter 2. For a study of Redman's theology, see Ashley Null, 'John Redman, the Gentle Ambler',

refutation of Redman would have required Cranmer to prove that solifidianism, and not Fisher's approach, was the true heir of Augustine—the heart of the great notebooks' argument. In any event, however, Redman's treatise articulated the common view of religious conservatives at Court with whom Cranmer had to contend after the fall of Cromwell, as can be seen from Gardiner's subsequent *A Declaration of such true articles* (1546). Cranmer clearly lost that debate, for the *King's Book* (1543) unreservedly rejected justification by faith. Not surprisingly, John Redman was a member of the drafting committee.[70]

Thus, Cranmer's political circumstances provided him ample reason to become the architect behind the Reformed interpretation of Augustine found in the great notebooks. As such, the suggestion that Cranmer's scholarly method relied on patristic gobbets for proof-texting rather than undertaking systematic study of the fathers must be revised.[71] In fact, internal evidence would suggest that Cranmer developed his defence over time,[72] incorporating new passages as he read through sections of Augustine's work.[73] Although the publication of the new formulary would have seemed to have settled the issue, Cranmer was still at work on the soteriological material in 1544, for a passage from the *Antididagma* is quoted on folio 93 *verso*. Ever the Cambridge don, Cranmer's response to the *King's Book* was to continue to gather evidence in favour of solifidianism until a more favourable time should arise. Without a thorough source-analysis of 'Cranmer's Great Commonplaces' as a whole, it is impossible to say how much of the soteriological material was prepared for any debate with Redman prior to the publication of the new formulary and how much afterwards. Nevertheless, the truly massive scale of

in *Westminster Abbey Reformed*, ed. C. S. Knighton, forthcoming. I remain grateful to Colin Armstrong for our discussions on Redman.

[70] Muller, *Letters of Gardiner*, 365. Cf. Collinson, 'Cranmer', 89, 93.

[71] K. J. Walsh, 'Cranmer and the Fathers', 246. Cf. S. L. Greenslade, *The English Reformers and the Fathers of the Church* (Oxford: Clarendon Press, 1960), 16. For an important critique of this view, see Selwyn, in Ayris and Selwyn, *Churchman and Scholar*, 68.

[72] A separately foliated group of *loci* were incorporated into the *tabula* as *loci* 53–57. One *locus*, 'Semper orandus est Deus, etc.' (CGC II, 302) was later expanded and included in a larger separately foliated collection; cf. 'Semper orandus est deus, etc.' (CGC II, 202v–204r) which is part of the brief numbered 1–24, (CGC II, 202r–225r). The brief also shows signs of development: folios 202r–215r being numbered 1–14 in the upper right-hand corner of the *recto* side of each leaf; folios 202r–225r being numbered 1–24 in the lower right-hand corner of the *recto* side of each leaf, and folio 226 bearing only that folio number.

[73] See, e.g., extracts from ten sermons (CGC II, 256r–261r) and from ten psalms (CGC II, 228r–232r).

the great notebooks' research would seem to be a natural scholarly response to such a serious political defeat. What can be stated with confidence is that the material associated with justification in the 'Great Commonplaces' was organized by Cranmer as a response to the theology espoused by conservatives like Redman and Gardiner, underwent considerable development, and achieved its final form sometime after the publication of the *King's Book*.

'DE SACRAMENTIS'

One of the great difficulties in ascertaining Cranmer's views during Henry's reign is the lack of direct evidence for his personal opinions on theological matters. In the tense, '*tertium-quid*' world of the Henrician church, Cranmer as its primate was not permitted to espouse public views more progressive than his king's. He could not publish books disseminating his Protestant views, as his fellow Reformers on the Continent did, and as he was himself to do under Edward. Under Henry his reforming energies had to work behind the scenes instead, using his position to shape policy and provide Protestant patronage. That he was only partially successful in these efforts left the Henrician church with doctrinal formularies which were neither clearly Catholic, nor clearly Protestant, and thus not very clear as to what Cranmer himself believed versus what he had conceded to his opponents. For written evidence of Cranmer's personal views at this time we must look behind these political agreements to the actual theological negotiations themselves. A few well-attested sources have survived: Cranmer's annotations to Henry's corrections of the *Bishops' Book*, his annotations to a draft of the Thirteen Articles, and his answers to queries about the sacraments.[74] Amongst Cranmer's papers, however, one anonymous product of this era also remains extant: 'De sacramentis', now bundled into LPL MS 1107 as folios 84–93.[75] Although seldom studied, this manuscript has its own contribution to make to Cranmer's story.[76]

---

[74] See Cox II, 80–117, 476–7.

[75] 'De sacramentis' has a curious double beginning. Folio 84 begins with its title and consists of a clearly composed essay that breaks off in mid-sentence on the bottom of the *verso* side. Folio 85 begins with another 'De sacramentis' title but the remaining folios through 93 *verso* consist of more of brief points on the sacramental debate rather than in the style of a developed essay as before. It would seem that folio 84 has been appended to folios 85–93, but since they are both in the same hand, this union could not but have happened fairly soon after the second section's composition.

[76] For a thorough examination of the manuscript, including a transcription and

Referring to Erasmus with the epithet 'bonae memoriae', 'De sacramentis' must have been written after his death on 11 July 1536.[77] Since the sections on the Eucharist and penance each contain a sub-section entitled 'concordia', followed by points of agreement, this manuscript most likely should be associated with the theological negotiations of the late 1530s. The Ten Articles were announced the same day as Erasmus's death. Yet, since these included only baptism, the Eucharist, and penance of the traditional seven sacraments, conservatives were unhappy, a situation to which folio 84 *verso* seems to allude.[78] A subsequent debate was held in convocation on the sacraments in February 1537 which eventually resulted in the *Bishops' Book* with its inclusion of all seven.[79] The negotiations with the Lutherans from May to September of the following year eventually foundered over the agenda. The conservative English bishops wanted to raise the issue of the four sacraments included in the *Bishops' Book* but rejected by the Lutherans; whereas the Lutherans wanted to discuss current English practices approved by Henry but rejected by them (private Masses, withholding of the cup from the laity, and mandatory celibacy for clergy).[80] Since the negotiations with the Lutherans in 1538 never reached a discussion of the disputed sacraments, it would seem most likely that 'De sacramentis' records the assessment and arguments of a participant in the sacramental debate leading up to the *Bishops' Book* of 1537.[81]

translation of the text, see Gordon Jeanes, 'A Reformation Treatise on the Sacraments', *Journal of Theological Studies* NS 46 (1995), 149–90. I have benefited from examining Jeanes's transcription of the abbreviated Latin text, revising my own version in some places accordingly, though small differences remain. I am grateful to Jeanes for rescuing this important manuscript from scholarly obscurity, even if my analysis may differ at points. The only other scholarly examination of this document of which I am aware is by Paul Bradshaw, *Anglican Ordinal*, 12, 16. Having assumed Cranmer was the author of the manuscript, Bradshaw described the section on ordination and noted that patristic authorities cited in 'De sacramentis' were also quoted in the great notebooks.

[77] LPL MS 1107, fol. 87v.

[78] 'Quare piissimus princeps, henricus octavus . . . in sua ecclesia concordiam constituit, cum episcoporum et omnium ordinum ecclesiasticorum consensu . . . Sed de numero sacramentorum contentio oritur', LPL MS 1107, fol. 84r.

[79] For this date and the delight of the conservatives that 'these four sacraments that were omitted be found again now', see Chapter 4.

[80] For a detailed study of English–Lutheran negotiations, see Rory S. McEntegart, 'Relations between England and the Schmalkaldic League', Ph.D. thesis (University of London, 1992).

[81] Jeanes, however, thinks 'it would be reasonable to suppose that the present document was written before the beginning of the negotiations [of 1538], at least partly with the intention of persuading the conservative English bishops to concede the issue of the sacraments to the Lutherans', 'Reformation Treatise', 152.

From the description of penance in 'De sacramentis', its longest section, this participant would seem to be an English Protestant engaged in negotiations with traditionalist opponents. The text has a strikingly Lutheran tone, drawing from such sources as the edition of *Loci communes* which Melanchthon dedicated to Henry VIII[82] and the Wittenberg Articles of 1536, which were also largely written by Melanchthon.[83] Consequently, the arguments consistently criticize traditional Catholic teachings, even calling those who held to the Catholic view of contrition, 'hypocrites'.[84]

---

[82] Melanchthon presented a copy of this edition to Cranmer via Alexander Alesius; Rupp, *Studies*, 95. The most striking example of the dependency of 'De sacramentis' on *Loci communes* is the almost verbatim transcription of the definition of a sacrament and the number of them:

'De sacramentis'	*Loci communes theologici* (1535)
1 Baptismus	Baptismus, coena Domini et absolu-
2 Coena Domini	tio. Nam hi ritus instituti sunt in Evan-
3 absolutio sunt ritus institui in evan-	gelio, et usurpantur ad significandam
gelio, et usurpantur ad significandam	hanc promissionem Evangelii pro-
hanc promissionem evangelii propriam	priam. Baptizamur enim, ut credamus
Baptizamur ut credamus nobis peccata	nobis peccata condonata esse. Sic et
condonata esse sic et coena domini et	coena Domini et absolutio admonent
absolutio certos nos faciunt de remis-	nos, ut credamus certo nobis remitti
sione peccatorum (LPL MS 1107, fol.	peccata (Philip Melanchthon, *LCT*
85r)	(1535), *CR* xxi. 470)

'Cranmer's Great Commonplaces' also included this passage within a more lengthy extract from Melanchthon; CGC I, 62. For Melanchthon's influence throughout 'De sacramentis', see Jeanes, 'Reformation Treatise', 167–80.

[83] The correlation on contrition is one example:

The Wittenberg Articles of 1536	'De sacramentis'
Cum igitur Christus clare manda-	Christus iussit praedicari poeniten-
verit, ut praedicentur poenitentia et	tiam et remissionem peccatorum in
remissio peccatorum in nomine ipsius	ipsius nomine
Ad haec plane et clare docemus, quod	haec duo semper coniungenda sunt
oporteat in omni vita conjungi haec duo	scilicet contritio et fides
contritionem et fidem.	
Haec sunt verba Divi Bernhardi in	bernardus haec coniungit, sermone
sermone de annunciatione, et huius-	tertio de annunciatione, et in aliis pler-
modi multa praeclara testimonia in	isque locis.
hanc sententiam extant passim in prae-	
cipuis patribus.	
Rursus contritio sine hac fide fit	et esset contritio, ipsa desperatio nisi
desperatio.	accederet spes veniae et fiducia miser-
(Mentz, *Wittenberger Artikel*, 24, 30,	icordiae.
32)	(LPL MS 1107, fol. 86v)

[84] '[Contritionem veram] hypocritae non habent qui putant poenitentiam in externis tantum castigationibus iuxta humanas traditiones positam esse', LPL MS 1107, fol. 87r. This section shows no 'loyalty to traditional Catholic sentiments' as suggested by Jeanes, 'Reformation Treatise', 152. Cf. 'falsissimum et hoc est,

This distinctly Protestant perspective renders it even more unlikely that 'De sacramentis' was the product of English–German negotiations of 1538. If the aim of the discussion on penance had been to record agreements between the German Lutherans and the Henrician church, the entire description should have been labelled 'concordia'. Yet agreement was specified on just two issues: the retention of confession for the purposes of absolution and the need for proper preparation for Communion—the only real points of accord possible between English conservatives and evangelicals on private confession. Should this then suggest that the penitential section was written to facilitate an agreement with the Germans by encouraging English traditionalists to go beyond mere consent to the 'concordia' and embrace the text's Lutheran sacramental view as a whole, calling them 'hypocrites' would have been decidedly unhelpful. The most reasonable conclusion is that 'De sacramentis' was the work of a convinced Protestant involved in an intra-English traditionalist–Reformer sacramental debate *circa* 1537.[85]

Who was this participant? One possible contender is Richard Moryson, a Protestant 'spin-doctor' on the payroll of Thomas Cromwell.[86] An unsigned manuscript discussion of the seven sacraments in his handwriting has several parallels with 'De sacramentis': (i) his first page is almost a verbatim English version of the first two Latin paragraphs of folio 84; (ii) both documents discuss the nature of New Testament sacraments and then give individual descriptions of each of the traditional seven; (iii) both documents conclude with a final, first-person commendation to an anonymous lord.[87] Nevertheless, their differences are significant

omnes posse continere, vel impetrare donum coelibatus, sicut, horribiles hypocritarum libidines clamant', ibid., fol. 91.

[85] Accordingly, the reference to the Lutherans in the third person in the discussion of marriage is simply an acknowledgement that their teaching was the doctrinal standard for the English Protestants' negotiations with their conservative colleagues; '[De sacramento matrimonii] Sed facilis est concordia de hoc sacramento quod ipsi lutherani magis cohonestant . . .', LPL MS 1107, 89v. Hence, the author can be said to have taken a 'funnel' approach to his introduction. He began his discussion of religion on the wider scale of the European controversy, narrowed the topic to King Henry's exemplary handling of these matters in England, and finally focused on the one issue at home that threatened to overturn the ecclesiastical equilibrium—the nature and number of the sacraments.

[86] For Moryson's relationship with Cromwell, see G. R. Elton, *Reform and Renewal: Thomas Cromwell and the Common Weal* (Cambridge: Cambridge University Press, 1973), 55–61.

[87] Moryson's 'Seven Sacraments' is found in PRO SP 6/8, pp. 273–302. Cf. 'I haue lost no labour, if your lordshyp vnto whomm I haue, asmoch as I can performe, take it thankefully', Moryson, 'Seven Sacraments', PRO SP 6/8, p. 302,

enough to establish them as separate works. Moryson's is a cogently argued treatise, systematically developed at greater length. Except for the clearly appended folio 84, 'De sacramentis' lacks the polish normally associated with a finished composition, its arguments being more noted than developed. Moryson refers to himself in the first person throughout. The person responsible for 'De sacramentis' never refers to himself except at the end. Although both documents describe the seven sacraments, their order is different, and Moryson's text has separated headings for 'sacrament of thaltare' and 'sacrament of masse'.[88] Although they cover much the same ground, including the same 'concordia' passages,[89] their common points often come at different stages in the discussion, and each has concerns not raised in the other.[90] Although they refer to many of the same sources and proof-texts, including reliance on Melanchthon's opinions, each makes references not found in the other. Clearly, 'De sacramentis' is not merely an abridged version of Moryson's manuscript. Rather Moryson's text would seem to be secondary to 'De sacramentis', a free adaptation at greater length with more systematic exposition.[91]

Since 'De sacramentis' has been preserved in a volume with Cranmer papers, along with others, the next possible contender for author of the manuscript is the Archbishop. While the hand is not Cranmer's nor that of Morice, the views on penance expressed in 'De sacramentis' agree with those in other documents known to be associated with him. Firstly, 'De sacramentis' argued that auricular confession was most beneficial but not necessary, the same position Cranmer took during the German embassy of 1538 and the debate over The Six Articles.[92] Secondly, both 'De sacramentis' and 'Cranmer's Great Commonplaces' defined *poenitentia* as consisting of contrition and faith.[93] Thirdly, all the

and 'mihi tamen non perit opera si tibi meo domino cui omnia mea studia debeo non fuerit ingrata', LPL MS 1107, fol. 93v.

[88] Moryson, 'Seven Sacraments', PRO SP 6/8, pp. 291–2.

[89] Cf. LPL MS 1107, fols. 87v, 90v–91r and Moryson, 'Seven Sacraments', PRO SP 6/8, pp. 290–4.

[90] e.g., Moryson is concerned about episcopal wealth: 'I dare boldely say, that bysshops owght to be contente with meate and clothe' ('Seven Sacraments', PRO SP 6/8, p. 296) but not 'De sacramentis'. 'De sacramentis' acknowledges patristic division over Communion: 'Sed cum patres sibi ipsis non constant in multis dogmatis, infirma sunt eorum testimonia, et in nullo loco infirmiora quam in hoc sacramento', LPL MS 1107, fol. 90r. Moryson has no similar passage.

[91] According to Jeanes, Moryson's manuscript is 'clearly secondary', 'Reformation Treatise', 151.   [92] LPL MS 1107, fols. 87v–88r; see Chapter 4.

[93] 'De poenitentia . . . haec duo semper coniungenda sunt scilicet contritio et

patristic passages concerning penance quoted in 'De sacramentis' appear in the great notebooks, three out of the four underlined.[94] In fact, Gordon Jeanes has recently shown that very many of the references included in 'De sacramentis' are also found in 'Cranmer's Great Commonplaces', although not all. Two parallels are of special note: (i) the references to Cajetan's opinion on extreme unction in 'De sacramentis', for Cranmer incorporated an extract from Cajetan in his homily of salvation;[95] (ii) the references to patristic opinions on the real presence and the Greek liturgy's understanding of spiritual sacrifice in the Eucharist, for both were of keen interest to Cranmer.[96] Neither Cajetan nor the patristic opinions on the real presence are mentioned by Moryson.[97] Jeanes has also noted the several parallels between Cranmer's recognized writings on the sacraments and their description in 'De sacramentis'.[98] Convinced by 'these multiple connections', Jeanes has concluded that Cranmer was the author of 'De sacramentis'.[99]

---

fides', LPL MS 1107, fol. 86v; 'In poenitentia occurrunt, Contritio et fides', CGC I, 133r.

[94] All the patristic quotations on penance in 'De sacramentis' appear in 'Cranmer's Great Commonplaces':

'De sacramentis'	'Cranmer's Great Commonplaces'
'verba Ambrosii lachrimae delent peccatum quod voce pudor est confiteri' (fol. 88v)	Ambrosius . . . lavat enim lachrima delictum, quod voce pudor est confiteri.' (fol. 138v)
'illa Chrisostomi solus deus te confitentem audiat' (fol. 88v)	'Chrisostomus . . . Solus te deus confitentem videat. . . .' (fol. 136r)
'non dico ut confitearis ea conservo tuo, etc. (fol. 88v)	'Non dico ut confitearis conservo tuo . . . ea.' (fol. 136r)
'tomo 7 homelia 9 de poenitentia medicinae inquit locus est non iudicii non poenas sed remissionem peccatorum tribuens' (fol. 88v)	'tomo. 7. ho. 5. Medicinae locus hic est, non iudicii, non poenas sed peccatorum remissionem tribuens, deo solo dic peccatum tuum.' (fol. 136v)

All the passages from the great notebooks were copied directly from the *Unio*. The first two quotations in 'De sacramentis' are inaccurate and the fourth uses the full correct ascription of the title found in the *Unio* but not the great notebooks. These discrepancies probably indicate that the author of 'De sacramentis' was dictating from memory, having at one time read the passages in the *Unio* itself. Since Cranmer had these passages copied out of the *Unio* for his great notebooks and is most likely the person who then underlined them, it would seem that the patristic quotations included in 'De sacramentis' were favourite proof-texts of Cranmer himself.

[95] Jeanes, 'Reformation Treatise', 169, 179–80. For Cajetan and Cranmer's homily, see Chapter 6.

[96] Jeanes, 'Reformation Treatise', 163, 165–7, 175–7.

[97] Cf. Moryson, 'Seven Sacraments', PRO SP 6/8, pp. 291–4, 299–301

[98] Jeanes, 'Reformation Treatise', 154–60, 168–80.

[99] Ibid., 159.

If so, a logical choice for the 'dominus' to whom 'De sacramentis' was submitted would be Thomas Cromwell, vice-gerent in spirituals and convenor of the debate on the sacraments.[100] Cromwell could easily have asked Cranmer for a Protestant position paper, as he or someone in his circle evidently asked Moryson to prepare in the light of 'De sacramentis'. Alternatively, 'De sacramentis' could be Cranmer's reflection on the current state of the debate, including noting the areas of agreement, in preparation for another round in front of the vice-gerent. Either way, the brevity of style, the occasional misquotations and the lack of a proper introduction on folios 85–93 suggests that 'De sacramentis' was quickly prepared, perhaps by dictation at the end of one day's debate in preparation for the next. If subsequently Cranmer was given Moryson's manuscript to read, he could easily have adapted its introduction as an addition to his own for future reference.[101]

While Jeanes has made an attractive case for Cranmer's direct authorship, other explanations of 'De sacramentis' remain possible, including that a research assistant familiar enough with Cranmer's views as well as the political situation and with access to his library did for the Archbishop what Moryson evidently did for the Vice-gerent. Moreover, the unusually blunt and unfavourable assessment of the value of patristic opinion on the Eucharist found in 'De sacramentis' is not a view normally associated with Cranmer at this time.[102] Nevertheless, at the very least, the

---

[100] Jeanes, however, thinks that this 'general "dominus" . . . hardly refers to any specific person but would be a general polite address', ibid., 152–3.

[101] If 'Seven Sacraments' is derived from 'De sacramentis', yet 'De sacramentis' was written in two stages, it would seem fairly straightforward to assume the following: (i) the original 'De sacramentis' of folios 85–93 was submitted to the 'dominus'; (ii) the 'dominus' asked Moryson to write a more complete essay, including a proper introduction; (iii) this new treatise was then read by the principle person associated with 'De sacramentis' and a new introduction was appended to the Lambeth text. Such a view, of course, is only a possibility. Jeanes thinks that there is nothing to suggest that fol. 84 was written by an author different from the rest of the text; 'Reformation Treatise', 151.

[102] '[S]ed cum patres sibi ipsi non constant in multis dogmatis, infirma sunt eorum testimonia et in nullo loco infirmiora quam in hoc sacramento [i.e. de sacramento Eucharistiae]', LPL MS 1107, fol. 90r; English translation, Jeanes, 'Reformation Treatise', 188. Cf. Cranmer's appeal to patristic authority when he rebuked Joachim Vadianus in 1537 for denying the real presence: 'veterum doctorum primorumque in ecclesias Christi scriptorum autoritatem una violassent! Nam ut ingenia vestra quantumcunque versaveritis, mihi tamen certe nunquam approbaveritis, nec cuiquam, opinor, aequo lectori, veteres illos auctores in hac controversia pro vestra facere sententia', Cox II, 342; English translation, ibid., 344. For Jeanes's view that the statement in 'De sacramentis' reflects Cranmer's personal opinion, see 'Reformation Treatise', 165–7. MacCulloch, however, is

common positions taken by 'De sacramentis' and the other manuscripts associated with Cranmer provide us with the evangelical
'party-line' in the debates with English traditionalists. Here we
see his shared negotiating strategy on penance.

CRANMER'S CROYDON COMMENTARY

With the advent of Edward's reign, Cranmer was able to turn his
attention to publishing sound Protestant doctrine without hin-
drance from traditionalists. One of his schemes was a new Latin
text of the Bible from which a definitive English translation could
be made. As part of this project, he enlisted Bucer's aid on the
Gospel of Matthew during the summer of 1549, and he made him
his house-guest at Croydon to further the work.[103] The unfinished
results are now included in Corpus Christi College, Cambridge,
MS 104.[104] Although attributed to Bucer by a title written in
Cranmer's own hand, internal evidence suggests that Cranmer
was responsible for the first three chapters and then had Bucer
continue with chapters 4–8: the two sections are written by
different secretaries; the last five chapters have a much more
detailed commentary than chapters 1–3 and include a translation
of the Gospel text which is lacking before chapter 4; and, most
importantly, the first three chapters have corrections in Cranmer's
hand and the last five have emendations by Bucer.[105] In this work,
the first three chapters have been styled as 'Cranmer's Croydon
Commentary on Matthew' or sometimes more simply as the
Croydon Commentary. It should be understood, however, that
the use of the shorter title still refers only to Cranmer's contribution.

The text of chapter 3 requires special note. After the conclusion
of the commentary, at the bottom of the same page Cranmer has
added in his own hand 'Commonplaces of this third chapter'.[106]
There then follows a discussion of the phrase 'the kingdom of
heaven'. Both the remaining text of page 32 and the phrase 'the

---

more cautious. He regards Jeanes's conclusion as 'not altogether secure'; *Cranmer*,
181 n. 19.

[103] MacCulloch, *Cranmer*, 426.

[104] For the circumstances of its composition, see *Martin Bucer und Thomas
Cranmer: Annotationes in Octo Priora Capita Evangelii secundum Matthaeum,
Croydon 1549*, ed. Herbert Vogt (Frankfurt: Athenäum, 1972), 12–13.

[105] For a detailed description of these differences see Vogt, *Bucer und Cranmer*,
13–16. NB, however, that his transcription of the text must be used with caution.

[106] 'Loci communes huius capitis tertii', CCCC MS 104, p. [32].

kingdom of heaven' written in the margin are in Cranmer's hand. The discussion continues on pages 33–4, but the hand is once again that of the secretary. It is important to note, however, that the last sentence in Cranmer's hand at the bottom of page 32 is completed by the secretary at the top of page 33.[107] Because of this significant link, the description of election on pages 32–4 can be assigned to Cranmer's authorship. As the manuscript is now bound, Cranmer's contribution ends on page 34.

According to Cranmer, however, what followed the commentary on Matthew 3 was not a 'commonplace' but 'commonplaces'. To find the second *locus*, the reader must turn to a manuscript commentary on Mark by Peter Alexander. There two leaves which discuss baptism have been bound in the midst of Alexander's work. The hand is not Alexander's but, in fact, that of the same secretary who transcribed the rest of Cranmer's Croydon Commentary, as the presence of his very distinctive abbreviation for 'quam' in both proves.[108] The text is a commentary on Matthew, not Mark, for its last line refers to Matthew 19 as 'Below, 19'.[109] And like the *locus* on the 'Kingdom of heaven', in the margin Cranmer has written the topic discussed: 'John's baptism and Christ's'—topics naturally associated with Matthew 3.[110] Since the first *locus* was originally written by Cranmer and then copied by the secretary, it seems only reasonable to conclude that the same procedure produced the second *locus* as well. One further manuscript detail adds support to this idea. If Cranmer wrote out the original text of pages 211–14 for the secretary to copy, he must have not included the title for the *locus* in the margin of the autograph, or else the secretary would have copied that as well. If Cranmer wrote the first *locus* at the same time as the second, the *marginalium* on page 32 would have to be a later addition, too. In fact, the title 'Kingdom of heaven' is not quite level with the first line of text of the *locus*, indicating that it also was an afterthought. Thus, like the discussion of election in the first, the reference to election in paedobaptism found in the second *locus* can be assigned to Cranmer's authorship as well.

[107] 'Hoc regnum et dei dicitur et caelorum, quia eo deus electos suos per filium suum [p. 33] liberos et volentes regit et ducit at [recte, ad] vitam caelestem, et divinam', CCCC MS 104, pp. [32]–3.

[108] CCCC MS 104, pp. 31, 213.

(page 31)   (page 213)

[109] 'Pertinent enim et hi ad regnum dei. Infr. 19', CCCC MS 104, p. [214]. This is a reference to Matthew 19: 14.

[110] 'Baptismus Johannis et Christi', CCCC MS 104, p. 211.

TRANSCRIPTION PRACTICES

Since much of the evidence for this book consists of numerous quotations from these unpublished sources, it is necessary to delineate the method of transcription followed. Firstly, due to the often uncertain nature of punctuation in the originals, quotations from manuscript sources do not use ellipses to give an indication of the larger context from which they have been taken. Secondly, in all quotations except those from 'Cranmer's Great Commonplaces' abbreviations have been expanded with the added letters signified by underlining. In the case of the great notebooks, however, no attempt has been made to convey the highly abbreviated nature of the original. Instead, underlining in a quotation from the 'Great Commonplaces' reproduces as closely as possible such markings in the manuscript. Hence, where only a portion of the word is underlined in the original, only those letters are underlined in the quotation. Thirdly, letters in brackets are no longer extant but can be reconstructed with confidence. Letters in brackets followed by a question mark are reasonable conjectures. However, in transcriptions from 'De sacramentis' letters in brackets have been supplied to correct spelling and in both 'De sacramentis' and 'Cranmer's Great Commonplaces', words in brackets represent words supplied to aid the sense of the quotation. Page or folio numbers in brackets have been supplied where lacking in the original. Fourthly, in transcribing the Latin 'i–j', 'v–u', 'ae–oe', and 'ti–ci' the following conventions have been adopted: for 'i–j', the preference of the original source has been followed; for 'v–u', 'ae–oe', and 'ti–ci' modern spelling practices have been used. Fifthly, citations from 'Cranmer's Great Commonplaces' follow the ascriptions in the original manuscript. Finally, all references to biblical texts follow the Vulgate ordering of material, unless otherwise noted. The Latin text of verses from Scripture have not been included in footnotes.

BIBLIOGRAPHY

MANUSCRIPT SOURCES

1. The British Library Department of Manuscripts:
   Royal MSS 7B.XI, 7B.XII, 'Cranmer's Great Commonplaces'.
   Cotton MSS Cleop. E.V, E.VI, Documents associated with the
   Henrician church.

2. The Library of Lambeth Palace:
   MS 1107, 'Cranmer's Collection of Canon Law'.
   MS 1108, A further collection of commonplaces.

3. The Parker Library, Corpus Christi College, Cambridge:
   MS 102, pp. 409–99, 529–[534], Cranmer's 'Sermon on Rebellion', text and notes.
   MS 104, pp. 15–[34], 211–[214], Cranmer's 'Croydon Commentary on Matthew'.
   MS 340, pp. 73–95, 115–31, Peter Martyr's sermons on
   rebellion.

4. The Public Record Office:
   State Papers 6/8, pp. 273–302, Richard Moryson's 'Seven
   Sacraments'.

5. The University Library, Cambridge:
   MS DD.5.27, Robert Ridley's commonplace book.
   MS EE.2.8, Peter Alexander's 'Collectanea ex libris Origenis
   Adamantii, Athanasii et Epiphanii una'.

OTHER CRANMER SOURCES

Bond, Ronald B. (ed.), *Certain Sermons or Homilies (1547)* AND *A
Homily against Disobedience and Wilful Rebellion (1570): A
Critical Edition* (Toronto: University of Toronto Press, 1987).
*The Byble in Englyshe, that is to saye the content of al the holy
scrypture, both of the olde, and newe testament, with a prologe
therinto, made by the reuerende father in God, Thomas archbysshop of Cantorbury* (London: Edward Whytchurche, Apryll
1540).

Burton, Edward (ed.), *A Short Instruction into Christian Religion, being a Catechism set forth by Archbishop Cranmer in 1548 together with the same in Latin, translated from the German by Justus Jonas in 1539* (Oxford: Oxford University Press, 1829).

Cardwell, Edward (ed.), *The Reformation of the Ecclesiastical Laws* (Oxford: Clarendon Press, 1850).

Cox, J. E. (ed.), *Miscellaneous Writings and Letters of Thomas Cranmer, Archbishop of Canterbury, Martyr, 1556* (Cambridge: Parker Society, 1846).

——*Writings and Disputations of Thomas Cranmer . . . relative to the Sacrament of the Lord's Supper* (Cambridge: Parker Society, 1844).

Duffield, G. E. (ed.), *The Work of Thomas Cranmer*, intro. J. I. Packer (Appleford: Sutton Courtenay Press, 1964).

Griffiths, John (ed.), *The Two Books of Homilies Appointed to be Read in Churches* (Oxford: Oxford University Press, 1859).

Jenkyns, Henry (ed.), *Remains of Thomas Cranmer*, 4 vols. (Oxford: Oxford University Press, 1833).

Ketley, Joseph (ed.), *The Two Liturgies . . . in the Reign of King Edward VI* (Cambridge: Parker Society, 1844).

Lloyd, Charles (ed.), *Formularies of Faith* (Oxford: Oxford University Press, 1825).

Selwyn, D. G. (ed.), *A Catechism set forth by Thomas Cranmer: From the Nuremberg Catechism translated into Latin by Justus Jonas* (Appleford: Sutton Courtenay Press, 1978).

Spalding, James C. (ed.), *The Reformation of the Ecclesiastical Laws of England, 1552* (Kirksville: Sixteenth Century Essays & Studies, 1992).

Vogt, Herbert (ed.), *Martin Bucer und Thomas Cranmer: Annotationes in Octo Priora Capita Evangelii secundum Matthaeum, Croydon 1549* (Frankfurt: Athenäum, 1972).

SECONDARY SOURCES

Adams, H. M., *Catalogue of Books Printed on the Continent of Europe 1501–1600 in Cambridge Libraries* (Cambridge: Cambridge University Press, 1967).

Alcock, John, *Mons Perfectionis* (Westmestre: Wynkin de Worde, 1497).

——*Ihesus clamabat Qui habet aures audiendi audiat, Luc. viii.* (Westmynstre: Wynkyn de Worde, n.d.).

Alesius, Alexander, *Of the auctorite of the word of god agaynst the bisshop of London* (n.p., n.d.).

Althaus, Paul, *The Theology of Martin Luther*, trans. Robert C. Schultz (Philadelphia, Pa.: Fortress Press, 1966).

Amann, E. and Michel, A. 'Pénitence', *Dictionnaire de théologie catholique*, ed. Jean Michel Alfred (Paris, 1899–1950), xii(i). 722–1050.

The Ante-Nicene Fathers, ed. Alexander Roberts and James Donaldson, 10 vols. (Grand Rapids, Mich.: Eerdmans, 1989).

Aquinas, Thomas, *Super Epistolas S. Pauli Lectura*, 2 vols. (Rome: Marietti, 1953).

The arte or crafte to lyue Well (London: Wynkyn de Worde, 1505).

Augustine, *Opera*, 5 vols. (Paris, 1531–2); Cranmer's annotated copy, BL C.79.i.1.

Ayris, Paul, 'Thomas Cranmer's Register: A Record of Archiepiscopal Administration in Diocese and Province', Ph.D. thesis (University of Cambridge, 1984).

Ayris, Paul, and Brooks, P. N., *Cranmer—Primate of all England: Catalogue of a Quincentenary Exhibition at The British Library, 27 October 1989–21 January 1990* (London: British Library, 1989).

Ayris, Paul, and Selwyn, David (eds.), *Thomas Cranmer: Churchman and Scholar* (Woodbridge: Boydell, 1993).

Bainton, Roland, *Erasmus of Christendom* (New York, N.Y.: Scribner, 1969).

Ball, R. M., 'The Education of the English Parish Clergy', Ph.D. thesis (University of Cambridge, 1977).

Barnes, Robert, *Supplicatyon* [London, 1531?].

Baron, Stephen, *Sermones Declamati coram alma vniuersitate Cantibrigiensi* (London: Wynkyn de Worde, n.d.).

Berlin, Isaiah, *The Hedgehog and the Fox: An essay on Tolstoy's View of History* (New York, N.Y.: Simon & Schuster, 1953).

Birch, David, *Early Reformation English Polemics* (Salzburg: Institut für Anglistik und Amerikanistik, Universität Salzburg, 1983).

Black, P. M. 'Matthew Parker's Search for Cranmer's "great notable written books"', *The Library*, Fifth Series, 29 (1974), 312–22.

Bodius, Hermann, *Unio Hermani Bodii in unum corpus redacta et diligenter recognita* (Venice, 1532).

Bonansea, Bernardine M., 'Duns Scotus' Voluntarism', in *John Duns Scotus, 1265–1965*, ed. John K. Ryan and Bernardine M. Bonansea, Studies in Philosophy and the History of

Philosophy, 3 (Washington, D.C.: Catholic University of America Press, 1965), 83–121.

Bonansea, Bernardine M., *Man and his Approach to God in John Duns Scotus* (Lanham, N.Y.: University Press of America, 1983).

Bond, Ronald B., 'Cranmer and the Controversy Surrounding Publication of *Certayne Sermons or Homilies* (1547)', *Renaissance and Reformation* 12 (1976), 28–35.

Bonner, Edmund, *Homelies . . . not onely promised before in his booke, intituled, A necessary doctrine, but also now of late adioyned therevnto* (London: Ihon Cawodde, 1555).

The Book of Concord: The Confessions of the Evangelical Lutheran Church, ed. Theodore G. Tappert (Philadelphia, Pa.: Fortress Press, 1959).

Booty, John E. (ed.), *The Book of Common Prayer 1559: The Elizabethan Prayer Book* (Washington D.C.: Folger Books, 1976).

Bradshaw, Brendan, and Duffy, Eamon (eds.), *Humanism, Reform and the Reformation: The Career of Bishop John Fisher* (Cambridge: Cambridge University Press, 1989).

Bradshaw, Paul F., *The Anglican Ordinal: Its History and Development from the Reformation to the Present Day* (London: SPCK, 1971).

Breen, Quirinus, 'The Terms "Loci Communes" and "Loci" in Melanchthon', *Christianity and Humanism*, ed. Nelson Peter Ross (Grand Rapids, Mich.: Eerdmans, 1973), 93–105.

Brightman, F. E., *The English Rite* (London: Rivingtons, 1915).

[——] 'Capitulum Coloniense: An Episode in the Reformation', *Church Quarterly Review* 31 (1891), 419–37.

Bromiley, G. W., *Thomas Cranmer, Archbishop and Martyr* (London: Church Book Room, 1956).

—— *Thomas Cranmer, Theologian* (London: Lutterworth, 1956).

Brooks, Peter Newman, 'Thomas Cranmer's Doctrine of the Sacraments', Ph.D. thesis (University of Cambridge, 1960).

—— *Cranmer in Context: Documents from the English Reformation* (Minneapolis, Minn.: Fortress Press, 1989).

—— 'Cranmer Studies in the Wake of the Quartercentenary', *Historical Magazine of the Protestant Episcopal Church* 31 (1962), 365–74.

—— *Thomas Cranmer's Doctrine of the Eucharist: An Essay in Historical Development*, 2nd edn. (London: Macmillan, 1992).

Brown, D. Catherine, *Pastor and Laity in the Theology of Jean Gerson* (Cambridge: Cambridge University Press, 1987).

Buchanan, Colin, *What did Cranmer Think he was Doing?*, 2nd edn. (Bramcote: Grove Books, 1982).

Burnet, Gilbert, *The History of the Reformation of the Church of England*, ed. Nicholas Pocock, 4 vols. (Oxford: Clarendon Press, 1865).

Burns, J. Patout, *The Development of Augustine's Doctrine of Operative Grace* (Paris: Études Augustiniennes, 1980).

Calvin, John, *Institutio Christianae Religionis, Corpus Reformatorum*, ed. C. G. Bretschneider and H. E. Bindseil, vol. xxix (Brunswick, 1853).

——*Calvin: Institutes of the Christian Religion*, ed. John T. McNeill, trans. Ford Lewis Battles, 2 vols. (Philadelphia, Pa.: Westminster, 1960).

Clifford, Alan C., 'Cranmer as Reformer', *The Evangelical Quarterly* 63 (1991), 99–122.

Cochlaeus, John, *Beati Isidori . . . De officiis ecclesiasticis* (Leipzig, 1534).

——*Commentaria . . . de actis et scriptis Martini Lutheri* (Mainz, 1549).

Collinson, Patrick, 'Thomas Cranmer', in *The English Religious Tradition and the Genius of Anglicanism*, ed. Geoffrey Rowell (Wantage: Ikon, 1992), 79–103.

Concilia Magnae Britanniae et Hiberniae, ed. David Wilkins, 4 vols. (London, 1737).

Councils and Synods with other Documents relating to the English Church, A. D. 1205–1313, ed. F. M. Powicke and C. R. Cheney, 2 vols. (Oxford: Clarendon Press, 1964).

Courtenay, William J., 'Cranmer as a Nominalist, *Sed Contra*', *Harvard Theological Review* 57 (1964), 367–80.

Cross, Richard, *Duns Scotus* (Oxford: Oxford University Press, 1999).

Cuming, G. J., *A History of Anglican Liturgy* (London: Macmillan, 1969).

De Burgh, John, *Pupilla oculi* (Paris: W. Hopylius for W. Bretton, 1510).

DeMolen, Richard L., *The Spirituality of Erasmus of Rotterdam* (Nieuwkoop: De Graaf Publishers, 1987).

Devereux, E. J., *Renaissance English Translations of Erasmus: A Bibliography to 1700* (Toronto: University of Toronto Press, 1983).

Dickens, A. G., *The English Reformation*, 2nd edn. (London: Batsford, 1989).

—— 'The Shape of Anti-clericalism and the English Reformation', in *Politics and Society in Reformation Europe: Essays for Sir Geoffrey Elton on his Sixty-Fifth Birthday*, ed. E. I. Kouri and Tom Scott (London: Macmillan, 1987), 379–410.

Dix, Gregory, *The Shape of the Liturgy* (Westminster: Dacre, 1945).

Dixon, R. W., *History of the Church of England from the Abolition of the Roman Jurisdiction*, 6 vols. (Oxford: Oxford University Press, 1878–1902).

Doctrinal of Sapience (London: William Caxton, 1487).

Donnelly, John Patrick, *Calvinism and Scholasticism in Vermigli's Doctrine of Man and Grace* (Leiden: Brill, 1976).

Dugmore, C. W., *The Mass and the English Reformers* (London: Macmillan, 1958).

Duffy, Eamon, *The Stripping of the Altars: Traditional Religion in England, c.1400–c.1580* (New Haven, Conn.: Yale University Press, 1992).

Duns Scotus, John, *Opera omnia*, 26 vols. (Paris: Vives, 1891–5).

—— *Quaestiones super quatuor libris Sententiarum*, 2 vols. (Venice, 1477); Cranmer's annotated copy, BL IB. 20307, IB. 20297.

Elliot, Maurice, 'The Giant and the Dwarfs', *Churchman* 109 (1995), 327–32.

Elton, G. R., *Reform and Reformation* (London: Arnold, 1977).

—— *Reform and Renewal: Thomas Cromwell and the Common Weal* (Cambridge: Cambridge University Press, 1973).

Emden, A. B., *Biographical Register of the University of Cambridge* (Cambridge: Cambridge University Press, 1963).

Erasmus, *Adages: I vi 1 to 1 x 100, Collected Works of Erasmus*, vol. xxxii, trans. R. A. B. Mynors (Toronto: University of Toronto Press, 1989).

—— *A ryght frutefull Epystle . . . in laude and prayse of matrymony*, trans. Richard Taverner (London: Robert Redman, 1532).

—— *The Handbook of the Christian Soldier*, trans. Charles Fantazzi, *Collected Works of Erasmus*, vol. lxvi, ed. John W. O'Malley (Toronto: University of Toronto Press, 1988), 93–107.

—— *De libero arbitrio* (Antwerp, 1524); Cranmer's annotated copy, BL 697.b.3.(1).

—— *A lytle treatise of the maner and forme of confession* (London: Iohn Byddell for Wyllyam Marshall, [1535]).

—— *Opera omnia Desiderii Erasmi Roterodami*, ed. J. Leclerc, 10 vols. (Leyden: Vander, 1703–6).

—— *Opus epistolarum Des. Erasmi Roterodami*, ed. P. S. Allen,

H. M. Allen, and H. W. Garrod, 12 vols. (Oxford: Clarendon Press, 1906–58).

Evans, G. R., 'Augustine on Justification', *Congresso Internazionale su S. Agostino nel XVI Centenario della Conversione*, Studia Ephemeridis 'Augustinianum' 26 (Rome: Institutum Patristicum 'Augustinianum', 1987), 275–84.

Fisher, John, *A sermon had at Paulis* (London: Berthelet, n.d.).

—— *Assertionis Lutheranae Confutatio* (Antwerp, 1523); Cranmer's annotated copy, BL C.81.f.2.

—— *Opera, quae hactenus inveniri potuerunt omnia* (Würzburg: Fleischmann, 1597).

—— *The English Works of John Fisher*, Part I, ed. J. E. B. Mayor (London: Early English Text Society, Extra Series, 27, 1876).

—— *Two fruytfull sermons*, ed. M. D. Sullivan (Ann Arbor: University of Michigan Microfilm Service, 1965).

Fisher, J. D. C., *Christian Initiation: Baptism in the Medieval West: A Study in the Disintegration of the Primitive Rite of Initiation* (London: SPCK, 1965).

Fitzgerald, William, *Lectures on Ecclesiastical History*, 2 vols. (London: Murry, 1885).

The floure of the commaundements of god (London: Wynkyn de Worde, 1510).

Fox, Alistair, *Thomas More: History and Providence* (Oxford: Basil Blackwell, 1982).

Fox, Alistair, and Guy, John, *Reassessing the Henrician Age: Humanism, Politics and Reform, 1500–1550* (Oxford: Basil Blackwell, 1986).

Foxe, John, *Acts and Monuments*, ed. Josiah Pratt, 8 vols. (London: Religious Tract Society, [1877]).

—— *Ecclesiasticall history contaynyng the Actes and Monumentes of thynges passed in every Kynges tyme in this Realme, especially in the Church of England principally to be noted* (London: Iohn Daye, 1570).

Frost, Ronald Norman, 'Richard Sibbes: Theology of Grace and the Division of English Reformed Theology', Ph.D. thesis (King's College, London, 1997).

Gallagher, Joseph E., 'The Sources of Caxton's *Ryal Book* and *Doctrinal of Sapience*', *Studies in Philology* 62 (1965), 40–62.

Gardiner, Stephen, *A declaration of such true articles as George Ioye hath gone about to confute as false* (London: Iohannes Herford, 1546).

Gerrish, B. A., *Grace and Gratitude: The Eucharistic Theology of John Calvin* (Edinburgh: T & T Clark, 1993).

Gerrish, B. A., *The Old Protestantism and the New: Essays on the Reformation Heritage* (Edinburgh: T & T Clark, 1982).

Gilbert, Neal W., *Renaissance Concepts of Method* (New York, N.Y.: Columbia University Press, 1960).

Gray, Arthur, and Brittain, Frederick, *A History of Jesus College Cambridge* (London: Heinemann, 1979).

Greenslade, S. L., *The English Reformers and the Fathers of the Church* (Oxford: Clarendon Press, 1960).

Grendler, Paul F., *The Roman Inquisition and the Venetian Press, 1540–1605* (Princeton, N.J.: Princeton University Press, 1977).

Guido, de Monte Rocherii, *Manipulus curatorum* (London: Pynson, 1508).

Hansberry, Lorraine, *A Raisin in the Sun* (New York, N.Y.: Signet, 1987).

Hardwick, Charles, *A History of the Articles of Religion* (London: Bell, 1904).

Hargrave, O. T., 'The Doctrine of Predestination in the English Reformation', Ph.D. dissertation (Vanderbilt University, 1966).

Harpsfield, Nicholas, *A Treatise on the Pretended Divorce between Henry VIII and Catharine of Aragon*, ed. Nicholas Pocock (Westminster: Camden Society, New Series, 21, 1878).

Henry VIII, *Assertio septem sacramentorum* (London: Pynson, 1521).

Holmes P. J., 'The Last Tudor Great Councils', *The Historical Journal* 33 (1990), 1–22.

Hudson, Anne, *The Premature Reformation: Wycliffite Texts and Lollard History* (Oxford: Clarendon Press, 1988).

Hughes, Philip, *The Reformation in England*, rev. edn., 3 vols. in 1 (London: Burns & Oates, 1963).

Hutchinson, F. E., *Cranmer and the English Reformation* (London: English Universities Press, 1951).

Ingham, Mary Elizabeth, 'Scotus and the Moral Order', *American Catholic Philosophical Quarterly* 67 (1993), 127–50.

Jacobs, Henry Eyster, *The Lutheran Movement in England during the Reigns of Henry VIII and Edward VI, and its Literary Monuments*, rev. edn. (Philadelphia, Pa.: Frederick, 1891).

James, Frank A., III, *Peter Martyr Vermigli and Predestination: The Augustinian Inheritance of an Italian Reformer* (Oxford: Clarendon Press, 1998).

Jarrott, C. A. L., 'Biblical Humanism', *Studies in the Renaissance* 17 (1970), 119–52.

Jeanes, Gordon, 'A Reformation Treatise on the Sacraments', *Journal of Theological Studies* NS 46 (1995), 14–90.

Jenkins, Robert C., *Pre-Tridentine Doctrine: A Review of the Commentary on the Scriptures of . . . Cardinal Cajetan* (London: Nutt, 1891).

Johnson, Margot (ed.), *Cranmer—a Living Influence for 500 Years: A Collection of Essays by Writers associated with Durham* (Durham: Turnstone Ventures, 1990).

Jones, Michael K., and Underwood, Malcolm G., *The King's Mother: Lady Margaret Beaufort, Countess of Richmond and Derby* (Cambridge: Cambridge University Press, 1992).

Journals of the House of Lords, 1509 to present (London).

Kaufman, Peter Iver, *Augustinian Piety and Catholic Reform: Augustine, Colet, and Erasmus* (Macon, Georgia: Mercer University Press, 1982).

Kelly, Henry Ansgar, *The Matrimonial Trials of Henry VIII* (Stanford: Stanford University Press, 1976).

Kempe, Margery, *The Book of Margery Kempe*, trans. B. A. Windeatt (London: Penguin, 1985).

Kidd, B. J. (ed.), *Documents Illustrative of the Continental Reformation* (Oxford: Oxford University Press, 1911).

King, John N., *English Reformation Literature: The Tudor Origins of the Protestant Tradition* (Princeton: Princeton University Press, 1982).

Knox, David B., *The Doctrine of Faith in the reign of Henry VIII* (London: James Clarke, 1961).

Lacey, T. A. (ed.), *The King's Book* (London: SPCK, 1932).

Lake, Peter, and Dowling, Maria (eds.), *Protestantism and the National Church in Sixteenth Century England* (London: Croom Helm, 1987).

Lane, Anthony N. S., 'Justification in Sixteenth-Century Patristic Anthologies', in *Auctoritas Patrum: Contributions on the reception of the Church Fathers in the 15th and 16th Century*, ed. Leif Grane, Alfred Schindler, and Markus Wriedt (Mainz: Philipp von Zabern, 1993), 69–95.

Laurence, Richard, *An Attempt to Illustrate Those Articles of the Church of England Which the Calvinists Improperly Consider as Calvinistical, in Eight Sermons*, 3rd edn. (Oxford: John Henry Parker, 1838).

Leader, D. R., *A History of the University of Cambridge*, i: *The University to 1546* (Cambridge: Cambridge University Press, 1988).

Lechner, Joan Marie, *Renaissance Concepts of the Commonplaces* (New York, N.Y.: Pageant, 1962).

Leedham-Green, E. S., *Books in Cambridge Inventories* (Cambridge: Cambridge University Press, 1986).

Lehmberg, Stanford E., *Sir Thomas Elyot: Tudor Humanist* (Austin, Tex.: University of Texas Press, 1960).

Letters and Papers, Foreign and Domestic, of the Reign of Henry VIII, 1509–47, ed. J. S. Brewer, J. Gairdner and R. H. Brodie, 21 vols. (London: HMSO, 1862–1910).

Leuenberger, Samuel, *Archbishop Cranmer's Immortal Bequest— The Book of Common Prayer of the Church of England: An Evangelistic Liturgy* (Grand Rapids, Mich.: Eerdmans, 1990).

Loane, Marcus L., *Masters of the English Reformation* (London: Church Book Room Press, 1954).

Luther, Martin, *D. Martin Luthers Werke: Kritische Gesamtausgabe*, ed. J. K. F. Knaake, G. Kawerau, et al. (Weimar, 1883–).

—— *Luther's Works*, ed. Jaroslav Pelikan and Helmut Lehmann, 55 vols. (Philadelphia, Pa.: Muhlenberg Press, 1958).

MacCulloch, Diarmaid, *Thomas Cranmer: A Life* (London: Yale University Press, 1996).

—— 'Two Dons in Politics: Thomas Cranmer and Stephen Gardiner, 1503–1533', *The Historical Journal* 37 (1994), 1–22.

MacLeod, Catharine, 'Archbishop Thomas Cranmer', in *Dynasties: Painting in Tudor and Jacobean England, 1530 –1630*, ed. Karen Hearn (London: Tate Publishing, 1995), 48–9.

Manschreck, Clyde L., *Melanchthon: The Quiet Reformer* (New York, N.Y.: Abingdon, 1958).

Marshall, Peter, *The Catholic Priesthood and the English Reformation* (Oxford: Clarendon Press, 1994).

Martyr, Peter, *An Unpublished Letter of Peter Martyr, Reg. Div. Prof. Oxford, to Henry Bullinger; written from Oxford just after the completion of the Second Prayer Book of Edward VI*, ed. William Goode (London: Hatchard, 1850).

Maskell, William, *Doctrine of Absolution* (London: Pickering, 1849).

Mason, Arthur James, *Thomas Cranmer* (London: Methuen, 1898).

Massaut, Jean-Pierre, 'La Position "Oecuménique" d'Érasme sur la pénitence', *Reforme et Humanisme* (Montpellier: Centre D'Histoire de la Reforme et du Protestantisme, 1977), 241–81.

Maxcey, Carl E., *Bona Opera: A Study in the Development of the Doctrine in Philip Melanchthon* (Nieuwkoop: De Graaf, 1980).

Maynard, Theodore, *The Life of Thomas Cranmer* (London: Staples, 1956).

McConica, J. K., *English Humanists and Reformation Politics Under Henry VIII and Edward VI* (Oxford: Clarendon Press, 1968).

McEntegart, Rory S., 'Relations between England and the Schmalkaldic League', Ph.D. thesis (University of London, 1992).

McEntire, Sandra J., *The Doctrine of Compunction in Medieval England: Holy Tears* (Lewiston, N.Y.: Edwin Mellen Press, 1990).

McGee, Eugene K., 'Cranmer and Nominalism', *Harvard Theological Review* 57 (1964), 189–216.

—— 'Cranmer's Nominalism Reaffirmed', *Harvard Theological Review* 59 (1966), 192–6.

McGrath, Alister E., 'The Anti-Pelagian Structure of "Nominalist" Doctrines of Justification', *Ephemerides Theologicae Lovanienses* 57 (1981), 107–19.

—— ' "Augustinianism"? A Critical Assessment of the So-called "Medieval Augustinian Tradition" on Justification', *Augustiniana* 31 (1981), 247–67.

—— *The Intellectual Origins of the European Reformation* (Oxford: Basil Blackwell, 1987).

—— *Iustitia Dei: A History of the Christian Doctrine of Justification*, 2nd edn. (Cambridge: Cambridge University Press, 1998).

McLelland, Joseph C., 'The Reformed Doctrine of Predestination According to Peter Martyr', *Scottish Journal of Theology* 8 (1955), 255–71.

—— *The Visible Words of God: An Exposition of the Sacramental Theology of Peter Martyr Vermigli, A.D. 1500–1562* (Edinburgh: Oliver and Boyd, 1957).

McNeill, John T., *A History of the Cure of Souls* (London: SCM, 1952).

McSorley, Harry J., *Luther: Right or Wrong? An Ecumenical-Theological Study of Luther's Major Work, The Bondage of the Will* (New York, N.Y.: Newman, 1969).

Melanchthon, Philip, *Philippi Melanchthonis opera, quae supersunt omnia, Corpus Reformatorum*, ed. C. G. Bretschneider and H. E. Bindseil, vols. i–xxviii (Brunswick, 1834–60).

Mentz, Georg (ed.), *Die Wittenberger Artikel von 1536* (Darmstadt: Wissenschaftliche Buchgesellschaft, 1968).

Meyer, Charles R., *The Thomistic Concept of Justifying Contrition* (Mundelein, Ill.: Seminarius Sanctae Mariae ad Lacum, 1949).

Mirk, John, *Instructions for Parish Priests*, ed. Gillis Kristensson (Lund: Gleerup, 1974).

—— *Festyuall* (London: Wynkyn de Worde, 1508).

More, Thomas, *The Confutation of Tyndale's Answer*, ed. Louis A. Schuster et al., *The Complete Works of St. Thomas More*, vol. viii in 3 parts (New Haven, Conn.: Yale University Press, 1973).

—— *Utopia*, ed. Edward Surtz and J. H. Hexter, *The Complete Works of St. Thomas More*, vol. iv (New Haven, Conn.: Yale University Press, 1964).

Muller, James Arthur (ed.), *The Letters of Stephen Gardiner* (Cambridge: Cambridge University Press, 1933).

Muller, Richard A., *Christ and the Decree: Christiology and Predestination in Reformed Theology from Calvin to Perkins* (Grand Rapids, Mich.: Baker Book House, 1988).

—— *Dictionary of Latin and Greek Theological Terms: Drawn Principally from Protestant Scholastic Theology* (Grand Rapids, Mich.: Baker Book House, 1985).

Nicene and Post-Nicene Fathers of the Christian Church, First Series, ed. Philip Schaff, 14 vols. (Grand Rapids, Mich.: Eerdmans, 1988).

—— Second Series, ed. Philip Schaff and Henry Wace, 14 vols. (Grand Rapids, Mich.: Eerdmans, 1989).

Nicholas, John Gray, 'A study of Piers Plowman in relation to the medieval Penitential Tradition', Ph.D. thesis (University of Cambridge, 1984).

Nichols, Ann Eljenholm, 'The Etiquette of Pre-Reformation Confession in East Anglia', *The Sixteenth Century Journal* 17 (1986), 145–63.

Nichols, John Gough (ed.), *Narratives of the Days of the Reformation* (London: Camden Society, First Series, 77, 1859).

Nicholson, Graham, 'The Act of Appeals and the English Reformation', in *Law and Government under the Tudors: Essays Presented to Sir Geoffrey Elton*, ed. C. Cross, D. Loades, and J. J. Scarisbrick (Cambridge: Cambridge University Press, 1988), 19–30.

Niesel, Wilhelm, *The Theology of Calvin*, trans. Harold Knight (London: Lutterworth, 1956).

Oates, J. C. T., *Studies in English Printing and Libraries* (London: Pindar, 1991).

Oberman, Heiko A., *Masters of the Reformation: The Emergence of a New Intellectual Climate in Europe* (Cambridge: Cambridge University Press, 1981).

The Ordynarye of Crystyanyte or of crysten men (London: Wynkyn de Worde, 1502).

Oxford Latin Dictionary, ed. P. G. W. Glare (Oxford: Clarendon Press, 1982).

Ozment, Steve, 'Marriage and the Ministry in the Protestant Churches', *Concilium: Theology in the Age of Renewal* 8/8 (October 1972), 39–55.

—— *The Reformation in the Cities* (New Haven, Conn.: Yale University Press, 1975).

Parker, T. H. L., *Commentaries on the Epistle to the Romans: 1532–1542* (Edinburgh: T & T Clark, 1986).

Parker, Matthew, *Correspondence of Matthew Parker, D. D.*, ed. J. Bruce and T. T. Perowne (Cambridge: Parker Society, 1853).

Patrologiae cursus completus, Series Latina, ed. J. P. Migne (Paris, 1878–90).

Pauck, Wilhelm (ed.), *Melanchthon and Bucer* (London: SCM Press, 1969).

Payne, John B., *Erasmus: His Theology of the Sacraments* ([Richmond, Virginia:] John Knox Press, 1970).

Peter the Lombard, *Sententiae in IV Libris Distinctae*, 2 vols. (Rome: Spicilegium Bonaventurianum, 1981).

Peters, Robert, 'The Use of the Fathers in the Reformation Handbook *Unio Dissidentium*', *Studia Patristica* 9, ed. F. L. Cross (1966), 570–7.

—— 'Who Compiled the Sixteenth-Century Patristic Handbook *Unio Dissidentium*?', *Studies in Church History* 2, ed. G. J. Cuming (1965), 237–50.

Pirenne, Henri, *Early Democracies in the Low Countries: Urban Society and Political Conflict in the Middle Ages and the Renaissance*, trans. J. V. Saunders (New York, N.Y.: Harper, 1963).

Pocock, Nicholas, *Records of the Reformation* (Oxford: Oxford University Press, 1870).

Pollard, A. F., *Thomas Cranmer and the English Reformation 1489–1556* (London: Putnam, 1905).

Pollard, A. W., and Redgrave, G. R. (eds.), *A Short-title Catalogue of Books Printed in England, Scotland, and Ireland, and of English Books Printed Abroad, 1475–1640*, 2nd edn., W. A. Jackson, F. S. Ferguson, and Katharine F. Pantzer, rev. eds., 3 vols. (London: Bibliographical Society, 1986).

Porter, H. C., *Reformation and Reaction in Tudor Cambridge* (Hamden, Conn.: Archon, 1972).

Poschmann, Bernhard, *Penance and the Anointing of the Sick,* trans. and rev. Francis Courtney (London: Burns & Oates, 1964).

Raitt, Jill, 'Three Inter-Related Principles in Calvin's Unique Doctrine of Infant Baptism', *The Sixteenth Century Journal* 11 (1980), 51–61.

Redman, John, *De iustificatione opus* (Antwerp: I. Withagius, 1555).

Redworth, Glyn, 'A Study in the Formulation of Policy: The Genesis and Evolution of the Act of Six Articles', *Journal of Ecclesiastical History* 37 (1986), 42–67.

Rex, Richard, 'The Crisis of Obedience: God's Word and Henry's Reformation', *The Historical Journal* 39 (1996), 863–94.

—— 'The English Campaign Against Luther in the 1520s', *Transactions of the Royal Historical Society*, Fifth Series, 39 (1989), 85–106.

—— *Henry VIII and the English Reformation* (London: Macmillan, 1993).

—— 'The New Learning', *Journal of Ecclesiastical History* 44 (1993), 26–44.

—— *The Theology of John Fisher* (Cambridge: Cambridge University Press, 1991).

Ridley, Jasper, *Thomas Cranmer* (Oxford: Clarendon Press, 1962).

Robinson, Hastings (ed.), *Original Letters Relative to the English Reformation*, 2 vols. (Cambridge: Parker Society, 1847).

Rummel, Erika, *Erasmus' Annotations on the New Testament: From Philologist to Theologian* (Toronto: University of Toronto Press, 1986).

Rupp, E. Gordon, *Studies in the Making of the English Protestant Tradition* (Cambridge: Cambridge University Press, 1947).

Rupp, Gordon, and Watson, Philip S. (eds.), *Luther and Erasmus: Free Will and Salvation* (Philadelphia, Pa.: Westminster, 1969).

Sawada, P. A., 'Two Anonymous Tudor Treatises on the General Council', *Journal of Ecclesiastical History* 12 (1961), 197–214.

Scarisbrick, J. J., *Henry VIII* (London: Methuen, 1968).

Selwyn, David G., *The Library of Thomas Cranmer* (Oxford: Oxford Bibliographical Society, 1996).

—— 'Review of *Thomas Cranmer: A Life* by Diarmaid MacCulloch', *Journal of Theological Studies*, NS 48 (1997), 323–30.

Spykman, Gordon J., *Attrition and Contrition at the Council of Trent* (Kampen: Kok, 1955).

Stafford, William S., 'Repentance on the Eve of the Reformation: John Fisher's Sermons of 1508 and 1509', *Historical Magazine of the Protestant Episcopal Church* 54 (1985), 297–338.

Statutes of the Realm, ed. Alexander Luders et al., 11 vols. (London, 1810–28).

Steinmetz, David C., *Reformers in the Wings* (Philadelphia, Pa.: Fortress Press, 1971).

Stephens, W. P., *The Holy Spirit in the Theology of Martin Bucer* (Cambridge: Cambridge University Press, 1970).

Strauss, Gerald, *Nuremberg in the Sixteenth Century* (New York, N.Y.: Wiley, 1966).

——'Protestant Dogma and City Government: The Case of Nuremberg', *Past and Present* 36 (1967), 38–58.

Strong, Roy, *Tudor and Jacobean Portraits* (London: HMSO, 1969).

Strype, John, *Memorials of . . . Thomas Cranmer, sometime Lord Archbishop of Canterbury*, 2 vols. in 1 (London: Richard Chiswell, 1694).

Sturge, Charles, *Cuthbert Tunstal: Churchman, Scholar, Statesman, Administrator* (London: Longmans Green, 1938).

Surtz, Edward, *The Works and Days of John Fisher* (Cambridge, Mass.: Harvard University Press, 1967).

Sykes, Stephen, 'Cranmer on the Open Heart', in *This Sacred History: Anglican Reflections for John Booty*, ed. Donald S. Armentrout (Cambridge, Mass.; Cowley Publications, 1990), 1–20.

Teetaert, Amédée, *La Confession aux laïques dans l'église latine depuis le VIIIe jusqu'au XVIe siècle* (Paris: Universitas Catholica Lovaniensis, 1926).

Tentler, Thomas N., 'Forgiveness and Consolation in the Religious Thought of Erasmus', *Studies in the Renaissance* 12 (1965), 110–19.

——*Sin and Confession on the Eve of the Reformation* (Princeton: Princeton University Press, 1977).

Tjernagel, Neelak Seawlook, *Henry VIII and the Lutherans* (St Louis, Mo.: Concordia, 1965).

Tomlinson, J. T., *The Prayer Book, Articles, and Homilies: Some forgotten facts in their history which may decide their interpretation* (London: Elliot Stock, 1897).

A Treatise concernynge generall councilles, the Byshoppes of Rome and the Clergy (London: Berthelet, 1538).

Trueman, Carl R., *Luther's Legacy: Salvation and English Reformers 1525–1556* (Oxford: Clarendon Press, 1994).

Wall, John T., 'Godly and Fruitful Lessons: The English Bible, Erasmus' Paraphrases, and the Book of Homilies', in *The Godly Kingdom of Tudor England: Great Books of the English*

Reformation, ed. John E. Booty (Wilton, Conn.: Morehouse-Barlow, 1981).

Wallace, Dewey D., Jr., 'The Doctrine of Predestination in the Early English Reformation', *Church History* 43 (1974), 201–15.

Wallace, Ronald S., *Calvin's Doctrine of the Word and Sacrament* (Edinburgh: Oliver and Boyd, 1953).

Walsh, K. J., 'Cranmer and the Fathers, especially in the *Defence*', *Journal of Religious History* 11 (1980), 227–47.

Warfield, Benjamin, B., *Calvin and Augustine* (Philadelphia, Pa.: Presbyterian and Reformed Publishing, 1956).

Warner, G. F., and Gilson, J. P., *Catalogue of Western Manuscripts in the Old Royal and King's Collections*, 4 vols. (Oxford: Oxford University Press, 1921).

Watkins, Oscar D., *A History of Penance*, 2 vols. (London: Longmans Green, 1920).

Wells-Cole, Anthony, *Art and Decoration in Elizabethan and Jacobean England: The Influence of Continental Prints, 1558–1625* (New Haven, Conn.: Yale University Press, 1997).

Wendel, François, *Calvin: The Origins and Development of his Religious Thought*, trans. Philip Mairet (London: Collins, 1963).

Whitaker, E. C., *Martin Bucer and The Book of Common Prayer* (Great Wakering: Alcuin Club, 1974).

White, Peter, *Predestination, Policy and Polemic: Conflict and Consensus in the English Church from the Reformation to the Civil War* (Cambridge: Cambridge University Press, 1992).

Whiting, Robert, *The Blind Devotion of the People* (Cambridge: Cambridge University Press, 1989).

Williams, Norman Powell, *The Ideas of the Fall and of Original Sin: A Historical and Critical Study* (London: Longmans Green, 1927).

Wolter, Allan B., *Duns Scotus on the Will and Morality*, translation edition ed. William A. Frank (Washington, D.C.: Catholic University of America Press, 1997).

—— *The Philosophical Theology of John Duns Scotus*, ed. Marilyn McCord Adams (Ithaca, N.Y.: Cornell University Press, 1990).

Yost, John K., 'The Reformation Defense of Clerical Marriage in the Reigns of Henry VIII and Edward VI', *Church History* 50 (1981), 152–65.

Zerner, Henri, *The School of Fontainebleau: Etchings and Engravings* (London: Thames and Hudson, 1969).

Index